PC
CONCEPTS

**SECOND
EDITION**

DRYDEN

soon to become

Harcourt
College Publishers

A Harcourt Higher Learning Company

Soon you will find The Dryden Press' distinguished innovation, leadership, and support under a different name . . . a new brand that continues our unsurpassed quality, service, and commitment to education.

We are combining the strengths of our college imprints into one worldwide brand: Harcourt Our mission is to make learning accessible to anyone, anywhere, anytime—reinforcing our commitment to lifelong learning.

We'll soon be Harcourt College Publishers. Ask for us by name.

One Company
"Where Learning
Comes to Life."

PC CONCEPTS

SECOND EDITION

EDWARD G. MARTIN

CHARLES S. PARKER

DEBORAH MORLEY
Editorial Consultant

THE DRYDEN PRESS
A DIVISION OF HARCOURT COLLEGE PUBLISHERS

FORT WORTH   PHILADELPHIA   SAN DIEGO   NEW YORK   ORLANDO   AUSTIN   SAN ANTONIO
TORONTO   MONTREAL   LONDON   SYDNEY   TOKYO

Publisher   Mike Roche

Executive Editor   Christina Martin

Developmental Editor   Elizabeth Hayes

Marketing Strategist   Bill Bernys

Art Director   Scott Baker

Production Manager   Linda McMillan

Project Management   GTS Publishing Services

Composition   GTS Graphics

Cover Image   Lamberto Alvarez

ISBN: 0-03-025969-X

Library of Congress Catalog Card Number: 99-074296

Address for Orders
Harcourt College Publishers, 6277 Sea Harbor Drive, Orlando, FL 32887-6777
1-800-782-4479

Address for Editorial Correspondence
Harcourt College Publishers, 301 Commerce Street, Suite 3700, Fort Worth, TX 76102

Web Site Address
http://www.harcourtcollege.com

THE DRYDEN PRESS SERIES IN COMPUTER TECHNOLOGY

Adams
First Steps Series
Word 2000
Word 97
Excel 2000
Excel 97
Access 2000
Access 97
PowerPoint 2000
PowerPoint 97
Outlook 2000
Windows 98

Coorough
Getting Started with Multimedia

Fenrich
Practical Guidelines for Creating
Instructional Multimedia Applications

Fuller/Manning
Getting Started with the Internet

Fuller
Getting Started with E-Commerce

Gordon and Gordon
Information Systems: A Management
Approach
Second Edition

Gray, King, McLean, and Watson
Management of Information Systems
Second Edition

Harris
Systems Analysis and Design for the Small
Enterprise
Second Edition

Larsen/Marold
Using Microsoft Works 4.0 for Windows 95:
An Introduction to Computing

Laudon and Laudon
Information Systems and the Internet: A
Problem-Solving Approach

Licker
Management Information Systems: A Strate-
gic Leadership Approach

Lorents and Morgan
Database Systems: Concepts, Management,
and Applications

Martin
Discovering Microsoft Office 2000
Discovering Microsoft Office 97

Martin/Parker
PC Concepts
Second Edition

Mason
Using Microsoft Excel 97 in Business

McKeown
Information Technology and the Networked
Economy

Millspaugh
Object-Oriented Programming with C++

Morley
Getting Started with Computers
Second Edition

Morley
Getting Started: Web Page Design with
Microsoft FrontPage 2000
Getting Started: Web Page Design with
Microsoft FrontPage 98
Getting Started: Web Page Design with
Microsoft FrontPage 97

Parker
Understanding Computers: Today and
Tomorrow
2000 Edition

Spear
Introduction to Computer Programming in
Visual Basic 6.0

Martin and Parker
Mastering Today's Software Series

**Texts available in any combination
of the following:**
Windows 98
Windows NT Workstation 4
Windows 95
Windows 3.1
Disk Operating System 6.0 (DOS 6.0)
Disk Operating System 5.0 (DOS 5.0)
Microsoft Office 2000
Microsoft Office 97 Professional Edition
Microsoft Office for Windows 95 Profes-
sional Edition
Word 2000
Word 97
Word 7.0 for Windows 95
Word 6.0 for Windows
Corel WordPerfect 7.0 for Windows 95
WordPerfect 6.1 for Windows
WordPerfect 6.0 for Windows
WordPerfect 5.1
Excel 2000
Excel 97
Excel 7.0 for Windows 95
Excel 5.0 for Windows
Lotus 1-2-3 97

Lotus 1-2-3 for Windows (5.0)
Lotus 1-2-3 for Windows (4.01)
Lotus 1-2-3 (2.4)
Lotus 1-2-3 (2.2/2.3)
Quattro Pro 4.0
Quattro Pro 6.0 for Windows
Access 2000
Access 97
Access 7.0 for Windows 95
Access 2.0 for Windows
Paradox 5.0 for Windows
Paradox 4.0
dBASE 5 for Windows
dBASE IV (1.5/2.0)
dBASE III PLUS
PowerPoint 2000
PowerPoint 97
PowerPoint 7.0 for Windows 95
Outlook 2000
A Beginner's Guide to QBASIC
A Beginner's Guide to BASIC
Netscape Navigator 4.0
Internet Explorer 2000
Internet Explorer 4.0

**The Dryden Online Series in
Information Technology**
Computers Online
Learning Office 2000
Learning Office 97
Learning Windows 98
Introduction to the Internet
Introduction to Multimedia
Introduction to Visual Basic 6.0
Systems Analysis and Design

PREFACE

Personal computers, or PCs, have become an integral part of our everyday lives. Today's writer or secretary is found at a PC keyboard rather than at a typewriter; today's artist, with a light pen in hand instead of a brush; today's businessperson, with electronic files that often replace bulky manila folders full of paper documents. In the commercial world, knowledge of PCs is becoming a prerequisite to success. Most skill-based jobs today depend heavily on the collection, use, creation, and dissemination of electronic information. Whether a person chooses to become an accountant, engineer, stockbroker, lawyer, architect, teacher, police officer, truck driver, doctor, or machine operator, he or she will probably be able to work both faster and smarter by knowing how to use a PC.

THE TEXTBOOK

PC Concepts was created to provide a highly compact and current presentation of the world of PCs for students taking a first course in computers. It contains the knowledge one absolutely needs to understand how PCs work and how they can be used to maximum benefit. The seven chapters of the book are devoted to such topics as storage and processing concepts, types of computer systems, PC hardware, PC software, communications and networking fundamentals, the Internet and the World Wide Web, shopping for a PC, and social issues regarding technology.

The best way for students to learn about technology is to use it. In its second edition, *PC Concepts* provides a truly interactive approach to learning computers with a text that is fully integrated with a completely updated, multimedia-enhanced Web site. Further, for instructors who want to progress to the next level, a full-content online course, *Computers Online*, is also available to be packaged with the text. *PC Concepts* is but one component of a complete and flexible instructional package—one that can easily be adapted to virtually any teaching format.

KEY FEATURES

Currency Perhaps more than textbooks in any other field, computer texts must reflect the latest technologies, trends, and classroom needs. The state-of-the-art content of this book and its multimedia support package reflects these considerations. Before the second edition was started, reviews were commissioned and meetings were held to identify key areas of change for the text and support package. Also, throughout the writing and production stages, enhancements were continually being made to ensure that the final product would be as current as possible throughout the life of the edition.

Readability We remember more about a subject if it is presented in a straightforward way and made interesting and exciting. This book is written in a conversational, down-to-earth style—one designed to be accurate without being intimidating. Concepts are explained clearly and simply, without use of overly technical terminology. Where complex points are presented, they are made understandable with realistic examples from everyday life.

Chapter Learning Tools Each chapter of the book contains a number of learning tools, described below, to help students master the materials.

1. **Outline** An outline of the headings in the chapter shows the major topics to be covered.
2. **Learning Objectives** A list of learning objectives is provided to serve as a guide while students read the chapter.
3. **Overview** Each chapter starts with an overview that puts the subject matter of the chapter in perspective and lets students know what they will be reading about.
4. **Boldfaced Key Terms and Running Glossary** Important terms appear in boldfaced type as they are introduced in the chapter. These terms are also defined at the bottom of the page on which they appear and in the end-of-text glossary.
5. **Illustrations and Photographs** Each chapter includes dynamic, fully annotated illustrations integrated with the text material as well as numerous screen shots that highlight the latest applications and programs. Many illustrations are rendered in a photo-realistic style to show students the close up details of computer components. In addition, instructive, full-color photographs appear throughout to help illustrate important concepts.
6. **Summary and Key Terms** This is a concise, section-by-section summary of the main points in the chapter. Every boldfaced key term in the chapter also appears in boldface type in the summary. Students will find the summary a valuable tool for study and review.
7. **Exercises** End-of-chapter exercises allow students to test themselves on what they have just read. The exercises include matching, fill-in, discussion, and true/false questions as well as problems in other formats.
8. **Projects** End-of-chapter projects require students to extend their knowledge by doing research beyond merely reading the book. Special icons denote projects that are recommended for groups, projects that are best done on the Internet, and projects that require hands-on computer skills (see margin).

PC Miniguides Three of the chapters contain PC Miniguides, special fold-out sections that can be useful to students in a classroom or lab setting or outside the course. The miniguides address sources for online software help, suggestions for using the Internet for classroom research, and tips for shopping for a PC.

End-of-Text Glossary The Glossary at the end of the book defines approximately 400 important computer terms mentioned in the text, including all boldfaced key terms. Each glossary item has a page reference indicating where it is boldfaced or where it first appears in the text.

NEW TO THIS EDITION

Although previous editions of this text have been highly successful, the relentless pace of technology has regularly necessitated a number of key changes in each new edition in order to keep content fresh. Among the noteworthy differences between the previous edition and the second edition of *PC Concepts* are the following:

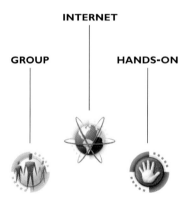

INTERNET

GROUP HANDS-ON

Web Tutor and Further Exploration Icons For an interactive experience in learning about computers, throughout each chapter students will find "Web Tutor" icons in the margins directing them to the *PC Concepts* Web site for multimedia-enhanced tutorials. "Further Exploration" icons point to Web sites with more in-depth information on a given topic.

Interactive Exercises. At the end of selected modules students can complete a multimedia-rich "Interactive Exercise." The text briefly describes this capstone exercise and then directs the student to the *PC Concepts* Web site to complete the exercise. Students can practice putting together a computer, sending e-mail, creating a PowerPoint presentation, and more.

Additional Interactive Review Material. At the end of each chapter, students can take advantage of more Web-related activities. Icons will direct students to the Online Glossary and Online Review, both at the *PC Concepts* Web site. The Online Reviews contain 50 study questions per chapter and provide immediate feedback. Also available at the site are updated Internet Lab Assignments.

Emphasis on the Internet and World Wide Web Continuing the trend from earlier editions, this book presents an increased emphasis on the Internet and the World Wide Web, PC-based processing, communications topics, and social issues regarding technology. This shift reflects the trend in applications as well as the reality of more and more people getting involved with technology in both their jobs and their personal lives.

New Topics Several topics have emerged in importance since the text was last published, and they receive greater attention here. Among these topics are extranets, Internet telephony and instant messaging, Linux, collaborative computing, DVD and new forms of secondary storage, and new forms of computer crime and cyberterrorism.

Art and Photo Program Both the art and photo programs have been extensively revised. Chapters include fully annotated illustrations integrated with the text material, as well as numerous screen shots showcasing the latest applications. Many illustrations are rendered in a photo-realistic style with close-up details of computer components. In addition, instructive, full-color photographs appear throughout to help illustrate important concepts.

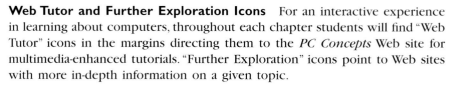

STUDENT AND TEACHER SUPPORT MATERIALS

PC Concepts is available with a complete package of support materials for instructors and students. Included in the package are the comprehensive *PC Concepts* Web site, a printed *Instructor's Manual and Test Bank with Transparency Masters*, a *Computerized Test Bank*, a set of *PowerPoint Presentations*, a set of *Electronic Transparencies*, a full-content online course, and a variety of software manuals to meet lab needs.

THE PC CONCEPTS WEB SITE

The *PC Concepts* Web site located at **www.harcourtcollege.com/infosys/pcc2e/** provides media-rich support for both instructors and students.

Students will find the following resources at the site:

Web Tutors The tutors are made up of a series of multimedia-enhanced tutorials that allow students to interact with the concepts discussed in the text.

Further Exploration This area provides links to Web sites with more in-depth information on a given topic from the text.

Interactive Exercises These multimedia-rich capstone exercises allow students to test their knowledge after completing a module.

Online Reviews Each review has fifty questions per chapter, some with graphics from the text, and provide immediate feedback.

Internet Lab Assignments Located here are updates for the end-of-chapter Internet projects as well as additional text-related projects and fun "Surfing on Your Own" activities.

Online Glossary The online glossary provides another venue for review of key concepts.

In the News These articles, which are updated monthly, will keep students informed of the latest happenings in the world of computers.

In the Instructor's section, teachers have access to the following:

Instructor's Manual Teachers can download an electronic version of the Instructor's Manual in Microsoft Word.

PowerPoint Presentation A PowerPoint presentation is available for each chapter in the text. Each presentation includes key points and illustrations from the text as well as embedded lecture notes from the Instructor's Manual.

Electronic Transparencies A set of over one hundred Electronic Transparencies for use in classroom presentations is available to help explain key points. The Electronic Transparencies cover key text figures, as well as illustrations not found in the text. The Teaching Outlines in the *Instructor's Manual* indicate when to show each of the Electronic Transparencies (as well as the Transparency Masters), and the Transparency Scripts in the *Instructor's Manual* list points to make about each.

THE INSTRUCTOR'S MANUAL

The instructor's-manual section of the *Instructor's Manual and Test Bank with Transparency Masters* contains materials useful to experienced instructors looking for new ideas, part-time or adjunct faculty needing tools to enable them to organize materials quickly, and teachers just breaking into the field who are seeking tips on how to set up or teach the course. For each of the seven chapters of the text, the instructor's-manual section provides a Chapter Outline and list of Learning Objectives, a brief Summary of the chapter materials, an alphabetical list of Key Terms, a Teaching Outline that provides an outlined summary of the chapter, Teaching Tips with recommendations for class discussion, Lecture Anecdotes with a number of additional materials for classroom use, scripts for each Electronic Transparency and Transparency Master included in the package, and answers or suggestions to end-of-chapter exercises and projects. A set of Transparency Masters is located at the end of this section.

THE TEST BANK

The test-bank section of the *Instructor's Manual and Test Bank* contains over a thousand questions and comes in both printed and computerized form.

The printed version of the test bank contains questions of five types: true/false, multiple-choice, fill-in, matching, and short-answer. Answers to the true/false, multiple choice, fill-in, and matching questions are given alongside each question; a page reference is provided with short-answer questions, showing where the answer can be found in the text. Alongside each true/false, multiple-choice, fill-in, and short-answer question in the test bank is a code key showing the section of the chapter from which the question was taken. This feature enables you to more quickly prepare tests with certain distribution requirements—say, tests covering each section equally, tests biased heavily toward certain sections, or tests that specifically avoid certain sections. There is also a 10-question multiple-choice quiz at the end of each chapter. Each quiz was created from some of the best questions from the chapter and covers the entire chapter. Each quiz has been produced in easy-to-copy-and-distribute form; also provided is a separate answer key to each quiz, which can be made into an overhead transparency.

The Computerized Test Bank—available for PC-compatible and Macintosh computers—contains all the questions found in the printed version of the test bank. It allows you to preview, add, delete, or edit test questions as well as to output questions in any order and to print answer keys.

SOFTWARE MANUALS

Lab manuals, covering hands-on use of software products, are available from Harcourt for a number of widely used products. Using Harcourt's custom-publishing option, you can have virtually any combination of components bound together for your classes. Check with your Harcourt sales representative about the configuration options currently possible.

COMPUTERS ONLINE

For instructors who want to add a richer online component to their course, *Computers Online*, by Merrill Wells of Red Rocks Community College, is available for packaging with the text. This new full-content online course can be used in a variety of ways: it can be used to supplement the text in a traditional classroom setting, or it can be used as a virtual classroom for distance-learning students. Students learn technology by interacting with the content in this rich, interactive multimedia environment. Each chapter of the course is filled with interactive activities, links, animations, demonstrations, collaborative classroom activities, critical-thinking exercises, and self-tests.

Computers Online has been designed using the WebCT course management system, one of the most popular tools used to provide virtual classroom environments. The WebCT environment provides instructors with such features as the ability to track student progress; timed, online quizzes; student management tools and the ability to customize course content. Student features include communication tools such as a bulletin board, electronic mail, and chat; student presentation areas which can be used for displaying course projects and other student work; student homepages; and much more. Visit **www.harcourtbrace online.com** to see a demo.

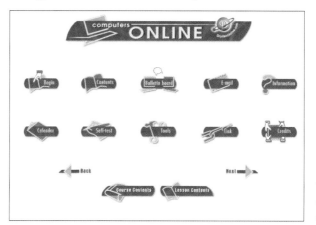

The *Computers Online* Course Homepage.

Harcourt will provide complimentary supplements or supplement packages to those adopters qualified under our adoption policy. Please contact your sales representative to learn how you may qualify. If as an adopter or potential user you receive supplements you do not need, please return them to your sales representative or send them to:

Attn: Returns Department
Troy Warehouse
465 South Lincoln Drive
Troy, MO 63379

ACKNOWLEDGMENTS

A project of this magnitude could never have been completed had it not been for the efforts of a large number of people, working in a variety of capacities.

First, we wish to thank the following reviewers on both editions of the text, whose thoughtful comments on preliminary drafts of *PC Concepts* improved both the technical accuracy of the text and its general marketability:

Second Edition:
Ray L. Cone, Odessa College
Terry Corwin, Valley City State University
Patricia L. Dreven, Community College of Southern Nevada
Lee A. Hunt, Collin County Community College
Lori L. Leonard, Worcester State College
Everett Martin, Heald College
Delfina C. Najera, El Paso Community College
Pam Ogaard, Bismark State College

First Edition:
David V. Bourque, Middlesex County College
Curtis Bring, Moorhead State University
Judy L. Cameron, Spokane Community College
Mark Ciampa, Volunteer State Community College
Donald L. Dersham, Mountain View College
Albert L. Harris, Appalachian State University
Joyce M. Koerfer, College of Du Page
Mary Veronica Kolesar, Utah State University
Michael A. Perl, Brookhaven College
Leonard Presby, William Paterson State College

We would also like to thank the following ancillary authors for their excellent work on the support package:

Beverly Amer, Northern Arizona University, *Online Reviews*
Wade Graves, Grayson County College, *Internet Lab Assignments*
Deborah R. Ludford, Glendale Community College, *PowerPoint Presentation*
Deborah Morley, College of the Sequoias, co-author, *Instructor's Manual and Test Bank with Transparency Masters*
Merrill Wells, Red Rocks Community College, *Computers Online*

We would especially like to thank Deborah Morley in her role as Editorial Consultant in this edition. Deborah contributed numerous insights and suggestions as the manuscript was developed; her expertise during all phases of the project is greatly appreciated.

We are indebted to scores of people at dozens of organizations for the photographs and screen shots they provided for this text. We would especially like to thank Jessie O. Kempter at IBM, Carol Parcels of Hewlett-Packard, and the many helpful people at Waggner Edstrom for their assistance.

At Harcourt, a special word of thanks to our publisher, Michael Roche, to our executive editor, Christina A. Martin, and to Elizabeth Hayes, associate editor, for the suggestions and accommodations they made to produce a better manuscript. Also we would like to thank Charlie Dierker, Linda McMillan, Scott Baker, Linda Blundell, Annette Coolidge, and the many others who worked hard on behalf of this book.

Charles S. Parker
Edward G. Martin

CONTENTS

Preface   vi

CHAPTER 1

Introduction to Personal Computers   1

Overview   2

PCs in the Workplace   3

What's a Personal Computer?   3

The Role of Data and Programs   6

Data: A Multimedia Perspective   6

Programs: The Instructions That Shape Data   7

A Closer Look at Storage   8

Memory   8

Secondary Storage   8

Hardware and Software   9

Hardware   9

Software   9

Organizing Data and Programs   12

Documents and Folders   12

Web-Page Organization   14

Fields, Records, Files, and Databases   14

Types of PCs   15

Desktop Units   15

Portables   16

PC-Compatible or Macintosh?   16

Computer Networks   17

Accessing Networks   18

Online and Offline   18

Using PCs: A Comprehensive Example   19

Summary and Key Terms   22

Exercises   23

Projects   25

Online Review   27

CHAPTER 2

Hardware   29

Overview   30

Input Hardware   31

Keyboards   31

Pointing Devices   31

Image Scanners   33

Processing Hardware   33

Bits and Bytes: The Building Blocks of Computer Logic   34

Looking Inside the System Unit   40

Secondary Storage Hardware   48

Properties of Secondary Storage Systems   48

Diskettes   49

Hard Disks   52

Optical Disks   54

Cartridge Tapes   56

Output Hardware   57

Monitors   57

Printers   59

Special-Purpose Output Devices   62

Summary and Key Terms   64

Exercises   66

Projects   68

Interactive Exercise   71

Online Review   71

CHAPTER 3

Software   73

Overview   74

Whose Software Is It?   75

Proprietary Software   75

Shareware   76

Freeware   76

The User Interface   77

Command Syntax   77

Shortcut Keystrokes   78

Graphical User Interfaces (GUIs)   78

Elements of a Graphical User Interface   80

Menus   80

Windows   86

Dialog Boxes   90

Online Help   91

Systems Software   92

Operating Systems   92

Utility Programs   98

Language Translators   99

Applications Software   100

Software Suites   100
Word Processors   101
Spreadsheets   101
Database Management Systems   106
Other Productivity Software   108

Summary and Key Terms   112

Exercises   114

Projects   116

Interactive Exercises   119

Online Review   119

CHAPTER 4

Communications and Networks   121

Overview   122

Telecommunications Applications   123

Electronic Mail and Messaging   123
Information Retrieval and the Web   125
Collaborative Computing   126
Transaction Processing   128

Telecommunications Media   129

Wire Media   129
Wireless Media   132

Adapting Computers to Telecommunications Media   134

Sending Data over Media   135
Network Interface Cards and Modems   136
ISDN and Beyond   139

Network Topologies   140

Local Networks   140

Local Area Networks (LANs)   142
Hierarchical Local Networks   144

Wide Area Networks (WANs)   145

Handling WAN Traffic   145

Communications Protocols   146

Summary and Key Terms   153

Exercises   155

Projects   156

Interactive Exercise   157

Online Review   157

CHAPTER 5

Introduction to the Internet and World Wide Web   159

Overview   160

Evolution of the Internet   161
From the ARPANET to the World Wide Web   161
The Internet Community Today   163
Myths about the Internet   165

What Does the Internet Have to Offer?   166
E-Mail   166
Information Retrieval and the World Wide Web   168
Mailing Lists   171
Newsgroups   172
Chat   173
Online Shopping   175

Internet Addresses   176

Desktop Tools for Accessing the Internet   178
Browsers and Plug-In Packages   178
Search Engines   188
Hardware Considerations   192

Connecting to the Internet   192
About Service Providers   192
Selecting a Provider   193
Setting Up Your System   195

Summary and Key Terms   197

Exercises   199

Projects   200

Interactive Exercises   203

Online Review   203

CHAPTER 6

Developing Your Own PC   205

Overview   206

The PC Marketplace   207
PC Products   207
Sales and Distribution   208

Selecting a PC   212
Analyzing Needs   213
Listing Alternatives   213
Evaluating Alternatives   215
Choosing a System   216

Hardware and Software Installation   217

Operating a PC   218

Backup Procedures   218

Equipment Maintenance   219

Security   222

Troubleshooting and Technical Assistance   222

Upgrading   226

Upgrading Hardware   227

Upgrading Software   227

Functional versus Technological Obsolescence   228

Learning More about PCs   229

Summary and Key Terms   231

Exercises   232

Projects   233

Online Review   236

CHAPTER 7

Social Issues Involving Computers   237

Overview   238

Computers, Work, and Our Well-Being   239

Stress-Related Concerns   239

Ergonomics-Related Concerns   240

Environment-Related Concerns   241

Computer Crime   241

Types of Computer Crime   242

Minimizing Computer Crime   246

Crime Legislation   250

Computers and Privacy   251

Privacy and Electronic Mail   251

Privacy and Marketing Databases   253

Privacy and the Internet   253

Caller Identification   254

Privacy Legislation   256

Ethical Issues Regarding Computers   256

Some Examples   258

Why Study Ethics?   258

Summary and Key Terms   259

Exercises   260

Projects   262

Interactive Exercise   265

Online Review   265

Glossary   267

Index   277

Credits   283

OUTLINE

Overview
PCs in the Workplace
What's a Personal Computer?
The Role of Data and Programs
>   Data: A Multimedia Perspective
>   Programs: The Instructions That Shape Data
A Closer Look at Storage
>   Memory
>   Secondary Storage
Hardware and Software
>   Hardware
>   Software
Organizing Data and Programs
>   Documents and Folders
>   Web-Page Organization
>   Fields, Records, Files, and Databases
Types of PCs
>   Desktop Units
>   Portables
>   PC-Compatible or Macintosh?
Computer Networks
>   Accessing Networks
>   Online and Offline
Using PCs: A Comprehensive Example

INTRODUCTION TO PERSONAL COMPUTERS

LEARNING OBJECTIVES

After completing this chapter, you will be able to:

1. Explain why it's especially important to learn about personal computers today.

2. Describe the role of a personal computer's input, processing, output, and storage functions.

3. Explain the functions performed by data, programs, memory (RAM), secondary storage, hardware, and software.

4. Name several types of hardware and software and explain the roles served by each.

5. Describe how data and programs are organized and accessed in a personal computer system.

6. Distinguish among the various types of personal computers.

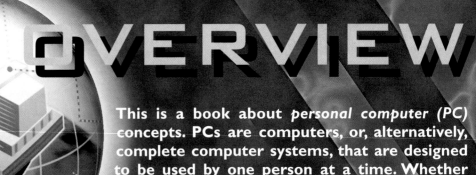

OVERVIEW

This is a book about *personal computer (PC)* concepts. PCs are computers, or, alternatively, complete computer systems, that are designed to be used by one person at a time. Whether you become an accountant, engineer, stockbroker, lawyer, architect, doctor, teacher, or even a truck driver or forklift operator, you will be able to work both faster and smarter if you know how to use a PC.

A major purpose of this chapter is to introduce you to how PCs work and to familiarize you with their usability. First, to get you excited about what PCs may be able to do for you, we look at several applications of PC technology in the workplace. Then, we describe formally and in detail what a PC is and how it works. Next, we cover in depth some important elements found in every personal computer system and, after that, several key technical concepts. Then, it's on to types of PCs and the usefulness of computer networks. Last, to tie together several of the chapter concepts, we look at an in-depth example of a PC user in action.

PCS IN THE WORKPLACE

Only a couple of decades ago, it was not critical for the average person to know how to use a computer in his or her job. Computers were large and expensive, and relatively few people in the working world had access to them. Furthermore, the use of these devices generally required a lot of technical knowledge. Most computers used in organizations were equipped to do little else but high-volume paperwork processing, such as issuing bills and keeping track of customer and product balances. Not only were most ordinary working people intimidated by computers, but there were few good reasons for becoming familiar with them.

Then, with the development of *microprocessors*—small, inexpensive computers that could fit on a fingernail-sized chip—daily life in the working world rapidly began to change. Developed in the early 1970s, microprocessors were rapidly assimilated into scores of products, from coffeemakers to entire personal computer systems that could fit on desktops. These PC systems consisted of the microprocessor chip itself (the computer) along with support devices such as disk drives, displays, and printers. Within a few years, there became thousands of times more computers and thousands of times more people involved with computers than was previously thought possible. This transition resulted in a flood of high-quality computing products in the marketplace. The products changed the way many organizations approach work and the types of skills they seek in the people they hire.

Today, with technology rapidly improving on multiple fronts, we are still in the midst of a computer and communications revolution in the workplace that is showing no signs of slowing down. If anything, the pace is accelerating. Most skill-based jobs depend heavily on the collection, use, creation, and dissemination of electronic information. Whatever your job, your performance will largely depend on such information and your ability to handle it. Figure 1-1 provides several examples of how PCs are being used in the workplace to enhance personal productivity.

For links to further information about information systems job opportunities, go to www.harcourtcollege. com/infosys/pcc2e/student/ explore/ and click on Chapter 1.

WHAT'S A PERSONAL COMPUTER?

Four words sum up the operation of every computer system, personal or otherwise: **input, processing, output,** and **storage.** To see what these words mean, let's look at something you probably have in your own home—a stereo sound system.

A simple sound system often consists of a compact disk (CD) player, an amplifier, and a pair of speakers. To use the system, you place a CD in the CD player and turn on the system. The CD player converts the patterns in the tracks into electronic signals and transmits them to the amplifier. The amplifier takes the signals, strengthens them, and transmits them to the speakers. The result is music. In computer terms, the CD player sends signals as *input* to the amplifier. The amplifier *processes* the signals and sends them to the

For a tutorial on the uses of computers, go to www. harcourtcollege.com/infosys/ pcc2e/student/tutor/ and click on Chapter 1.

■ **Input.** What is supplied to a computer process. ■ **Processing.** The conversion of input to output. ■ **Output.** The results of a computer process. ■ **Storage.** An area that holds materials going to or coming from the computer.

MULTIPURPOSE WORKSTATION
Most business professionals today require their own desktop computer in the office or at home to prepare budgets and reports, exchange electronic mail, organize their work, and collect information from computer networks.

PRESENTATION TOOL
Increasingly, computers are being used to make presentations in front of an audience. The content of the presentation might be stored on a local disk drive or on a remote drive on a computer network.

NETWORKING
At many hotel chains, local desktop PCs at registration desks are hooked into a global communications network that keeps track of guest reservations and rooms.

DESIGN TOOL
The computer has become a vital creative tool in fields such as advertising art, architecture, and engineering. Affordable computers can quickly produce stunning photorealistic renderings that help designers sell ideas to clients.

FIGURE 1-1

Computers shaping the workplace.

speakers, which produce a musical *output*. The CD player is an **input device,** the amplifier is a processing unit, and the speakers are **output devices.** The amplifier is the heart of the system, whereas the CD player and speakers are examples of **peripheral equipment.**

Most sound systems have a variety of other peripheral equipment. An antenna, for example, is another kind of input device. Headphones are another type of output device. A tape deck is both an input and output device—you can use it to send signals to the amplifier or to receive signals from it. The

■ **Input device.** Equipment that supplies materials to the computer. ■ **Output device.** Equipment that accepts materials from the computer. ■ **Peripheral equipment.** The devices that work with a computer.

tapes and CDs in your collection are, in computer terms, **storage media.** They store music in a **machine-readable form**—a form that the associated input device (tape deck or CD player) can recognize (that is, "read") and convert into signals for the amplifier to process.

All the elements in a sound system have their counterparts in a computer system. At a minimum, a **computer system** consists of the computer itself and its peripheral equipment. Also included are the instructions and facts the computer processes, as well as operating manuals, procedures, and the people who use the computer. In other words, all the components that contribute to making the computer a useful tool can be said to be parts of a computer system. When a computer system is controlled by a small chip called a *microprocessor*, it is called a **microcomputer system** and, particularly when it is designed to be used by one person at a time, a *personal computer system* or **personal computer (PC).** Figure 1-2 features a desktop personal computer system typical of those being sold today.

At the heart of every PC is its microprocessor, which is also commonly known as the PC's **central processing unit (CPU).** In a word, it's the **computer** itself. The CPU is analogous to the stereo amplifier. Like its counterpart, the CPU can't do anything useful without peripheral equipment—for input, output, and storage functions—and storage media, which contain the

FIGURE 1-2

A computer system.

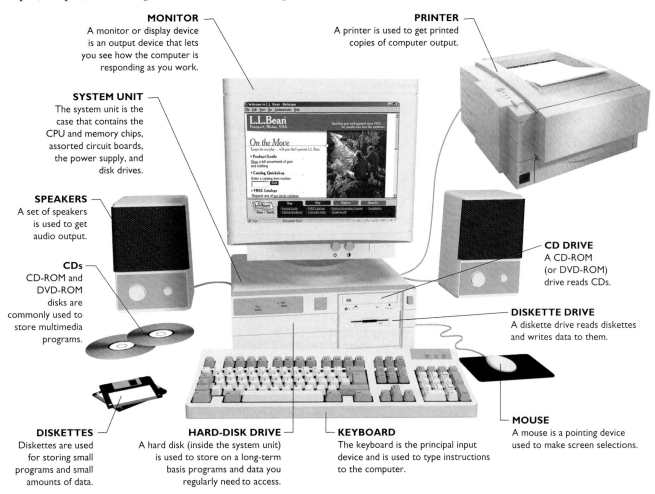

MONITOR
A monitor or display device is an output device that lets you see how the computer is responding as you work.

PRINTER
A printer is used to get printed copies of computer output.

SYSTEM UNIT
The system unit is the case that contains the CPU and memory chips, assorted circuit boards, the power supply, and disk drives.

SPEAKERS
A set of speakers is used to get audio output.

CDs
CD-ROM and DVD-ROM disks are commonly used to store multimedia programs.

CD DRIVE
A CD-ROM (or DVD-ROM) drive reads CDs.

DISKETTE DRIVE
A diskette drive reads diskettes and writes data to them.

MOUSE
A mouse is a pointing device used to make screen selections.

DISKETTES
Diskettes are used for storing small programs and small amounts of data.

HARD-DISK DRIVE
A hard disk (inside the system unit) is used to store on a long-term basis programs and data you regularly need to access.

KEYBOARD
The keyboard is the principal input device and is used to type instructions to the computer.

■ **Storage media.** Objects that store computer-processed materials. ■ **Machine-readable form.** Any form that represents data so that computer equipment can read them. ■ **Computer system.** A collection of elements that includes the computer and components that contribute to making it a useful tool. ■ **Microcomputer system.** A computer system driven by a microprocessor. ■ **Personal computer (PC).** A microcomputer system designed to be used by one person at a time. ■ **Computer.** The piece of equipment, also known as the **central processing unit (CPU),** that interprets and executes program instructions and communicates with peripheral devices.

programs and data the computer crunches to produce results. Computer *input* and *output (I/O) devices* include, to name only a few, keyboards, mice, display devices, speakers, and printers. *Storage devices* include the drives that hold disks and tapes—the storage media. The storage devices featured in Figure 1-2 are a diskette drive, a hard-disk drive, and a CD drive.

A computer system, of course, is not a stereo sound system, and a computer is much more versatile than a stereo amplifier. For example, a computer system can perform an enormous variety of processing tasks and a stereo system only a few. Also, a computer can support a much greater variety of input and output devices than can a stereo amplifier.

Two things that give a computer its flexibility are its memory and its ability to be programmed. The computer's *memory*, or "workspace," is an electronic storage area that allows the computer to retain whatever inputs it receives and the results it produces from the input. An ordinary home sound system has no such memory; what's playing on the CD player or tape deck passes directly through the amplifier to the speakers. Because computers can hold materials in such a workspace, they can be directed by *programs* to rearrange or recombine those materials in an amazing variety of ways before sending them along to you as output.

THE ROLE OF DATA AND PROGRAMS

A computer receives two kinds of material as input: data and programs. If data are like clay, then programs are the hands that mold the clay from a lump into something meaningful.

DATA: A MULTIMEDIA PERSPECTIVE

Data are essentially raw, unorganized facts. Almost any kind of fact or set of facts can become computer data: a collection of personal observations, last year's sales figures, a colorful graph, or a set of employee records.

Data can exist in many forms. The four types of data commonly handled by computer systems are text, graphics, audio, and video.

Text data have been around the longest. These data usually consist of standard alphabetic, numeric, and special characters—that is, the symbols one normally sees in a simple word-processed letter, a budget, or a printed report.

Graphics data consist of still pictures such as drawings, graphs, photographs, and illustrations. Graphics data often require a more sophisticated representation inside the computer than that used by text because they are naturally more complicated and are often multicolored.

An example of *audio* data is an ordinary telephone conversation. Any type of sound—including music and voice—is considered audio data. Modern computers can store sounds in machine-readable form just as they store any other type of data.

Video data consist of motion pictures, such as a movie clip, a feature-length film, or a live conference. Put another way, video data are graphics data that move. Two common types of video are *computer animation* and *full-motion video*. The former are a series of similar two-dimensional drawings or three-dimensional computer models that are displayed one right after another to

For a tutorial on multimedia hardware go to www. harcourtcollege.com/infosys/ pcc2e/student/tutor/ and click on Chapter 1.

■ **Data.** A collection of raw, unorganized facts.

produce the illusion of motion, as you see in TV cartoons, whereas the latter are usually a series of photographic frames such as those that comprise most motion pictures. Many PCs today are capable of handling video data in one form or another.

MULTIMEDIA COMPUTING   Most PCs sold today are *multimedia computer systems*. That is, they can combine any or all of the four data types. Multimedia computer systems display conventional text and graphics on a display screen, they play audio output over speakers, they can run video clips stored on CDs—such as CD-ROM and its higher-capacity successor, DVD-ROM—and they have special circuit boards and processor chips that enhance multimedia output. Figure 1-3 features a multimedia application. CD-ROM and DVD-ROM will be covered in more detail later in the chapter.

PROGRAMS: THE INSTRUCTIONS THAT SHAPE DATA

Programs are instructions that tell the computer how to process data to produce *meaningful information*—the results that you, the computer system user, want. Like many other devices, the amplifier in your home sound system is *special-purpose*. It is designed to perform only a few specific tasks—interact with a CD player, play music into speakers or headphones, and the like. These functions are built into its circuitry. To put it another way, the amplifier is "hardwired" to perform a very limited number of specific tasks.

Most computers, in contrast, are *general-purpose* devices. They are able to perform a large variety of tasks—for instance, preparing letters to clients, analyzing sales figures, and creating slide presentations, to name a few. Because most computers must be flexible, they can't be hardwired to do the hundreds of tasks they may be required to do. Instead, they rely on programs for guidance. Every program contains instructions that tell the computer exactly what to do. As each program is being processed by the computer system, it is provided a specific set of data by the user. The program and its data input then direct the computer to perform in the manner needed to do whatever task needs to be done.

Programs are created in a particular **programming language**—a code the computer system can read and translate into the electronic pulses that make it work. Programming languages come in many varieties—Visual BASIC, C++, and Java are a few that you may have heard about in the news. Today, it is possible for millions of people to use computers without having to write their own programs, leaving that task to computer professionals. All most users need to do to operate a program is be able to make intuitive screen selections (which pass on the proper instructions to the computer) and be able to enter data from time to time (when the computer says on the screen to do so). It is also common for computer systems to supply forms for users to follow so that they can enter words and numbers in the right places, thus simplifying the data-entry task considerably.

For links to further information about programming languages, go to www. harcourtcollege.com/ infosys/pcc2e/student/ explore/ and click on Chapter 1.

FIGURE 1-3

Multimedia computing. Most of the computers sold today have a multimedia capability, which means that they can handle audio and video data in addition to conventional text and graphics.

■ **Program.** A set of instructions that causes the computer system to perform specific actions. ■ **Programming language.** A set of rules used to write computer programs.

A CLOSER LOOK AT STORAGE

So far we've seen that if you want to get something done on a computer system, you must present it with both facts (data) and instructions (a program) specifying how to process those facts. For example, if you want the system to write payroll checks, you must supply such data as employees' names, Social Security numbers, and salaries. The program instructions "tell" the system how to compute taxes, how to take deductions, where and how to print the checks, and so forth. The computer relies on storage to remember all these details as it is doing the work. Actually, computer systems contain two types of storage.

MEMORY

Primary storage—often called **memory** or **RAM** (for **random access memory**)—holds the data and programs that the computer is currently processing. RAM functions like a scratch pad; the data are stored only temporarily, as they are needed for processing. When data are "captured" in the computer's memory, they can be rearranged or recombined by the instructions in the program. Memory is contained within the *system unit*—the case that houses the computer (refer again to Figure 1-2).

More often than not, the work that you create in a computer session needs to be used at a later time, say, tomorrow or next week. Because turning off the computer destroys any data left in RAM, another means of storage—called *secondary storage*—is needed so that work can be *saved*.

SECONDARY STORAGE

Data and programs the computer-system user needs from session to session are stored in **secondary storage.** On PCs, the most common type of *secondary storage device* is the disk drive—more specifically, diskette, hard-disk, and CD drives, all of which are usually fitted into the system unit. These devices and their media enable you to save large quantities of data and programs conveniently in machine-readable form, on a relatively long-term basis, so that you need not retype them into the system or reinstall them every time you need to use them. Secondary storage devices on microcomputer systems are usually capable of storing thousands of programs and millions of pieces of data.

When the CPU needs a certain program and set of data, it requests them from the secondary storage device—much as you might request a particular song from a jukebox—and reads them into RAM for processing. Unlike a jukebox, however, which puts the original copy of the CD or phonograph record into play, the CPU puts a duplicate of the original program or data into RAM for use. As you finish with the duplicate, you can save it separately from the original or save it so that it replaces the original.

The difference between RAM and secondary storage is similar to the difference between your own memory and this textbook. You read this textbook by bringing a few facts at a time into your memory and processing them through your brain. As you read, there become two copies of many of the

---

■ **Memory.** Also known as **random access memory (RAM)**, the section of the computer system that temporarily holds data and program instructions awaiting processing, intermediate results, and processed output. ■ **Secondary storage.** Storage on media such as disk and tape that supplements memory.

SECONDARY STORAGE
Secondary storage such as disk and tape are used by the computer like a library; the computer finds the material it needs on them and adds new materials from time to time.

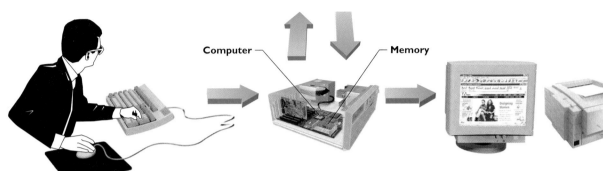

Computer —  — Memory

INPUT
The user deploys a mouse and a keyboard to enter input to the computer.

PROCESSING
Every time the user inputs something, the computer must respond. For instance, when a program from secondary storage is requested, the computer must find it and load it into memory. Similarly, when a document is to be saved or output, the computer must transfer it from memory to secondary storage or to an output device.

OUTPUT
Output devices such as a monitor and a printer present computer results to the user.

facts—the copy in the textbook and the copy in your memory. The facts in the textbook, like data in secondary storage, are long term; they will not disappear if you take the weekend off to go camping. Many of the facts saved in your own memory, however, will disappear as soon as your mind moves on to something else—just like data in RAM.

Figure 1-4 illustrates the relationships among input, processing, output, memory, and secondary storage.

FIGURE 1-4

Input, processing, output, and storage. These tasks are repeatedly performed when the user and computer are engaged in an interactive dialog.

HARDWARE AND SOFTWARE

In the world of computers, it is common to distinguish between hardware and software.

HARDWARE

The word **hardware** refers to the actual machinery that makes up a computer system—for example, the CPU, input and output devices, and storage devices. We've already spent a good portion of this chapter on the hardware parts of a computer system, so we won't dwell on them here.

SOFTWARE

The word **software** refers to computer programs. As already mentioned, programs direct the computer system to do specific tasks, just as your thoughts

■ **Hardware.** Physical equipment in a computing environment, such as the computer and its peripheral devices.
■ **Software.** Computer programs.

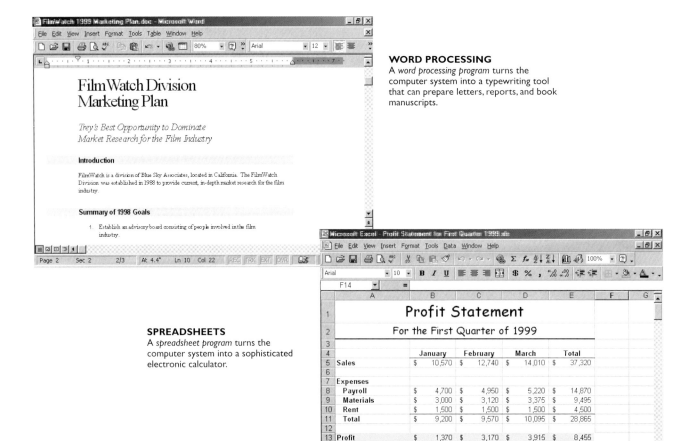

WORD PROCESSING
A *word processing program* turns the computer system into a typewriting tool that can prepare letters, reports, and book manuscripts.

SPREADSHEETS
A *spreadsheet program* turns the computer system into a sophisticated electronic calculator.

PRESENTATION GRAPHICS
Presentation graphics programs turn the computer system into a tool that can be used to prepare slides, overheads, and other presentation materials for meetings.

 **FIGURE 1-5**

Productivity software. Productivity software is designed to make both ordinary users and computer professionals more productive at their jobs.

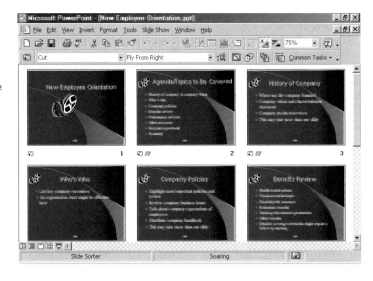

direct your body to speak or move in certain ways. Software comes in two basic varieties: applications software and systems software.

APPLICATIONS SOFTWARE **Applications software** is designed to assist with such tasks as creating letters and books, preparing and analyzing budgets, managing files and databases, playing games, scheduling airline flights, or diagnosing hospital patients' illnesses. In other words, applications software makes

---

■ **Applications software.** Programs that help with the type of work that people acquire computer systems to do.

DATABASE MANAGEMENT
A *database management system* turns the computer system into an electronic research assistant, capable of searching through mounds of data to prepare reports and answer queries.

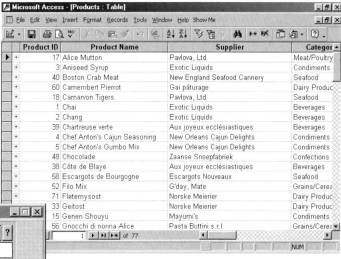

E-MAIL
An *electronic mail (e-mail) program* enables people to compose and send, receive, and manage electronic mail messages.

WEB BROWSER
Web browsers enable people to get to any of the thousands of sites on the Internet's World Wide Web and to output Web pages on a display screen.

possible the types of "computer work" most people have in mind when they acquire a computer system. **Productivity software** is the class of applications software designed to help workers be more productive at their jobs. Some important types of productivity software are described in Figure 1-5; in Chapter 3, we cover productivity software in far more detail.

SYSTEMS SOFTWARE   **Systems software** consists of "background" programs that enable applications software to run on a computer system's hardware devices. One of the most important pieces of systems software is the *operating*

■ **Productivity software.** Computer programs, such as word processors and spreadsheets, designed to make workers more productive in their jobs. ■ **Systems software.** Background programs, such as the operating system, that enable applications programs to run on a computer system's hardware.

FIGURE 1-6

Software package. A typical software package consists of one or more program disks, a printed user's guide, and a printed user's license inside a shrink-wrapped box.

system, a set of control programs that supervises the computer system's work. Many recent Hollywood movies have portrayed the role of the operating system in an overly exaggerated manner—for example, as a demon master-control program that tries to take over the world. Fortunately, operating systems don't control people; rather, people control operating systems. Two common operating systems used with PCs are Microsoft Windows and Mac OS.

The software you buy today in a store or through the mail is often in package form (see Figure 1-6). Typically, such a *software package* consists of program disks, operating instructions, training tutorials, a warranty, and printed or electronic reference manuals inside a shrink-wrapped box or plastic case. All the programs on the disks have been written in a programming language, though, as a general rule, you do not have to learn the language in which the package is written—or, for that matter, learn any language at all—to be able to use the package. Increasingly, software is being distributed over computer networks like the Internet, and it is quite possible that someday in the near future, the software package that you buy in the box will be a rarity. Such software may be available for free or you may have to pay a one-time fee or monthly subscription fee to use it.

The most widely used software products are revised every year or two to keep up with changes in technology, such as bigger disk drives, faster microprocessor chips, larger memories, and the like. Each revision is commonly referred to as a *version* or *release* and is assigned a number—for instance, Windows 98, Office 2000, and WordPerfect 9.

ORGANIZING DATA AND PROGRAMS

Data, as we said earlier, are essentially facts, and programs are the instructions that shape those facts into meaningful information. Unfortunately, you can't randomly input a collection of facts and instructions into a computer system and expect to get the desired results. To be processed by any type of computer system, data and programs must be organized in a systematic way (see Figure 1-7).

DOCUMENTS AND FOLDERS

One of the fundamental ways that data and programs are organized is through documents and folders. For instance, when you are working with a word processor, each memo, letter, or report that you create is stored as a separate electronic **document.** Related documents are, in turn, stored in an

---

■ **Document.** Any single piece of work that's created with software and then given a name by which it may be accessed.

DOCUMENTS AND FOLDERS
Documents and folders are handy for organizing such outputs as memos, letters, reports, budgets, and programs.

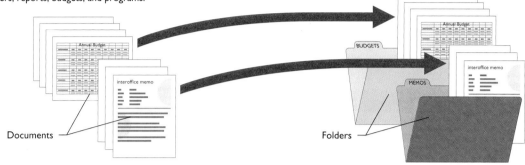

Documents   Folders

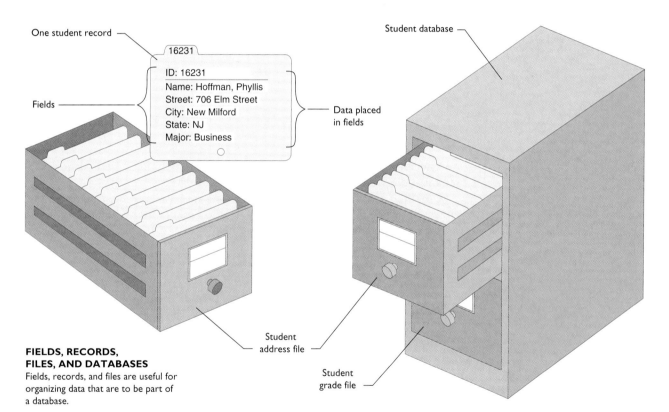

One student record

16231

ID: 16231
Name: Hoffman, Phyllis
Street: 706 Elm Street
City: New Milford
State: NJ
Major: Business

Fields

Data placed in fields

Student database

Student address file

Student grade file

FIELDS, RECORDS, FILES, AND DATABASES
Fields, records, and files are useful for organizing data that are to be part of a database.

electronic **folder.** Thus, one folder might contain memos to business associates while another holds a set of budgets for a specific project. Related programs are stored in their own folders, too. Organizing into documents and folders is natural for most office workers, a number of whom were using cardboard file folders to organize paperwork well before PCs became a fixture on desktops.

In the documents-folders method of organization used by computers, you can also create *subfolders* within each folder. Consequently, you might create a "Letters" folder that contains one subfolder with letters sent to friends and a second with letters sent to business associates. A folder can contain any mixture of subfolders and independent documents.

△ **FIGURE 1-7**

Organizing data and programs.

■ **Folder.** A container for documents.

WEB-PAGE ORGANIZATION

Many of you may have had the experience of looking at screen pages from the Internet's World Wide Web, or Web. A *Web page* is a document that is assigned a unique address on the computer on which it is stored. The *Disney.com* page in Figure 1-5 is such an example. By entering its address on your own local computer, you can access such a page over ordinary phone lines if your PC is connected to the Internet. Usually Web pages are a little bigger than the size of a screen, and you will have to scroll the page up or down on your PC to see parts of the page that are currently off the screen. When you click your mouse in special places on the page, the page is usually replaced with another that is linked to it.

Related Web pages are usually stored in the same folder on the remote computer, and the complete collection of such pages and folders is called a *Web site*. For instance, at the Disney Web site you will find pages about Disney movies (stored in a Movies folder), pages about Disney TV shows (stored in a TV folder), pages about Disney merchandise for sale (stored in a Shopping folder), and so on.

To gain access to a specific page at a Web site, type in the appropriate address, or click your mouse on an appropriate descriptor. For instance, to get to pages about Disney movies, click on the word "Movies" on the Disney.com Web page. A detailed discussion of the Internet and Web is reserved for a later chapter.

FIELDS, RECORDS, FILES, AND DATABASES

Another common procedure—which is most widely used with data—is to organize the data into fields, records, files, and databases.

A **field** is a collection of characters (such as a single digit, letter of the alphabet, or special symbol such as a decimal point) that represents a single type of data. Two examples are a person's name and the price of a product. A **record** is a collection of related fields—say, the ID number, name, address, and phone number of John Q. Jones. A **file** is a collection of related records, and a **database** is a set of related files.

Your school, for example, probably has a *file*, stored on disk, of all students currently enrolled. The file contains a *record* for each student. Each record has several *fields* containing various types of data about a particular student: ID number, name, street, city and state of residence, major subject area, and the like. What's more, your school probably even has a student *database* that consists of several files—say, a student address file (such as the one in Figure 1-7), a student grade file (containing courses completed and grades earned by each student), and possibly other student-oriented files. Put another way, most of the information about students would be found in such a student database.

Documents, folders, fields, records, files, and databases usually have names and other ways of being uniquely identified. Both you and the computer system use such identifiers to find the entity when you wish to access, modify, or delete it.

Be aware that many of the terms you've learned about in this section can be used interchangeably or used in different contexts. For instance, a "word-processed file" and a "word-processed document" generally refer to the same thing—the output that a user creates and names with a word-processing program. Also, the term "file," traditionally used to mean "group of records," is commonly extended to programs (which are groups of instructions). Thus, the term

---

■ **Field.** A collection of related characters. ■ **Record.** A collection of related fields. ■ **File.** A collection of related records. ■ **Database.** A collection of related files.

"program file" is in common usage and used interchangeably with "program." As you learn more about computers, you'll get to see that it's not unusual for several terms to mean the same thing or for one term to mean several things.

TYPES OF PCS

As illustrated in Figure 1-8, the system units accompanying most PCs are classified as being either desktop or portable.

DESKTOP UNITS

Desktop computers are those found most often sitting on desktops in schools, homes, and businesses. These are the computer systems that have become household names—IBM Aptiva and ValuePoint; Apple Macintosh; Compaq Presario; and so on.

Desktop PCs come in two styles. In the *desktop-case model,* the system-unit case is designed specifically to be placed on a desktop. In the *tower-case model*, the system-unit case is upright and can be placed on either a desktop or floor. Tower cases have more room in which to mount secondary storage units and leave more space on the desktop for people to work. But because

 FIGURE 1-8

PCs. (from left to right, top to bottom) Desktop PC with desktop-style case. Desktop PC with tower-style case. Notebook computer. Hand-held computer.

■ **Desktop computer.** A computer system that is designed to reside on an ordinary desktop. Contrasts with portable computer.

store copies of the programs and data they regularly use on their hard disks. Copies (backups) of these programs and data, as well as less frequently used materials, are typically stored off the computer, such as on diskette or CD.

Lydia's hard disk already has everything she needs for beginning her work-day, so all she has to do to get started is to turn on the PC's power. As soon as the computer system is turned on, it automatically loads portions of the operating system into RAM. Within a minute, the operating system returns a screen indicating that it is ready to receive directives from Lydia (see the first screen of Figure 1-10). This process of the computer system readying itself for processing is called *booting*.

Next, after the system is booted up, Lydia must make a selection with her mouse that tells the computer which applications program she wishes to work on—say, her word-processing program or her spreadsheet program. Once she makes her choice, certain portions of the selected applications program are loaded from hard disk into RAM. At

FIGURE 1-10

Lydia getting started on her computer system.

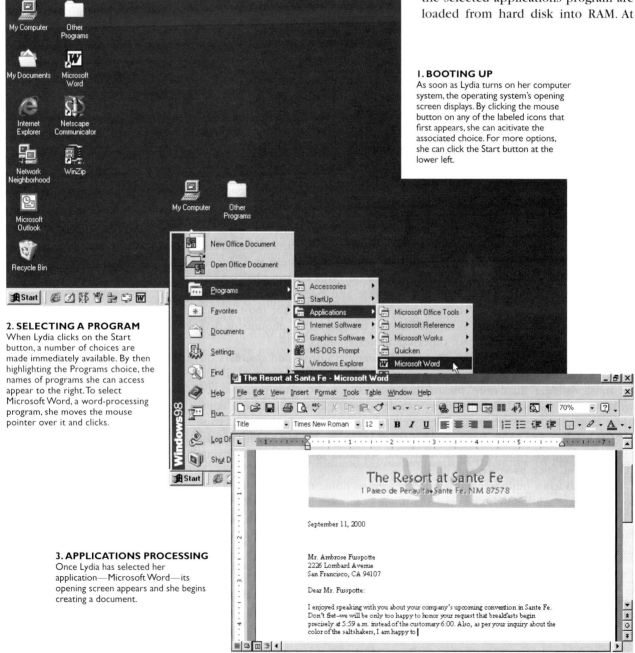

1. BOOTING UP
As soon as Lydia turns on her computer system, the operating system's opening screen displays. By clicking the mouse button on any of the labeled icons that first appears, she can acitvate the associated choice. For more options, she can click the Start button at the lower left.

2. SELECTING A PROGRAM
When Lydia clicks on the Start button, a number of choices are made immediately available. By then highlighting the Programs choice, the names of programs she can access appear to the right. To select Microsoft Word, a word-processing program, she moves the mouse pointer over it and clicks.

3. APPLICATIONS PROCESSING
Once Lydia has selected her application—Microsoft Word—its opening screen appears and she begins creating a document.

this point, the applications program temporarily takes control of the computer system from the operating system. Once an applications program is activated, the computer is transformed into a powerful, useful tool that is defined by the capabilities of the program.

APPLICATIONS PROCESSING   One use for which Lydia finds her computer system indispensable is *word processing*. When a letter must be quickly prepared and sent to a client to confirm a booking date or to thank the client for his or her business, Lydia uses Microsoft Word—her word-processing program.

To begin, Lydia selects the Word icon with her mouse so that the proper operating-system routine (in RAM) will retrieve Word for her (see the second screen in Figure 1-10). She does this by rolling her mouse along its mouse pad and, when the onscreen mouse pointer (arrow) is pointing to Word, clicking the left mouse button. Then, when the initial Word screen appears, she begins typing a letter (see the third screen in Figure 1-10).

The panels at the top of the standard Word screen let her choose among dozens of typeface styles and sizes, as well as among such special effects as boldface and italic text. When she finishes the letter, she will select with her mouse a printer-shaped icon to have it printed out on her printer and, also, a disk-shaped icon to save the letter to the proper folder on her hard disk. These operations, too, are activated from the top-of-screen panels. To save the letter onto her hard disk, she may ask her PC to save the document using the name Fusspotte and to place the document on the C drive. Lydia likes giving documents meaningful names so that she doesn't have to think twice about what the documents contain when she sees their names listed on the screen.

Lydia also frequently uses her PC to prepare budgets, a task that requires her to use a *spreadsheet* program. To work with the program, Lydia again needs to summon a program menu from her operating system and follow the same types of steps as she did when she accessed her word-processing program. A few years ago, the operating system she used then (called MS-DOS) required her to shut down, or *close*, her word-processing program before launching another applications program, but these days she uses a newer operating system (Windows 98), which enables her to keep several applications open at the same time and move among them freely.

With her spreadsheet program open and ready to go, she is ready to prepare budgets. After she creates them, she can send the completed budgets to her printer or save them to her hard disk. With a few mouse clicks, she can even import tables from the budgets into letters that she's creating with her word-processing program.

To plan meals, Lydia uses a *database management system*. To get this application up and running, she again summons the operating system to open it for her. The database program is especially useful in assisting Lydia with searches through descriptions of food dishes to find ones that will fit a particular client's needs. On her hard disk is stored a *file* of recipe *records*, one for each food dish she can offer to guests. If Lydia is helping a client plan a Saturday-night banquet over the phone, for instance, she can summon the database program to search for all "main-course" recipes in the file in which "beef" and "mushrooms" are included among the ingredients. Then she can have the names of these dishes displayed on her monitor—and eventually send specific recipes to her printer.

Lydia could rely on her memory, but having the computer system do the search for her often turns up good alternatives that did not cross her mind. Also, she can save a lot of time by having her computer system do the searching in the background while she attends to other matters with the client.

Lydia also has a *modem*, which enables her PC to get data from or send data to other computers located miles away. For instance, Lydia uses her computer to place food and beverage orders automatically with a distributor located in another state. Through the Internet, Lydia can use her Web browser to look up the *home page* for the distributor. She can read the page for items of interest and then place a food or beverage order on an electronic form and transmit the order over regular telephone lines. The distributor's *Web site*, which consists of several related screen pages that can be reached through the Internet, provides a confirmation of the order and also allows Lydia to inspect the stock selection and prices before she orders. Recently, Lydia acquired an *intelligent agent* program that inspects sites on the Internet automatically and looks for the lowest prices on certain items.

Resort employees, including Lydia, are particularly excited about the new opportunities the Internet has created. For instance, travelers with home PCs can access the hotel's Web site and get room rates as well as detailed restaurant and facility information. The site has cut down on phone calls, which has saved money on staffing. Recently, resort management decided to use the Internet for competitive advantage by providing an online service that enables guests to book rooms on their PCs at a cost lower than if a clerk had to do the same task manually.

THE BOTTOM LINE: DOING WORK FASTER AND BETTER One reason for Lydia's success at her job is her skill at quickly pulling together key information when dealing with clients, managers, and suppliers. The database management system and word processor allow Lydia to give clients first-class service. The resort's management appreciates the value of this; a $20,000 booking can easily be won or lost on the quality of service. The spreadsheet allows Lydia to quickly prepare important financial information for management and to analyze that information in ways that would not be feasible if she had to do it by hand. Also, the ability to network enables Lydia to save time and lower costs when placing orders and to explore new channels for marketing the resort's services. These are but a few of the benefits that PCs and their productivity software provide.

SUMMARY AND KEY TERMS

Go to the Online Glossary at www.harcourtcollege.com/infosys/pcc2e/student/ to review key terms.

Whatever profession you choose, you will be able to work both faster and smarter if you know how to use a personal computer, or PC.

PCs IN THE WORKPLACE The PC revolution that started about two decades ago and is still in full swing has resulted in a flood of high-quality computing products in the marketplace. These products have changed the way many organizations do work and the type of skills they seek in the people they hire.

WHAT'S A PERSONAL COMPUTER? Four words summarize the operation of any computer system: **input, processing, output,** and **storage.**

The processing function is performed by the **computer** itself, which is sometimes called the **central processing unit,** or **CPU.**

The input and output functions are performed by **peripheral equipment,** such as **input devices** and **output devices.** Mounted on some of the peripheral equipment are **storage media.** Storage media retain materials in **machine-readable** form, which the computer system can recognize and process.

At a minimum, a **computer system** consists of the computer itself and its peripheral equipment. When a computer system is controlled by a small chip called a microprocessor and is designed to be used by one person at a time, it is commonly called a **microcomputer system** or, sometimes, a **personal computer** or **PC.**

THE ROLE OF DATA AND PROGRAMS   The material that a computer receives as input is of two kinds: data and programs. **Data** are the raw, unorganized facts the computer has at its disposal; **programs** are instructions that explain to the computer what to do with these facts. Programs must be written in a **programming language** that the computer can understand.

A CLOSER LOOK AT STORAGE   Computer systems have two types of storage. *Primary storage* (which is often called **memory** or **RAM,** for **random access memory**) is often built into the unit housing the computer itself; it temporarily holds the programs and data that the system is currently processing. **Secondary storage** is used to store programs and data that are needed from session to session.

HARDWARE AND SOFTWARE   In the world of computers, it is common to distinguish between hardware and software. **Hardware** refers to the actual machinery that makes up the computer system, such as the CPU, input and output devices, and secondary storage devices. **Software** refers to computer programs. Software comes in two basic forms: **applications software** and **systems software.** The class of applications software that helps make people more productive in doing their jobs is called **productivity software.**

ORGANIZING DATA AND PROGRAMS   One of the fundamental ways that data and programs are organized is into **documents** and **folders.** On the Internet's World Wide Web, folders are used to store related *Web pages*, and the complete collection of Web pages and folders is called a *Web site.* Another common procedure is to organize data into fields, records, and files. A **field** is a collection of characters that represents a single type of data. A **record** is a collection of related fields. A **file** is a collection of related records, and a **database** is a collection of related files.

TYPES OF PCs   Many PCs in use today are **desktop computers** or **notebook computers.** Each type of computer is usually a **PC-compatible** or Macintosh-compatible **platform.**

COMPUTER NETWORKS   The need to share hardware, software, and data is met by tying together computers into a computer network. To gain access to such a network you need a hardware adapter such as a *modem*, communications software, and possibly an access provider. Any computer that is in a state in which it can send data to or receive data from a computer network is said to be **online** to the network. If a computer isn't online, it's **offline.**

USING PCs: A COMPREHENSIVE EXAMPLE   Chapter 1 concludes with a comprehensive example that ties together many of the materials presented earlier in the chapter.

EXERCISES

1. From smallest to largest, place the following terms in the correct order: file, record, database, field.

2. Define the following terms:
   a. Peripheral equipment
   b. Central processing unit (CPU)
   c. Platform
   d. Offline
   e. Secondary storage

3. What is the difference between a file and a database? Provide an example of each.

4. Select the term that best matches each phrase:
   - a. Software   f. RAM
   - b. Hardware   g. Diskette
   - c. Folder   h. File
   - d. Computer   i. Network computer
   - e. Data   j. Programming language
   - _____ Equipment in a computer system
   - _____ Another name for memory
   - _____ A set of rules used to create software
   - _____ A collection of related records
   - _____ A collection of related documents
   - _____ Another name for the CPU
   - _____ A collection of unorganized facts
   - _____ A type of secondary storage
   - _____ Another name for programs
   - _____ A diskless PC

5. For the following list of computer hardware, write the principal function of each device in the space provided. Choices include input device, output device, storage device, and processing device.
   - a. CPU _____
   - b. Mouse _____
   - c. Monitor _____
   - d. CD-ROM drive _____
   - e. Keyboard _____
   - f. Diskette drive _____
   - g. System unit _____
   - h. Printer _____
   - i. Subnotebook computer _____

6. Fill in the blanks.
   - a. Four words sum up the operation of a computer system: input, processing, output, and _____.
   - b. Computer systems that can handle text, graphics, audio, and video data are called _____ computer systems.
   - c. RAM is an acronym for _____.
   - d. PC-compatible and Macintosh-compatible are two types of _____.
   - e. Memory is sometimes called _____ storage, whereas tape and disk are examples of _____ storage.
   - f. Another name for programs is _____.
   - g. Programs are written using a programming _____.

7. Match each term with the description that best fits.
   - a. Word-processing program
   - b. Operating system
   - c. Web browser
   - d. Spreadsheet program
   - e. Database management system
   - _____ Helps search through a large bank of facts, such as airline flight schedules
   - _____ Supervises the running of all other programs on the computer
   - _____ Helps prepare letters and text reports
   - _____ Turns the computer into a sophisticated electronic calculator and analysis tool
   - _____ Helps to display parts of the Internet

8. **Correct the Definition** Each of the following definitions is not strictly true in some regard. In each case, identify how the definition is false. Then, correct the error by defining the term in the right way.
   - a. Memory: Another name for computer storage.
   - b. Hardware: The peripheral equipment in a computer system.
   - c. Computer: A term that refers to the CPU and all of the storage and input/output equipment that supports it.
   - d. Processing: The conversion of output to input.
   - e. Productivity software: Applications software.

9. Identify the following as either true (T) or false (F).
   - _____ Data and programs are essentially the same thing.
   - _____ Word processors are types of computer operating systems.
   - _____ A device can be online to a computer network even when the power to the device is shut off.
   - _____ A folder can consist of both files and other folders.
   - _____ The operating system is an example of productivity software.

10. Order the following list of PCs by size, from the largest to the smallest.
    - a. Notebook computer
    - b. PDA
    - c. Laptop computer
    - d. Desktop computer
    - e. Subnotebook computer

11. Name the four types of data covered in the chapter, and answer the following questions:
    - a. How are these types of data related to the term *multimedia*?
    - b. You type a letter to a friend and include with it a computerized picture of your dog. What types of data does the letter include?

12. How does memory differ from secondary storage? Name the secondary storage media covered in this chapter.

PROJECTS

1. THE INTERNET The Internet and World Wide Web are both handy tools that can help you research topics covered in this textbook and also help you with many of the projects. While a detailed explanation of how the Internet and the Web work is beyond the scope of this chapter—read Chapter 5 if you want to know more—it would be to your advantage to learn how to use these tools right from the outset. That's not a difficult task. It's simply a matter of finding an Internet-enabled computer on your campus, logging on to the Internet from this computer, typing an address to get to a specific information site, and then making selections at the site.

a. Find a computer at your school that has access to the Internet. Then, follow the directions provided by your instructor or lab aide to log on to the Internet.

b. What is the name of the software package—used by the computer you are working on—that helps people browse through Internet information?

c. Access the "home page" of your school. What is the *Web address* of this page; that is, the string of characters that anyone at any location can type into a computer to locate your school? (You should see a box on the screen that displays a long string of characters beginning with *http://*, and right after this set of characters—beginning with *www* and often ending with *.edu*—is the address of your school's home page.)

d. What types of information did you find at your school's Web site? (To see information beyond the home page, select—with a mouse or a keyboard—one of the highlighted pieces of text on the page. Each piece of highlighted text—which is distinguished by coloring, boldfacing, and underlining—is called a *hyperlink*. It is by selecting hyperlinks that you move to other pages.)

e. Access the home pages of at least two other schools. You can get to other schools by first accessing an Internet *search site* such as any of the five below (the Web address you need to type into the computer is in the second column). These search sites let you type in key words to find information or, alternatively, let you use a comprehensive menu system.

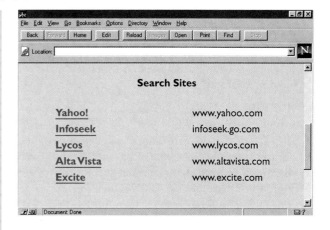

When you've reached the home page of the search site you've chosen, select the highlighted text that says "Colleges and Universities" (or something similar to that). Then, keep making selections on subsequent screens until you find the school you are seeking. What types of information or features did you find at these other college sites that were different from your own school's Web site?

f. What are the Web addresses of the two schools you looked up in part e of this exercise?

g. To get to the Parker home page, type

www.harcourtcollege.com/infosys/pcc2/

Here you will find updated information on the projects contained in this book as well as other items of interest. Make a preliminary exploration of the information available by selecting hyperlinks.

h. "Log off" the Internet, and turn off your computer.

2. PRODUCTIVITY SOFTWARE Figure 1-5 shows several types of productivity software. For this project, find the names of two commercial programs that fit into each category listed below, and identify the company that produces each program you choose.

a. Word-processing program
b. Spreadsheet program
c. Database management program
d. Web browser

3. COMPUTER JOURNALS Go to your school library or to a local bookstore, and find five journals (magazines or newspapers) that focus on PCs. For each journal, list the following information on the following page:

a. The name of the journal

b. The frequency with which the journal is published (e.g., weekly, monthly, bimonthly)

c. The audience the journal specifically targets (for instance, word-processor users, users of Macintosh computers, people who use the Internet)

d. Many journals are also published in online versions that appear on the Internet's World Wide Web. If any of the five journals you have chosen exist in an online form, provide their Web addresses. (You do not need Internet access to get this information.)

4. **COMPUTER ADVERTISEMENTS** Look in a computer journal—such as *PC Magazine* or *MacWorld*—for an advertisement featuring a personal computer system for sale. What are the principal hardware components of this system and their functions? What systems and applications software does the ad offer as part of the purchase price and what—specifically—does each of these programs do? Do the hardware and software systems provide complete capabilities for performing simple chores such as creating letters and writing term reports, or would you have to purchase additional hardware or software?

5. **ONLINE BOOKSTORES** Online bookstores are appearing on the World Wide Web with increasing frequency. Two popular ones are the Amazon Bookstore (www.amazon.com), which offers one of the largest collections of book titles you'll find in a single place, and Fatbrain.com (www.fatbrain.com), which has one of the largest collections of computer books and magazines available anywhere.

a. Get onto the Web, and visit one of these bookstores (or perhaps another of your own choosing). Compare the online bookstore's prices on two computer books (of your own choosing) with those of a conventional bookstore in your area. Are the online bookstore's prices higher or lower? (*Hint:* You can search for other online bookstores through a search site such as Yahoo! or Excite. Type "online bookstores" into the space that offers a keyword search to see what is currently available.)

b. The software at many online bookstores lets you search for books by typing in an author's name, a book's subject area, or a keyword contained in a book's title. Try as many book-search tools as you can while visiting at least one online bookstore site, and make a list of those available. Do you find the Internet useful as a search tool for book titles and prices?

c. The Amazon site currently lets visitors access book reviews of titles in which they're interested and even write their own reviews of

books for others to read. At the bookstore site you've chosen to visit, list as many features like this as you can that aren't typically available at conventional bookstores.

6. **ONLINE SHOPPING** The accompanying figure shows the Web site for L.L. Bean, a mail-order seller of outdoor clothing and equipment. The company is famous for its printed catalogs, received annually by millions of people, which it still sends out to supplement its Web site. For this project, visit the L.L. Bean site at

www.llbean.com

Report to the class how shoppers can electronically search for items of interest and how they can select a certain size or color of an apparel item. What are the advantages and disadvantages or an online catalog, relative to a printed one?

7. **COMPUTER CASE STUDY: REGISTERING FOR CLASSES** One of the ways computers have helped colleges and universities throughout the years is registering students for classes every semester.

a. On your own campus, how do computers help out in the registration process? Make a list of the individual tasks that computers perform that would otherwise be done manually.

b. News reports regularly feature stories about colleges using leading-edge technologies to help out in the registration process. For instance, some colleges let students register over the Internet or by Touch-Tone phone. Find one such story in a computer magazine or newspaper, and report to your class about it.

8. **WHAT'S MY LINE?** By looking at advertisements in computer journals or by going on the Internet and visiting the Web sites of computer companies, state whether each of the computer lines or models listed below is exclusively portable, exclusively desktop, both portable and desktop, or neither portable nor desktop.
   a. IBM Aptiva series
   b. IBM ThinkPad series
   c. Apple Mac
   d. Apple Powerbook series
   e. IBM WordPad
   f. Compaq Presario series
   g. IBM 3090 series

PC magazines and newspapers containing the information needed for this exercise may be available in your college or town library; such journals are also carried by many bookstores and computer stores. Apple, Compaq, and IBM are located at the following Web addresses:

COMPANY	WEB ADDRESS
Apple Computer	www.apple.com
Compaq	www.compaq.com
IBM	www.ibm.com

9. **BENEFITS PROVIDED BY COMPUTERS** Organizations acquire computers for many reasons. Most of them first flocked to computers because these awesome devices could do certain types of jobs much faster than humans and with far fewer errors. Such capabilities enabled computers to displace humans in many types of work at a great savings in labor costs. Eventually, computers gained capabilities to do far more than just faster, more accurate, and cheaper work. They could also provide better information to decision makers, improve customer service, and create products that few dreamed possible before the age of computers. For this project, provide at least one real-world example—from a computer journal or from your personal experience—

that illustrates how PCs can help an organization achieve one of these latter benefits.

10. **PALMTOP COMPUTERS** Hardware vendors today collectively sell a variety of palmtop computers, including personal digital assistants (PDAs). Choose a palmtop computer, and report to your class about its features and price. Articles about palmtop computers appear regularly in computer journals such as *Computerworld* and *PC Magazine*; check your campus library or the Internet.

11. **MULTIMEDIA TITLES** Name at least three current multimedia CD products that fit into each of the following categories: computer games, educational products, and reference works. For each CD, describe its contents, name the company that publishes it, and write down its suggested list price. Several computer journals (including *PC Magazine*) and software stores regularly identify best-selling CDs.

 12. **WEATHER SITES** A veritable blizzard of weather sites exists on the World Wide Web. Besides getting forecasts for selected cities at home and around the world, you can use your PC to track storms, inspect Doppler radar, and pore over historical weather data. And that's not all. At some sites you can get information about the best areas of the country to golf on a given day or delays at the nation's busiest airports.

Visit at least three weather sites, and write a short report, not to exceed a total of three pages, describing their features. Also explain which of the sites you liked the best. The accompanying list provides the addresses of some sites you may wish to visit.

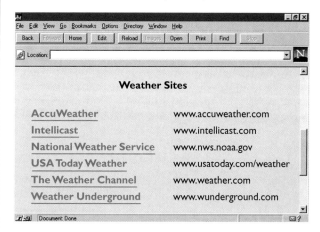

Weather Sites

AccuWeather	www.accuweather.com
Intellicast	www.intellicast.com
National Weather Service	www.nws.noaa.gov
USA Today Weather	www.usatoday.com/weather
The Weather Channel	www.weather.com
Weather Underground	www.wunderground.com

ONLINE REVIEW

 Go to the Online Review at www.harcourtcollege.com/infosys/pcc2e/student/ to test your understanding of this chapter's concepts.

OUTLINE

Overview
Input Hardware
     Keyboards
     Pointing Devices
     Image Scanners
Processing Hardware
     Bits and Bytes: The Building Blocks of Computer Logic
     Looking Inside the System Unit
Secondary Storage Hardware
     Properties of Secondary Storage Systems
     Diskettes
     Hard Disks
     Optical Disks
     Cartridge Tapes
Output Hardware
     Monitors
     Printers
     Special-Purpose Output Devices

2 CHAPTER

HARDWARE

LEARNING OBJECTIVES

After completing this chapter, you will be able to:

1. Describe several types of input, output, and storage devices and the purpose served by each.

2. Explain how programs and data are represented in computer logic.

3. Identify the components of the system unit and explain the roles they perform.

4. Name several properties of disks and appreciate situations in which each type of disk is appropriate.

5. Describe several of the key features of keyboards, monitors, printers, and other input and output devices, as well as some of the differences among them.

OVERVIEW

When people think of computers or computer systems, hardware seems to come to mind most readily. Hardware refers to the exciting pieces of equipment that make your computer system look, well, like a computer system. As you will learn in this chapter, a rich variety of PC hardware is available in today's marketplace.

The discussion of hardware in this chapter is divided into four areas. First you will learn about input hardware, the devices used to enter data and programs into the computer system. Then we address the processing function of the computer system. Here you will learn about how data and programs are represented in logic the computer understands. We will also cover the devices—chips and boards, for instance—that account for the lion's share of the performance of a typical PC hardware system. Next we cover secondary storage, with an emphasis on disk systems—the secondary storage alternative with which you are most likely to interact. The chapter closes with a discussion of output equipment, by far the most diverse class of hardware in terms of the functions it performs. Discussion of communications hardware is deferred until Chapter 4.

INPUT HARDWARE

Input hardware devices enable users to enter data into the computer system. A variety of hardware is available for input. Among the most popular devices for PC users are keyboards, pointing devices, and image scanners.

KEYBOARDS

For most people, a PC would be useless without a **keyboard,** which is the main vehicle for input. Keyboards vary tremendously with respect to such factors as number of keys, key arrangement, types of special keys, and touch. Figure 2-1 shows a typical PC keyboard.

The keyboards accompanying most PCs have several special keys that perform specific software routines. The Delete key and the Backspace key, for example, erase characters from the screen, and the Insert key enables characters to be inserted. The Enter key is commonly used to enter text and instructions into the computer.

Ctrl, Alt, and Shift keys are on virtually all PC keyboards. These keys work by being held down while another key is pressed. If you hold down the Alt key and strike a letter key, for instance, the command corresponding to an underlined letter on an active menu is invoked.

Usually, several *function keys* (see the top part of Figure 2-1) are available to users. These keys, labeled F1, F2, F3, and so on, are typically located across the top of the keyboard. When pressed by the operator, these keys initiate a command or even an entire computer program. Generally speaking, each software package you work with defines the function keys differently. For example, pressing the F2 key in your word processing program may enable you to indent text, but the same keystroke in your spreadsheet program may let you edit cells.

Most keyboards also have a *numeric keypad* (see the right part of Figure 2-1), which is activated by the Num Lock key and makes it easy to enter numbers quickly.

POINTING DEVICES

The term **pointing device** refers to input hardware that moves an onscreen pointer such as an arrow, cursor, or insertion point. As the pointing device moves along a surface or, alternatively, as it remains stationary while a finger or hand operates it, the pointing device determines the position, distance, or speed of the movement and repositions the onscreen pointer accordingly. Some common types of pointing devices are the mouse, light pen, touch screen, joystick, trackball, and graphics tablet.

MICE Most people supplement keyboard operations on their desktop PCs with a **mouse** (see Figure 2-2). When you move the mouse along a flat surface, its onscreen pointer—often referred to as the *mouse pointer*—moves correspondingly. Mice are very useful for moving quickly from one location to another on a display screen, for making screen selections, and for moving and

For a tutorial on the various parts of a keyboard, go to www.harcourtcollege.com/infosys/pcc2e/student/tutor/ and click on **Chapter 2.**

For a tutorial on the mouse and other types of input devices, go to www.harcourt college.com/infosys/pcc2e/ student/tutor/ and click on **Chapter 2.**

■ **Keyboard.** An input device composed of numerous keys, arrange in a configuration similar to that of a typewriter, that generate letters, numbers, and other symbols when depressed. ■ **Pointing device.** A piece of input hardware that moves an onscreen pointer such as an arrow, cursor, or insertion point. ■ **Mouse.** A common pointing device that you slide along a flat surface to move a pointer around a display screen and make selections.

QWERTY
These keys identify the keyboard as being of the QWERTY type

FUNCTION KEYS
Invoke short programs

ENTER KEY
Enters commands into the computer and creates blank lines in a document

BACKSPACE KEY
Erases one character to the left of the cursor position

PRINT SCREEN KEY
Used to print the display-screen contents

ESCAPE KEY
Used to cancel an operation

TAB KEY
Accesses tab stops

CAPS LOCK KEY
Works like the Shift-lock key on a typewriter

CONTROL KEY AND ALT KEY
Used in combination with other keys to enter commands into the computer

SPACE BAR
Enters a blank space

SHIFT KEY
Produces uppercase letters and symbols on upper part of certain keys

ARROW KEYS
Move the cursor around the display screen

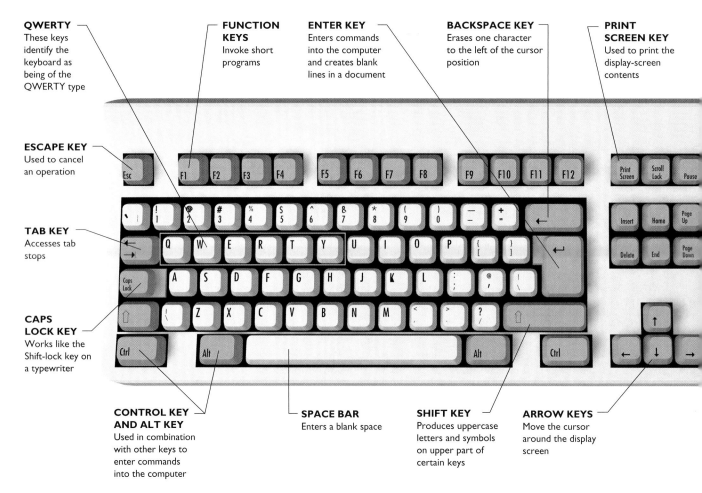

FIGURE 2-1

PC keyboard. This keyboard typifies those sold with many personal computers. For operational convenience, the keyboard features duplicates of many keys.

resizing text and images. Using a mouse is often much faster than pressing combinations of keys on the keyboard.

Mice are especially handy when working with *icons* on the screen—small graphics symbols that represent commands or program options. When you use the mouse to *select* an icon, you point to it on the screen and press—or "click"—the left mouse button once or twice. To *move* an icon from one part of the screen to another, you position the mouse pointer on the icon, hold down the left button while dragging the icon to its new position, and release the button once the icon is there. This operation is commonly known as *dragging and dropping*. Many mice today come with a wheel on top of them, which enables you to more easily *scroll* the display-screen contents.

LIGHT PEN   A *light pen* contains a light-sensitive cell at its tip. When the tip of the pen is placed close to the screen, the display device can identify the pen's position, and the pen can be used to select items. One of the most common applications of light pens is notebook-sized PCs targeted to workers who might otherwise use a clipboard and paper form to enter data while on the move. Figure 2-3 shows a pen-based computer in use.

JOYSTICK   A *joystick* (see again Figure 2-3), which looks like a car's stick shift, is often used for playing computer games. With many joysticks, the speed at which they move and the distance they travel determine the speed and distance traveled by the onscreen pointer. Today, some electronic games employ gloves with built-in sensors instead of joysticks to enable the computer to detect hand movements directly.

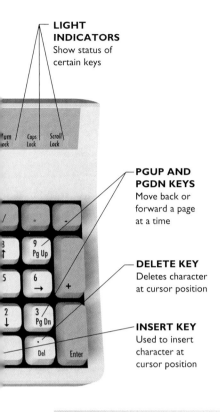

LIGHT INDICATORS
Show status of certain keys

PGUP AND PGDN KEYS
Move back or forward a page at a time

DELETE KEY
Deletes character at cursor position

INSERT KEY
Used to insert character at cursor position

TRACKBALL A *trackball* consists of a sphere resting on rollers, with only the top of the sphere exposed outside its case (see again Figure 2-3). The onscreen pointer travels in whichever direction you spin the sphere. A mouse is merely a trackball turned upside-down. Many people prefer a trackball to a mouse because it requires less desk space to use. Some keyboards have built-in trackballs. On many laptop and notebook computers, a highly compact, trackball-like device called a *pointing stick* is placed within the keyboard to enable onscreen pointer movement.

GRAPHICS TABLET A *graphics tablet* often employs a penlike stylus or a mouselike device called a *crosshair cursor*. The operator uses one or the other to trace over an image on a flat tablet (see again Figure 2-3, which features four pens and a single crosshair cursor). The image is read into the computer system's memory as the pen or cursor passes over it.

IMAGE SCANNERS

Image scanners, such as the ones in Figure 2-4, are used to convert images such as photographs, drawings, and documents into a collection of tiny dots and store them in computer memory. Many image scanners sold with PCs scan at a resolution of 300, 600, or 1,200 dots per inch (dpi). As you might expect, the more dots the computer uses to store the image, the better the resolution will be when the image is finally output. Many image scanners are "dumb," meaning that they cannot recognize any of the text they read. "Intelligent" image scanners, by contrast, are accompanied by *optical character recognition (OCR) software* that enables them to identify as well as read characters. The recognized text can then be manipulated with a word processor, spreadsheet, or other program.

For links to further information about input devices, go to www.harcourtcollege.com/infosys/pcc2e/student/explore/ and click on Chapter 2.

PROCESSING HARDWARE

The case in which the microprocessor (CPU) chip and its memory are housed is called the **system unit.** As mentioned briefly in Chapter 1, this device usually contains the disk drives, circuitry such as chips and boards, and a number of other components.

In this section, we look closer at some of the hardware contained in a typical system unit. Before we do that, however, it's important to digress for a few moments into a discussion of how computer systems store programs and data. In the process, you'll see how you can determine the amount of space a PC needs to do its work.

■ **Image scanner.** A device that can read into computer memory a hard-copy image such as a text page, photograph, map or drawing. ■ **System unit.** The hardware unit that houses the CPU and memory, as well as a number of other devices.

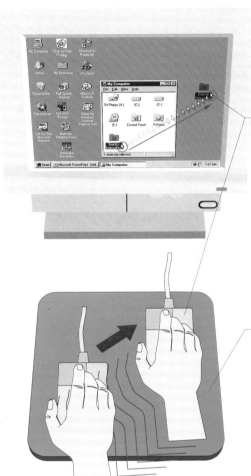

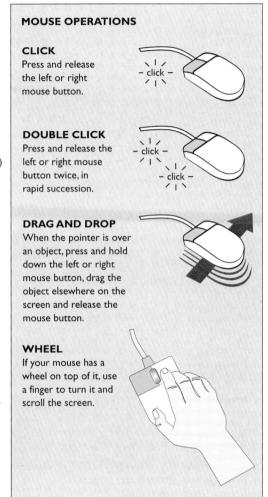

MOUSE OPERATIONS

CLICK
Press and release the left or right mouse button.

DOUBLE CLICK
Press and release the left or right mouse button twice, in rapid succession.

DRAG AND DROP
When the pointer is over an object, press and hold down the left or right mouse button, drag the object elsewhere on the screen and release the mouse button.

WHEEL
If your mouse has a wheel on top of it, use a finger to turn it and scroll the screen.

MOUSE POINTER
When the mouse (below) is moved along a flat surface, a pointer (top) on the display screen moves correspondingly.

MOUSE PAD
A mouse pad provides a smooth surface upon which to slide the mouse.

FIGURE 2-2

Using a mouse.

For links to further information about binary and other types of data representation, go to www.harcourtcollege.com/infosys/pcc2e/student/explore/ and click on Chapter 2.

BITS AND BYTES: THE BUILDING BLOCKS OF COMPUTER LOGIC

The electronic components of the PCs used by most people work in only two states: a circuit is either open or closed, a magnetic spot is either present or absent, and so on. It is convenient to think of these *binary* states—binary means *two*—as the 0-state and the 1-state. Computer professionals refer to such 0s and 1s as **bits** (a contraction of the term *bi*nary dig*its*). Being primarily electronic, computers do all their processing and communicating by representing programs and data in bit form.

People, of course, do not speak binary. You are not likely to go up to a friend and say,

$$0100100001001001$$

which in one binary-based coding system translates as "HI." People communicate with one another in *natural languages*, such as English, Chinese, and Spanish. In our part of the world, most of us speak English. Also, we write

■ **Bit.** A binary digit, such as 0 or 1.

LIGHT PEN
A light pen is sometimes used with a portable computer.

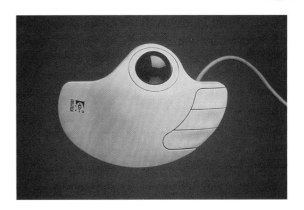

TRACKBALL
Many people use a trackball as
an alternative to a mouse.

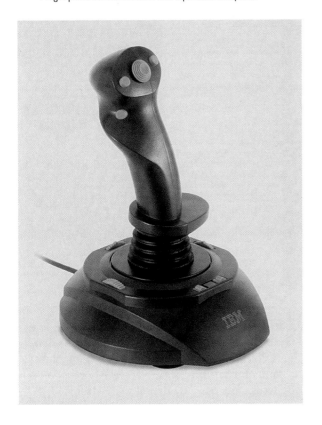

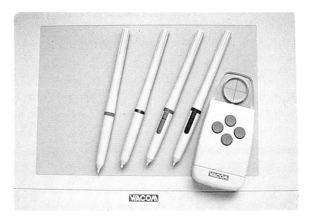

GRAPHICS TABLET
A graphics tablet is often used in combination
with a pen or with a crosshair cursor.

JOYSTICK
Joysticks are commonly used
with computer games.

 **FIGURE 2-3**

Pointing devices. The wide variety of
pointing devices on the market today
powerfully illustrates the many ways for
ordinary users to input data to their
PCs.

with a 26-character alphabet, and we use a number system with 10 rather than 2 digits. Computers, however, understand only 0 and 1. So, for us to interact with a computer, our messages to it must be translated into binary form, and its messages to us must be translated from binary into a natural language.

People often interact with computer systems at a keyboard, whose keys consist of a wide variety of natural-language symbols. When we press keys, the computer system must translate all the natural-language symbols that the keys represent into strings of 0s and 1s. Later, when the computer system provides us the results of its processing, it must translate the 0s and 1s it has used to internally represent the results back into natural language (see Figure 2-5).

TEXT DATA PCs use a variety of binary-based codes to represent programs and data. For example, when a person at a keyboard enters data and programs,

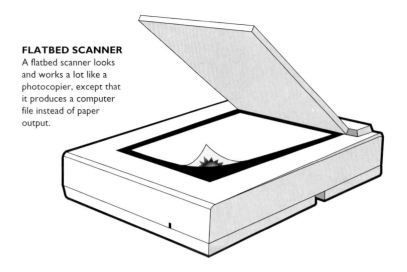

FLATBED SCANNER
A flatbed scanner looks and works a lot like a photocopier, except that it produces a computer file instead of paper output.

RESOLUTION
Many scanners let you specify the resolution (in dpi) at which you wish to scan. High-resolution images look sharper but take more time to input and require more bytes to store.

DRUM SCANNER
Drum scanners, such as this one that attaches to an ordinary keyboard, use a roller as opposed to a flatbed mechanism to input images.

HANDHELD SCANNER
Handheld scanners are useful for inputting small amounts of information and work by sliding over images.

FIGURE 2-4

Image scanners.

a fixed-length, binary-based code called *ASCII* (American Standard Code for Information Interchange) is used for each character. ASCII represents each printable character as a unique combination of a fixed number of eight bits—for instance, 01000001 stands for an uppercase *A* (see Figure 2-6).

Most computers we use for work and play, incidentally, are designed to handle data in chunks of eight bits. A group of eight bits has 256 (2^8) different combinations; therefore, ASCII can represent up to 256 characters, more than enough to account for the 26 uppercase and 26 lowercase characters, the 10 decimal digits, and all the special characters—like &, %, and $—on the keyboard.

The eight bits used to represent a character are collectively referred to as a **byte.** In PCs, one byte represents a single character of data. For this reason, PC manufacturers use the byte measure to define their machines' storage capacity. Thus, when you type a message such as

        All work and no play make Jack a dull boy

you've just entered 41 bytes into your computer system (counting spaces—the space character also has a byte representation).

■ **Byte.** A configuration of 8 bits that represents a single character of data.

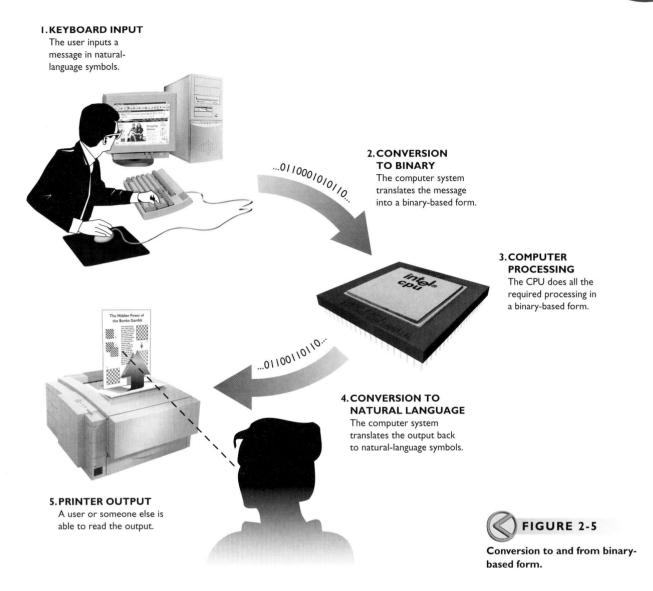

1. KEYBOARD INPUT
The user inputs a message in natural-language symbols.

...0110001010110...

2. CONVERSION TO BINARY
The computer system translates the message into a binary-based form.

3. COMPUTER PROCESSING
The CPU does all the required processing in a binary-based form.

...0110011011010...

4. CONVERSION TO NATURAL LANGUAGE
The computer system translates the output back to natural-language symbols.

5. PRINTER OUTPUT
A user or someone else is able to read the output.

FIGURE 2-5

Conversion to and from binary-based form.

As you may have noticed, computer advertisements are filled with references to kilobytes, megabytes, gigabytes, and terabytes. One **kilobyte (KB)** is equal to a little over 1,000 bytes (1,024, to be precise), one **megabyte (MB** or *meg*) equals about one million bytes, one **gigabyte (GB)** equals about one billion bytes, and one **terabyte (TB)** equals about one trillion bytes. The typical PC sold today has a memory of about 64 or 128 megabytes and a hard disk of several gigabytes.

As hinted at in Figure 2-5, the conversion from natural-language words and numbers to their ASCII equivalents and back again usually takes place on an input/output device. When a user types a message at a keyboard, an encoder chip inside the keyboard usually translates it into ASCII and sends it as a series of bytes to the CPU. The output that the CPU sends back to the display or printer is also in ASCII, which the display or printer—with the aid of a decoder chip—translates into natural-language words and numbers. Therefore, if the CPU sent the ASCII message

`0100100001001001`

to your display device, "HI" would appear on your screen.

■ **Kilobyte (KB).** Approximately 1,000 bytes (1,024, to be exact). ■ **Megabyte (MB).** Approximately 1 million bytes.
■ **Gigabyte (GB).** Approximately 1 billion bytes. ■ **Terabyte (TB).** Approximately 1 trillion bytes.

Character	ASCII Representation	Character	ASCII Representation
0	00110000	I	01001001
1	00110001	J	01001010
2	00110010	K	01001011
3	00110011	L	01001100
4	00110100	M	01001101
5	00110101	N	01001110
6	00110110	O	01001111
7	00110111	P	01010000
8	00111000	Q	01010001
9	00111001	R	01010010
A	01000001	S	01010011
B	01000010	T	01010100
C	01000011	U	01010101
D	01000100	V	01010110
E	01000101	W	01010111
F	01000110	X	01011000
G	01000111	Y	01011001
H	01001000	Z	01011010

FIGURE 2-6

ASCII.

PCs usually handle data in byte multiples. For instance, a 32-bit computer is built to process data in chunks of four bytes; a (faster) 64-bit computer processes data in chunks of eight bytes. These byte multiples are commonly called *words*.

NONTEXT DATA   So far, we've limited the discussion to text data, which consists of digits, letters, and special symbols such as the percent sign and dollar sign. Graphics, audio, and video data are also represented in binary form inside the computer system.

GRAPHICS DATA   One of the most common methods for storing graphics data is in the form of a bitmap. Images produced on a display screen are composed of thousands of tiny dots, called **pixels** (a contraction of the two words *picture elements*). With *bitmap* graphics, each of the pixels is assigned some combination of 0s and 1s that represents a unique shade or color. On the screen of a typical monitor sold with PCs today, there may be as many as 1,024 columns by 768 rows of pixels, or 786,432 pixels, providing images on the screen.

The simplest type of bitmap is *monochrome*, in which there is only a foreground and background color. Thus, each screen pixel is either one color or the other. If we respectively let these colors be black and white and let black be represented by the 0 bit and white be represented by the 1 bit, we can translate any picture into a black-and-white electronic bitmap, as shown in top part of Figure 2-7.

Next higher up on the scale of realism are *grayscale* images, in which each pixel can be not only pure black or pure white but also any of 254 shades of gray in between. Thus, there are 256 possibilities for each screen dot. You may remember from an earlier discussion that a single byte can represent any of 256 states. So, 11111111 could represent a pure white pixel, 00000000 a pure black one, and any byte in between—such as 11001000 and 00001010—some shade of gray (see the middle part of Figure 2-7).

■ **Pixel.** A single dot on a display screen.

MONOCHROME GRAPHICS

With monochrome graphics, each pixel is represented by a single bit.

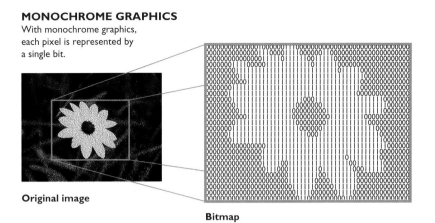

Original image

Bitmap

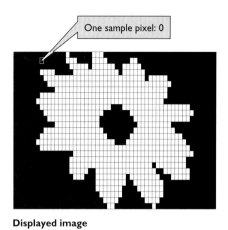

One sample pixel: 0

Displayed image

GRAYSCALE GRAPHICS

With 256-shade grayscale graphics, each pixel is represented by one byte. Different bytes represent different shades of gray.

One sample pixel:
01101110

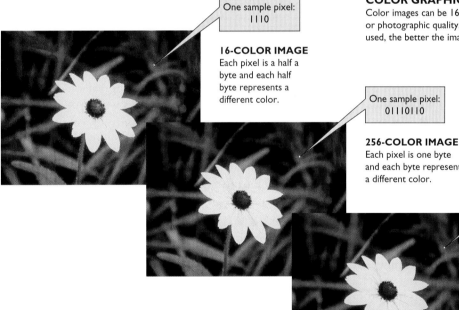

One sample pixel:
1110

16-COLOR IMAGE

Each pixel is a half a byte and each half byte represents a different color.

COLOR GRAPHICS

Color images can be 16-color, 256-color, or photographic quality. The more colors used, the better the image quality.

One sample pixel:
01110110

256-COLOR IMAGE

Each pixel is one byte and each byte represents a different color.

One sample pixel:
101001100100110111001011

PHOTOGRAPHIC-QUALITY IMAGE
(16.7 million colors)

Each pixel is three bytes and each three-byte string represents a different color.

Color coding works like grayscale—each pixel is represented by some number of bytes. Computers often display color graphics using 16 colors, 256 colors, or 16,777,216 colors. A 16-color image needs only a half byte assigned to each pixel (e.g., 0000 or 1111 or a combination in between), a 256-color image requires one byte, and a 16.78-million-color (photographic-quality) image requires three bytes (see the bottom part of Figure 2-7).

 FIGURE 2-7

Bitmap graphics. With bitmap graphics, each of the hundreds of thousands of pixels on a display screen is assigned some combination of 0s and 1s that represent a unique shade or color.

AUDIO DATA   Audio data—such as someone speaking or a symphony playing—are often digitally encoded by a method called *waveform audio*. Waveform audio consists of taking several thousand digital snapshots, called *samples*, of a real-life sound piece every second. At the end of the piece, the played-back collection of samples becomes the voice or music.

The audio CDs you typically buy in music stores, for instance, sample at a rate of 44,100 times per second. Each sample is two bytes long and corresponds to a unique "sound." Thus, 0011100100101010 corresponds to one sound and 1111000001010101 to another. When these sounds are played back at a rate of 44,100 times per second, it's impossible for the human ear to distinguish each one, and they collectively sound like real voice or music.

The port on an add-in board extends through the back of the system unit's case.

PORTS
Ports located at the back of the system unit enable you to plug in peripherals that work with the add-in boards.

VIDEO DATA   Films that you normally see in the movies or on TV are merely *moving* graphical data. Typically, films are shown at a rate of 30 frames (each frame consisting of a still graphic) per second. As you can imagine, the amount of data involved for a two-hour color feature film can be quite taxing for a computer system. For instance, just a single 256-color image shown on a 1,024-by-768-pixel display requires 786,432 bytes. When you multiply that by 30 times per second, 60 seconds per minute, and 120 minutes, you get about 170 gigabytes. Methods exist to compress video data—in fact, any sort of data—so that computers can handle them more efficiently.

RUNNING PROGRAMS   So far we've covered representing data and programs in byte form. Data and programs are converted into bytes when you enter them into the computer. When the computer wants to run a program, however, it must further translate it into a binary form known as machine language.

Every program contains instructions that tell the computer precisely what to do. Before any program instruction can be executed by your computer, it must be converted into the **machine language** that is native to the type of computer you are using. An example of a typical machine-language instruction appears below:

01011000011100000000000010000010

A machine-language instruction may look like a meaningless string of 0s and 1s, but it actually consists of groups of bits that represent specific operations and storage locations. The 32-bit instruction shown here, for instance, moves data between two specific memory locations. The set of machine-language instructions available to a computer is known as that computer's *instruction set*.

In early computers, including the first PCs, users had to write all their own programs in machine language. Today, of course, hardly anyone knows how to code in machine language, and most users don't even write their own programs. Instead, those who use or write applications programs rely on *language translators*—special programs that automatically convert instructions into

■ **Machine language.** A binary-based programming language that the computer can execute directly.

POWER SUPPLY
The power supply converts standard electrical power into a form the computer can use.

MEMORY (RAM)
Memory temporarily stores data while you are working on them.

SYSTEM BOARD
The system board is the main circuit board of the computer, and all components of the computer system connect to it.

RD-DISK DRIVE
hard-disk drive is principal secondary age medium.

STORAGE BAYS
Other secondary storage devices usually include a diskette drive and CD-ROM or DVD drive.

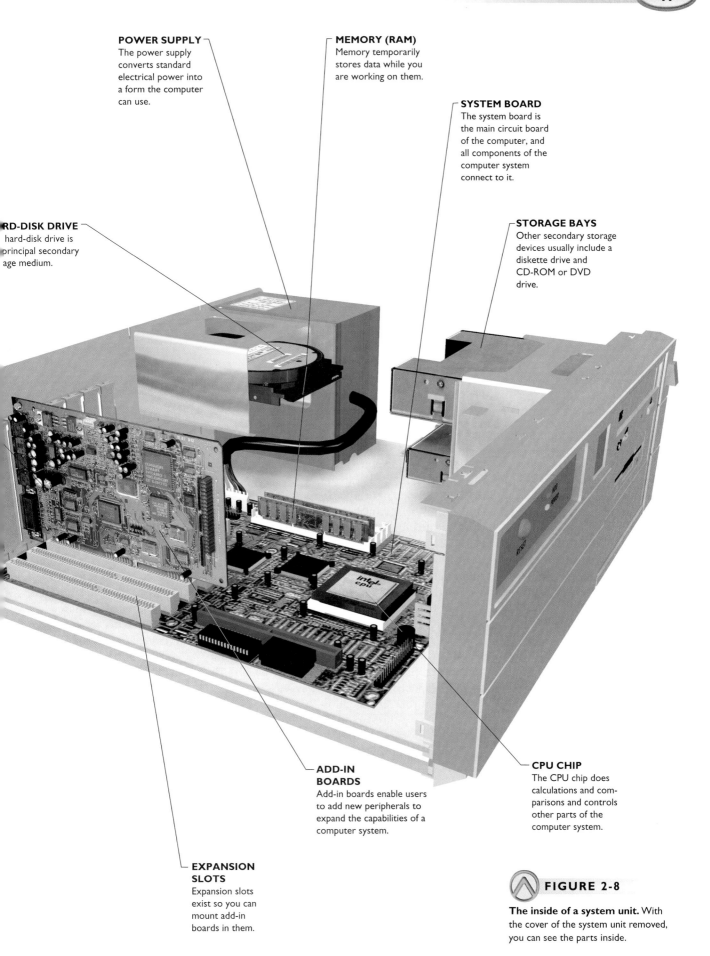

ADD-IN BOARDS
Add-in boards enable users to add new peripherals to expand the capabilities of a computer system.

CPU CHIP
The CPU chip does calculations and comparisons and controls other parts of the computer system.

EXPANSION SLOTS
Expansion slots exist so you can mount add-in boards in them.

FIGURE 2-8

The inside of a system unit. With the cover of the system unit removed, you can see the parts inside.

machine language. The translation is so transparent that most people aren't even aware that it is taking place.

Each type of microprocessor chip has its own machine language. Thus, a code used on a PC-compatible computer is totally foreign to an Apple Macintosh. This is why, when you buy a program such as a word processor or spreadsheet, you must get one intended for your specific type of computer system.

LOOKING INSIDE THE SYSTEM UNIT

In this section we "flip the lid" off a typical system unit to see how the parts inside fit together. Almost all computers sold today use a modular hardware approach—related circuitry is etched onto memory or processor chips, the chips are mounted onto carrier packages that are plugged into boards, and the boards are fitted into slots inside the system unit.

The system unit usually consists of at least a CPU chip, memory (RAM and ROM) chips, boards on which these and other chips are mounted, ports that provide connections for external devices, a power supply, and internal circuitry to hook everything together (see Figure 2-8). In addition, system units often have built-in hard-disk drives and *bays*—open areas into which additional secondary-storage equipment can be mounted. Such devices as a diskette drive, a CD-ROM or DVD drive, a Zip or Jaz drive, a tape drive, and even a second hard-disk drive are among the most common candidates for mounting into empty bays. Disks and tapes are covered later in the chapter.

For a tutorial on CPUs and how they are made, go to www.harcourtcollege.com/ infosys/pcc2e/student/tutor/ and click on Chapter 2.

MICROPROCESSOR CHIPS Every PC contains a specific microprocessor chip as its CPU. This chip is put into a carrier package, and the carrier package is mounted onto a special board—the **system board** or *motherboard*—that fits inside the system unit. This board is located on the floor of the system unit shown in Figure 2-8.

Most microcomputer systems made today use CPU chips manufactured by either Intel or Motorola. The Intel line of chips—such as the 80386, 80486, Pentium, Pentium Pro, Pentium II, Celeron, and Pentium III—is used on the PCs made by IBM as well as by Compaq, Dell, and scores of other companies that make PC-compatible computer systems. Many of the older Intel chips are commonly referred to by their last three digits—for instance, a 486 refers to an 80486 chip. Most of the newer Pentium chips are "MMX-enabled," meaning they are expressly configured for the high-speed graphics and video required of leading-edge multimedia applications. In recent years, a number of *clone chips* have appeared on the market—made by companies such as Cyrix and Advanced Micro Devices (AMD)—that for all intents and purposes are functionally compatible with Intel chips; AMD chips have become quite prominent recently, especially in lower-priced PCs.

The Motorola line of chips—including those in the 68xxx family—is found primarily in Apple Macintosh computers made before 1994. In recent years, Apple, Motorola, and IBM have teamed up on the PowerPC chip, which has become the standard CPU on Macintosh computers. Some CPU chips in the PowerPC line are the 601, 603, 604, 620, and 750. Apple's Power Macintosh (or *Power Mac*) is one computer line based on PowerPC chips.

The type of CPU chip in a computer's system unit greatly affects what a person can do with the computer system. Software is optimized to work with a specific chip or chip family, and a program that works with one chip may not function with another unless modified. For instance, software is not easily portable between the Intel and PowerPC chip families as these families employ a somewhat dissimilar design philosophy. Also, a program designed for

---

■ **System board.** The main circuit board of the computer to which all computer-system components connect. Also called a *motherboard*.

a speedy Pentium III chip may crawl at a snail's pace (or even not work at all) with the earlier and less capable 80486 chip.

Different terms are used to rate speeds in different types of CPU chips. In the PC world, speeds are most commonly rated in *megahertz (MHz)*. Each MHz represents one million "clock ticks" per second. PCs are regulated by a system clock, which determines how quickly data and program instructions can be transmitted across circuitry. The faster the clock, the faster the data and program instructions move. Many PCs sold today run at 500 MHz or more.

Working alongside the CPU chip in many system units are *specialized processor chips*, such as a numeric coprocessor chip, a graphics accelerator chip, and several DSP chips. The role of these "slave chips" is to perform specialized tasks for the CPU, thereby enhancing overall system performance.

A *numeric (math) coprocessor chip* helps the CPU perform arithmetic, whereas a *graphics accelerator* chip helps the CPU with the computationally intensive chore of creating complex screen displays. *DSP chips*—DSP is for *digital signal processor*—handle such chores as sending data to and from the hard disk as well as controlling the modem and sound card. For instance, a DSP chip is what converts the signals coming in over telephone lines into the bits and bytes the computer can understand, thereby enabling you to see Web pages on your PC. It is not unusual to boost the speed of a computer system several times over by using specialized chips.

For links to further information about **CPU chips**, go to www.harcourtcollege.com/ infosys/pcc2e/student/ explore/ and click on Chapter 2.

RAM RAM (for **random access memory**) is used to store the programs and data on which the computer is currently working. Like the microprocessor, the RAM of a PC consists of circuits etched onto silicon chips. These chips are mounted in carrier packages, just as the CPU is, and the packages are often arranged onto boards—called *single in-line memory modules*, or *SIMMs*— which are then plugged into the system board.

Most PCs sold today have enough RAM to store several megabytes of data. Most PCs also allow memory expansion through add-in boards (discussed shortly) when RAM is insufficient. RAM is *volatile*, meaning that the contents of memory are lost when the computer is turned off. This is in contrast to secondary storage, which is *nonvolatile*.

To speed processing, most PCs employ a technique called *cache memory*. Cache memory stores frequently accessed data so that they can be fetched more rapidly than they can be in RAM. An analogy can be made to the way many people work at their desks, placing the papers they need the most within an arm's length and leaving others farther away. The fastest type of cache memory (called *internal cache*) is built directly onto the CPU chip. A slower but larger type of cache memory (called *external cache*) is located off the chip. Internal and external cache are sometimes respectively referred to as Level 1 (L1) and Level 2 (L2) cache.

ROM ROM, which stands for **read-only memory,** consists of nonerasable hardware modules that contain programs. Like RAM, these software-in-hardware modules are mounted into carrier packages that, in turn, are plugged into one or more boards inside the system unit. You can neither write over these ROM programs (that's why they're called *read-only*) nor destroy their contents when you turn off the computer's power (that is, they're nonvolatile). The CPU can fetch a program stored in ROM more quickly than if it were stored on disk, where it would have to be loaded into memory before the computer could start to work on it.

Important pieces of systems software are often stored in ROM. For instance,

---

■ **Random access memory (RAM).** The computer system's main memory .■ **Read-only memory (ROM).** A software-in-hardware module from which the computer can read data, but to which it cannot write data.

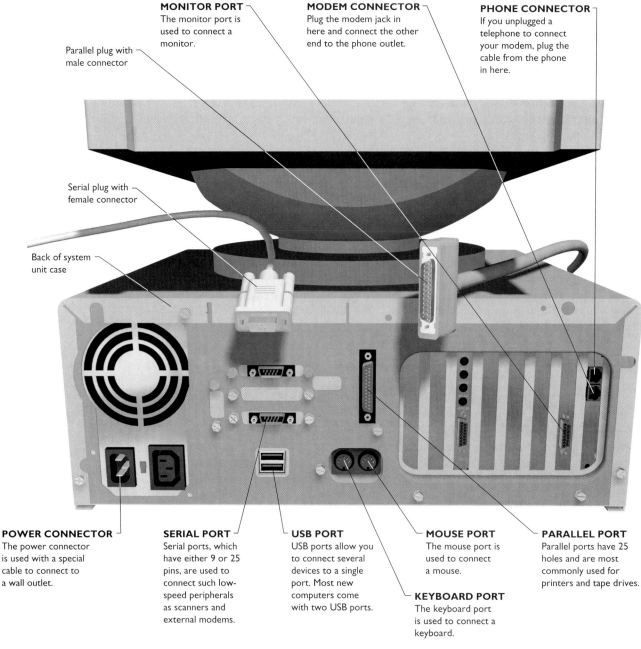

MONITOR PORT
The monitor port is used to connect a monitor.

MODEM CONNECTOR
Plug the modem jack in here and connect the other end to the phone outlet.

PHONE CONNECTOR
If you unplugged a telephone to connect your modem, plug the cable from the phone in here.

Parallel plug with male connector

Serial plug with female connector

Back of system unit case

POWER CONNECTOR
The power connector is used with a special cable to connect to a wall outlet.

SERIAL PORT
Serial ports, which have either 9 or 25 pins, are used to connect such low-speed peripherals as scanners and external modems.

USB PORT
USB ports allow you to connect several devices to a single port. Most new computers come with two USB ports.

MOUSE PORT
The mouse port is used to connect a mouse.

KEYBOARD PORT
The keyboard port is used to connect a keyboard.

PARALLEL PORT
Parallel ports have 25 holes and are most commonly used for printers and tape drives.

FIGURE 2-9

Ports.

one of the things a computer does when it is first turned on is perform a power-on self test (POST). The POST program is stored in ROM, and it produces the beeps you hear as your computer system begins operation, or "boots up." POST takes an inventory of the components in your computer system, initializes system settings, and checks each component to see that it's working properly.

PORTS Most system units contain built-in sockets that enable you to plug in external hardware devices. These sockets, which are on the exterior of the system unit, are known as **ports** (see Figure 2-9).

Serial ports can transmit data only a single bit at a time; however, they require the least expensive type of cabling and can reliably send data at distances of up to about 1,000 feet. In contrast, *parallel ports* can transmit

Port. A socket on the exterior of a computer's system unit into which a peripheral device may be plugged.

data a byte at a time—making them several times faster than serial ports—but they use more expensive cables and cannot reliably send data farther than 50 feet. Parallel ports are typically used to connect nearby printers and tape drives to a PC, whereas serial ports are used for such devices as scanners and modems. Keyboards and mice usually come with their own, dedicated serial ports; displays, their own, dedicated parallel ports.

When a peripheral device needs to be plugged into a desktop system unit but there is no built-in port for it, you normally must buy a special *add-in board* that has a port on it. When you install the board, the port typically extends through a hole in the back of the system unit so that you can plug the peripheral device into it. For notebook and hand-held computers, *PC cards* are used instead of boards. Add-in boards and PC cards are discussed next.

SYSTEM EXPANSION Not everyone wants the same type of computer system. One group of people may be satisfied with 64 MB of RAM, while another may want 128 MB or 256 MB in the same model of computer. Similarly, while many people need only average sound capabilities from their computer systems, musicians and music buffs may desire top-of-the-line audio. To account for the variety of needs in the marketplace, most PC-system vendors enable you to customize the system you buy from them with either add-in boards or PC cards.

ADD-IN BOARDS **Add-in boards** are used in desktop PCs. They are cardlike pieces of electronic circuitry that plug into *expansion slots* in the PC's system unit (refer again to Figure 2-8). Add-in boards enable you to add specific types of peripheral devices or otherwise expand the capabilities of a computer system.

Many types of add-in boards are available. For example, displays usually come with their own *video-adapter boards*, which both translate instructions from the CPU into a form the display can understand and temporarily store information before it goes to the screen. Similarly, you can get your computer system to communicate with the Internet or with remote facsimile (fax) machines by getting a *fax/modem board*. For sound and graphics capabilities, you would acquire a certain type of *sound board* and *graphics board*. SIMMs are boards, too. To add more memory to your system, for instance, you might plug in a SIMM board containing 64 more megabytes of RAM.

You can buy your computer customized with the right boards at the time of system purchase or, as new needs evolve, you can add boards at a later time. Because adding boards later can be time consuming and problematic—many users are nervous about taking the cover off their system units and poking around inside—many vendors have drifted toward a plug-and-play strategy to make it easier than ever to install new devices. **Plug-and-play** means that your computer system has the ability to automatically detect and to help configure new hardware devices.

PC CARDS For many years, users of laptop and notebook PCs were not able to expand their machines much. Most portable PCs don't have enough room to accommodate either the standard desktop input/output bus or its big internal boards. Then came PCMCIA. *PCMCIA*—which stands for Personal Computer Memory Card International Association—refers to a standard way to connect peripheral devices to portable computers.

The mainstay of PCMCIA is a credit-card-sized adapter card known as the *PCMCIA card*, or more commonly, the **PC card** (see Figure 2-10). PC cards, which typically plug into a slot in the side of a notebook or laptop computer, come in three basic thicknesses. A Type I card, the thinnest of the lot, is often

For a tutorial on the various ports found on a PC, go to www.harcourtcollege.com/infosys/pcc2e/student/tutor/ and click on Chapter 2.

■ **Add-in board.** A circuit board that may be inserted into a slot within a desktop computer's system unit to add one or more functions.■ **Plug-and-play.** The ability of a computer to detect and configure new hardware components.
■ **PC card.** A small card that fits into a slot on the exterior of a portable computer to provide new functions.

46 CHAPTER 2: HARDWARE

 FIGURE 2-10

PC cards. PC cards provide a way for notebook-PC users to enhance their computing environments. The Type III card shown here has a built-in modem and separate ports for a phone jack and local-network connection.

used to add more memory. A Type II card typically adds networking capabilities or sound. Type III cards, the thickest type, often contain a removable hard drive, or perhaps several communications functions. Many notebook and laptop PCs have a multipurpose slot that can accommodate two Type I cards, two Type II cards, or a single Type III card. Because the cards are removable, taking them out when you don't need them is as easy as unplugging a table lamp.

There is a practical limit to the number of peripheral devices a CPU can handle. Generally, each new device interfaced through a port, an add-in board, or a PC card adds to the burden the CPU must manage, thereby possibly degrading system performance.

BUSES A **bus** is any path along which bits are transmitted. As shown in Figure 2-11, several types of buses operate within the system unit. The *internal bus* moves data around the CPU chip. A *data bus* links the CPU to RAM. From RAM, an *expansion bus* extends the data bus so that it links with peripherals.

Today, a number of expansion-bus standards are in existence. The most widely used is *ISA* (for *Industry Standard Architecture*), which has been around since 1984. Three newer (and wider) buses commonly seen on PCs are EISA, or *Enhanced Industry Standard Architecture* (used on many 486 PCs), IBM's *Micro Channel Architecture* (used on some IBM PCs), and Apple's *NuBus* (until recently, used on many Macintoshes). Only a few years ago, many people in the computer industry figured that ISA would be eclipsed by newer bus designs, but the large base of ISA boards in use and the recent popularity of local buses—which have diminished the demands placed on the standard expansion bus—have given ISA new life.

A drawback with early PCs was that a single expansion bus had to do all the bussing between the RAM and peripheral devices. That wasn't a problem in the days when text was nearly the only thing that monitors displayed and data could creep along at a snail's pace. But times have changed. Graphical user interfaces (GUIs) have come to the fore, and they demand a lot of speed in order to constantly redraw complex screens. Multimedia systems—with their video clips—especially require lightning quickness. Adding fuel to the fire, many more devices are competing for expansion-bus space these days:

■ **Bus.** An electronic path within a computer system along which bits are transmitted.

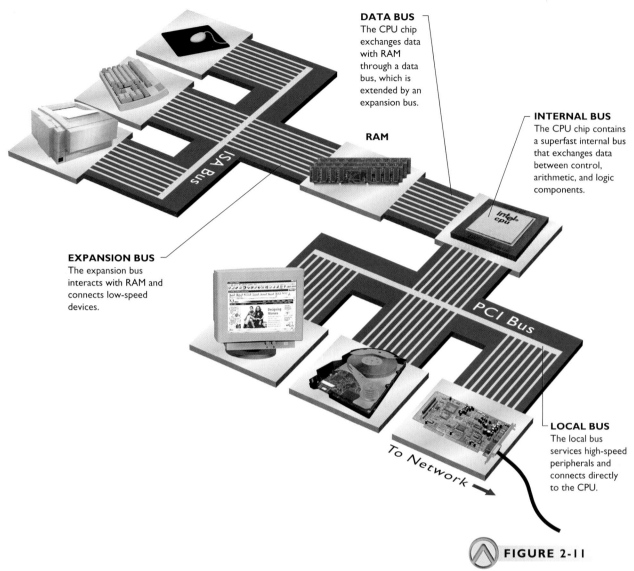

DATA BUS
The CPU chip exchanges data with RAM through a data bus, which is extended by an expansion bus.

INTERNAL BUS
The CPU chip contains a superfast internal bus that exchanges data between control, arithmetic, and logic components.

RAM

EXPANSION BUS
The expansion bus interacts with RAM and connects low-speed devices.

LOCAL BUS
The local bus services high-speed peripherals and connects directly to the CPU.

FIGURE 2-11

Buses. The task of buses is to transport bits and bytes from one computer-system component to another.

mice, scanners, backup tape devices, sound boards, graphics boards—you name it.

To provide faster system response time, hardware producers have taken peripherals that need extremely fast response time—such as the display, disk drives, and boards connecting to high-speed local networks—and given them their own bus. This type of bus is called a *local bus*, and it links directly to the CPU. All other (slower) devices—such as the mouse, modems, and sound boards—work off the traditional expansion bus. The local bus carries data in larger chunks and at faster clock speeds than the regular expansion bus, which is constrained by the slowest peripherals attached to it. The local bus standard most commonly used today is *PCI*, for Peripheral Component Interconnect.

The most important recent development in bus architectures is the *universal serial bus (USB)*. USBs enable up to 128 devices—all of which use the same type of plug—to connect to a PC through a single port. You can link peripheral devices to a single port by chaining them together—say, by plugging the printer into a port and then plugging a modem or a scanner into the printer, and so on. USB makes devices *hot swappable*, which means that you can add or unplug devices with the system power on. USB is still too new to predict its eventual success. USB requires USB-enabled peripheral devices to work.

SECONDARY STORAGE HARDWARE

The most popular secondary storage alternatives for PCs are diskettes, hard disks, and CD-ROM optical disks. Less widely used alternatives are other types of disks as well as magnetic tape cartridges. But before we look in depth at any of these secondary storage alternatives, let's turn first to the properties that define and differentiate them.

For a tutorial on various types of secondary storage systems, go to www. harcourt college.com/ infosys/pcc2e/student/tutor/ and click on Chapter 2.

PROPERTIES OF SECONDARY STORAGE SYSTEMS

Secondary storage systems are often discussed in terms of their physical parts, media removability, and access capabilities.

PHYSICAL PARTS   Any secondary storage system involves two physical parts: a *peripheral device* and a *storage medium*. A disk unit and a tape drive are examples of peripheral devices; magnetic disk platters and magnetic tape cartridges are types of media. Data and programs are written onto and read from some type of medium. A medium must be situated on or inserted into a peripheral device in order for the CPU to process its contents. Diskettes and hard disks are magnetically sensed media; CD-ROMs are read by laser (light) beams.

The peripheral storage device can be internal or external. *Internal devices*—such as diskette, hard-disk, and CD drives—typically come configured in the system unit when you buy a PC. These devices can also be installed in empty bays in the system unit when necessary. *External devices* are stand-alone hardware components that connect via cable to a port on the back of the system unit.

In most secondary storage systems, media must pass by a *read/write head* inside the peripheral device to be read from or written to.

REMOVABLE VERSUS NONREMOVABLE MEDIA   In many secondary storage systems, although the peripheral device is online to the computer, the associated medium must be loaded into the device before the computer can read from it or write to it. These are called *removable-media* secondary storage systems. Diskettes, CDs, and magnetic tape cartridges are examples of removable media used on such systems. Other secondary storage systems, such as most hard disks, are *fixed-media* secondary storage systems—the disk is encased in a sealed unit and cannot be easily removed.

Fixed media generally provide higher speed and better reliability at a lower cost. Removability has its advantages, too. Several are listed below:

- UNLIMITED STORAGE CAPACITY   The medium on the storage device can be replaced when full.
- TRANSPORTABILITY   Stored programs and data can be swapped among computers and people.
- BACKUP   A duplicate set of data or programs can be created and stored away from the computer, for use if the originals are destroyed.
- SECURITY   Stored programs or data can be placed in a controlled area.

As you can see, the advantages for removability are compelling. But so are speed and price. Consequently, virtually all PCs have both removable- and fixed-storage components.

SEQUENTIAL VERSUS DIRECT ACCESS   When a PC is instructed to use data or programs residing in secondary storage, it first must be able to find the materials. The process of retrieving data and programs from storage is called *access*.

Two basic access methods are available: sequential and direct. With **sequential access,** the records in a file can be retrieved only in the order in which they are physically stored. With **direct access,** also called *random access*, records can be retrieved in any order.

On computer systems, tape allows only sequential access to data. A computer tape works like a cassette tape in your stereo system—to get to some item in the middle of the tape, you must pass through all the preceding ones. Computer disks, in contrast, allow both sequential and direct access to data. They work like music CDs—you can play items in sequence or go directly to a particular one.

Media that can be accessed directly—such as memory and disk—are *addressable*. This means that each stored data record or program may later be randomly accessed through a unique *address*, which is automatically determined by the computer system. Tape systems, in contrast, are generally not addressable.

DISKETTES

Diskettes, or *floppy disks*, are small, round platters encased in plastic jackets. The platters are made of tough Mylar plastic and coated with a magnetizable substance. Each side of the diskette contains concentric tracks, which are encoded with 0- and 1-bits when you write data and programs to them.

On both diskette and hard-disk systems, the 0s and 1s are written by read/write heads magnetizing particles a certain way on the medium's surface (see Figure 2-12). The particles retain their magnetic orientation when they are later read, and the orientation can be changed at any time by rewriting to the medium.

FIGURE 2-12

Storing data on a magnetic disk.

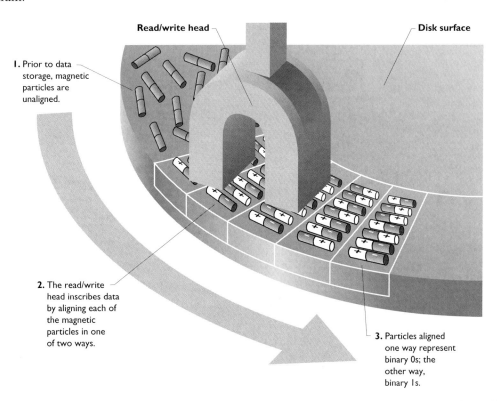

Read/write head

Disk surface

1. Prior to data storage, magnetic particles are unaligned.

2. The read/write head inscribes data by aligning each of the magnetic particles in one of two ways.

3. Particles aligned one way represent binary 0s; the other way, binary 1s.

■ **Sequential access.** Fetching stored records in the same order in which they are physically arranged on the medium.
■ **Direct access.** Reading or writing data in storage so that the access time is independent of the physical location of the data. Also known as *random access*. ■ **Diskette.** A low-capacity, removable disk made of a tough, flexible plastic and coated with a magnetizable substance.

DISKETTE SIZES Most diskettes in use are $3\frac{1}{2}$ inches in diameter. They are contained in rugged plastic cases that can fit into a shirt pocket. Strange as it may seem, $3\frac{1}{2}$-inch diskettes are faster and store more data than the $5\frac{1}{4}$-inch diskettes that were prevalent only a few years ago—not to mention that they get to those data faster. Today, $5\frac{1}{4}$-inch diskettes have all but disappeared from the marketplace.

Despite their small size, $3\frac{1}{2}$-inch diskettes can store a respectable amount of data. The most common capacity is 1.44 megabytes. The 1.44-megabyte diskettes are often called *high-density* diskettes; the older and less-prevalent 720-kilobyte diskettes, *double-density* or *low-density*. Density, incidentally, refers to how tightly bits of data are packed on the diskette. A diskette with 1.44 megabytes has enough room to store about 700 pages of double-spaced text, or several images.

PHYSICAL PROPERTIES Figure 2-13 illustrates the physical properties of a diskette. The plastic surfaces of a diskette are coated with a magnetizable substance. The jacket is lined with a soft liner that wipes the disk clean as it spins. To further protect data, diskettes contain a *write-protect square* to prevent users from accidentally writing on the disk. Exposing this square opening makes writing impossible. When the disk is placed into a drive, it is rotated when the drive engages its hub and begins to spin.

DISKETTE ADDRESSES Each side of a diskette platter contains a specific number of concentric **tracks,** which are encoded with 0- and 1-bits when data and programs are written to them. To be used by a particular computer system,

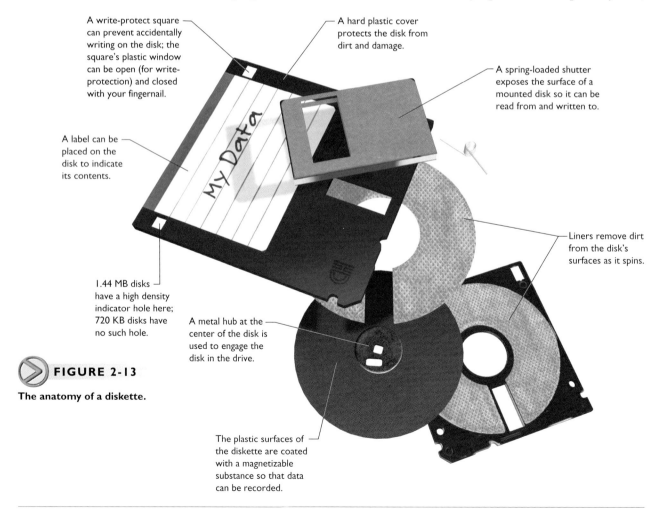

A write-protect square can prevent accidentally writing on the disk; the square's plastic window can be open (for write-protection) and closed with your fingernail.

A hard plastic cover protects the disk from dirt and damage.

A spring-loaded shutter exposes the surface of a mounted disk so it can be read from and written to.

A label can be placed on the disk to indicate its contents.

Liners remove dirt from the disk's surfaces as it spins.

1.44 MB disks have a high density indicator hole here; 720 KB disks have no such hole.

A metal hub at the center of the disk is used to engage the disk in the drive.

FIGURE 2-13

The anatomy of a diskette.

The plastic surfaces of the diskette are coated with a magnetizable substance so that data can be recorded.

■ **Track.** A path on a storage medium where data are recorded.

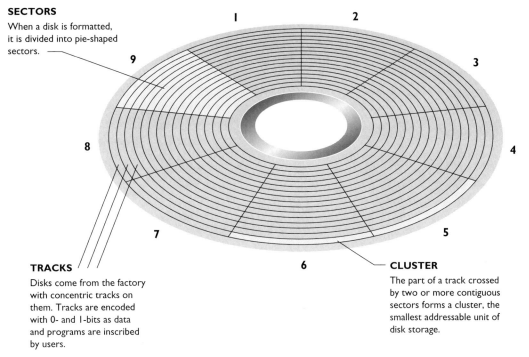

SECTORS
When a disk is formatted, it is divided into pie-shaped sectors.

TRACKS
Disks come from the factory with concentric tracks on them. Tracks are encoded with 0- and 1-bits as data and programs are inscribed by users.

CLUSTER
The part of a track crossed by two or more contiguous sectors forms a cluster, the smallest addressable unit of disk storage.

FIGURE 2-14

Diskette organization.

disks must be formatted. *Formatting* divides the disk into pie-shaped **sectors** and thereby prepares the disk for use with a particular operating system. On many microcomputer systems, the part of any track crossed by two or more contiguous sectors forms a cluster. A **cluster** is used to represent a single disk address (see Figure 2-14). Diskettes can be bought preformatted, and you can also use your computer's operating system to format the diskette for you. A diskette is not usable for storage unless it has been formatted.

A **file directory** on the diskette, which the PC automatically maintains, keeps track of the diskette's contents. This directory shows the name of each diskette file, its size, and the cluster number at which it begins.

USING DISKETTES To use a diskette, you insert it into a device called a **disk drive** or *disk unit* (see Figure 2-15). Disk doors on 3½-inch drives automatically accept a diskette that has been inserted properly—you'll hear a click when this happens—and possibly require you to press an *eject button* to remove the disk. There is only one correct way to insert the diskette into the drive—with the disk label facing up and the metallic, shutter-mechanism end going in first.

While the diskette is rotating, the read/write heads access tracks through the shutter's *recording window*. If the *indicator light* for a drive is on, meaning that the read/write heads are accessing the diskette in the drive, do not try to remove the diskette.

SUPERDISKETTES A drawback to diskettes is their storage capacity. Not too long ago, 1.44 megabytes was considered a reasonable amount of storage, but storage demands are increasing rapidly, and 1.44 MB is looking smaller and

FIGURE 2-15

Inserting a diskette into a drive. Diskettes go into a drive only one way—label side up, with the disk shutter facing the drive door.

■ **Sector.** A pie-shaped area on a disk surface. ■ **Cluster.** An area formed where a fixed number of contiguous sectors intersect a track. ■ **File directory.** A listing on a storage medium that provides such data as name, length, and starting address for each stored file. ■ **Disk drive.** A direct-access secondary storage device that uses a magnetic or optical disk as the principal medium.

 FIGURE 2-16

Superdiskette drives with cartridges. Disk-cartridge products with capacities of 100 megabytes or more are commonly sold either as replacements for standard diskettes or as supplemental storage solutions. (Left: 250 MB Iomega Zip drive and cartridges, Right: 120 MB Imation SuperDisk drive and cartridges.)

smaller with each passing year. Consequently, a number of other storage products have been introduced in recent years as either replacements for the standard diskette or as supplemental storage solutions. Among such products are *Zip disks, laser servo* (LS) disks, and *HiFD disks,* each of which has a capacity of 100 or more megabytes (see Figure 2-16). Each of these disk products is 3½ inches in diameter and requires its own special drive. LS and HiFD drives can read standard diskettes; Zip drives cannot. All three types of drives sell for about $100, and their disk cartridges for $15 or so.

HARD DISKS

Most PCs made today have some type of hard disk. Typically, a **hard disk** consists of one or more rigid metal platters that are mounted onto a shaft and sealed in a box along with an access mechanism (see Figure 2-17). Thus, on PCs, the terms *hard disk* and *hard-disk drive* commonly refer to the same thing—a single *pack* of disks as well as accompanying read/write heads, circuit board, and outside casing.

In most PCs, the hard disk is hermetically sealed. This keeps the disk surfaces completely free of air contamination, thereby enabling the disks to spin faster and to encounter fewer operational problems. Whereas a standard diskette spins at about 300 revolutions per minute (rpm), hard disks typically spin at anywhere from 3,600 to 9,600 rpm.

Hard disks provide far greater amounts of online storage and significantly faster access to programs and data than diskettes. Microcomputer hard disks are most commonly found in capacities of one gigabyte or more. Thus, if you have a 20-gigabyte hard disk, you have the storage equivalent of over 13,800 3½-inch diskettes available the minute you turn on the power. Also, you don't have to constantly shuffle diskettes in and out of drives. Speedwise, hard-disk drives can access data at least ten times faster than diskette drives. That's because the hard disk both rotates faster and is constantly spinning whenever your computer is turned on. A diskette, in contrast, does not spin when it is not being accessed.

Hard disks on PCs can be internal or external. An *internal* hard-disk system, such as the one in Figure 2-17, is standard on virtually all PCs sold and is by far the most common type. An *external* hard-disk system is a detached drive that can supplement the storage that comes with the computer. External disks are often slightly slower and more expensive than their internal counterparts but provide the flexibility of being shared by two or more computers.

For links to further information about nonremovable storage devices and media, go to www.harcourtcollege. com/infosys/pcc2e/student/ explore/ and click on Chapter 2.

■ **Hard disk.** A system consisting of one or more rigid platters and an access mechanism.

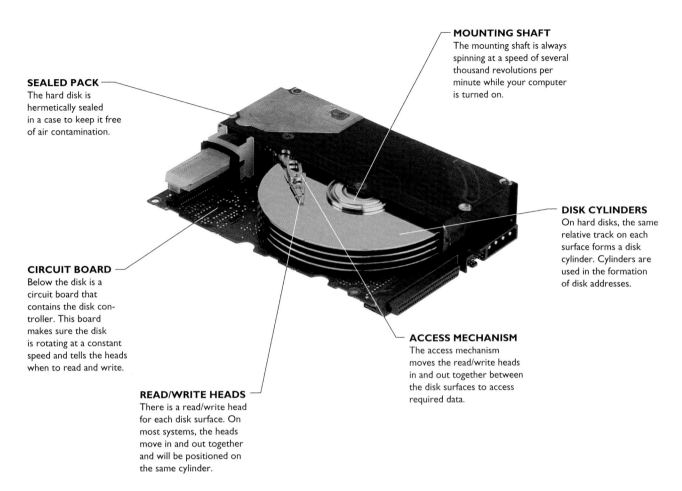

SEALED PACK
The hard disk is hermetically sealed in a case to keep it free of air contamination.

MOUNTING SHAFT
The mounting shaft is always spinning at a speed of several thousand revolutions per minute while your computer is turned on.

DISK CYLINDERS
On hard disks, the same relative track on each surface forms a disk cylinder. Cylinders are used in the formation of disk addresses.

CIRCUIT BOARD
Below the disk is a circuit board that contains the disk controller. This board makes sure the disk is rotating at a constant speed and tells the heads when to read and write.

ACCESS MECHANISM
The access mechanism moves the read/write heads in and out together between the disk surfaces to access required data.

READ/WRITE HEADS
There is a read/write head for each disk surface. On most systems, the heads move in and out together and will be positioned on the same cylinder.

While most hard disks are "fixed," meaning you cannot separate them from their drives, systems that use removable hard-disk cartridges are gaining in popularity (see Figure 2-18). One of the most widely used of these is Iomega's *Jaz drive.* A Jaz cartridge, which can store one or two gigabytes, takes slightly longer to access than a conventional fixed hard disk. The Jaz drive comes in both an internal and an external version, each available for less than $400.

Like diskettes, hard disks contain tracks and sectors—but many more of both. Each new hard disk is typically formatted for use at the factory before it is sold. On most desktop PCs, hard disks are 3½ inches in diameter; on most notebook computers, 2½ inches.

FIGURE 2-17

A hard-disk drive. Hard-disk systems for PCs often have capacities in the gigabyte range. Featured here is an *internal* hard-disk system.

FIGURE 2-18

Removable hard disk. Iomega's Jaz drive, which works with removable, high-capacity gigabyte-range cartridges to deliver performance close to a computer system's native fixed hard disk. The Jaz drive is available in external (pictured here) and internal models.

OPTICAL DISKS

FIGURE 2-19

Optical-disk drives and their storage media.

Optical disk systems are also in wide use on PCs. Data are placed onto these disks with high-intensity laser beams that typically burn tiny holes into the surface. Then a lower-intensity laser beam reads the data inscribed. Three common types of optical-disk systems in use today are CD-ROM, WORM, and rewritable CDs (see Figure 2-19). An up-and-coming standard that many people expect to shortly inherit the roles of both CD-ROM technology and video-cassette recorders connected to television sets is DVD.

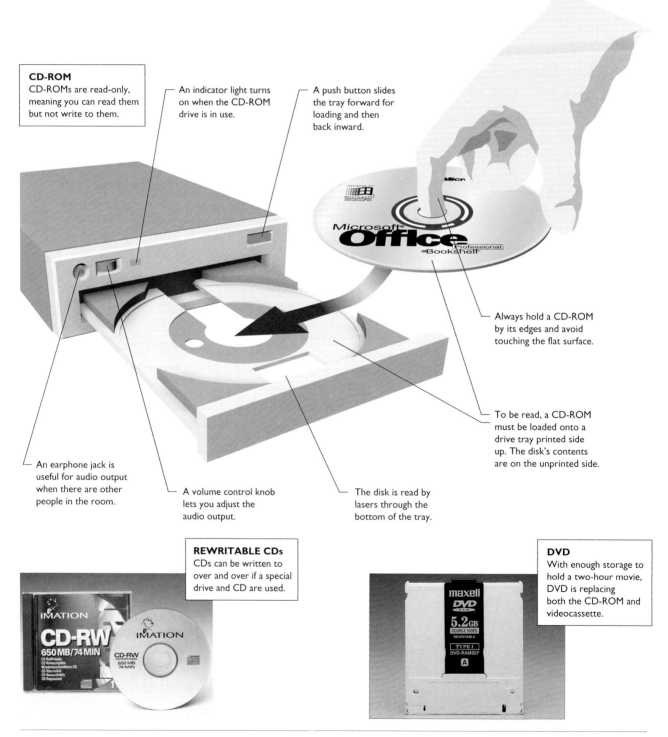

CD-ROM
CD-ROMs are read-only, meaning you can read them but not write to them.

An indicator light turns on when the CD-ROM drive is in use.

A push button slides the tray forward for loading and then back inward.

Always hold a CD-ROM by its edges and avoid touching the flat surface.

To be read, a CD-ROM must be loaded onto a drive tray printed side up. The disk's contents are on the unprinted side.

An earphone jack is useful for audio output when there are other people in the room.

A volume control knob lets you adjust the audio output.

The disk is read by lasers through the bottom of the tray.

REWRITABLE CDs
CDs can be written to over and over if a special drive and CD are used.

DVD
With enough storage to hold a two-hour movie, DVD is replacing both the CD-ROM and videocassette.

■ **Optical disk.** A disk read by reflecting pulses of laser beams.

CD-ROM Most optical disk units on PCs are of the **CD-ROM** (compact disk/read-only memory) type. Specialized equipment stores data on CD-ROMs at the factory by burning tiny holes into the disks' surfaces with high-intensity laser beams. Then, your PC drive's lower-intensity laser beam reads the data so inscribed. Because the storage process permanently etches the surface of the CD-ROM, you cannot write new data to the disk in any way.

Internal CD-ROM optical-disk drives costing about $100 are standard items on PCs today. Most CD-ROM disk drives available on the market are touted as 24X, 32X, 36X, and so on. These labels convey the speed of the drive. For instance, 36X is for 36 times the speed of the baseline unit that was originally manufactured.

Only one side of a CD-ROM contains data—the side opposite the one with the printing on it. When you mount a CD-ROM on a drive tray, you place it with the printed side up. Be careful not to get dirt, fingerprints, or anything else that might hinder light reflectivity on the CD's surface.

While many computer-industry forecasters have for years been predicting the CD-ROM would be replaced by newer CD technologies, it is instead still going strong. Tie-ins with the Internet have been able to extend the power of CD-ROMs, and the millions of new owners of sub-$1,000 PCs have also swelled the ranks of potential CD-ROM buyers.

WORM Optical-disk systems are available that will let you write once to the disk. Once written, the data cannot be erased. These are called **WORM** (write once, read many) CD systems. The most widely used WORM standard is *CD-R*, the *R* standing for "recordable." CD-R lets users create their own CD-ROM master disks, which can be used to create inexpensive CD-ROMs for distribution purposes. WORM disks have a built-in security measure; because others can't rewrite to the disk, you know that what you put on it can't be accidentally erased or altered in any way. In recent years, with drives selling for $500 or less and blank CDs going for about $5 apiece, CD-R has seen a new application—home users making high-quality music CDs on their own.

REWRITABLE CDs Optical-disk systems that allow you to both write and erase data—possibly hundreds of thousands of times—have also recently become available. **Rewritable CDs** use either an *MO* (for magneto-optical) or *phase-change* technology. Phase-change drives are generally faster than MO drives and, unlike MO drives, can sometimes also read CD-ROMs. However, the various MO drives in the marketplace are more compatible with one another, making it easier for users to exchange information. CD PD (the *PD* is for *power drive*) and CD-RW (the *RW* is for *rewritable*) are the two prevailing phase-change standards. CD PD's cartridge technology enables CDs to be read far more often before the disk degrades, but CD-RW disks and drives are more compatible with other CD standards—such as CD-ROM, CD-R, and DVD.

DVDs The acronym **DVD** (for *digital versatile disk*) refers to a relatively new high-capacity CD storage format that was initially developed to store the full contents of a standard two-hour movie. The acronym DVD originally stood for *digital video disk*. Proponents of the technology later felt that the word *video* was too limiting—the disks can also store text, graphics, and audio data—so the longer name is often dropped or, alternatively, the word *versatile* substituted for *video*.

DVD-ROM technology is seen by many as the successor to music CDs, computer CD-ROMs, and prerecorded VHS videotapes that people buy or rent for

For links to further information about removable storage devices and media, go to www.harcourtcollege.com/infosys/pcc2e/student/explore/ and click on Chapter 2.

■ **CD-ROM.** A low-end optical disk that can be read but not written to. ■ **WORM.** An optical disk that can be written to only once, but read an unlimited number of times. ■ **Rewritable CDs.** An optical disk that allows users to repeatedly write to and read from its surface. ■ **DVD.** An optical-disk standard that enables very high capacities.

TAPE DRIVES
Cartridge tape drives
are available as both
internal and external
devices.

CARTRIDGE TAPES
There are a very large number of tape
formats in use—QIC-80, TR-1, DAT,
and so on. When buying tapes, be sure
that they conform to the format specified
by the drive's manufacturer.

As a tape is being
processed, it spools
from one reel onto
another and then
back again.

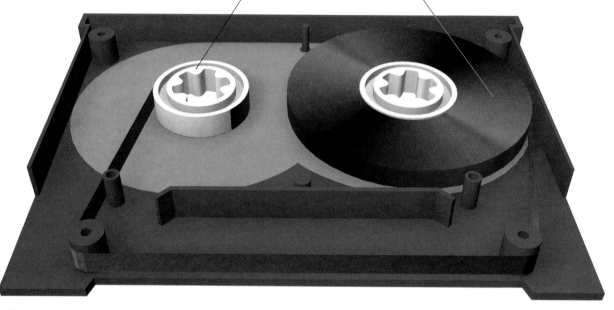

 FIGURE 2-20

Cartridge tapes. On PCs, cartridge
tapes are most frequently used to back
up the contents of a hard disk.

home viewing—in other words, read-only products. As consumers begin to
appreciate the extra value that 4.7, 9.4, and 18.8 GB DVD-ROM can offer,
expect to see rewritable DVDs—called *DVD-RAM*—following into the market. In a few years, it is likely that many people will be recording television
programs at home on blank DVDs, just as they do today on blank VHS tapes.

DVDs require DVD-enabled disk drives. DVD is backward compatible, which
means that you can play CD-ROMs on DVD drives. You can also play audio
CDs on DVD drives.

CARTRIDGE TAPES

Cartridge tape is useful for transporting data between PCs and for backing up
the contents of a hard disk (see Figure 2-20). The tape, which is enclosed in a
plastic cartridge, is made of a thin plastic that is coated with a magnetizable
substance. To be read from or written to, the tape must be mounted on a device
called a **tape drive.** Like disk drives, tape drives can be internal or external.

Today, a variety of cartridge-tape standards are on the market, including QIC-
80, Travan 1 and Travan 4, and DAT (for digital-audio tape). Tapes conforming
to one standard often cannot be read in drives that conform to another

■ **Cartridge tape.** Magnetic tape in which the supply and take-up reels are contained in a small plastic case. ■ **Tape
drive.** A secondary storage device that reads from and writes to mounted magnetic tapes.

standard. Tapes used with PCs typically can store at least a gigabyte of data and cost from $20 upward. When buying a tape drive, be sure it accepts tapes with a capacity large enough to back up your entire hard disk. Hard-disk backup on tape often takes an hour or more.

OUTPUT HARDWARE

Output devices are perhaps the most diverse type of hardware. Most of them convert strings of bits the computer uses back into natural-language form or picture form to make them understandable to humans.

Most output devices produce output for screen display or send output onto paper or film. The term **soft copy** often refers to display output—that is, output that is temporary and of limited portability. **Hard copy,** on the other hand, refers to output that has been recorded onto a medium such as paper or microfilm—in other words, output that is in a permanent and highly portable form.

MONITORS

Monitors, or *display devices*, are computer hardware that contains a viewing screen. One commonly finds them plugged into and sitting on top of the system units of PCs. As each key on the keyboard is pressed, the corresponding character representation of the key appears on the monitor screen at the insertion point position. The *insertion point* is a highlighted position on the screen indicating where the next character to be typed will be placed.

Most monitors sold with desktop computers today can output text, graphics, and video. They are widely available with screens of 14, 15, 17, 19, 20, or 21 inches, with size measured diagonally along the screen surface. Many features other than size differentiate the hundreds of display devices currently on the market (see Figure 2-21). A discussion of the more noteworthy features follows.

FIGURE 2-21

Monitors. A wide variety of monitors is available in today's equipment marketplace. Two common types of PC monitors are (left to right) the CRT, which resembles a standard television screen, and the flat-panel display.

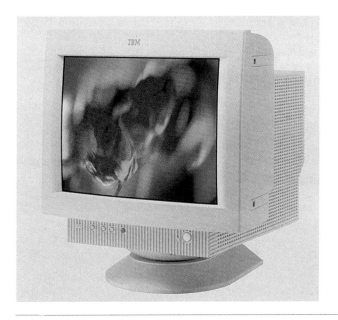

■ **Soft copy.** A nonpermanent form of computer system output—for example, a screen display. ■ **Hard copy.** A permanent form of computer system output—for example, information printed on paper or film. ■ **Monitor.** A display device without a kcyboard.

RESOLUTION A key characteristic of any display device is *resolution*, or sharpness of the screen image. Resolution is measured by the density of the pixels, or dot pitch. A display's *dot pitch*, the distance between pixels in millimeters, is typically .26 or .28. The smaller the dot pitch, the better the resolution—that is, the crisper the picture.

Resolution is often also specified as a matrix of pixels. A display resolution of, say, 640 by 480 means that the screen consists of 640 columns by 480 rows of pixels—that is, 307,200 pixels.

Text characters, as well as graphics and video images, are formed by configurations of pixels (see Figure 2-22). Because pixels are so finely packed and are viewed by users from a distance, they appear to blend together to form continuous images.

In the typical desktop display, pixels are electronically maintained and manipulated at lightning-fast speeds by an electron gun. Pixels on the screen are *refreshed*—that is, redrawn with the gun so that they will remain bright— at a rate of 60 times each second.

COLOR DISPLAY By far, most desktop PC monitors being sold today produce *color* output and are of the *red-green-blue (RGB)* type. With an RGB monitor, all colors available on the screen are formed by mixing combinations of only these three colors. Mixing only three colors may not sound like much, but when red, green, and blue light of varying intensities are blended—for each of the hundreds of thousands of pixels on the screen—a very wide range of colors is possible.

Most desktop monitors being sold today with PCs are also *noninterlaced*. This means that the monitor draws every screen line each time it refreshes the screen in order to provide a more stable image. *Interlaced displays*—used with most television sets—instead draw every other line of the image each time the screen is refreshed and fill in the alternate lines on the next refresh. While interlaced monitors are cheaper, they can produce some screen flicker. That's why it's easier to read small text on a computer monitor than on a television set. Figure 2-23 illustrates the difference between interlaced and non-interlaced monitors.

CRT AND FLAT-PANEL DISPLAY DEVICES Most desktop monitors use a large picture-tube element similar to the one inside a standard television set. This type of monitor, shown in the leftmost part of Figure 2-21, is commonly called

Each pixel on a screen is individually assigned a color to form the screen image. The higher the pixel density, or resolution, the crisper the screen image.

▶ **FIGURE 2-22**

Pixels.

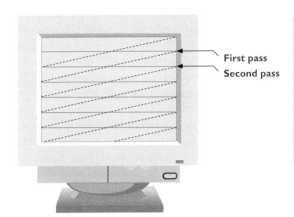

First pass
Second pass

INTERLACED MONITOR
Every other line of the image is drawn on a refresh and alternate lines are filled in on the next pass.

NONINTERLACED MONITOR
Every screen line is redrawn on each screen refresh.

FIGURE 2-23

Interlaced and noninterlaced monitors.

a **CRT (cathode-ray tube).** CRT technology is relatively mature. Over the years, CRTs have become inexpensive and capable of providing excellent color output. These features notwithstanding, CRTs are bulky and fragile, and they consume a great deal of power.

Over the past 15 years or so, monitors that use charged chemicals or gases sandwiched between panes of glass have become popular alternatives to CRTs—especially on portable computers. These slim-profile devices are called **flat-panel displays** (see the right-most image in Figure 2-21). Although they can be relatively expensive, flat-panel displays take up little space, are lightweight, require less power than CRT monitors, and produce a sharp picture.

Most flat-panel displays on ordinary computer systems use a *liquid crystal display (LCD)* and either an *active-matrix* or *passive-matrix* color-display technology. Active-matrix displays provide a much sharper screen image, but they do so at a higher cost.

GRAPHICS STANDARDS Graphics standards are used to specify "modes" in which a display device can operate. For example, *VGA* (for video graphics array)—the standard used on many of the older 386 and 486 PCs with 14- and 15-inch displays—can output at a maximum resolution of 640 by 480 pixels. VGA allows, at most, 256 colors to be displayed simultaneously.

SVGA (for Super VGA), the standard that took over when Pentium-based PCs and 17-inch monitors became popular, allows even larger pixel matrices. Most SVGA monitors display at either a resolution of 800 by 600 pixels or 1,024 by 768 pixels—and up to 16,777,216 colors. Thus, an SVGA display can show two-and-a-half times the amount of information that a VGA display of the same size can show, though the information appears smaller.

For links to further information about display devices, go to www.harcourtcollege. com/infosys/pcc2e/student/ explore/ and click on Chapter 2.

PRINTERS

Monitors have two major limitations as output devices: (1) Only a small amount of data can be shown on the screen at one time, and (2) output, being in soft-copy form, is not portable. You must be physically present at a monitor to get any results. **Printers** overcome these limitations by producing hard copy—a permanent record of output.

■ **Cathode-ray tube (CRT).** A display device that projects images on a long-necked display tube similar to that in a television set. ■ **Flat-panel display.** A slim-profile display device. ■ **Printer.** A device that records computer output on paper.

DOT-MATRIX CHARACTERS   If you look at the spokes on the print head of an old typewriter, you'll notice that they contain embossed, solid characters—called solid fonts. Many of the earliest computer printers used solid-font print heads to output onto paper—and some modern printers still do—but today, most characters and graphics images are formed by a matrix of dots.

The output resolution produced by such printers is measured in dpi, and often hundreds of thousands of dots can be packed into a single square inch of output. Resolution from dot-matrix printers has become so good in recent years that the characters on paper look like smooth, continuous strokes rather than collections of dots—even under close inspection (see Figure 2-24).

By far the most popular printers for PCs today utilize either laser or ink-jet technology, which we'll cover in some depth shortly. Both of these types of printers employ a *nonimpact printing* technology in that the print-head mechanism makes no contact at all with paper or film. For many years, most PC printers relied on *impact printing*; in an impact dot-matrix printer, one or more vertical columns of pins in the print head are repeatedly activated, striking characters onto paper (see Figure 2-25).

LASER PRINTERS   Relatively inexpensive personal **laser printers**—costing between $300 and $1,500 and printing 4 to 12 pages per minute (ppm)—are widely available for PCs. Most of these generate resolutions of at least 600 dpi. At 600 dpi, every square inch of the output image is broken down into a 600-by-600 matrix of dots. That's 360,000 dots packed into every inch! Laser devices are especially popular in business because of their speed and crisp-looking text output, and they are the most common type of printer sold to that market segment.

Laser printers form images in the same way as copying machines—by charging thousands of dots on a drum with a very-high-intensity laser beam. Toner from a cartridge is affixed to the charged positions and, when paper is pressed against the drum, an image is formed. A heating unit fuses the image permanently onto the paper (see Figure 2-26).

FIGURE 2-24

Print resolution. Print resolution is commonly measured by the number of dots per inch (dpi). The higher the dpi, the harder it is to tell that dots were used to compose the image.

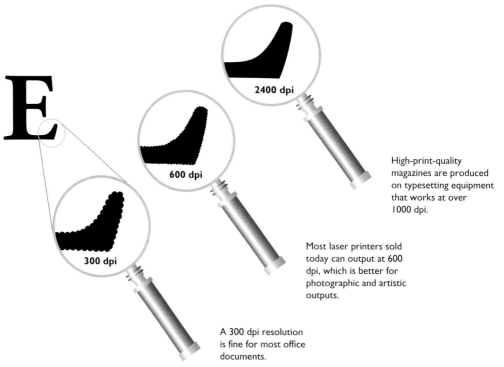

2400 dpi

600 dpi

300 dpi

High-print-quality magazines are produced on typesetting equipment that works at over 1000 dpi.

Most laser printers sold today can output at 600 dpi, which is better for photographic and artistic outputs.

A 300 dpi resolution is fine for most office documents.

■ **Laser printer.** A printer that works on a principle similar to that of a photocopier.

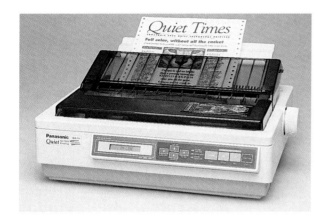

IMPACT DOT-MATRIX PRINTING
Because of the force of the print head on paper, impact dot-matrix printers are ideal for printing multipart forms. Many impact dot-matrix printers cost less than $200 and cost about a penny a page to operate.

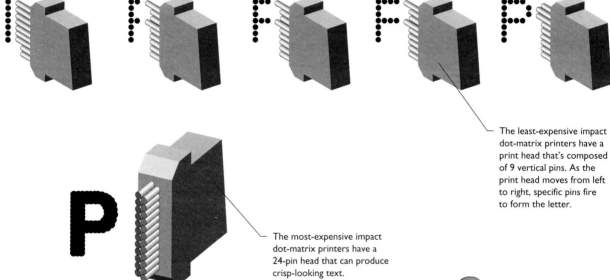

The least-expensive impact dot-matrix printers have a print head that's composed of 9 vertical pins. As the print head moves from left to right, specific pins fire to form the letter.

The most-expensive impact dot-matrix printers have a 24-pin head that can produce crisp-looking text.

FIGURE 2-25

Impact dot-matrix printing.

While most laser printers, such as the one featured in Figure 2-26, produce only monochrome and gray-scale outputs, color laser printers costing only a few thousand dollars have recently become available. While output is not of photographic quality, color laser printers are faster than many other types of color printers. Also, the output quality is quite acceptable if the page image is simple enough or (if complex) is going to be used only for proofing purposes.

INK-JET PRINTERS **Ink-jet printers** work by spraying thousands of small droplets of electrically charged ink onto a page to form images (see Figure 2-27). For the past several years, ink-jet printing has been the technology of choice for those who want to produce affordable color with a PC. Most ink-jet printers made today will produce black-and-white, gray-scale, and color output.

The principal advantage to ink-jet printing is cost: You can buy a color ink-jet printer for as little as $100 or so, whereas printers using other technologies are generally more expensive. There are disadvantages, however. Text can take longer to output than on a laser printer and may not look as crisp. Ink-jet printers use replaceable color cartridges, and their cost can mount up over time if you use a lot of color in your work.

For links to further information about printers, go to www.harcourtcollege.com/infosys/pcc2e/student/explore/ and click on Chapter 2.

■ **Ink-jet printer.** A printer that forms images by spraying droplets of charged ink onto a page.

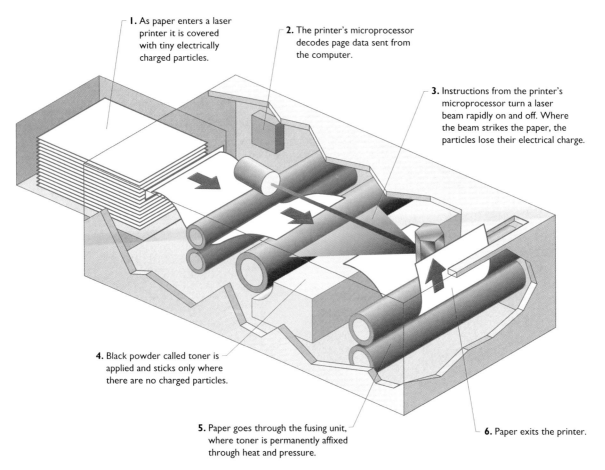

1. As paper enters a laser printer it is covered with tiny electrically charged particles.

2. The printer's microprocessor decodes page data sent from the computer.

3. Instructions from the printer's microprocessor turn a laser beam rapidly on and off. Where the beam strikes the paper, the particles lose their electrical charge.

4. Black powder called toner is applied and sticks only where there are no charged particles.

5. Paper goes through the fusing unit, where toner is permanently affixed through heat and pressure.

6. Paper exits the printer.

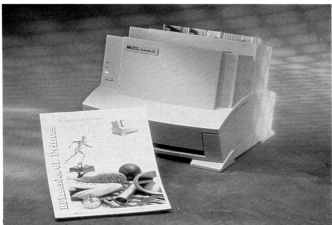

ABOUT LASER PRINTERS

Because of their speed and output quality, laser printers are by far the most popular type of printer for business applications.

Common speeds for personal laser printers are 4, 6, 8, and 12 pages per minute (ppm).

Many personal printers come with at least 1 MB RAM. While this is fine for text, 4 MB is better for intensive graphics work.

FIGURE 2-26

Laser printing. Costing less than $500, personal laser printers are useful for production, routine business reports, correspondence, and also for graphics outputs.

SPECIAL-PURPOSE OUTPUT DEVICES

A large number of output devices are available for other uses than those already covered. Two such devices are speakers and plotters.

SPEAKERS Most computer systems targeted for home use today come with a set of **speakers**. Speakers provide audio output for such consumer-oriented multimedia applications as playing computer games, listening to audio tracks on CD and the Internet, engaging in Internet voice chat, and receiving audio e-mail. Common business applications include audio-video demonstrations and presentations as well as computer videoconferencing.

■ **Speaker.** An output device that produces sound.

If you have Internet access, there are a variety of helpful resources available through Microsoft's Office Update site. Available resources include product updates, downloads, answers to common questions, and access to newsgroups.

1. Select *Office on the Web* from the Help menu to launch your browser and connect to the Office Update site.

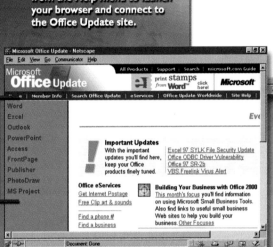

2. Select the desired Office program.

3. Select options on the Office Update site to locate a variety of helpful information and resources.

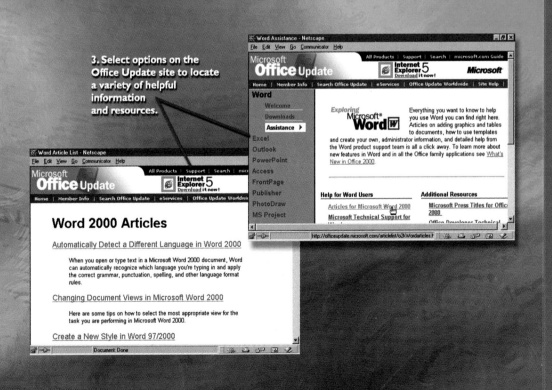

Many programs have a variety of helpful templates and wizards to help you create documents quickly. Microsoft Word templates include letters, memos, fax cover sheets, brochures, calendars, and so forth.

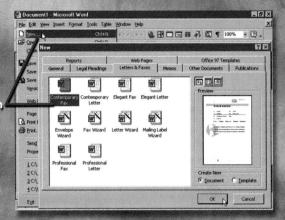

1. Select New from the File menu and then select the desired template.

✔ TRY THIS

If all templates and wizards are not displayed, insert your Microsoft Office installation disk and run Setup to install the additional templates and wizards for each desired Office program.

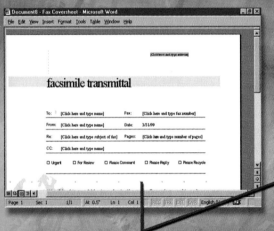

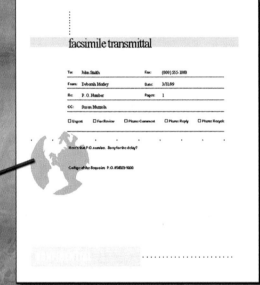

2. If a template was selected, the document will be created with placeholder text that should be edited to finish the document.

3. If a wizard was selected, the wizard will prompt you for specific information to be used when creating the document. After all wizard screens have been completed, the finished document will be displayed.

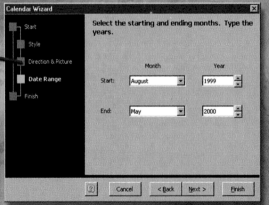

FIGURE 2-27

Ink-jet printing.

INK-JET PRINTING

Ink-jet printers create colors by mixing different combinations of ink. Devices targeted to personal use output text at a rate of one-to-five pages per minute but are far slower for color output.

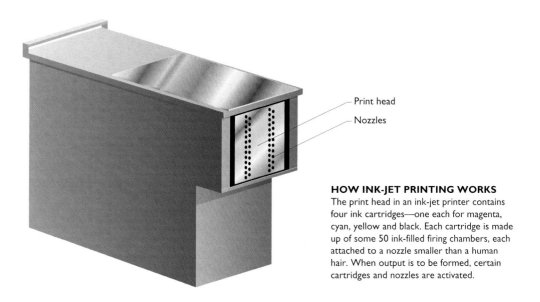

Print head

Nozzles

HOW INK-JET PRINTING WORKS

The print head in an ink-jet printer contains four ink cartridges—one each for magenta, cyan, yellow and black. Each cartridge is made up of some 50 ink-filled firing chambers, each attached to a nozzle smaller than a human hair. When output is to be formed, certain cartridges and nozzles are activated.

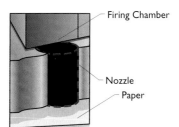

Firing Chamber

Nozzle

Paper

1. An electric current flows along the bottom of a firing chamber. This makes the ink boil and a steam bubble forms.

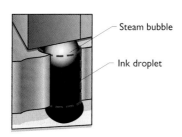

Steam bubble

Ink droplet

2. As a bubble expands, it pushes ink through the nozzle. The pressure of the bubble forces an ink droplet to be ejected onto the paper (see Step 3).

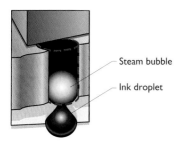

Steam bubble

Ink droplet

3. The volume of ink deposited is about one millionth that of a drop of water from an eyedropper. A typical character is formed by a 20-by-20 array of drops.

FIGURE 2-28

Plotter. Ink-jet plotters, by far the most prevalent type today, are useful for wide-format graphics that are too big for a standard ink-jet printer.

PLOTTERS A **plotter** is an output device used primarily to produce charts, drawings, maps, three-dimensional illustrations, and other forms of graphics-oriented hard copy (see Figure 2-28). While many ink-jet printers double as plotters, users with specialized graphics needs—such as artists who make posters and engineers who produce oversized drawings—will want to consider a device that is principally targeted to plotting rather than general applications. The two most common types of plotters are ink-jet and electrostatic plotters. An *ink-jet plotter,* which is by far the most prevalent type, is an output device that uses ink-jet technology to create images, whereas an *electrostatic plotter* works through principles similar to those of a copying machine. Electrostatic plotters are much faster than ink-jet plotters but tend to be more expensive. Whether they employ ink-jet or electrostatic printing, plotters are of either the flatbed or drum type. *Flatbed plotters* resemble drafting boards, whereas *drum plotters*, such as those in Figure 2-28, draw on paper that is rolled onto a drumlike mechanism.

SUMMARY AND KEY TERMS

Go to the Online Glossary at www.harcourtcollege.com/infosys/pcc2e/student/ to review key terms.

INPUT HARDWARE For most people, a PC would be useless without a **keyboard,** which is often the main vehicle for input. **Pointing devices** are a type of input hardware that moves an onscreen pointer such as an arrow, cursor, or insertion point. The most widely used pointing device is the **mouse.** Some other widely used pointing devices are the *light pen, joystick, trackball,* and *graphics tablet.* An **image scanner** is used to input such images as photographs, drawings, and documents into the computer system.

PROCESSING HARDWARE Almost all computer systems sold today use a modular hardware approach; that is, related circuitry is etched onto processor

■ **Plotter.** An output device that prints graphs and diagrams.

chips or memory chips, the chips are mounted onto carrier packages that are later fitted into boards, and the boards are positioned into slots inside the **system unit.**

The electronic components of most computers used for work or play operate in a two-state, or *binary*, fashion. It is convenient to think of these binary states as the 0-state and the 1-state. Computer professionals refer to such 0s and 1s as **bits.**

PCs use a fixed-length code called *ASCII* for sending and storing data. ASCII represents any single character of data—a digit, alphabetic character, or special symbol—as a string of eight bits called a **byte.**

The storage capacity of PCs often is expressed in **kilobytes (KB),** or thousands of bytes; **megabytes (MB** or *meg*), or millions of bytes; **gigabytes (GB),** or billions of bytes; and **terabytes (TB),** or trillions of bytes.

Binary data can be used to represent not only text data but also graphics, audio, and video data. With graphics and video data, each screen **pixel** is stored as some byte multiple. A program must be translated into **machine language** before the computer can execute it.

Every PC system unit contains a specific microprocessor chip as its CPU, which is mounted onto the **system board.** The main memory chips on PCs are commonly referred to as **RAM,** for **random access memory.** Memory chips that contain nonerasable programs are referred to as **ROM,** for **read-only memory.**

Many system units have external **ports** into which peripheral devices may be plugged. Also, many desktop PCs contain a limited number of internal expansion slots into which **add-in boards** can be mounted by the user. **Plug-and-play** provides a PC with the ability to detect and to help configure new hardware as it is manually added. On portable computers, expansion is normally done with **PC cards.**

The CPU connects to RAM, ROM, and peripherals through circuitry called a **bus.** The most widely used *expansion bus* architecture is ISA, and the most widely used *local bus* architecture is PCI.

SECONDARY STORAGE HARDWARE Among the most common types of secondary storage are magnetic disk, optical disk, and magnetic tape.

Any secondary storage system involves two physical parts: a *peripheral device* and an *input/output medium.* In most systems, media must pass by a *read/write head* in the peripheral device to be read from or written to. Media on secondary storage devices can be either *removable* or *fixed.* Two basic *access* methods are used on secondary storage systems: **sequential access** and **direct access.**

Diskettes are commonly used because of their removability and low cost. Each side of a diskette contains concentric **tracks,** which are encoded with 0- and 1-bits when data and programs are written to them. **Sectors** divide a diskette into pie-shaped pieces. The part of a track composed of two or more contiguous sectors is called a **cluster.** The disk's **file directory,** which the PC maintains automatically, keeps track of the contents at each disk address. To use a diskette, the operator inserts it into a **disk drive.** Today, diskettes are being challenged by other removable media—such as Zip, LS and HiFD disks—with much higher storage capacities.

Hard disks are faster and have greater data-carrying capacity than diskettes. Hard disks that accompany PCs are most commonly found in capacities of one gigabyte or more and can be either internal or external and either fixed or removable.

Optical disks, which work with laser read/write devices, are a relatively recent secondary storage technology. Most optical-disk systems available today are **CD-ROM,** write-once **(WORM),** rewritable **CD,** or **DVD** systems.

Cartridge tape is useful for transporting data between systems and for backing up the contents of a hard disk. To be read from or written to, the tape must be mounted on a device called a **tape drive.** Tape drives can be internal or external.

OUTPUT HARDWARE   Most output devices produce output for screen display or output onto paper or film. **Soft copy** generally refers to display output. **Hard copy,** on the other hand, refers to output that has been recorded onto a medium such as paper or microfilm.

Monitors are hardware devices that contain a viewing screen. Most desktop monitors being sold today with PCs are *noninterlaced*, provide color output, use either a **CRT** (for **cathode-ray tube**) or **flat-panel display** and adhere to a graphics standard known as SVGA.

Printers produce hard-copy output, in which text and graphics output are formed by a matrix of dots. The two most popular printers for PCs today are **laser printers** and **ink-jet printers,** both of which are of the nonimpact type.

A large number of output devices are available for uses other than those already covered. Two such devices are **speakers** and **plotters.**

EXERCISES

1. What is the purpose of the following keyboard keys?
   a. Escape key
   b. Function keys
   c. Ctrl key
   d. Backspace key
   e. Arrow keys
   f. Del key
   g. Ins key
   h. Numeric keypad keys

2. Identify at least six pointing devices that are used in conjunction with display devices for entering data into the computer system.

3. Below are listed several pieces of computer hardware. In each of the spaces provided, write the principal function of the given device—in other words, whether it is primarily an input device, output device, storage device, or processing device.
   a. CPU _____
   b. Mouse _____
   c. Monitor _____
   d. CD-ROM drive _____
   e. Trackball _____
   f. Diskette drive _____
   g. System unit _____
   h. Printer _____
   i. Image scanner _____
   j. Plotter _____

4. Identify each of the following statements as true or false.
   a. Most PC printers sold today are of the impact type.
   b. A Zip disk physically resembles a diskette more than it does a CD-ROM.
   c. QWERTY refers to the way some keyboards are arranged.
   d. "System board" and "motherboard" refer to essentially the same thing.
   e. Interlaced monitors are superior to noninterlaced ones.

5. Fill in the blanks:
   a. The term _____ generally refers to output that has been recorded onto a medium such as paper or film.

b. Resolution on a monitor screen is often measured by the number of dots, or _____, per unit of area.

c. A monitor that outputs images in a single foreground color is known as a(n) _____ display.

d. A(n) _____ printer does not rely on metal or a ribbon striking paper.

e. The Pentium III chip is made by _____ Corporation.

6. From smallest to largest, place the following terms in the correct order: kilobyte, gigabyte, byte, terabyte, bit, megabyte.

7. Match each term with the description that best fits.
   a. CD-ROM
   b. Mouse
   c. Image scanner
   d. Keyboard
   e. SIMM
   f. Plotter
   g. Local bus
   h. High-density
   i. Dot pitch
   j. Ports

_____ PCI is an example
_____ A term that describes a type of optical disk
_____ A term that describes a type of diskette
_____ The most widely used type of input device
_____ A device that can be used to input the likeness of a drawing into computer storage
_____ Users of this device might double-click it
_____ Parallel and serial are two types
_____ A term commonly used to describe the resolution of a monitor
_____ A block of RAM
_____ Two types are ink-jet and electrostatic

8. Name at least eight devices located under the cover of the system unit. What function does each of these devices perform?

9. Each of the following definitions is not strictly true in some regard. In each case, identify how the definition is false. Then, correct the error by defining the term in the right way.
   a. Cluster: The intersection of a disk sector and track.
   b. Optical disk: A CD-ROM disk.
   c. Dot pitch: Commonly referred to as dpi, it's the amount of space, measured in millimeters, between pixels on a monitor screen.
   d. DVD: An acronym for digital video disk.
   e. Dot-matrix printer: A printer that uses hammers to produce output onto paper as a configuration of dots.

10. Match the terms below with the pictures that follow. Note that each term can match one or two pictures, or none at all.

_____ VGA   _____ Trackball
_____ Noninterlacing   _____ Cluster
_____ SVGA   _____ Port
_____ Joystick   _____ PC card
_____ Image scanner _____ Crosshair cursor

a.
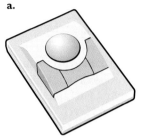

d.

b.

e.

c.

11. Why do color images—such as those that appear on a monitor's screen—take up more storage space than monochrome ones?

12. Assume, for simplicity's sake, that a kilobyte is 1,000 bytes, a megabyte is $1,000 \times 1,000$ bytes, and a gigabyte is $1,000 \times 1,000 \times 1,000$ bytes. You have a 10 gigabyte hard disk with the following usage:

PROGRAMS AND APPLICATIONS	BYTES
Operating system	7,600,453
Other systems software	2,184,605
Office suite	63,701,460
Other software	479,842,809
Documents	27,904,668

What percentage of the hard disk is used up?

PROJECTS

1. **Keyboards** One interesting story claims that the QWERTY keyboard, which became a typewriter standard more than a century ago, was actually created to slow down typists so that they wouldn't get their fingers stuck between the keys. Despite the QWERTY keyboard's somewhat controversial design, it has managed to survive through the years, becoming the standard keyboard arrangement for computer systems as well. For this project, answer the questions below. Feel free to consult Internet resources in your research as well as journal articles and books.

   a. Why has QWERTY prevailed over other, more highly praised keyboard designs?
   b. Many people prefer the Dvorak keyboard over QWERTY. How does the Dvorak keyboard differ, and why do many people prefer it?
   c. What is the least expensive way to implement a Dvorak keyboard?

2. **Image Scanners** Image scanners have become very popular peripheral devices in recent years for home and office use. Scanners convert flat images—such as a page of text or a photograph—into digital files that you can manipulate on your computer. For this project, choose a recent scanner designed for a PC, and answer the following questions about it. Feel free to consult Internet resources in your research as well as journal articles and product brochures.

   a. What is the name and/or model number of the PC scanner you have chosen? Who manufactures the product?
   b. How does a scanner handle source documents—through a flatbed or drum mechanism, by moving a handheld unit over the documents, or in some other way?
   c. Can the scanner input color information to the CPU?
   d. Does any software come with the scanner? If it does, describe the types of capabilities the software provides.
   e. At what maximum resolution (stated in dpi) does the scanner accept inputs?
   f. What is the list price of the scanner?

3. **Intel** Intel is the world's largest producer of CPU chips and also the leading chip vendor for PC-compatible computers. Consult either computer periodicals in a library available to you or Intel's Web site (www.intel.com) to answer the following questions.

   a. What is the name of the fastest Intel CPU chip currently being sold with PCs?
   b. At what speed does this chip run? State the answer in MHz.
   c. What other products does Intel produce besides CPU chips?

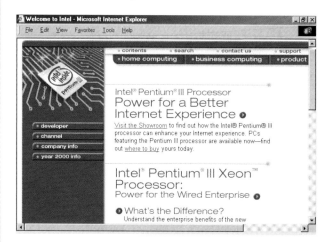

4. **PC Makers** Virtually all the leading PC makers maintain Web sites and regularly run advertisements in computer journals. For any three of the PC makers listed in the following figure, answer the questions that follow. Feel free to do this project using either Web-based information or information found in computer journals. You can do the exercise in groups of three students each if your instructor permits.

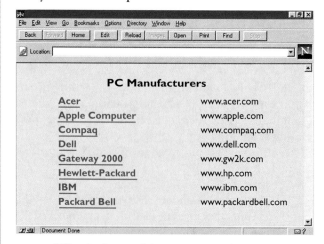

   a. What is the model name or number of a current desktop PC sold by each vendor? A current notebook computer?
   b. What processing speeds do these computers achieve? Give your answer in MHz.

c. What type of CPU powers each of these computers—for instance, a Pentium II or PowerPC 750?

d. How many megabytes of RAM does each type of PC include?

e. How large is each PC's native hard disk (measured in megabytes)?

5. Inspecting a System Unit Open up a system unit and look at the parts inside. Make one or two diagrams labeling components that you recognize. Be sure to include the following components: CPU chip, RAM SIMMs, expansion slots, expansion boards, hard-disk drive, diskette drive(s), CD drive (if present), power supply, and ports.

 6. Audio Data on the Web Several Web sites cater to users who want their Web pages talking or playing music. Three major categories of audio sites are those that let you download audio software for your Web browser, those that let you listen to radio stations over the Internet, and those that let you download such audio products as books, courses, and music singles. For this project, pick one of these three categories and write a paper (three to five pages) describing the audio resources it provides to interested users. The figure below lists several sites, any of which might be a good starting point for your research.

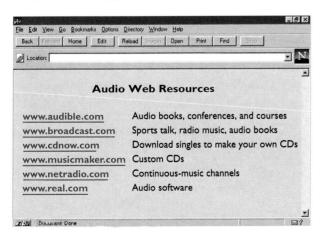

7. Secondary Storage Companies The figure below lists the Web sites of several companies that make secondary storage devices. Choose any company on the list and determine the types of storage products it makes.

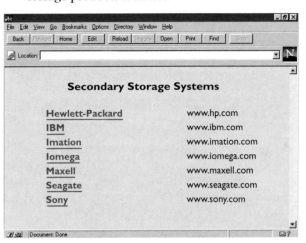

Hint: If you can't get the product information you need over the Internet, you may be able to get it though the mail or have it faxed to you. Many companies also have toll-free phone numbers, which you can find by dialing directory assistance at 800-555-1212.

8. CD Product Review Thousands of CD titles compete for attention in today's commercial marketplace. Some, such as *Myst*, have become runaway bestsellers, while some others are arguably not worth the plastic needed to publish them. For this project, choose any CD title and write a short review about it, not exceeding three pages. In the review, cover both good and bad points that you see in the product. Also, be sure that your critique has a "bottom line"; in other words, after you weigh the pros and cons, would you recommend the CD to others or suggest that people stay away?

9. **Making Your Own CD-ROMs** Technology is now available so that you can download music over the Internet directly onto your hard disk and, from there, burn the music onto a local CD. Do the necessary research so that you can describe to your classmates exactly how homemade CDs can be produced on an ordinary computer system and what sorts of special equipment you need to do it. Make sure that the procedure you come up with is legal; remember that most music is copyrighted.

10. **CD-ROM Books** In recent years, many books have been published not only in traditional print format but also as CD-ROMs. Electronic books have certain advantages and disadvantages over printed ones. Identify as many as you can of both of these.

11. **PC Printers** For any three PC printer models from any of the following series—HP LaserJet series, Epson Stylus series, Canon BJC series, HP DeskJet series—determine the information listed below. The three printer models you choose can come from the same or a different series.
    a. The printing technology in use (for example, ink-jet or laser)
    b. The approximate cost
    c. The approximate speed
    d. Whether or not color output is possible

    Facts about specific printer models are available on the World Wide Web and in PC journals such as *PC Magazine* (see especially the annual printer issue that usually appears around November). PC journals containing the information needed for this exercise may be available in your college or town library or in a local bookstore. The companies producing the printer lines named in this project are available at the following Web addresses:

COMPANY	WEB ADDRESS
Canon	www.canon.com
Epson	www.epson.com
Hewlett-Packard	www.hp.com

12. **Ink-Jet Printers** Ink-jet printers have become very popular in recent years for PCs, for both home and office use. Three important factors contributing to their acceptance are low cost, low noise level, and color capability. For this project, choose a vendor of ink-jet printers, and answer the following questions about the products in its current line. Feel free to consult the Internet for your research as well as journal articles and product brochures (see the previous project for a list of useful Web sites and the hint about *PC Magazine*).
    a. What are the names and/or model numbers of the ink-jet printers produced by the manufacturer you have chosen?
    b. Provide as many of the following statistics as you can about each of these printers: list price, rated speed for text pages, rated speed for color pages, number of ink cartridges used, colors of ink cartridges used, and maximum resolution possible.

13. **Digital Cameras** Digital cameras are beginning to appear more often for various types of image-input applications. For this project, choose a digital camera that costs less than $1,000, and answer the following questions about it. Feel free to consult Internet resources in your research as well as journal articles and product brochures.
    a. What is the name and/or model number of the camera you have chosen? Who manufactures the product?
    b. What is the street or list price of the camera?
    c. How does a digital camera take pictures? In other words, describe the storage medium the camera substitutes for conventional film.
    d. At what maximum resolution can the camera take pictures? At what minimum resolution? Also determine the number of pictures that can be taken at each resolution.
    e. How do you transfer the pictures the camera takes into a desktop computer's storage?
    f. What can you do if the pictures you take turn out too light?
    g. For what types of applications is a digital camera suitable and unsuitable?

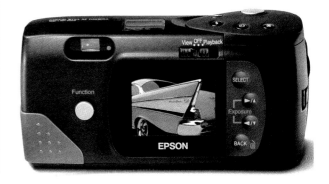

Hint: Among the companies currently making digital cameras are Kodak, Sony, Epson, Canon, and Casio. Each of these companies maintains Web sites, any of which you can easily get to by typing the company name in between the "www." and ".com" in the Web address [for instance, www.kodak.com]. Most of these companies also maintain toll-free phone numbers for product information, which you can obtain for free from Directory Assistance.

14. **Flat-Panel Screens**   Flat-panel displays have become extremely popular during the last several years for a variety of applications. Some uses are described in the chapter, and another is shown below. Can you come up with five others?

15. **Multifunction Devices**   Some printers today are marketed as *multifunction devices*. Such printers not only print, but they also perform a number of other duties as well—for instance, copying documents, faxing, and/or scanning. For this project,

find an example of a multifunction device currently on the market, and report the following to the class.

a. The name of the device and its maker
b. The suggested retail price of the device
c. The capabilities of the device

ONLINE REVIEW

Go to the Online Review at www.harcourtcollege.com/infosys/pcc2e/student/ to test your understanding of this chapter's concepts.

INTERACTIVE EXERCISE

PUTTING TOGETHER YOUR NEW PC

You've just gotten your brand new PC, and it is time to get it up and running. Go to the Interactive Exercise section at www.harcourtcollege.com/infosys/pcc2e/student/exercise/ to complete this exercise.

OUTLINE

Overview
Whose Software Is It?
    Proprietary Software
    Shareware
    Freeware
The User Interface
    Command Syntax
    Shortcut Keystrokes
    Graphical User Interfaces (GUIs)
Elements of a Graphical User Interface
    Menus
    Windows
    Dialog Boxes
    Online Help
Systems Software
    Operating Systems
    Utility Programs
    Language Translators
Applications Software
    Software Suites
    Word Processors
    Spreadsheets
    Database Management Systems
    Other Productivity Software
PC Miniguide: Online Help

3 CHAPTER

SOFTWARE

LEARNING OBJECTIVES

After completing this chapter, you will be able to:

1. Explain how users gain access to software and the restrictions that sometimes limit their activities.

2. Describe the differences among user interfaces.

3. Identify the elements commonly found in a graphical user interface and explain their functions.

4. Describe the roles played by such systems software as operating systems, language translators, and utility programs.

5. Describe what word processors, spreadsheets, database management systems, and a number of other types of applications software programs are designed to do.

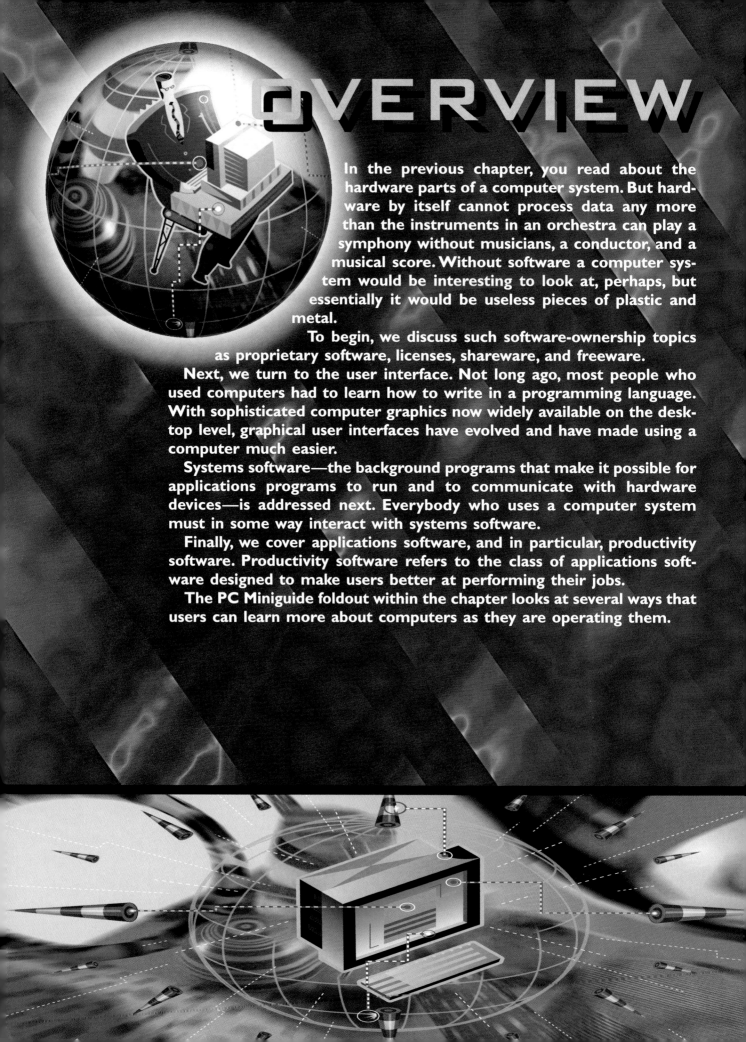

OVERVIEW

In the previous chapter, you read about the hardware parts of a computer system. But hardware by itself cannot process data any more than the instruments in an orchestra can play a symphony without musicians, a conductor, and a musical score. Without software a computer system would be interesting to look at, perhaps, but essentially it would be useless pieces of plastic and metal.

To begin, we discuss such software-ownership topics as proprietary software, licenses, shareware, and freeware.

Next, we turn to the user interface. Not long ago, most people who used computers had to learn how to write in a programming language. With sophisticated computer graphics now widely available on the desktop level, graphical user interfaces have evolved and have made using a computer much easier.

Systems software—the background programs that make it possible for applications programs to run and to communicate with hardware devices—is addressed next. Everybody who uses a computer system must in some way interact with systems software.

Finally, we cover applications software, and in particular, productivity software. Productivity software refers to the class of applications software designed to make users better at performing their jobs.

The **PC Miniguide** foldout within the chapter looks at several ways that users can learn more about computers as they are operating them.

WHOSE SOFTWARE IS IT?

Who owns a particular software product and how it can be used can be potentially sensitive issues. Often, when a software publisher creates a program and offers it for sale, the publisher secures a copyright on the software and then owns the rights to it. But who is then allowed to use it? Here, we discuss various classes of ownership and use.

For a tutorial on various types of software, go to www. harcourtcollege.com/ infosys/pcc2e/student/tutor/ and click on **Chapter 3**.

PROPRIETARY SOFTWARE

By far, most of the applications and systems software used today are **proprietary software**. This means that the rights to it are owned by someone and that the owner expects potential users to buy a copy of it in order to use it.

Microsoft Office is a typical example. If you want to acquire this product to write letters or to produce budgets, you must purchase a registered copy of it in a store, through a mail-order reseller, or over the Internet. In buying the software, you thereby acquire a **software license** to become an authorized user (see Figure 3-1). Organizations such as businesses or schools, who

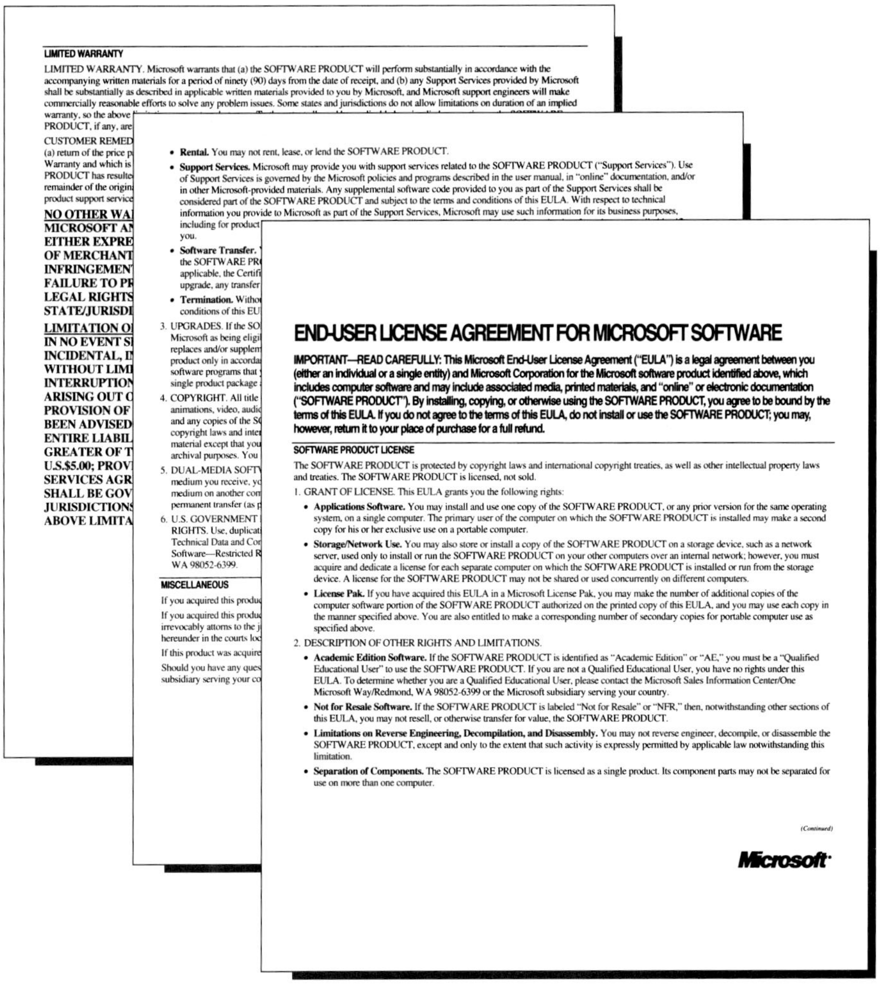

FIGURE 3-1

User license for a proprietary software product. Shown here is the English-language portion of a standard Microsoft license.

■ **Proprietary software.** A software product to which someone owns the rights. ■ **Software license.** An agreement that enables someone to use a proprietary software product.

may require several people to work with the software, generally acquire a *site license* that enables multiple users access to the software.

If you buy a copy of Microsoft Office (or any other proprietary software) for your own use, you cannot make copies of it to give to your friends. Nor can you reproduce parts of Office's code to build your own suite program. Nor can you rent or lease the software to others. You and you alone have bought only the right to operate the software for its intended use—creating your own documents. Part of the sticker price that you pay for the program goes back to the software publisher—Microsoft Corporation—for its efforts in bringing the product to the marketplace.

In general, the advantages of licensed proprietary software are quality, ongoing product support, and a large base of users. If, for instance, you buy a product from a well-known software maker such as Microsoft, Corel, or Lotus Development, you generally know that millions of dollars went into its creation, that the product is likely to be around several years from now, and that you can turn to several places for help. For instance, many large software makers *beta test* their key software on thousands of users working on scores of different computer platforms before it is released to the public. This practice virtually ensures that it will be free of major problems when it gets into the hands of paying users.

SHAREWARE

Some software is available as **shareware**. While you don't have to pay to use shareware, you must pay for support of any type. That is, you are expected to pay a nominal "contribution" or "registration fee" to the software publisher if you want written or online documentation, software updates, and/or technical help and advice. The amount charged is typically anywhere from $5 to $75. Many shareware creators also ask that you register their software after you use it for a certain period of time—usually about a month.

The shareware creator normally doesn't mind if you make copies of the program for your friends. That's because even though you may choose not to register or to continue to use the program, your friends may like it more than you do and decide to pay the creator for support items. After all, support is how this type of software publisher makes money, so the more exposure its programs get, the better. Keep in mind that many shareware products are copyrighted and, therefore, their rights are owned by someone. Thus, you cannot copy code from the program to make your own competing program.

Many shareware and freeware programs—the latter covered next—are available over the Internet (see Figure 3-2).

For links to further information about shareware, go to www.harcourtcollege.com/ infosys/pcc2e/student/ explore/ and click on Chapter 3.

FREEWARE

Freeware, or *public-domain software,* refers to programs that you can use free of charge with no strings attached.

Who, you may ask, would want to give away software and not make so much as a dime off of it? Plenty of people, it so happens. College and university professors, as well as graduate students, are motivated to develop freeware because they are doing something academic institutions promote—advancing the state of the art of computer science and making new breakthroughs available as soon as possible to the public. Others may want to inspire as many people as possible to test the software's marketability. If the freeware turns out to be popular, the developer may polish it up a bit and include documentation and support—and then start selling the program for profit.

■ **Shareware.** Software that people can copy and use in exchange for a nominal fee. ■ **Freeware.** Software offered for use without charge.

FIGURE 3-2

Shareware. Shareware and freeware are plentiful on the Internet.

In recent years, even established software publishers have started embracing the freeware concept, giving it greater respectability with mainstream users. For instance, Netscape and Microsoft both give away their browser software for free on the Internet. Also, users of word processing and spreadsheet programs can often find several free applications that enhance working with these programs at their software publisher's Web site. And for users of Linux—a freeware version of the Unix operating system—Corel and Oracle have many applications available for free. With freeware like Linux, support is often available through a loose confederation of software developers, Internet newsgroups, and Web sites.

THE USER INTERFACE

Users interact with software in a variety of ways. Those still working with Microsoft's now-discontinued MS-DOS operating system, for instance, often type in DOS-language commands at a prompting character in order to perform their work. A Microsoft Windows user, on the other hand, makes selections from menus and icons using a mouse to perform similar operations. The manner in which a program makes its resources available to users is known as its **user interface**.

By issuing commands, you get a program to perform a desired action. Commands are often invoked by typing statements that conform to a command syntax, by using shortcut keystrokes, or by making selections from a graphical user interface (GUI) with a mouse or keyboard.

COMMAND SYNTAX

Typing precise instructions that told the computer exactly what you wanted to do was the first type of user interface, and until the 1980s, it was by and

---

■ **User interface.** The manner in which a computer program makes its resources available to users.

large the only type available. At some type of system **prompt**, the user types in a command that conforms to a strict command syntax. **Syntax** refers to the grammatical rules that govern the structure and content of statements in a particular language.

For instance, when you are using the MS-DOS operating system, you generally type commands at the operating-system prompt. If you are currently in the DOS section on the C drive and want to erase a file named FRED from the A drive, then at the

```
C:\DOS>
```

operating-system prompt, you must type

```
ERASE A:FRED
```

If you instead type

```
ERADICATE A:FRED
```

or

```
ERASE FRED FROM A
```

an error message will appear on the screen, indicating that the command does not conform to the official syntax of the MS-DOS language.

Unfortunately, using a command syntax effectively is often beyond the patience and capabilities of most users. Syntax can be both exacting and unforgiving, and the average person tends to be casual with regard to the rigors imposed by a command syntax. To make software available to as wide an audience as possible, software publishers have added features such as shortcut keystrokes and GUIs to simplify entering commands. While such developments have not completely eliminated the use of command syntax, they have been successful in bringing computers within the reach of virtually everyone.

SHORTCUT KEYSTROKES

Shortcut keystrokes enable you to invoke commands with a minimal number of keystrokes. For instance, when you want to indent text with many versions of the WordPerfect word processing program, you strike the F4 function key. Next, you type the text you want indented. To turn off the indent, you press the Enter key. To perform the same type of task using a command syntax—something people had to do during the early days of word processing—would take much greater effort (see Figure 3-3).

In Microsoft Word, you can change from single-spacing to double-spacing in a document just as easily—just hold down the Control key and press 2 (Ctrl+2).

Shortcut keystrokes are a major time saver when compared with conventional command syntax. However, they can also tax the user's memory. If the user can't remember the shortcut keystroke for a seldom-used command, then he or she may have to look it up in a printed manual or an online help system.

GRAPHICAL USER INTERFACES (GUIs)

Graphical user interfaces (GUIs) have become popular in recent years with the availability of high-resolution display screens, faster CPUs, and larger capacity RAM and hard disks. Before these types of hardware were available, GUIs—which feature graphical icons and windows as well as

---

■ **Prompt.** Displayed text or symbols indicating the computer system's readiness to receive user input. ■ **Syntax.** The grammatical rules that govern a language. ■ **Shortcut keystrokes.** Keystrokes that make it possible for commands to be entered with minimal keystroking. ■ **Graphical user interface (GUI).** A term that refers to the graphical screens that make it easier for users to interact with software.

Indenting a paragraph

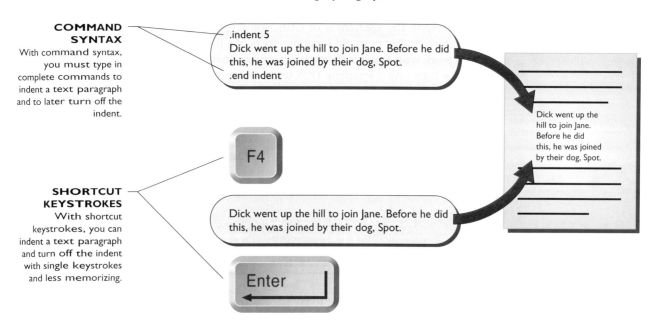

COMMAND SYNTAX
With command syntax, you must type in complete commands to indent a text paragraph and to later turn off the indent.

.indent 5
Dick went up the hill to join Jane. Before he did this, he was joined by their dog, Spot.
.end indent

F4

SHORTCUT KEYSTROKES
With shortcut keystrokes, you can indent a text paragraph and turn off the indent with single keystrokes and less memorizing.

Dick went up the hill to join Jane. Before he did this, he was joined by their dog, Spot.

Enter

Dick went up the hill to join Jane. Before he did this, he was joined by their dog, Spot.

WYSIWYG (for "*what you see is what you get*") document displays that resemble printed documents—were not practical. Early graphics monitors displayed output that looked too crude. And when screen outputs first started to become acceptable, the graphics simply took too long to generate on the computer. These days, of course, most computers can rapidly display desktop graphics, and the most constraining factor is when graphics have to travel at slow modem speeds to reach one's desktop from afar.

Today's most widely used GUIs are Microsoft Windows and the Apple Macintosh interface. Virtually all modern PC software follows at least one of these standards. Thus, if you are comfortable with the applicable standard, a conforming software package will have an immediate familiarity to it when you first use it. A growing trend is for each of the standards to borrow from one another, increasingly giving all software the same look and feel.

GUIs employ such devices as pull-down menus, windows, icons, and toolbars to make it easier than ever for users to navigate successfully through software packages (see Figure 3-4). Each of these devices will be explained shortly. Instead of having to remember a complicated command syntax or shortcut-keystroke sequence, all the GUI user has to do is look for the command on a menu, point to it using a mouse or keyboard, and select it. Online tools are available to assist users who cannot recall instantly the command necessary to perform a specific operation.

GUIs also provide a means of customizing screens to suit each user's personal work style. Menus and toolbars can often be personalized with favorite commands and moved anywhere on the screen, and elements can be made to appear or disappear. For instance, with a couple of mouse actions, users can temporarily get rid of the bottom-of-screen Windows *taskbar* (containing the Start button and time) and any of the *toolbars*

FIGURE 3-3

Shortcut keystrokes. Key combinations help users issue commands—such as indenting a paragraph—with minimal input from the keyboard.

FIGURE 3-4

Graphical user interfaces. GUIs employ such devices as pull-down menus, windows, icons, and toolbars to make it easy for users to navigate successfully through their favorite software packages.

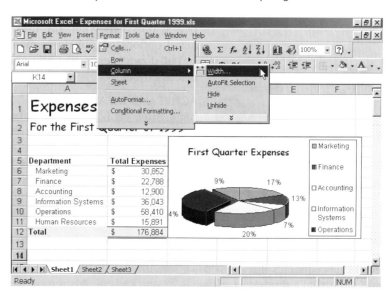

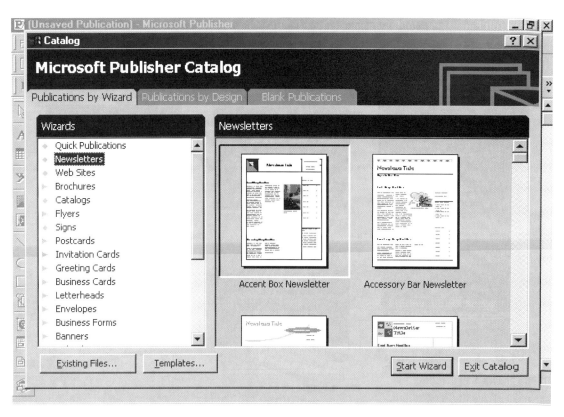

 FIGURE 3-30

Desktop publishing. Desktop publishing programs turn the computer system into a tool that can produce layouts for magazines and books.

ACCOUNTING Virtually every business must support a number of routine operations, most of which involve some form of tedious recordkeeping. Because these operations—such as paying employees, recording customer purchases and payments, and recording vendor receipts and payments—involve the processing of business transactions, they are called *transaction processing systems*. **Accounting packages** are specialized software-suite products that pull together a number of related transaction processing functions (see Figure 3-31). In many cases, the packages also enable management to get up-to-the-minute reporting on transaction volume during a particular

 **FIGURE 3-31**

Accounting software. An important function of accounting software is invoicing customers.

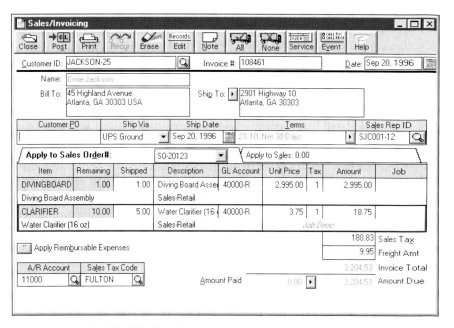

■ **Accounting package.** A software package that processes an organization's business transactions, such as those coming from payroll, order entry, accounts receivable and payable, and so forth.

period, as well as key decision-making information about inventories, open orders, and overdue payments or rental merchandise.

CAD SOFTWARE Using **computer-aided design (CAD) software**, people can dramatically reduce the time it takes to design products, as well as improve the way products are presented to consumers. Using the computer, designers can electronically modify design alternatives onscreen until they achieve the desired results. CAD is especially helpful in designing products such as automobiles, aircraft, ships, structures, electrical circuits and computer chips, and even shoes and clothes (see Figure 3-32). Although not long ago CAD was confined to large computer systems, it now represents a major applications area in the PC world.

VERTICAL-MARKET SOFTWARE Applications software products such as word processors, spreadsheets, and DBMSs are broadly targeted to a general class of users. Spreadsheets, for instance, are used by accountants, financial analysts, salespeople, teachers, and people in many other professions. Furthermore, spreadsheet users come from a number of industries—banking, the automotive industry, chemicals, pharmaceuticals, academia, and so on. **Vertical-market software**, on the other hand, refers to software targeted to a narrow group

FIGURE 3-32

Computer-aided design (CAD).

ARCHITECTURE
In the field of architecture, CAD programs enable architects to render photorealistic images of exteriors and interiors of buildings.

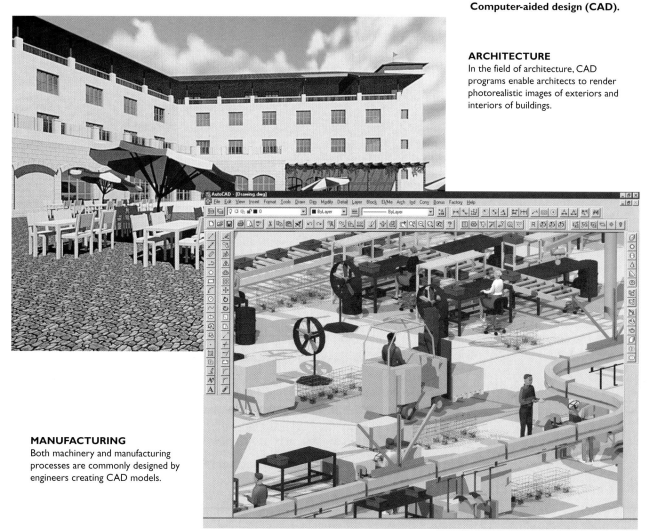

MANUFACTURING
Both machinery and manufacturing processes are commonly designed by engineers creating CAD models.

■ **Computer-aided design (CAD) software.** A general term applied to the use of computer technology to automate design functions. ■ **Vertical-market software.** Productivity software products designed to meet the needs of niche markets, such as medical and dental offices and videotape-rental stores.

of users—that is, a "niche market." One example is medical-office software. Such programs consist of customized accounting systems that are targeted to the particular type of record management faced by doctors and dentists. Some other examples of vertical-market products are the programs used to run videotape-rental stores, auto dealerships, and restaurants.

ARTIFICIAL INTELLIGENCE AND EXPERT SYSTEMS   The ability of computer systems to perform in ways that would be considered intelligent if observed in humans is commonly referred to as *artificial intelligence (AI)*. The field of AI evolved from attempts to write programs that would enable computers to rival skilled humans at games such as chess and checkers, to prove difficult mathematical theorems, and so forth.

Expert systems—programs that incorporate the knowledge base and reasoning patterns of human experts—are an outgrowth of the chess-playing programs of the 1950s and 1960s. Today expert systems are successfully used on PCs in many fields. In medicine, for instance, an expert system might be used to incorporate the thinking patterns of some of the world's leading physicians. For example, a system might be given a list of symptoms exhibited by a patient. If these symptoms might lead to the diagnosis of a disease the program knows something about, the program might ask the attending physician for information about specific details. Ultimately, through questioning and checking the patient's condition against a large database of successfully diagnosed cases, the program might quickly draw conclusions that the attending physician might have reached much more slowly, if at all. Expert systems also have enormous potential in business.

SUMMARY AND KEY TERMS

Go to the Online Glossary at www.harcourtcollege.com/infosys/pcc2e/ student/ to review key terms.

In Chapter 3 we explore several fundamental software concepts.

WHOSE SOFTWARE IS IT?   Most of the well-known applications and systems software on the market today is **proprietary software.** Individual buyers get **software licenses** authorizing them to use proprietary software; businesses often seek *site licenses*. Some software is also available as **shareware.** Still another class of software is **freeware.**

THE USER INTERFACE   The manner in which a program makes its resources available to users is known as its **user interface.**

Command **syntax** relies on users typing, at some sort of software **prompt,** statements that conform to strict grammatical rules and structure. **Shortcut keystrokes,** which represent commands, are designed to be both easier and faster than using a command syntax. **Graphical user interfaces (GUIs)** employ such screen-oriented recall devices as pull-down menus, windows, and icons to make it easy for users to execute commands.

ELEMENTS OF A GRAPHICAL USER INTERFACE   Most users work with software that has a graphical user interface.

Menus are often one of several principal types. At the top of many GUI screens or windows is a **menu bar** showing the governing command set.

■ **Expert system.** A program or computer system that provides the type of advice that would be expected of a human expert.

Pull-down menus unfurl on the screen when the user makes a choice from a menu bar or another pull-down menu. Menus also exist in the form of a set of **icons;** names such as **toolbars,** command buttons, navigation bars, and **hyperlinks** refer to *icon menus*. Additionally, **palettes,** tab menus, and dialog boxes are other types of menus.

The staple of the GUI is the **window**—a box of related information that appears overlaid on the display screen. A window is normally titled through a banded *title bar* that appears at the top of it. Windows can be customized onscreen to meet applications needs in a variety of ways. The *mouse pointer* is **context sensitive** and changes with respect to the operation the user is performing onscreen. When the information available in a window cannot fit on the screen at one time, **scroll bars** can be used to get to other parts of it.

Dialog boxes are special windows that prompt the user for further information. They employ a variety of tools, including radio buttons, check boxes, text boxes, list boxes, message boxes, sliders, and the like.

Many GUIs have an *online help* feature to make it easy for users to get help when they are sitting at their display screens.

SYSTEMS SOFTWARE   The basic role of **systems software** is to act as a mediator between applications programs and the computer system's hardware.

An **operating system** is a collection of programs that manages the computer's activities. Many operating systems exist in the marketplace. **PC-DOS** and **MS-DOS** are commonly found on older PC-compatible computers. Today, many DOS users have gravitated to Windows and its graphical user interface. **Windows 3.x** and its successors, **Windows 95** and **Windows 98,** are the main personal versions of Windows that have replaced DOS's syntax-oriented interface. *Windows CE* is a compact version of Windows 95/98 that runs on portable devices. **Windows NT** and **Windows 2000,** which resemble Windows 95 and 98 in many ways but are more powerful, exist in both personal and network-server editions. Newer operating systems are capable of **multitasking,** enabling users to work on more than a single program at a time.

Mac OS is the operating system native to the Apple Macintosh line of computers. **Unix** is the most widely used operating system on Internet server computers. **NetWare** is an operating system that's widely used for the operation of server computers on local-area networks (LANs).

A **utility program** is a type of systems program written to perform repetitive processing tasks. A **language translator** is a systems program that converts an applications program into machine language. The two most common types of language translators are **compilers** and **interpreters.**

APPLICATIONS SOFTWARE   **Applications software** makes possible the types of "computer work" that users have in mind when they acquire a computer system. **Productivity software** is the type of applications software that people use in order to be more productive at their jobs. Today, many types of productivity software are bundled with other related applications software and sold as a **software suite.**

One of the most widespread applications of computers today is **word processing**—the use of computer technology to create, manipulate, and print the sort of material that traditionally has been prepared with typewriters. An electronic **spreadsheet** is a software program that produces computerized counterparts to the ruled, ledger-style worksheets with which accountants frequently work. A **database management system (DBMS)** is a software system that integrates data in storage and provides easy access to them.

Other types of productivity software include **presentation graphics software,** communications-oriented software such as Web **browsers** and **e-mail** programs, **desktop publishing** programs, **accounting packages, computer-aided design (CAD) software, vertical-market software,** and **expert systems.**

EXERCISES

1. Describe the purpose of each of the following GUI elements:
   a. Ghosted type
   b. Imagemap
   c. Command button
   d. Ellipses
   e. Spin box
   f. Checkmark

2. Identify each of the following statements as true or false
   _____ Shareware is generally more expensive and more restrictive than proprietary software.
   _____ A palette is a menu that works with file-folder tabs.
   _____ A maximized window fills the entire screen.
   _____ The successor to Windows NT is called Net-Ware.
   _____ The principal purpose of CAD software is helping designers perform their jobs.

3. Using your own words, define the following:
   a. Hypertext
   b. Path
   c. Toolbar
   d. Palette
   e. Access key

4. Match each term with the description that fits best.
   a. Menu bar
   b. Pull-down menu
   c. Cascading
   d. Tiling
   e. Toolbar
   f. Scroll bar
   g. Radio button
   h. Text box
   _____ A method of arranging windows side by side
   _____ A dialog-box feature that provides a set of options preceded by round symbols, only one of which can be darkened
   _____ A dialog box that requires you type input
   _____ A horizontally arranged menu that appears at the top of the screen
   _____ A method of arranging windows so that they overlap
   _____ A feature that lets you move offscreen information into a window
   _____ A type of icon menu
   _____ A menu that drops vertically below a choice made on a menu bar

5. Describe and compare the three basic approaches software designers have employed to enable users to enter commands.

6. Match the dialog box elements below with the terms that follow.
   _____ Radio buttons
   _____ Simple list box
   _____ Check boxes
   _____ Command buttons
   _____ Message box
   _____ Drop-down list box

7. Match the GUI elements below with the terms that follow.
   _____ Options aren't available in the current context
   _____ A toolbar
   _____ Restores the previous screen size
   _____ Closes an application
   _____ Lets you see offscreen information
   _____ Expands an application window to fill the entire screen

8. Identify the operating system or operating environment covered in the chapter described in each sentence.
   a. Windows 3.x provides a graphical user interface for it.
   b. Microsoft designed it to run in organizations, on both office-desktop machines and the network administrator's workstation.
   c. It was originally developed at Bell Labs more than 20 years ago.
   d. This product by Novell is designed to manage local networks.
   e. This product immediately replaced Windows 3.x.

9. Fill in the blanks:
   a. A group of related programs that is bundled for sale at a price that is less than the individual components purchased separately is called a software _____.
   b. The manner in which a program package makes its resources available to the user is known as its _____.
   c. The grammatical rules that govern a language are called the language's _____.
   d. A(n)_____ is one that lets you enter keystrokes such as Alt + F1 or Del instead of typing a command.
   e. GUI is an acronym for _____.
   f. A command _____ is a horizontal line that is used to group related commands.

   g. _____ programs are systems programs written to perform repetitive processing tasks such as sorting data and formatting disks.
   h. DBMS is an acronym for _____.

10. Select the term that best matches each phrase:
   a. AI
   b. Paradox
   c. DOS
   d. WordPerfect
   e. Linux
   f. 1-2-3
   g. NetWare
   h. PowerPoint
   i. Works
   j. CAD
   _____ The name of a presentation graphics software product
   _____ Applications software that caters to product designers
   _____ An operating system available free over the Internet
   _____ A word-processing program
   _____ An early PC operating system, now technologically obsolete
   _____ A contemporary spreadsheet program
   _____ A DBMS
   _____ An integrated software program
   _____ An operating system targeted specifically to PC-based networks
   _____ An expert system uses this technology

PROJECTS

1. **MICROSOFT OFFICE** Microsoft Office is by far the best-selling software suite, with more than an 80 percent share of the office-suite market. For the version of Microsoft Office at your school, answer the following questions:
   a. What version number does your school run?
   b. What are the names and functions of the main component programs in the suite?
   c. How many toolbars can you summon through the Toolbars command? What are the names and purposes of these toolbars? Where, exactly, is the Toolbar command located? How do you get rid of one toolbar and replace it with another?
   d. Identify the name and purpose of each toolbar button pictured below. Also, name the toolbar on which each button appears.

   i.   iii.   v.

   ii.   iv.

2. **SHAREWARE AND FREEWARE** Using computer magazines and newspapers, or the Internet, find a shareware or freeware product that falls into each of the following categories. Describe each product briefly, providing its name, facts about what it does, and the company or individual that publishes it.

CATEGORY	PRODUCT/FUNCTION/PUBLISHER
Computer game	_____
Educational software	_____
Productivity software	_____
Systems software	_____
Internet software	_____

3. **SLIDERS** Many programs use sliders, which let users choose a setting within a range. Describe at least three different uses for sliders, and for each one, identify a program that illustrates the use. Your descriptions should be detailed enough so that anyone reading them has a good idea of not only what the slider is used for but also what types of choices the slider provides.

4. **ONLINE HELP** Choose any current applications program—such as a word processor or a spreadsheet—and research its online help feature. For the package you have chosen, report the following characteristics to your class:
   a. The types of online help available within the program
   b. How you would access each type of help you described in part *a*
   c. The duties of the wizards available within the program

   You may wish to consult the PC Miniguide foldout in this chapter as you do this project.

5. **THE OPERATING SYSTEM AT YOUR SCHOOL** Gather the following information about the operating system that runs your school's PC lab:
   a. Find out the name of the operating system, the name of the company that makes it, and the version your class uses. You should be able to find out the version number from the operating system itself, by clicking on a menu choice or typing a command.
   b. How many bytes of RAM does the operating system require in order to work effectively?
   c. How many bytes of disk space does the operating system consume?

6. **USING AN OPERATING SYSTEM** Using the operating system on your own computer or the computers in your school's PC lab, complete the following tasks:
   a. Format a diskette.
   b. Copy a file from the hard disk to a diskette.
   c. Make a copy of a diskette.

7. **UTILITY SOFTWARE** Look through computer journals or consult the Internet to identify at least one independent software product in each of the listed categories. Besides giving the name of each product, also name the company that sells it, and state its list or street price. In addition, write a sentence or two describing the capabilities of the product.
   a. Desktop enhancer
   b. Uninstaller
   c. Antivirus
   d. File viewer
   e. Memory manager

8. **MICROSOFT CORPORATION** Microsoft Corporation began in humble fashion in the 1970s, as a small company making language compilers for PCs. In the early 1980s it produced DOS—its flagship product for many years—and success snowballed from

there. Microsoft branched from systems software into applications software, and soon thereafter into a variety of other ventures—communications, travel, car-buying, television, to name just a few. Microsoft spends over $2.5 billion a year on product development, which is more than the combined annual profits of several of its closest competitors.

For this project, write a paper (five to eight pages) describing the many business activities in which Microsoft is involved. Try to be as specific as possible. In other words, break down each category of business as closely as you can and provide examples—for instance, operating systems (Windows 2000), productivity software (Office 2000), etc.

9. **APPLE COMPUTER: WHAT COULD HAVE BEEN** Not too many years ago, before the world even heard of Microsoft Windows, close to one out of every five computers sold was made by Apple. Throughout most of the 1980s, the Apple Macintosh had a wildly successful graphical user interface (GUI) and loyal following of users, while PC-compatibles were stuck with non-GUI DOS. By the late 1990s, however, Apple's share of the PC market was down to 3 percent and close to 90 percent of all PCs used Windows. What went wrong for Apple? Since 1998, Apple has been staging a comeback. Do you think it will ever be able to recapture the market share it lost?

10. **USING A WIZARD TO CREATE A JOB RÉSUMÉ** Many word-processing programs—such as Microsoft Word, Corel WordPerfect, and Lotus WordPro—contain wizard software that enables people to create attractive-looking résumés for seeking jobs.

Résumé and cover letter

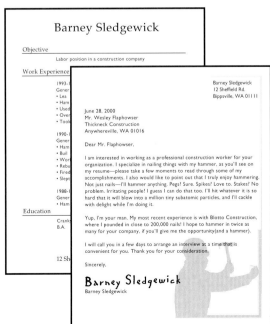

a. Using the word-processing software available at your school, create a résumé that includes your name, address, and phone number, as well as your job objective, work experience, and education.

b. Create an attractive cover letter to send with the résumé. Many wizards that produce résumés also have a routine for preparing cover letters.

11. **THE WORD-PROCESSING SOFTWARE AT YOUR SCHOOL** For the word-processing program on your own PC or that available on the PCs in your school's lab, describe how to do the following tasks:

a. Change from single spacing to double spacing
b. Summon the thesaurus feature
c. Preview a document before printing it
d. Change from full to left justification
e. Change the typeface and typesize on a printed document
f. Create a two-column text page
g. Insert a watermark behind a text page
h. Insert a piece of clip art into a text page
i. Change a printed-page orientation from portrait (8½ by 11 inches) to landscape (11 by 8½ inches)
j. Create a style sheet
k. Mark your place in a document with a bookmark
l. Direct the software to automatically insert the current date

12. **THE SPREADSHEET PROGRAM AT YOUR SCHOOL** For the spreadsheet program that comes with your own PC or the PCs in your school's lab, describe how to do the following tasks:

a. Insert columns and rows
b. Adjust the width of columns and the height of rows
c. Delete columns and rows
d. Change the alignment data in cell A8 from left justified to centered
e. Change the typeface and typesize on the top row of a worksheet
f. Filter records
g. Place borders around a worksheet
h. Sort worksheet rows
i. Print worksheets

13. **CREATING WORKSHEETS** Refer to the worksheets on the following page, and complete the activities that follow.

a. Prepare the worksheet in the top part of the figure. Note that Expenses is a row that must be totaled and that Profit is the difference between Sales and Expenses.

b. *Extra credit:* Dress up the worksheet you prepared so that it resembles the worksheet at the bottom. Note that you have several tools to help make the transition, including applying an autoformat, boldfacing and increasing the size of type, widening columns and rows (notice that you will have to add text to cell A9), centering text, and applying fill colors and colored fonts to selected cells.

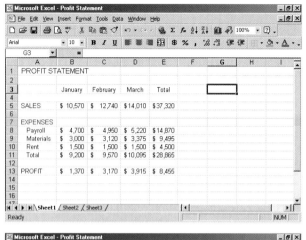

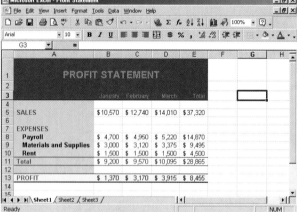

14. PREPARING A PIE CHART Using the spreadsheet program on your own PC or the spreadsheet program available at your school's computer lab, produce a pie chart for the following data. Assume that each slice of the pie represents the percentage of employees in each department.

DEPARTMENT	NUMBER OF EMPLOYEES
Finance	100
Systems	160
Sales	50
Production	175

15. CREATING A DATABASE AND PERFORMING DATABASE OPERATIONS Using the database management system available on your own PC or in your school's PC lab, create a table for the records in the accompanying figure. Count the maximum number of characters, and decide on the width of each of the fields. Define monthly Salary as a num-

ber field, Employed as a date field, and all other fields as text. Then, do the exercises that follow.

a. Display the names of all persons in the Personnel department.

b. Display the names of all persons earning more than $1,600 per month.

c. Display the names of all persons who are either working in MIS or making more than $1,700 a month.

d. *Extra credit:* Sort the file alphabetically by department and, within department, by last name.

e. Arrange the file from highest- to lowest-salaried employee. If there is a tie for Salary, list tied employees in alphabetical order. On the screen, have only the name of the employee and the salary show, with all other information hidden.

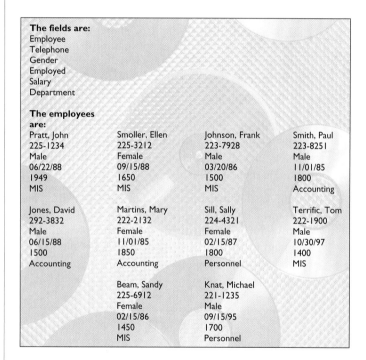

16. DOING AN ELECTRONIC SLIDE PRESENTATION Using the presentation graphics program on your own PC or the program available in your school's PC lab, do the following:

a. Produce a series of text-oriented electronic slides—at least a half-dozen or so—that are similar in style to the six shown on the screen in Figure 3-29.

b. Arrange the slides into an automated presentation that can be shown to the class.

c. *Extra credit:* Use the timer available in the package to automatically run the presentation. Also, add transition effects—both visual and sound—between each slide.

INTERACTIVE EXERCISES

USING YOUR NEW PC

Your new PC is up and running—now it's time to try it out. Go to the Interactive Exercise at www.harcourtcollege.com/infosys/pcc2e/student/exercise/ to complete this exercise.

PREPARING A MULTIMEDIA PRESENTATION

You've been asked to prepare a PowerPoint presentation for the company sales meeting. Go to the Interactive Exercise section at www.harcourtcollege. com/infosys/pcc2e/student/exercise/ to complete this exercise.

ONLINE REVIEW

Go to the Online Review at www.harcourtcollege.com/infosys/pcc2e/student/ to test your understanding of this chapter's concepts.

OUTLINE

Overview
Telecommunications Applications
      Electronic Mail and Messaging
      Information Retrieval and the Web
      Collaborative Computing
      Transaction Processing
Telecommunications Media
      Wire Media
      Wireless Media
Adapting Computers to Telecommunications Media
      Sending Data over Media
      Network Interface Cards and Modems
      ISDN and Beyond
Network Topologies
Local Networks
      Local Area Networks (LANs)
      Hierarchical Local Networks
Wide Area Networks (WANs)
      Handling WAN Traffic
Communications Protocols

4
CHAPTER

COMMUNICATIONS AND NETWORKS

LEARNING OBJECTIVES

After completing this chapter, you will be able to:

1. Describe several uses of telecommunications technology.

2. Name various types of communications media and explain how they carry messages.

3. Identify the hardware, software, and procedural components that link telecommunications systems.

4. Describe several types of local networks and how they work.

5. Explain how users transmit data over wide area networks.

OVERVIEW

The term *telecommunications,* or telecom, refers to communications over a distance—over long-distance phone lines, privately owned cables, or satellites, for instance. Telecommunications has both extended the usefulness of the PC in the workplace and boosted its popularity as a fixture in the home.

In business, telecommunications has become an integral part of operations. Business people throughout the world regularly use electronic mail and messaging systems to communicate with fellow employees and distant associates. Documents that companies once maintained in dog-eared file folders and hand delivered from person to person now zip along at electronic speeds from one PC to another at the press of a button. The list of applications is virtually endless.

In the home, the biggest telecom happening in recent years has been the whirlwind popularity of the Internet and World Wide Web. Almost overnight, the PC has evolved into a vehicle through which people communicate with faraway friends and "surf" to exciting places. Information on virtually any topic, stored on computers located almost anywhere on the globe, can be retrieved within seconds. With telecom companies scrambling to bring faster transmissions into the home and with the Internet evolving to deliver new forms of entertainment, many experts predict that the best is yet to come.

In Chapter 4, we look first at several critical business applications of telecommunications. Next, we touch on a number of technical issues, including the various ways in which computers transmit data and how networked devices connect to one another. From there, we proceed to the two major types of networks, local networks and wide area networks. The Internet is treated in depth in Chapter 5.

TELECOMMUNICATIONS APPLICATIONS

Today, a wide variety of important business applications involve **telecommunications**, and the roster of uses is growing rapidly.

ELECTRONIC MAIL AND MESSAGING

One of the biggest applications for telecommunications today is electronic mail and messaging. Several technologies play key roles.

ELECTRONIC MAIL   **Electronic mail**, or **e-mail**, is an application in which users employ software known as *e-mail programs* to exchange electronic messages. The user often composes a message within such a program at a PC and then sends it over long-distance wires or interoffice cable by clicking a Send button. The software deposits the message in an electronic mailbox maintained by the receiver's network, where it can be retrieved and read by the receiver at a convenient time. **Electronic mailboxes** are the computer equivalents of traditional mailboxes. They represent space on some computer's hard disk set aside to store e-mail messages. Figure 4-1 shows briefly how using e-mail software works. E-mail will be covered in depth in the next chapter.

VOICE MAIL   **Voice mail** is a telecommunications technology that takes electronic mailboxes one step further. A voice-mail system digitizes the sender's

For a tutorial on the uses of telecommunications and networks, go to www. harcourtcollege.com/infosys/ pcc2e/student/tutor/ and click on Chapter 4.

FIGURE 4-1

Electronic mail.

A Save command lets you save messages.

An address book lets you maintain a list of e-mail addresses and attach them automatically to mail.

There are often separate panes for address information and for the message.

A Send command lets you send messages.

cc is for carbon copy; it means sending the same message to several people.

bcc is for blind carbon copy; it's for when you don't want recipients to know who else was sent the message.

Your e-mail program can place a short "signature" on every message you send.

```
┌─────────────────────────────────────────────────────────────┐
│  Send Mail                                          _ □ ✕     │
├─────────────────────────────────────────────────────────────┤
│   Edit    Signature  Attachment                               │
│  ──────────────────────────────────────────────────────────  │
│   Send   Cancel  Save   Address Book    Help                  │
│  ──────────────────────────────────────────────────────────  │
│                 To:   Mary Jones <mjones@dryden.com>          │
│               From:   Zorch Zubars <zzubars@aol.com>          │
│            Subject:   Upcoming meeting                        │
│                 cc:   J.J. King <jjk@amalgamated.com>         │
│                bcc:   Damita Williams <dmw@amalgated.com>     │
│  ──────────────────────────────────────────────────────────  │
│         Mary,                                                 │
│                                                               │
│         Just a quick note to remind you that I will be        │
│         bringing the artwork to our meeting next week.        │
│         I think you'll be pleased to see it.                  │
│                                                               │
│         Hope all is going well.                               │
│                                                               │
│         Zorch Zubars                                          │
│         Zubars Art Studio, The Virtual Reality Place          │
│         214-920-1234                                          │
│                                                               │
└─────────────────────────────────────────────────────────────┘
```

■ **Telecommunications.** Transmission of data over a distance. ■ **Electronic mail.** The computer-to-computer counterpart for interoffice mail or the post office. Also called **e-mail.** ■ **Electronic mailbox.** A storage area on a hard disk that holds messages, memos, and other documents for the receiver. ■ **Voice mail.** An electronic mail system that digitally records spoken phone messages and stores them in an electronic mailbox.

spoken message and stores it in bit form on an answering device at the receiver's location. When the receiver presses a Listen key, the digitized message is reconverted to voice data.

BULLETIN BOARDS Unlike an electronic mailbox, which restricts access to an area on disk to only a single individual, an electronic **bulletin board system (BBS)** sets up an area to which several people have access. Functionally, BBSs work like the bulletin boards at supermarkets or health-foods stores—people post notices that may interest others, any of whom may respond. Typically, a single computer bulletin board focuses on a particular interest area. For instance, a company may set up one bulletin board for employees to post computer-related questions and another for customers to ask questions about particular products, while a bulletin board set up by a college professor may encourage members of a class to share ideas about projects or assignments. Bulletin boards are also commonly called *newsgroups* or *discussion groups*.

FACSIMILE Facsimile, or **fax,** technology resembles e-mail, except that it employs different methods and it can be more convenient or less convenient for certain types of uses (see Figure 4-2).

Facsimile (fax) machines allow users to send images of hard-copy documents from one location to another over ordinary phone lines. For example, a secretary in Seattle may place a short document containing both text and pictures into a fax machine like the one in Figure 4-2. The fax machine

FIGURE 4-2

Faxing.

FAX MACHINES
Facsimile (fax) machines make it possible for hard-copy images of documents to be sent from one location to another over ordinary phone lines.

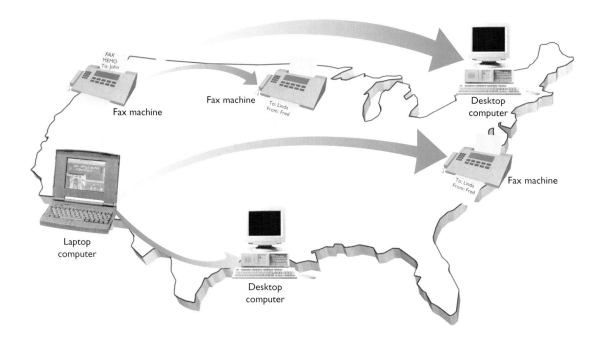

FAX MODEMS
Fax modems and fax software make it possible for PCs to communicate with both fax machines and other PCs with faxing capabilities.

■ **Bulletin board system (BBS).** A computer file shared by several people, that enables them to post or broadcast messages. ■ **Facsimile.** A method for transmitting text documents, pictures, maps, diagrams, and the like over the phone lines. Abbreviated as **fax.**

digitizes the page images and transmits the resulting data over the phone lines to Chicago and Boston. In Chicago, another fax machine receives the electronic page images and reproduces them in hard-copy form. In Boston, a PC's hard disk picks up the fax image in soft-copy form for later viewing on a display screen. All of this data exchange may take place in less than a minute.

PCs need *fax modems* and *fax software* to communicate with both fax machines and other computers with faxing capabilities. Computer-to-computer faxing brings certain advantages, including saving paper, preventing time lost waiting in line for the office fax machine, and allowing recipients to electronically save and modify faxed documents and to route them elsewhere.

Faxing capabilities are often integrated with other mail and messaging technologies. For instance, e-mail-to-fax software lets users turn their e-mail messages into faxes, and free *e-faxing* services are available on the Internet to allow a person to receive faxes as e-mail messages.

PAGING   Through a pocket-sized wireless device called a *pager,* someone can send short messages to another person who is on the move, even across the world (see Figure 4-3). Pagers provide either send-only or send-and-receive capabilities, and they often communicate over special wireless networks. Many newer pagers will also let users exchange e-mail messages with anyone having an e-mail connection—including other pager users. About 50 million people use pagers in the United States alone, and that number is growing.

FIGURE 4-3

Paging. Pagers are carried by people on the move. Close to 50 million people use pagers in the United States alone.

INFORMATION RETRIEVAL AND THE WEB

The assortment of information you can get over ordinary phone lines today is, in a word, amazing. Thousands of public and private databases are currently available for online *information retrieval,* many over the Internet's World Wide Web.

The **Internet** (named as a contraction of the two words *inter*connected *net*works) is a global "network of networks." It links thousands of networks and millions of individual users, businesses, schools, government agencies, and other organizations. It is a favorite source of information today because its resources include a vast storehouse of facts that people can easily obtain. The *World Wide Web,* or *Web,* is the most widely used feature on the Internet for accessing information. It is used by both individuals and businesses to collect facts on such a wide range of subjects as news and weather, business and the economy, travel, entertainment, and shopping (see Figure 4-4). The Internet is also used for e-mail and a variety of other applications.

Individuals access the Internet through a company known as an *Internet service provider (ISP),* sometimes called a *service provider* or an *access provider,* for short. Today's most widely used ISP is America Online (AOL), featured in Figure 4-5. Other ISPs with a strong national following are the Microsoft Network (MSN), CompuServe (now owned by AOL), Prodigy, Earth-Link, and MCI WorldCom. In addition, there are thousands of small, local ISPs located in cities and towns throughout the United States, serving local audiences with local or toll-free telephone numbers and possibly faster lines or better service than the bigger providers.

Most ISPs charge individuals between $15 and $25 per month for Internet access. People can bypass signing up with their own service provider by getting access to the Internet through their school, employer, or local library.

We will be covering the Internet in depth in Chapter 5.

■ **Internet.** A global network linking thousands of networks and millions of individual users, schools, businesses, and government agencies.

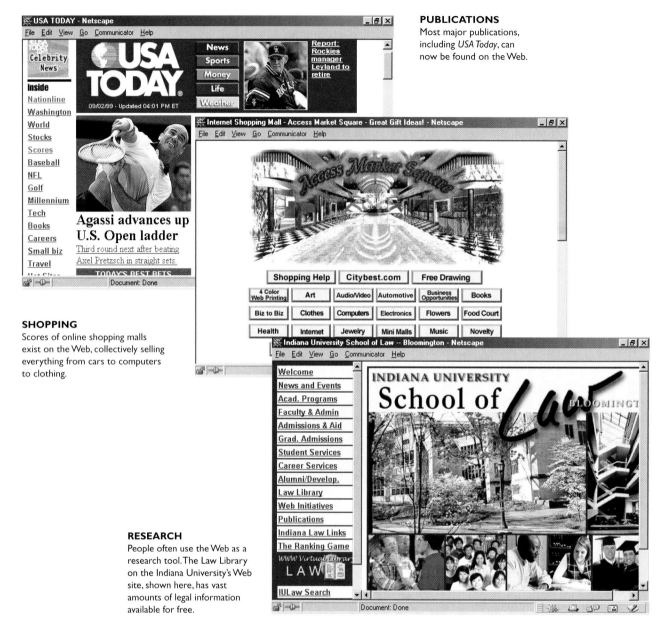

PUBLICATIONS
Most major publications, including *USA Today*, can now be found on the Web.

SHOPPING
Scores of online shopping malls exist on the Web, collectively selling everything from cars to computers to clothing.

RESEARCH
People often use the Web as a research tool. The Law Library on the Indiana University's Web site, shown here, has vast amounts of legal information available for free.

 FIGURE 4-4

The Internet's World Wide Web.
One of the most popular features of the Internet is the World Wide Web, which brings virtually any sort of information anyone could imagine to a computer's display screen in the form of easy-to-read pages.

COLLABORATIVE COMPUTING

In addition to ordinary electronic mail and messaging, modern communications technology and the Internet enable geographically scattered workers to collaborate in their work tasks in other, more sophisticated ways. Three such uses of technology are briefly covered here: workgroup computing, teleconferencing, and telecommuting (see Figure 4-6).

WORKGROUP COMPUTING **Workgroup computing** allows several people to use their desktop workstations or PCs to collaborate in their job tasks, without ever leaving their offices. The insurance industry provides a good example. Years ago, clerks would have processed an accident claim by filling out forms by hand and manually walking file folders around from desk to desk for approvals and signatures. Today, such claims are processed electronically with special *workgroup-computing software,* or *groupware* as it is more commonly known. The software generates electronic forms and displays them as

■ **Workgroup computing.** Several people using desktop workstations to collaborate in their job tasks.

necessary so workers can fill them in with data, review their work, and approve payment at their desktop workstations. The software can automatically route and monitor the progress of forms as well. Consequently, insurers can process claims more rapidly and reliably and with far fewer errors than they could before groupware was available. Better service is often provided, too, because an adjuster can give claimants progress reports after pressing only a few keystrokes. Alternatively, claimants can get reports themselves over the Internet.

Groupware is getting attention wherever people need to collaborate on their jobs. Engineers and architects commonly use groupware to collaborate on designs, newspapers use it to circulate pieces among writers and editors, and so on.

TELECONFERENCING **Teleconferencing** refers to the use of computer and communications technology to conduct meetings between people in different locations. Such meetings may take place via sophisticated computer-messaging techniques, through video technology that lets people see and hear each other, and by a number of other means. For instance, using relatively inexpensive *videoconferencing* software and hardware, people in contact by computer can see and hear each other on their PCs. Or workers can engage in a virtual conference at their PC workstations by using *conferencing software* that organizes comments typed during online discussions.

TELECOMMUTING **Telecommuting** refers to people working at home and being connected to their employers through such means as the Internet, modems, fax machines, personal computers, and pagers. With such tools, the employee can read e-mail sent to them at the office, access database information and presentation materials when making on-site pitches to clients, and get in touch with callers almost immediately while on the road. Telecommuting enables a company to save on office and parking space and offers an employee considerable freedom in choosing to work when, and where, he or she wishes to work.

FIGURE 4-5

America Online (AOL). With millions of subscribers, AOL is the world's biggest Internet service provider.

For links to further information about teleconferencing and telecommuting, go to www.harcourtcollege.com/ infosys/pcc2e/student/ explore/ and click on Chapter 4.

■ **Teleconferencing**. Using computer and communications technology to carry out a meeting between people in different locations. ■ **Telecommuting**. Working through one's home and being connected by means of electronic devices to coworkers in remote locations.

OFFICE AT WORK
At a company work site, employees can meet with coworkers without ever leaving their offices by teleconferencing, by using e-mail, or by using workgroup software that lets them share documents.

HOME OFFICE
Through the Internet, you can complete many tasks at home as easily as you could in the office. What's more, with no commute, you have the freedom to live almost anywhere you would like.

MOBILE OFFICE
Telecommunications hardware and software is near the point where workers can keep in touch by satellite almost anywhere on the globe.

 FIGURE 4-6

Collaborative computing in the twenty-first century. Computer networks enable people to work where they wish and to collaborate on tasks without having to get together physically in a single place, at the same time.

TRANSACTION PROCESSING

Transaction-processing operations, such as entering orders and handling accounts receivable, are the lifeblood of most companies. If you were to pull the plug on the computers doing these tasks, the companies would go out of business.

At one time, transaction-processing operations were totally centralized. As communications systems allowed firms to distribute workloads to multiple sites, many organizations modified their transaction-processing systems accordingly. The airlines' passenger reservation systems offer a noteworthy example; thousands of ticketing agents located across the globe use display workstations to tap into distant computerized databases full of flight, hotel, and rental-car information. While a computer in, say, Chicago is gathering flight information for an agent in Cerritos, California, that same agent may be completing local processing of a ticket for another client. With today's Internet, the airlines' passenger reservations systems are more distributed than ever before, enabling ordinary people to bypass travel agents and book flights from their home PCs.

Virtually every large organization today maintains several types of distributed transaction-processing systems. For instance, chain stores often collect and process data locally and then transmit the data to headquarters sites for timely analysis. Mail-order firms frequently process orders at central sites and then transmit transaction data to warehouse sites to initiate packing and delivery. The applications are countless.

Many companies have extended their distributed transaction-processing systems a step further by creating *interorganizational systems (IOSs),* which strategically link their computers to the computers of key customers or suppliers. One common type of interorganizational system, *electronic data interchange (EDI),* facilitates the exchange of standard business documents—such as purchase orders and invoices—from one company's computer system to the system of another company. What's more, the company doing the purchasing often uses EDI to electronically track an order's progress on the seller's computer system. At such giant companies as General Motors and DuPont, large suppliers of key items no longer even have to wait for purchase orders. When the suppliers see low stocks of materials on General Motors' or DuPont's computers, they automatically ship the goods and send electronic invoices.

TELECOMMUNICATIONS MEDIA

Figure 4-7 shows a simple telecommunications system in which two distant hardware units transfer messages over some type of **communications medium.** The hardware units may be two PCs, a PC and a mainframe, or some other combination of two devices. The medium may be a privately operated set of cables, or it may consist of public phone lines, microwaves, or some other alternative. When a message is transmitted, one of the hardware units is designated as the *sender* and the other as the *receiver.* The message may be sent over the medium in several ways, as this section will demonstrate.

FIGURE 4-7

A simple telecommunications system.

As complicated as telecommunications systems may seem, at their simplest level they allow one device to communicate effectively with another.

SENDER

MESSAGE

RECEIVER

Communications media fall into one of two classes, wire and wireless media.

WIRE MEDIA

Telecommunications systems commonly carry messages using one or more of these three types of wiring: twisted-pair wires, coaxial cable, and fiber-optic cable (see Figure 4-8).

TWISTED-PAIR WIRES Twisted-pair wires, in which thin strands of wire are twisted together in sets of two, is the communications medium that has been in use the longest. The telephone

---

■ **Communications medium**. The intervening link, such as a telephone wire or cable, that connects two physically distant hardware devices. ■ **Twisted-pair wire**. A communications medium consisting of wire strands twisted in sets of two and bound into a cable.

COAXIAL CABLE

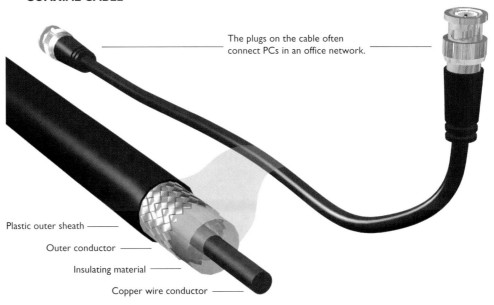

The plugs on the cable often connect PCs in an office network.

Plastic outer sheath

Outer conductor

Insulating material

Copper wire conductor

TWISTED-PAIR WIRES

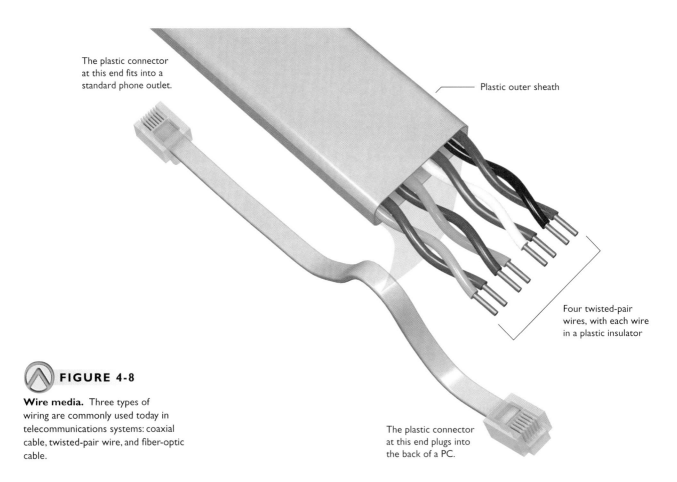

The plastic connector at this end fits into a standard phone outlet.

Plastic outer sheath

Four twisted-pair wires, with each wire in a plastic insulator

The plastic connector at this end plugs into the back of a PC.

FIGURE 4-8

Wire media. Three types of wiring are commonly used today in telecommunications systems: coaxial cable, twisted-pair wire, and fiber-optic cable.

system still carries most of the data transmitted in this country and abroad primarily over inexpensive twisted-pair wires. In some cases, several thousand pairs may be bound together into single cables to connect switching stations within a city. By contrast, only a few pairs are needed to connect a home phone to the closest telephone pole.

FIBER-OPTIC CABLE

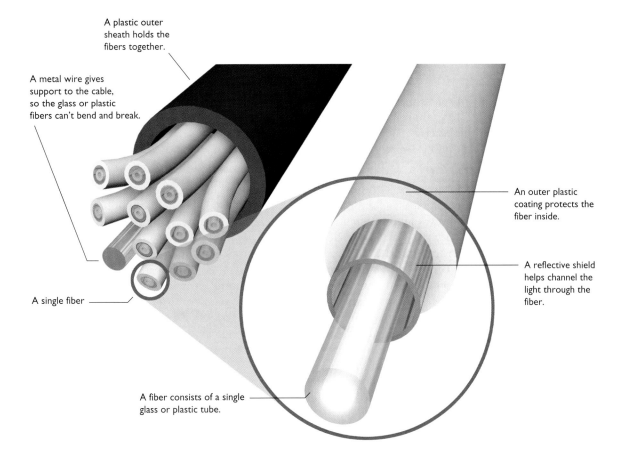

A plastic outer sheath holds the fibers together.

A metal wire gives support to the cable, so the glass or plastic fibers can't bend and break.

A single fiber

A fiber consists of a single glass or plastic tube.

An outer plastic coating protects the fiber inside.

A reflective shield helps channel the light through the fiber.

COAXIAL CABLE   Coaxial cable, the medium pioneered by the cable television industry, was originally developed to carry high-speed, interference-free video transmissions. Coaxial cable is now also widely used in other types of communication applications, such as linking computers in office networks. Additionally, phone companies rely heavily on coaxial cable.

FIBER-OPTIC CABLE   One of the most successful developments in transmission media in recent years has been fiber optics. **Fiber-optic cables** often consist of hundreds of clear glass or plastic fiber strands, each approximately the thickness of a human hair. Transmission requires the transformation of data into light beams, which are sent through the cable by a laser device at speeds on the order of billions or even trillions of bits per second. Each hairlike fiber has the capacity to carry data for several television stations or thousands of two-way voice conversations. Cables that link big cities often carry several hundred fibers in a single cable.

The advantages of fiber optics over other wire media include speed, size, weight, security, and longevity. In particular, enormous speed differences separate conventional wire and fiber-optic cable. In the second or two it takes to transmit a single page of Webster's unabridged dictionary over conventional wire, more than a dozen copies of the entire 2,000-plus pages of the work can be transmitted over a single fiber-optic strand.

A stunning new advance in fiber-optic technology may someday yield speeds far greater than those available today. Through a technology called wavelength

For a tutorial on the different types of cabling and other telecommunications media, go to www.harcourtcollege.com/infosys/pcc2e/student/tutor/ and click on Chapter 4.

■ **Coaxial cable.** A transmission medium, consisting of a center wire inside a grounded, cylindrical shield, capable of sending data at high speeds. ■ **Fiber-optic cable**. A transmission medium composed of hundreds of hair-thin, transparent fibers along which lasers carry data as light waves.

division multiplexing (WDM), laser devices exist that can now simultaneously transmit multiple, *color* beams—perhaps a hundred or more—through a single fiber. With speeds of up to 200 trillions of bits per second, the entire contents of the Library of Congress can pass through a single fiber in a single second.

WIRELESS MEDIA

Wireless transmission media have become especially popular in recent years. They support communications in situations in which physical wiring is impractical. What's more, the lack of wiring can serve to make devices highly portable. Three widely used media for wireless communications are microwave technology, cellular technology, and infrared technology.

MICROWAVE TECHNOLOGY   Microwaves are high-frequency radio signals. Text, graphics, audio, and video data can all be converted to microwave impulses and transmitted through the air. Microwave signals can be sent in two ways, via terrestrial stations or by way of satellites (see Figure 4-9). Both can transmit data in large quantities and at high speeds.

Terrestrial microwave stations can communicate with each other directly over distances of no more than about 30 miles. The stations need not be within actual sight of each other; however, they should have a clear path along which to communicate. To avoid obstacles like mountains and Earth's curvature, the stations often are placed on tall buildings and mountaintops. When one station receives a message from another, it amplifies it and passes it on to the next station.

Communications satellites were developed to reduce the cost of long-distance transmission via terrestrial microwave repeater stations and to pro-

FIGURE 4-9

Microwave transmission. Microwave signals can move in two ways: via terrestrial stations or by way of satellites.

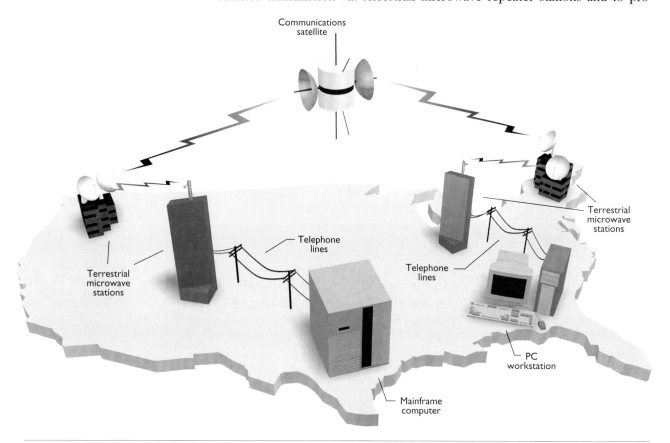

■ **Microwave.** An electromagnetic wave in the high-frequency range. ■ **Terrestrial microwave station.** A ground station that receives microwave signals, amplifies them, and passes them on to another station. ■ **Communications satellite.** An earth-orbiting device that relays communications signals over long distances.

vide a cheaper and better overseas communications medium than undersea cable. Many older satellites maintain *geosynchronous orbits* 22,300 miles above Earth. "Geosynchronous" means that, because the satellites travel at the same speed as Earth's rotation, they appear to remain stationary over a given spot on the globe. Such satellites are so far above Earth's surface that it takes only three of them to blanket the planet with signals.

Not all satellites travel thousands of miles above Earth. Two relatively new satellite projects that use a low-Earth-orbit (LEO) strategy are IRIDIUM and Teledesic. LEO satellites circle the globe at an altitude of less than 500 feet. They are cheaper to build, and, because of their lower orbits, they provide faster message transmission than traditional satellites.

The *IRIDIUM* project, spearheaded by Motorola, uses about 60 satellites and provides global wireless communications service for phoning, faxing, paging, and low-speed data transmission. The creation of Craig McCaw, a cellular-phone pioneer, *Teledesic* will become operational in 2003 with 288 satellites, and data will be able to travel at screamingly fast, fiber-optic-cable-caliber speeds. Both IRIDIUM and Teledesic are designed to provide contact between any two points on the globe.

Both communications satellites and terrestrial microwave stations work best when they transmit large amounts of data one way at a time. Thus, they are ideal for applications such as television and radio broadcasting and getting information from the Internet.

CELLULAR TECHNOLOGY **Cellular phones** are special mobile telephones that do not need hookups to standard phone outlets in order to work. They can put two people into communication with each other almost anywhere, even if the parties are in motion.

Cellular phones, which use radio waves, operate by keeping in contact with cellular antennae (see Figure 4-10). These antennae, which resemble tall metal telephone poles, are strategically placed throughout a calling area. Calling areas are divided into zones measuring ten miles wide or so-called *cells,* each with its own antenna. The antennae perform two essential functions: (1) They enable a moving cellular phone to transmit and receive signals without interruption by passing signals off to antennae in contiguous cells into which the phones are moving, and (2) they provide an interface with the regular public phone network via a switching office.

Cellular phone use has increased from 1.6 million users to 66.5 million users in the last decade and is expected to reach over 100 million users by the year 2002. Currently, those who most benefit from the cellular phone boom are people who need to maintain constant contact with the office or clients but must be on the move, as well—such as a busy executive, salesperson, truck driver, or real-estate agent. Farmers, refinery workers, and others who work outdoors are reaping the benefits of cellular technology to stay in contact with others when they cannot afford the time it would take to get to a regular phone. Cellular phones that enable busy families and teenagers to keep in touch are also becoming more popular. The latest generation of cellular phones has adopted several functions found in handheld computers and pagers.

The transmission networks that support cellular phones are also useful for sending business data. Through a laptop computer with a cellular modem, you can gain access to huge databases of information and the Internet while you are far from an office or a regular phone. Cellular networks are a hit internationally, too, especially in less-developed countries such as Poland and China. In places like these, communication systems are crude by

For links to further information about wire and wireless telecommunications media, go to www.harcourtcollege. com/infosys/pcc2e/student/ explore/ and click on Chapter 4.

■ **Cellular phone.** A mobile phone that transmits calls through special ground stations that cover areas called *cells* to communicate with the regular phone system.

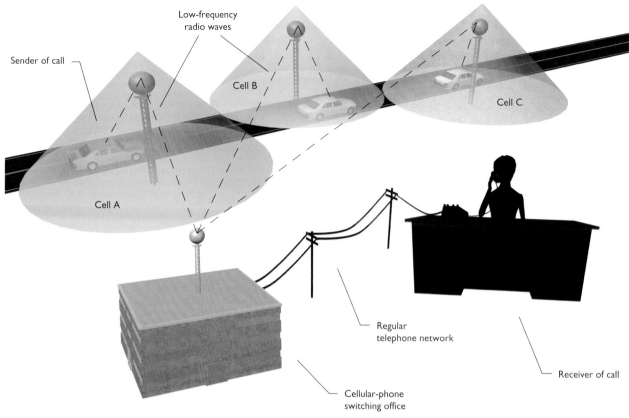

Low-frequency
radio waves

Sender of call

Cell B

Cell C

Cell A

Regular
telephone network

Receiver of call

Cellular-phone
switching office

ABOUT CELLULAR CALLS
When you make a cellular call from your car, it is
picked up by the antenna in the cell from which
you are calling. As you move from one cell to another,
the call is switched seamlessly to the new cell's antenna—
which broadcasts at a different frequency.

 **FIGURE 4-10**

Cellular phones.

North American standards, and it is much easier to build new cellular networks than to fix current facilities or to install wired systems.

INFRARED TECHNOLOGY *Infrared technology* has gained popularity in recent years as a way to set up wireless links between office PCs. As opposed to microwave and cellular technologies, which use *radio* waves, infrared technology sends data as *light* rays. One system, for instance, places a device on each computer through which it can send and receive messages via a transmitter located on the office ceiling. This setup provides an unobstructed, line-of-sight path to and from the computers. Recently, a beaming device has become available that hooks up with a PC card and cable to a laptop's infrared port. The device relays print commands to a desktop computer's display screen, which wires the message to its attached laser printer.

ADAPTING COMPUTERS TO TELECOMMUNICATIONS MEDIA

A computer needs special equipment to send messages over a communications medium. The type of equipment depends on such factors as the medium itself and how data are sent over it.

SENDING DATA OVER MEDIA

Data travel over communications media in various ways. The following paragraphs describe several of them.

ANALOG OR DIGITAL? One of the most fundamental distinctions in data communications is the difference between analog and digital transmissions (see Figure 4-11).

The regular phone system, established many years ago to handle voice traffic, carries **analog** signals—that is, *continuous* waves over a certain frequency range. Changes in the continuous wave reflect the myriad variations in the pitch of the human voice. Transmissions for cable TV and large satellite dishes also use analog signals, as do many wireless networks.

Most business computing equipment, in contrast, transmits **digital** signals, which handle data coded in two *discrete* states: 0-bits and 1-bits. Your desktop computer is a digital device; so, too, are midrange and mainframe computers. Also, networks often carry digitally encoded data transmissions within office buildings. Whenever communications require an interface between digital computers and analog networks, an adaptive device called a *modem* (covered in more detail shortly) is needed to translate between the two.

BANDWIDTH AND SPEED Over an analog medium, data travel at various frequencies. The difference between the highest and lowest frequencies available on such a medium is known as the medium's **bandwidth.** For example, many telephone lines have a bandwidth of 3,000 hertz (Hz), which is the difference between the highest (3,300 Hz) and lowest (300 Hz) frequencies at which they can send data. Transmissions of text data require the least amount of bandwidth, and video data need the most.

Just as a wide firehose permits more water to pass through it per unit of time than a narrow garden hose, a medium with great bandwidth allows more data to pass through it per unit of time than a medium of small bandwidth. Put another way, greater bandwidth allows data to travel at higher speeds. The speed at which data travel over both analog and digital media is often given in **bits per second (bps),** kbps (thousands of bits per second), or mbps (millions of bits per second).

Figure 4-12 compares the speeds of several media. As the figure shows, twisted-pair wire has the lowest speed, with increasingly better rates for coaxial cable, radio waves, and fiber-optic cable. Twisted-pair wire is often called a "low-bandwidth" medium; fiber-optic cable, a "high-bandwidth" medium. Increasingly, high-bandwidth media are being installed in many homes and businesses to accommodate the growing number of byte-hungry, information-related products coming into the marketplace.

PARALLEL VERSUS SERIAL TRANSMISSION In most communications networks, and especially where long distances are involved, data travel serially. In **serial transmission,** all of the bits in a message are sent one after another along a single path. On the other hand, **parallel transmission** sends each set of eight bits (plus a check bit called a parity bit, discussed shortly) needed to convey each byte in a message at one time over nine separate paths. Figure 4-13 illustrates the difference between the two.

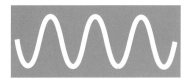
Analog mode

Digital mode

FIGURE 4-11

Analog and digital transmissions.

■ **Analog.** Transmission of data as continuous-wave patterns. ■ **Digital.** Transmission of data as 0- and 1-bits. ■ **Bandwidth.** The difference between the highest and lowest frequencies that a transmission medium can accommodate. ■ **Bits per second (bps).** A measure of a transmission medium's speed. ■ **Serial transmission.** Data transmission in which every bit in a byte must travel down the same path in succession. ■ **Parallel transmission.** Data transmission in which each bit in a byte follows its own path simultaneously with all other bits.

Speed Comparison

	Type	Speed
Wire Media	Twisted-pair wire (dial-up lines)	300 bps to 56 kbps
	Twisted-pair wire (dedicated lines)	1 to 10 mbps
	Coaxial cable	1 to 20 mbps
	Fiber-optic cable	up to 200 mbps
Wireless Media	Radio wave	4.8 to 19.2 kbps
	Satellite	64 to 512 kbps
	Terrestrial microwave	1.544 mbps
	Infrared (laptop ports)	115 kbps to 4 mbps

FIGURE 4-12

Speed. A wider bandwidth allows a medium to carry more data per unit of time and to support more powerful communications applications.

As the figure suggests, parallel transmission is much faster than serial transmission. However, because it requires a cable with several tracks rather than one, it is also much more expensive. Thus, parallel transmission usually is limited to short distances, such as computer-to-printer communications.

NETWORK INTERFACE CARDS AND MODEMS

Workstations such as PCs and display terminals—a *display terminal* is a display device with an attached keyboard—are usually connected to a network with either a network interface card or a modem. The type of connection required often depends on whether the workstation accesses the network through a *dedicated line* that is set up for private use (which plugs into a network interface card) or through a conventional *dial-up line* (which plugs into a modem).

FIGURE 4-13

Serial and parallel transmissions. The figure illustrates a transmission of the ASCII representation of the letter A.

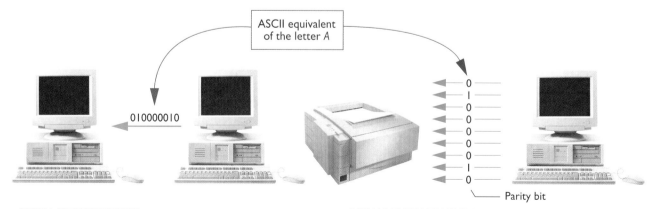

SERIAL TRANSMISSION
In serial transmission, all of the bits of a byte follow one another over a single path.

PARALLEL TRANSMISSION
In parallel transmission, the bits of a byte are split into separate paths and transmitted along the paths at the same time.

Rear view of workstation, with case removed

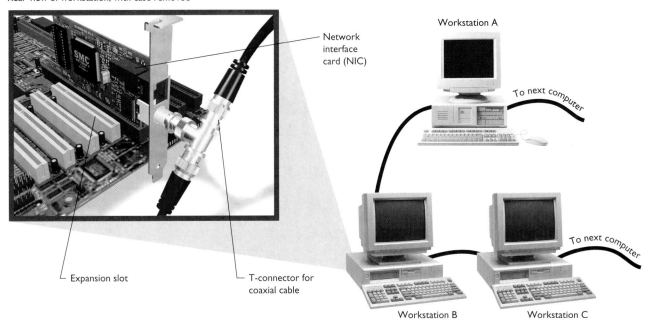

Network interface card (NIC)

Expansion slot

T-connector for coaxial cable

Workstation A

Workstation B

Workstation C

Dial-up lines—the type of telephone connections found in most homes and many small businesses—let you call anywhere in the world. They are sometimes called "switched lines" because switching stations within the phone network route your call to the desired destination. A dedicated line, on the other hand, provides a permanent connection between two points. Although dial-up lines are much cheaper, they are slower, and busy signals often prevent connections.

NETWORK INTERFACE CARDS A **network interface card (NIC)** is an add-in board that plugs into an expansion slot within the system unit (see Figure 4-14). These cards often connect to coaxial cables between the workstations in *local networks,* which span small areas like an office building or a college campus. NICs pass on to the network any outgoing data from workstations, and they also collect incoming data to the workstations.

MODEMS Because digital impulses—such as those sent by desktop workstations—cannot be transmitted over analog phone lines, communications require some means of translating each kind of signal into the other. Conversion of signals from digital to continuous-wave form is called *modulation,* and translation from continuous waves back to digital impulses is termed *demodulation.* A **modem** (coined from the terms *mo*dulation and *dem*odulation) takes care of both operations.

Modems are most often used to connect PCs to *wide area networks,* such as the Internet. Wide area networks join devices spread much farther apart than just a few miles. As Figure 4-15 shows, when a workstation sends a message to a remote CPU over an analog line, a modem at the sending end converts from digital to analog, and another at the receiving end converts from analog to digital.

Modems are most commonly available as add-in boards, which are designed to be inserted into an expansion slot within a desktop PC's system unit, and as standalone hardware devices (see Figure 4-16). The former type, called *internal modems,* are popular because they don't take up extra desk space

FIGURE 4-14

Network interface cards (NICs). NICs are often used to connect workstations via coaxial cable to networks that span small areas, like office buildings or college campuses.

WebTutor

For a tutorial on connecting computers to telecommunications media, go to www.harcourtcollege.com/infosys/pcc2e/student/tutor/ and click on Chapter 4.

■ **Network interface card (NIC).** An add-in board though which a workstation connects to a local network. ■ **Modem.** A communications device that enables digital computers and their support devices to communicate over analog media.

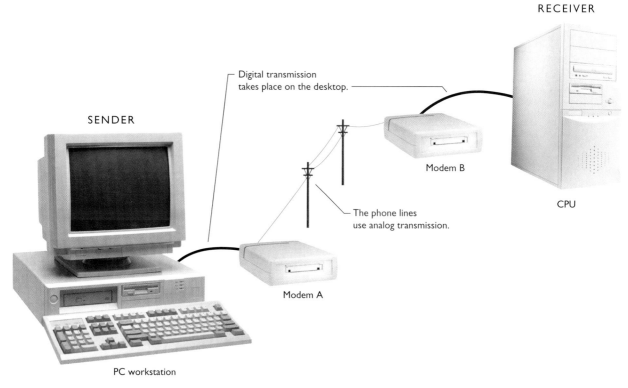

FIGURE 4-15

How modems work. An operator of a PC workstation types in data that become digitally encoded. Modem A converts these digital data to analog form and sends them over the phone lines to Modem B. Modem B reconverts the data to digital form and delivers them to the receiving CPU. This latter CPU transmits back to the workstation by reversing these steps.

and are generally cheaper. Some prefer the latter type, called *external modems,* because they can be moved from one computer to another and because they have display panels that can provide useful diagnostics. PC-card modems for laptop computers are also available. Common transmission rates found on modems are 14.4, 28.8, 33.6, and 56 kbps. Modems capable of higher speeds can function at the lower rates as well.

A few words of caution about modems: Your Internet service provider may not support your calling area with the highest possible speeds, even though your modem is capable of them. Also, your phone company may not be able to deliver data at your modem's top speed because of line loads. What's more, data compression can slow down considerably the rate at which information is handled.

FIGURE 4-16

Types of modems. Modems are either external or internal.

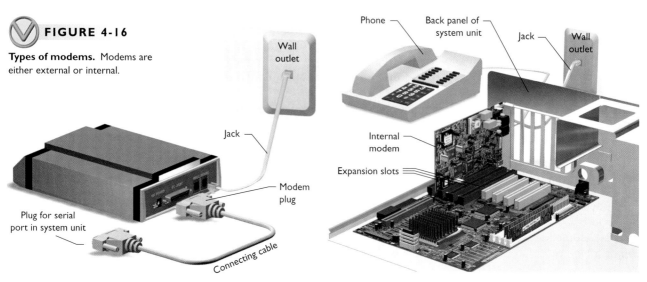

EXTERNAL MODEM
External modems are detached from the system unit and can be moved from computer to computer.

INTERNAL MODEM
Internal modems are boards that fit in an expansion slot within the system unit and are the type of modem recommended for most personal uses.

Modems can now deliver data as fast as the present phone system can carry it. To achieve more speed, you need either an ISDN line or some other, faster alternative.

MODEM SOFTWARE The programs that work with modems to enable your PC to communicate with the Internet and remote databases are commonly referred to in the PC world as *modem software*. When you buy a new PC with a modem, you will usually get modem software as part of the bundle. Although products in the modem-software marketplace provide different features, most of them let you access the Internet and service providers, receive and send electronic mail and faxes, and exchange files with other computers.

In addition, many modem programs will automatically place and answer calls for you, interface with voice machines, provide security for your files, and simplify a number of routine, phone-related tasks (such as accessing phone directories and keying in IDs and passwords to online service providers or newsgroups).

ISDN AND BEYOND

If you need more speed than you can squeeze out of a modem, your best bet is an ISDN line or something even faster.

ISDN (for *integrated services digital network*) is a digital phone service that operates over ordinary dial-up phone lines or over dedicated lines leased for private use. ISDN gives access to one or two 64 kbps channels. With two channels, you can use each separately—say, one to talk to a friend about a homework assignment while you watch as a Web page downloads from the Internet over the other. You can also combine the two lines into one for a full 128 kbps of bandwidth. To use ISDN, a special *ISDN adapter*—the ISDN counterpart of a modem—must be connected to your computer. The adapter allows you to communicate with other ISDN devices, such as the ISDN adapter owned by your Internet service provider.

ISDN is more expensive than modem transmission. An adapter can easily cost more than $300, and the installation charge on an ISDN line—if you don't live too far out in the country—can run another couple of hundred dollars or so. Also, you must often pay a per-minute connect charge for your time on the line, even for a local call.

DirecPC works with a small, $200 satellite dish that is similar to the one used with digital television's DirecTV service. DirecPC can provide up to 400 kbps speeds when data are downloaded but only modem-fast speeds when data are sent the other way, up to the satellite. Fortunately, most applications require far more data sent down than up. Typical monthly costs, which include an Internet connection and an e-mail account, are $30 for 25 hours of access per week or $50 for 100 hours.

Businesses often require faster speeds than any of the alternatives mentioned so far. Such options offer more speed than ISDN and DirecPC, but—no surprise—they also bring higher prices. With a *T1 dedicated line* or a *frame-relay service,* for instance, a company can get speeds up to a few mbps over coaxial cable. Companies often lease these lines and then split the bandwidth among several users. *T3 fiber-optic dedicated lines* are even faster and can reach 45 mbps and upward. Also, lines that follow the *asynchronous transfer mode (ATM)* standard can deliver speeds of 155 mbps over fiber-optic lines—and perhaps over 600 mbps in the near future. T3 and ATM are most often used by communications companies for network *backbones*—those parts of a network that carry the most traffic.

■ **ISDN.** A digital phone service that offers high-speed transmissions over ordinary phone lines.

NETWORK TOPOLOGIES

For a tutorial on the various types of network topologies, go to www.harcourtcollege.com/infosys/pcc2e/student/tutor/ and click on Chapter 4.

Telecommunications networks can be classified in terms of their *topologies,* or patterns (see Figure 4-17). Three common topologies are the star, bus, and ring.

STAR NETWORKS The **star network**—the oldest topology for computer networks—often consists of a large computer hierarchically connected to several workstations through point-to-point links. Star networks are common in traditional mainframe environments, as shown in the first diagram of Figure 4-17. The mainframe serves as the *host computer,* and it hooks up to several PC workstations or to several display terminals. The display terminals are sometimes referred to as *dumb terminals* because they are workstations that can do little more than send and receive data; the mainframe does virtually everything else.

BUS NETWORKS A **bus network** operates a lot like ordinary city buses in a ground transportation system. The hardware devices are like bus stops, and the data move like passengers. For example, the bus network labeled in Figure 4-17 contains four workstations (bus stops) at which the system picks up or lets off data (passengers). The bus line commonly consists of a high-speed cable with inexpensive twisted-pair wires dropped off each workstation. A bus network contains no host computer.

RING NETWORKS A less common and more expensive alternative to the star and bus is the **ring network,** which lacks any host computer; instead, a number of computers or other devices are connected by a loop. A ring network is also shown in Figure 4-17.

Networks often combine topologies, in effect turning several smaller networks into a larger one. Figure 4-17 shows two star networks *daisy chained* together with a bus. In the figure, cluster stations—or *hubs*—coordinate the traffic of sent and received messages on workstations that are hooked up to them. Figure 4-17 also shows three star networks linked together in a ring by a high-speed *fiber-optic backbone.* Additionally, network topologies can contain redundant links, as the Internet does, so that they conform to no well-known geometric pattern.

Workstations send and receive messages according to some predefined method or *protocol.* The topic of communications protocols is discussed later in this chapter.

LOCAL NETWORKS

Organizations need communications facilities that connect geographically close resources, such as PCs located in the same college campus or classroom or workstations located in the same office. Such networks are known as **local networks.** Two common types of local networks are host-independent local area networks (LANs) and hierarchical local networks.

■ **Star network.** A telecommunications network consisting of a host device connected directly to several other devices.
■ **Bus network.** A telecommunications network consisting of a transmission line with lines dropped off for several devices. ■ **Ring network.** A telecommunications network that connects machines serially in a closed loop. ■ **Local network.** A privately run communications network of several machines located within a few miles or so of one another.

BASIC TOPOLOGIES

Most network topologies follow a simple star, bus, or ring pattern.

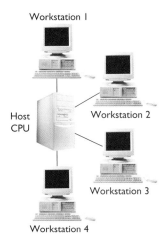

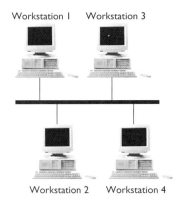

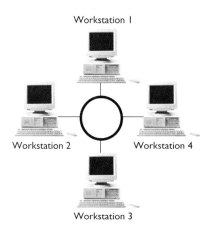

STAR NETWORK

A star network often consists of a mainframe host that's connected to several workstations in a point-to-point fashion.

BUS NETWORK

A bus network uses a high-speed cable that workstations tap into—in the manner shown—to pick up and drop off messages.

RING NETWORK

In a ring network, computers and other devices are connected in a loop.

COMBINATION TOPOLOGIES

Many networks are formed by combining topologies—such as the bus and star.

FIGURE 4-17

Network topologies. Networks follow either a basic topology or a more complex combination—such as a daisy chain or backbone.

DAISY CHAINING

Daisy chaining refers to connecting devices serially with a bus line. Here, two hubs (cluster stations that manage workstations) coordinate the sending and receiving of messages from two star networks.

continued

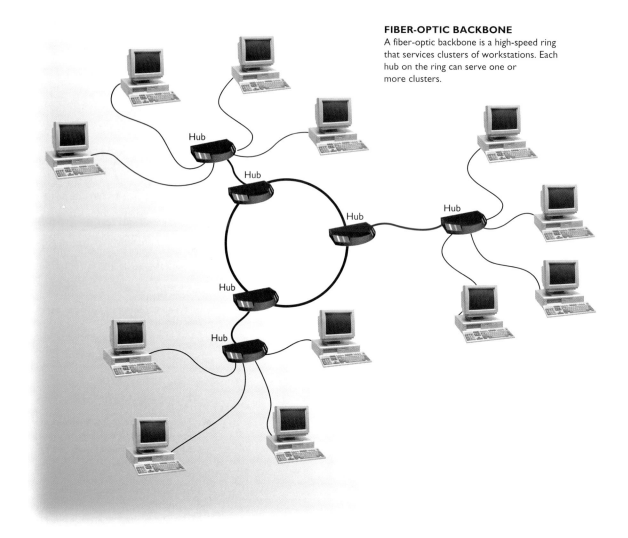

FIBER-OPTIC BACKBONE
A fiber-optic backbone is a high-speed ring that services clusters of workstations. Each hub on the ring can serve one or more clusters.

FIGURE 4-17

continued

LOCAL AREA NETWORKS (LANs)

The term **local area networks (LANs)** typically refers to local networks without any host computer as such. Instead, most LANs use either a bus or ring topology, and computers within the network itself manage workstations' demands for shared facilities. LANs are available principally in the client-server and peer-to-peer varieties.

CLIENT-SERVER LANs Client-server LANs are so named because each workstation that receives network service is called a **client,** while the computers that manage the requests for facilities within the network are called **servers** (see Figure 4-18). For example, a *file server* might manage disk-storage activities, enabling workstation users to access any of several available operating systems, applications programs, or data files. Similarly, a *print server* handles printing-related activities, such as managing user outputs on a high-quality network printer. LANs also incorporate such devices as *mail servers*

■ **Local area network (LAN).** A local network without a host computer, usually composed of PC workstations and shared peripherals. ■ **Client-server LAN.** A LAN composed of *client* devices, which receive network services, and *server* devices, which provide the services. ■ **Client.** A device designed to receive service in a client-server network. ■ **Server.** A computer that manages shared devices, such as laser printers or high-capacity hard disks, in a client-server network.

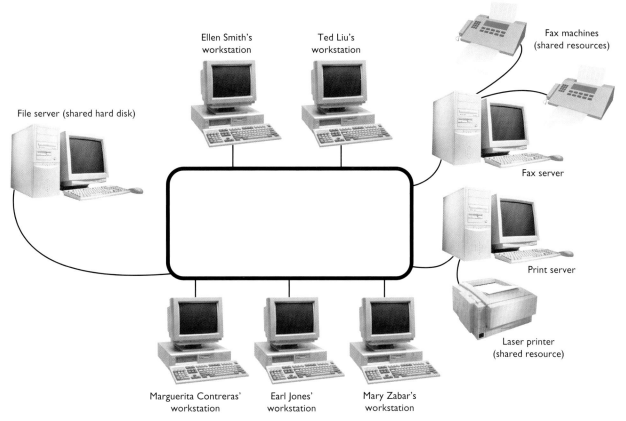

Ellen Smith's workstation

Ted Liu's workstation

Fax machines (shared resources)

File server (shared hard disk)

Fax server

Print server

Laser printer (shared resource)

Marguerita Contreras' workstation

Earl Jones' workstation

Mary Zabar's workstation

FIGURE 4-18

Client-server LAN. In a client-server LAN, each workstation that receives network service is called a *client*, while the computers that manage requests for network services are called *servers*.

and *fax servers,* which are dedicated to managing electronic mail and facsimile transmissions, respectively.

Because servers often manage large databases, perform certain types of processing chores for clients, and interact with several other computers, LANs often include powerful PCs like those based on the latest Intel and PowerPC processor chips to perform server duties. In very large LANs, midrange and mainframe computers often function as servers.

PEER-TO-PEER LANS Applications that require small networks often use **peer-to-peer LANs.** These LANs do not predesignate computers as clients and servers per se. Instead, all of the user workstations and shared peripherals work on the same level, and users have direct access to each other's workstations and shared peripherals. Peer-to-peer LANs were designed as a way to bring networking to small groups without the complexity and expense that normally accompany client-server systems. Peer-to-peer capabilities are built into many personal operating systems.

LANs are used for a variety of applications, the simplest of which involve just sharing expensive hard disks and laser printers. LAN technology has evolved beyond these initial applications to include numerous other uses (see Figure 4-19).

One of the newest functions is the intranet. An **intranet** is a private LAN—set up by a company for its employees—that implements the infrastructure and standards of the Internet and its World Wide Web. Intranets today serve a variety of purposes, such as making company phone books and procedure manuals available to employees, disseminating forms, and enabling employees

■ **Peer-to-peer LAN.** A LAN in which all of the user workstations and shared peripheral devices operate on the same level. ■ **Intranet.** A private network—often one set up by a company for employees—that implements the infrastructure and standards of the Internet and World Wide Web.

Uses for LANs

Sharing expensive devices like network printers among several users

Handling certain types of applications better than mainframes

Performing electronic mail operations

Implementing an intranet

FIGURE 4-19

Uses for LANs.

FIGURE 4-20

Uses for intranets. Companies can get an intranet up and running on a local-area network by following the standards and guidelines of the Internet and World Wide Web. Any or all of the applications listed here can become part of a company intranet.

USES FOR INTRANETS

Facilitating electronic mail

Maintaining internal phone books

Storing procedure manuals

Posting training materials

Disseminating employee forms

Posting internal job listings

Providing electronic catalogs for ordering supplies

Facilitating workgroup computing

Scheduling meetings and appointments

Making available critical expertise

Disseminating newsletters

Posting reports and other types of information

to communicate and work together on projects (see Figure 4-20). Because many company sites are fitted with high-bandwidth cable media, intranets make possible much richer multimedia displays than the Internet at large, which is constrained by the speeds available through dial-up modems and ordinary phone lines.

In many ways, intranets provide the logical framework with which to build a company LAN. Many employees are already familiar with the Internet and its World Wide Web, so the similar-looking intranets minimize training requirements. Also, Internet technology (and therefore intranets) can function on almost any computer platform, and many companies have diverse mixtures of computers that need to communicate with one another. What's more, development costs are relatively small—no highly unique, proprietary system has to be designed.

Much newer to the scene than intranets are *extranets,* extensions of intranets out onto the Internet itself. Extranets provide such people as mobile workers and selected customers and suppliers access to a company's internal data and applications via the Web. Because they generally cover long distances, extranets are examples of wide-area networks (WANs). WANs are covered later in the chapter.

PC-based LANs have a big advantage over host-based hierarchical systems, which we'll be looking at next: Organizations can inexpensively add small increments of extra computing power to their LANs as needs grow. For instance, companies can add extra workstations or more servers at any time. Also, expandable machines called *scalable superserver computers,* which cater to LANs, have designs expressly intended for easy additions of processing power and memory. On the disadvantage side, security on LANs still lags behind that on mainframe-based host systems, and LANs often run up higher costs for development and support.

HIERARCHICAL LOCAL NETWORKS

Hierarchical local networks are the oldest type of local network. They follow a star topology. At the top of the hierarchy is a host computer such as a mainframe or midrange computer that controls virtually all of the processing. At the bottom are user workstations. Between the top and bottom, devices such as communications controllers manage exchanges between the host and workstations.

■ **Hierarchical local network.** A local network in which a relatively powerful host CPU at the top of the hierarchy interacts with workstations at the bottom.

Workstations in hierarchical local networks can either download files from the host or upload files to it. **Downloading** means that copies of existing files move from the host to the PC workstations. **Uploading** means that new data created at the PC workstations move to the host system.

Both downloading and uploading usually require stringent organizational control. Downloading presents the danger of unauthorized access to data, whereas uploading entails the risk of garbage data corrupting other applications. Uploading and downloading are also common operations in client-server LANs, where clients download files off of a server or upload files to it.

A major difference between a hierarchical local network and a host-independent client-server LAN is *where* the processing takes place. In the client-server LAN, a lot of the processing can be done at the client or desktop level. Except for database retrievals, possibly very little other processing is done at the server end. In the hierarchical local network, by contrast, the processing is typically concentrated at the host or server level. In many such systems, the client is a dumb terminal that has very little processing capability beyond sending and receiving data.

WIDE AREA NETWORKS (WANS)

Wide area networks (WANs) are communications networks that encompass relatively wide geographical areas. Many WANs link together geographically dispersed LANs or LAN clusters. The mix also often includes hundreds or thousands—or, in the case of the Internet, millions—of independent user workstations that connect from remote locations. WANs may be publicly accessible, like the Internet, or privately owned and operated.

HANDLING WAN TRAFFIC

Two big issues with WANs are interconnectivity and network management (see Figure 4-21). Because these networks tie together so many devices across such long distances, they need a number of special pieces of equipment. These devices are discussed in the paragraphs that follow.

REPEATERS *Repeaters* are devices that amplify signals along a network. WANs need them because signals often have to travel farther than the wires or cables that carry them are designed to support. Repeaters are also commonly used on LANs when longer distances are involved.

ROUTERS **Routers** work in large, switched networks—like the Internet—to pass messages along to their destinations. Each router along the path to the destination passes any message it receives along to the next router, and the routers work together to share information about the network. If one part of the network is congested or out of service, a router can choose to send a message by an alternate route. Routers are to networks like the Internet what

---

■ **Downloading.** The process of transferring a file from a remote computer to a requesting computer over a network. ■ **Uploading.** The process of transferring a file from a local computer to a remote computer over a network. ■ **Wide area network (WAN).** A network that spans a large geographic area. ■ **Router.** A device used on WANs to decide the paths along which to send messages.

FIGURE 4-21

Wide area networks (WANs). To provide reliable service while reducing costs, WAN traffic is often monitored, analyzed, and managed at sophisticated control centers.

switching stations are to the phone system, with one important exception: The phone network predetermines the message path, whereas routers on the Internet make their own decisions, and one never knows ahead of time the path a message will take.

GATEWAYS AND BRIDGES Local networks often must communicate with outside resources, such as those on wide area networks and other local networks. Messages sent between two distinct networks reach their destinations via gateways and bridges.

A **gateway** is a collection of hardware and software resources that enables devices on one network to communicate with those on another, *dissimilar* network. Workstations on a LAN, for instance, require a gateway to access the Internet. Suppose, for example, an executive working at an office workstation on a LAN wishes to access the Internet through America Online; a gateway is necessary to link the two kinds of networks.

Two networks based on similar technology—such as a LAN in one city and a LAN in another—communicate via a device called a bridge. A **bridge** is a collection of hardware and software resources that enables devices on one network to communicate with devices on another, *similar* network. Bridges can also partition a large LAN into two smaller ones and connect two LANs that are nearby each other.

MULTIPLEXERS Communications lines almost always have far greater capacity than a single workstation can use. Because communications lines are expensive, networks can run efficiently if several low-speed devices share the same line. A special device called a **multiplexer** makes this possible by interleaving the messages of several low-speed devices and sending them along a single high-speed path.

CONCENTRATORS A **concentrator** is a multiplexer with a store-and-forward capability. Messages from slow devices accumulate at the concentrator until it collects enough characters to make a message worth forwarding to another device. In airline reservation systems, for instance, concentrators placed at such key sites as New York and Los Angeles allow travel agents to share communications lines economically. Messages initiated by agents are sent to the concentrator, stored, multiplexed with messages from other agents, and transmitted at very high speeds over long-distance lines to central processing sites. In the world of LANs, concentrators are known as *hubs*.

COMMUNICATIONS PROTOCOLS

Because manufacturers have long produced devices that use a variety of transmission techniques, the telecommunications industry has adopted standards called protocols to rectify the problem of conflicting procedures.

■ **Gateway.** An interface that enables two dissimilar networks to communicate. ■ **Bridge.** An interface that enables two similar networks to communicate. ■ **Multiplexer.** A communications device that interleaves the messages of several low-speed devices and sends them along a single high-speed path. ■ **Concentrator.** A communications device that combines control and multiplexing functions.

The term *protocol* comes from the areas of diplomacy and etiquette. For instance, at a dinner party in the elegant home of a family on the Social Register, the protocol in effect may be formal attire, impeccable table manners, and remaining at the table until beckoned to the parlor by the host or hostess. At a casual backyard barbecue, a different protocol will probably exist. In the communications field, protocols have comparable roles.

A communications **protocol** is a collection of procedures to establish, maintain, and terminate transmissions between devices. Protocols specify how devices will physically connect to a network, how data will be packaged for transmission, how receiver devices will acknowledge signals from sender devices (a process called *handshaking*), how errors will be handled, and so on. Just as people need an agreed-upon set of rules to communicate effectively, machines also need a common set of rules to help them get along with one another.

Protocols are found in all types of networks. How many protocols are there? Thousands. The following paragraphs discuss a few of the most common ones. As you will shortly see, each protocol addresses a highly specific type of situation.

For a tutorial on the various types of communications protocols, go to www. harcourtcollege.com/infosys/ pcc2e/student/tutor/ and click on Chapter 4.

SIMPLEX, HALF DUPLEX, OR FULL DUPLEX?   One level of protocol found in virtually all types of telecommunications addresses the direction in which transmitted data move (see Figure 4-22).

Simplex transmission allows data to travel only in a single, prespecified direction. An example from everyday life is a doorbell—the signal can go only from the button to the chime. Two other examples are television and radio broadcasting. The simplex standard is relatively uncommon for most types of computer-based telecommunications applications; even devices that are designed primarily to receive information, such as printers, must be able to communicate acknowledgment signals back to the sender devices.

In **half-duplex transmission,** messages can move in either direction but only one way at a time. The press-to-talk radio phones used in police cars employ the half-duplex standard; only one person can talk at a time. Often the line between a desktop workstation and a remote CPU conforms to the half-duplex pattern, as well. If another computer is transmitting to a workstation, the operator cannot send new messages until the other computer finishes its message or pauses to acknowledge an interruption.

Full-duplex transmission works like traffic on a busy two-way street— the flow moves in two directions at the same time. Full-duplexing is ideal for hardware units that need to pass large amounts of data between each other, as in mainframe-to-mainframe communications.

FIGURE 4-22

Simplex, half-duplex, and full-duplex transmissions.

| Infrared device | Desktop computer | Desktop computer | Server computer | Mainframe | Mainframe |

SIMPLEX
Messages can only go in a single, prespecified direction.

HALF DUPLEX
Messages can go both ways, but only one way at a time.

FULL DUPLEX
Messages can go both ways, simultaneously.

■ **Protocol.** A set of conventions by which machines establish communication with one another in a telecommunications environment. ■ **Simplex transmission.** Any type of transmission in which a message can move along a path in only a single, prespecified direction. ■ **Half-duplex transmission.** Any type of transmission in which messages may move in two directions—but only one way at a time—along a communications path. ■ **Full-duplex transmission.** A type of transmission in which messages may travel in two directions simultaneously along a communications path.

ASYNCHRONOUS VERSUS SYNCHRONOUS TRANSMISSION Another level of protocol commonly encountered by PC owners addresses packaging of data for serial transmission. As mentioned earlier, most data are transmitted serially in communications networks.

In **asynchronous transmission,** one character at a time is sent over a line. When the operator strikes a key on a keyboard, the character's byte representation moves up the line to the computer. Striking a second key sends the byte for a second character, and so forth. But because even the fastest typist can generate only a very small amount of data relative to what the line can accept, the line sits idle a lot of the time. Furthermore, each character sent must be packaged with a "start bit" and "stop bit," resulting in substantial transmission overhead.

When large blocks of data have to be sent, asynchronous transmission is too slow. **Synchronous transmission** increases speed on a line by dispatching data in blocks of characters rather than one at a time. Each block can consist of thousands of characters. The blocks are timed so that the receiving device knows that it will be getting them at regular intervals. Because no idle time occurs between transmission of individual characters in the block—and because less transmission overhead is required—this method allows more efficient utilization of the line. Synchronous transmission is made possible by a *buffer* at the workstation, a storage area large enough to hold a block of characters. As soon as the buffer is filled, all the characters in it are sent up the line to the destination computer.

Figure 4-23 shows the difference between asynchronous and synchronous transmission. Synchronous transmission is available on most high-speed modems.

THE PARITY BIT The parity bit is an error-checking protocol that looks for mistransmitted bits. For example, suppose you are at a keyboard and

FIGURE 4-23

Asynchronous and synchronous transmissions.

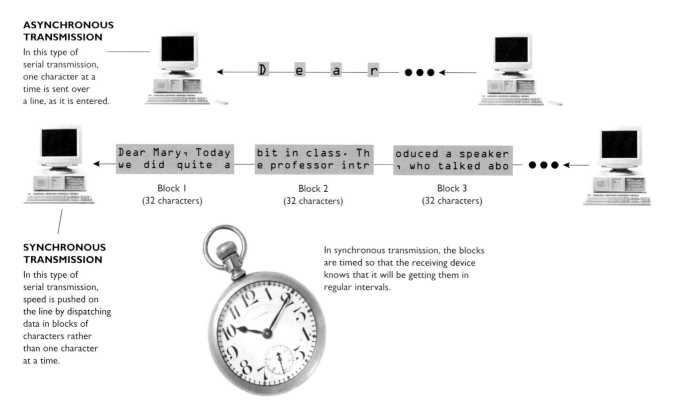

ASYNCHRONOUS TRANSMISSION

In this type of serial transmission, one character at a time is sent over a line, as it is entered.

D e a r ●●●

Dear Mary, Today we did quite a | bit in class. The professor intr | oduced a speaker , who talked abo ●●●

Block 1 (32 characters)   Block 2 (32 characters)   Block 3 (32 characters)

SYNCHRONOUS TRANSMISSION

In this type of serial transmission, speed is pushed on the line by dispatching data in blocks of characters rather than one character at a time.

In synchronous transmission, the blocks are timed so that the receiving device knows that it will be getting them in regular intervals.

■ **Asynchronous transmission.** The transmission of data over a line one character at a time, with variable time intervals between characters. ■ **Synchronous transmission.** The timed transmission of data over a line one block of characters at a time.

press the *B* key. If the keyboard processor supports ASCII coding, it will transmit the byte "01000010" up the line to the CPU. Interference on the line, however, might cause the sixth bit to change from 0 to 1 so that the CPU instead receives the message "01000110." Unless the CPU had some way of knowing that a mistake was made, it would wrongly interpret this byte as the letter *F.*

To enable the CPU to detect such transmission errors, ASCII has an additional bit position. This bit, called the **parity bit,** is automatically set to either 0 or 1 to make all the 1-bits in a byte add up to either an even or an odd number. In odd-parity systems, the parity bit makes all the 1-bits in a byte add up to an odd number; in even-parity systems, it makes them add up to an even number (see Figure 4-24). The parity bit is automatically generated by the computer system, so its existence is transparent to most users.

LAN PROTOCOLS In the LAN world, the protocols in effect depend on the particular type of network architecture used. The term *network architecture* refers to both the particular topology the network follows—say, bus or ring—as well as scores of little details, only a few of which we'll talk about here. By far, the two most common LAN architectures are Ethernet and token ring.

ETHERNET **Ethernet** is a collection of protocols that specify a standard way of setting up a bus LAN. It specifies the types and lengths of cables, how the cables connect, how devices communicate data, how the system detects and corrects problems, and so on.

Data communications and problem checking in an Ethernet network require a set of procedures collectively called *CSMA/CD,* which stands for *carrier sense multiple access with collision detection* (see Figure 4-25). "Carrier sense" means that, when a workstation has to send a message, it first "listens" for other messages on the line. If it senses no messages, it sends one. "Multiple access" means that two workstations might want to send a message at the same time. "Collision detection" means that after a workstation sends a message, it listens to see if the message might have collided with one from another workstation.

A collision takes place when two messages are sent at exactly the same time, so they temporarily jam the network. When they suspect a collision, the two sending workstations wait for short, random periods of time and send their messages again. The chance of the messages colliding a second time is extremely small.

A standard Ethernet system can send data at a rate of up to 10 mbps, and newer versions can transmit even faster. *Fast Ethernet,* for instance, runs at 100 mbps, and *gigabit Ethernet* is even faster.

TOKEN RING Like Ethernet, **token ring** is a network architecture. It is used with a ring network topology and employs a *token-passing* protocol.

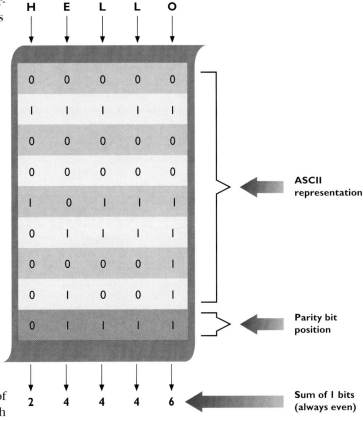

FIGURE 4-24

The parity bit. If a system supports even parity, as shown here, the number of 1-bits in every byte must always be an even number. The parity bit is set to either 0 or 1 in each byte to force an even number of 1-bits.

■ **Parity bit.** An extra bit added to the byte representation of a character to ensure that either an odd or an even number of 1-bits transmitted with every character. ■ **Ethernet.** A collection of protocols that specify a standard way of setting up a bus-based LAN. ■ **Token ring.** A ring-based LAN that uses token passing to control transmission of messages.

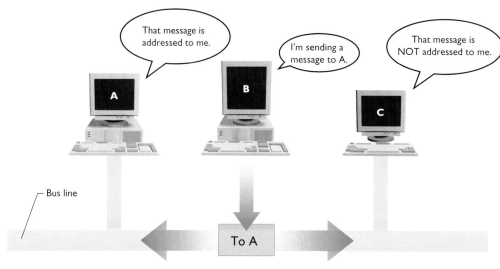

SENDING MESSAGES

Workstation B checks to see if the network is free and sends a message if it thinks it is. The message is broadcast across the network to all workstations, but only the one it is addressed to, A, can pick it up.

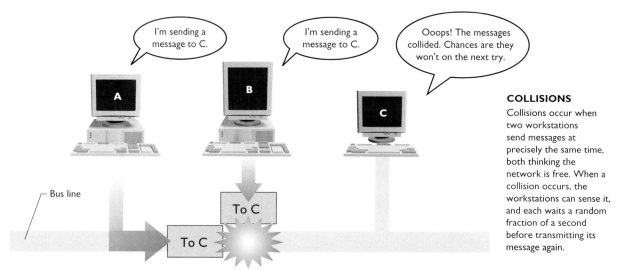

COLLISIONS

Collisions occur when two workstations send messages at precisely the same time, both thinking the network is free. When a collision occurs, the workstations can sense it, and each waits a random fraction of a second before transmitting its message again.

 **FIGURE 4-25**

Ethernet's **CSMA/CD** protocol.

Here's how a token-ring network works (see also Figure 4-26): A small packet called a *token*—which has room for messages and addresses—is sent around the ring. As the token circulates, workstations either check to see if the token is addressed to them or try to seize it so that they can assign messages to it. A token contains a control area, which specifies whether the token is free or carries a message. When a sender device captures a free token, it changes the status of the token from free to busy, adds an addressed message, and releases the token. The message then travels around the ring to the receiver location. The receiver copies the message and changes the status of the token back to free. Then, it releases the token.

Although the token ring architecture maintains more order than Ethernet in that it allows no collisions, sometimes a computer with a defective network interface card will swallow a token. If the token is gone for too long, the LAN assumes it's vanished and generates another. Several versions of the token ring architecture exist, the newer ones being faster and allowing more than a single token. Typical speeds run from a few mbps to several mbps.

1. A carrier called a token circulates around the ring. The token is "free" if a message is not attached to it; "busy," otherwise.

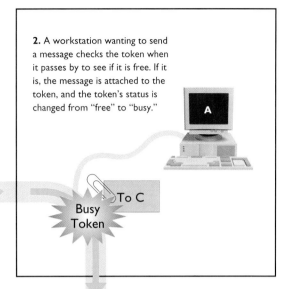

2. A workstation wanting to send a message checks the token when it passes by to see if it is free. If it is, the message is attached to the token, and the token's status is changed from "free" to "busy."

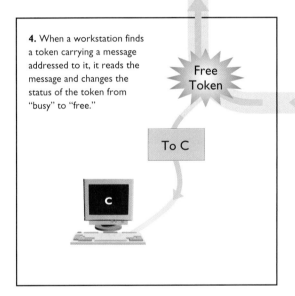

4. When a workstation finds a token carrying a message addressed to it, it reads the message and changes the status of the token from "busy" to "free."

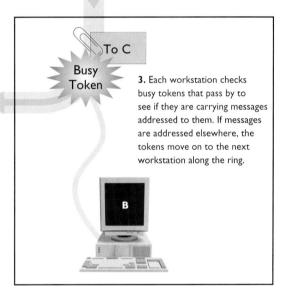

3. Each workstation checks busy tokens that pass by to see if they are carrying messages addressed to them. If messages are addressed elsewhere, the tokens move on to the next workstation along the ring.

FIGURE 4-26

Token ring and the token-passing protocol.

WAN PROTOCOLS Like LANs, WANs also conform to particular network architectures. One rather common architecture, *Systems Network Architecture (SNA),* has operated for years in the IBM mainframe world. SNA is most commonly used for private networks—such as airlines' reservation systems and large banking networks—that have tens of thousands of workstations. Instead of CSMA/CD or token passing, SNA often runs a *polling* protocol to transmit data. With polling, devices are asked—one by one and over and over again—if they have messages to send.

Another widely used architecture, *Fiber Distributed Data Interface (FDDI),* is commonly used to set up the fiber-optic backbones that connect dispersed campus LANs at large universities. These backbones use a ring topology and a token-passing protocol similar to token-ring networks to span over a hundred miles or more and run at speeds of over 100 mbps.

The Internet, too, relies on many protocols. One, called *transmission control protocol/Internet protocol (TCP/IP),* specifies how to package and send messages for the hundreds of different types of computers that hook up to the Internet. TCP/IP relies on a procedure known as packet switching to do

1. Each message is split into packets.

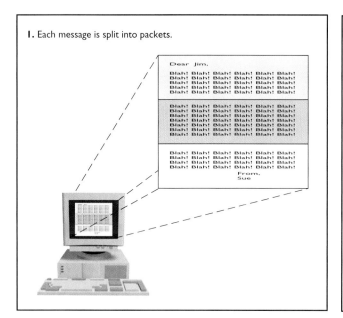

2. The packets are addressed to the same destination.

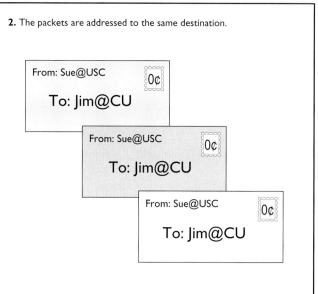

3. The packets may travel the same or different routes to the destination.

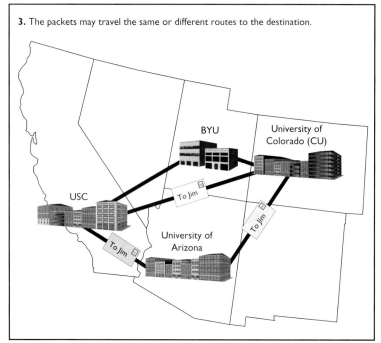

4. The packets are reassembled into the message at the destination.

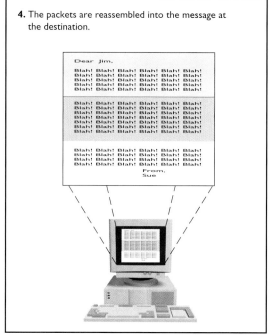

FIGURE 4-27

Packet switching.

this. **Packet switching** (see Figure 4-27) divides messages into smaller units called *packets*. Packets may travel along the Internet to their destination by the shortest path, but sometimes links along this path are heavily congested or broken due to the weather or an accident. Consequently, packets can be routed through any feasible link—and not necessarily all together—to reach their destination. They are reassembled when they arrive. A typical router can handle about 10,000 packets per second, and some routers are rated at 200,000 or more packets per second.

Note that just because a network divides data into packets, it does not necessarily mean that packet switching is in effect. Strictly speaking, any block of data—from a single asynchronous bit to several thousand bytes—can be referred to as a packet.

■ **Packet switching.** A transmission technique that breaks messages into smaller units that travel to a destination along possibly different paths.

SUMMARY AND KEY TERMS

Go to the Online Glossary at www.harcourtcollege.com/infosys/pcc2e/student/ to review key terms.

Telecommunications, or *telecom,* refers to communications over a distance—over long-distance phone lines, via privately owned cables, or by satellite, for instance.

TELECOMMUNICATIONS APPLICATIONS   A wide variety of important business applications involve telecommunications. Among these are **electronic mail** or **e-mail** (exchanging messages through **electronic mailboxes), voice mail, bulletin board systems (BBSs), facsimile** or **fax,** paging, information retrieval (including **Internet** access), **workgroup computing, teleconferencing, telecommuting,** transaction processing, and interorganizational systems such as *electronic data interchange.*

TELECOMMUNICATIONS MEDIA   Messages sent in a telecommunications system are transmitted over some type of **communications medium.** Wiring, such as **twisted-pair wires, coaxial cable,** and **fiber-optic cable,** constitutes one major class of media. Messages also are commonly sent through the air in the form of **microwave** signals or over cellular or infrared networks. **Terrestrial microwave stations** accommodate microwave transmissions when either the sender or the receiver is on the ground. **Communications satellites** reduce the cost of long-distance transmissions via terrestrial microwave stations and provide overseas communications. **Cellular phones** use special ground stations that cover areas called *cells* to enable users to communicate with others. *Infrared technology* relies on infrared light beams to transmit data.

ADAPTING COMPUTERS TO TELECOMMUNICATIONS MEDIA   Signals sent along a phone line travel in an **analog** fashion—that is, as continuous waves. Computers and their support equipment, however, are **digital** devices that handle data coded into 0s and 1s.

The difference between the highest and lowest frequencies on an analog medium is known as the medium's **bandwidth.** A higher bandwidth allows a medium to support more powerful communications applications. Media speed is often measured in **bits per second (bps),** kbps (thousands of bits per second), or mbps (millions of bits per second).

Messages move between machines either in **parallel transmissions,** in which each bit of a byte follows a different path, or in **serial transmissions,** in which bits of a byte follow one another in series along a single path.

Workstations are usually connected to a network through either a **network interface card (NIC)** or a **modem.** Typically, NICs connect workstations to local networks with dedicated lines, whereas modems connect workstations to wide-area networks with dial-up lines. If you need more bandwidth than you can squeeze out of a modem, your best bet is an **ISDN** line or something beyond.

NETWORK TOPOLOGIES   Telecommunications networks can be classified in terms of their *topologies,* or geometrical patterns. Three common topologies are the **star network,** the **bus network,** and the **ring network.** Network topologies are often combined to aggregate smaller networks into larger ones.

LOCAL NETWORKS   Many organizations build their own **local networks,** which connect devices in a single building or at a single site. Two common types of local networks are local area networks and hierarchical local networks.

Local area networks (LANs) fall into two categories. The first, **client-server LANs,** consist of **server** devices that provide network services to **client** workstations. Services often include access to expensive printers and vast amounts of secondary storage, database access, and computing power. In the second type of LANs, **peer-to-peer LANs,** the user workstations and shared peripherals in the network operate at the same level. The term **intranet** refers to a private LAN that implements the infrastructure and standards of the Internet and World Wide Web.

A **hierarchical local network** consists of a powerful *host* CPU at the top level of the hierarchy and microcomputer workstations or display terminals at lower levels. The workstations or terminals can either **download** data from the host or **upload** data to it.

WIDE AREA NETWORKS   Wide area networks (WANs) are communications networks that span relatively wide geographical areas. Because they tie together so many devices over such long distances, they require a number of special pieces of equipment.

Repeaters amplify signals along a network. **Routers** work in large switched networks like the Internet to pass messages along to their destinations. Devices on two dissimilar networks can communicate with each other if the networks are connected by a **gateway.** Devices on two similar networks can communicate with each other if they are connected by a **bridge.** A **multiplexer** enables two or more low-speed devices to share a high-speed line. A **concentrator** is a multiplexer with a store-and-forward capability.

COMMUNICATIONS PROTOCOLS   A communications **protocol** is a collection of procedures to establish, maintain, and terminate transmissions between devices. Because devices transmit data in so many ways, they collectively employ scores of different protocols.

One type of protocol classifies transmissions in the **simplex, half-duplex,** or **full-duplex** modes.

Serially transmitted data are packaged either **asynchronously** (one byte to a package) or **synchronously** (several bytes to a package). Synchronous transmissions use a timing mechanism to coordinate exchanges of data packets between senders and receivers.

A **parity bit** is tacked on to each byte to ensure that either an odd or an even number of 1-bits is transmitted with every character.

Two major LAN architectures are **Ethernet** and **token ring.** Each of these architectures is specified in a detailed set of protocols. Ethernet LANs commonly use a protocol called *CSMA/CD* to exchange messages, whereas token ring LANs use a protocol called *token passing.*

Like LANs, WANs also conform to particular network architectures. Three such architectures are *SNA, FDDI,* and *TCP/IP.* TCP/IP relies on a procedure known as **packet switching.**

EXERCISES

1. Define the following terms and answer the questions that follow.
   a. E-mail
   b. Voice mail
   c. Fax
   d. Paging

   Which of the four would most effectively transmit a 15-page business report that has several handwritten comments by the boss? Which of the four would most effectively remind a person walking in a park of an important phone call that must be made this afternoon?

2. Fill in the blanks:
   a. Two types of modems are _____ modems and _____ modems.
   b. _____ is the process of transferring a file from a host or server computer to a requesting workstation over a network.
   c. A(n) _____ is a private LAN that uses the standards of the Internet and World Wide Web.
   d. All the bits in a byte follow each other in succession over a single path in _____ transmission.
   e. In _____-duplex transmission, messages may travel in two directions simultaneously.

3. List the types of telecommunications media covered in the chapter. Which is the most appropriate for each of the following situations?
   a. Getting a report from a hard disk on a laptop computer onto a nearby desktop printer without the use of wire
   b. Transmitting data as quickly as possible, regardless of the cost
   c. Establishing contact between two people on the move
   d. Connecting a modem to a wall in the cheapest way possible
   e. Connecting workstations in a LAN

4. Many types of communications software will tell you how long you will spend downloading a particular file. Answer the questions below, assuming that a 10-page document occupies about 35 kilobytes (35,000 bytes) of storage space. Assume also eight bits in a byte, and that each byte is transmitted with an extra parity bit for error checking—in other words, a byte actually takes up nine bits.
   a. How long will a 56 kbps modem take to download 100 pages of information? A 28.8 kbps modem?

   b. How much faster could you complete the transfer in part a over an ISDN line that runs at 128 kbps? Over a 1.54 mbps T1 connection? Over a fiber-optic backbone that runs at 100 mbps?
   c. All of the calculations you have made so far reflect maximum speeds. What real-world conditions would slow the rate of transfer?

5. Identify the three most basic network topologies, and answer the following questions.
   a. Which is most appropriate to link a host mainframe computer with dumb terminals?
   b. Which most commonly uses a token-passing protocol?
   c. On which does Ethernet most commonly run?

6. What terms do the following acronyms represent?
   a. Bps
   b. LAN
   c. ATM
   d. EDI
   e. NIC
   f. CSMA/CD

7. Describe in your own words the functions of each of the following types of equipment.
   a. Router
   b. Repeater
   c. Gateway
   d. Bridge
   e. Concentrator

8. How does CSMA/CD work? How does it differ from token passing?

9. Match each term with the description that fits best.
   a. NIC
   b. Analog
   c. Token passing
   d. Bps
   e. ISDN
   f. Uploading
   _____ A protocol used in a type of LAN
   _____ The process of transferring a file from a local computer to a remote computer over a network
   _____ A digital phone service that offers high-speed transmission over ordinary phone lines
   _____ An add-in board through which a workstation connects to a local network
   _____ A measure of a transmission medium's speed
   _____ The transmission of data as continuous wave patterns

10. Determine whether the following statements are true or false.
   a. Most modems plug into dedicated lines.
   b. Infrared transmission is a wireless transmission technique that works with radio waves.
   c. A ring network connects devices serially in a closed loop.
   d. An intranet is a type of private LAN.
   e. A bridge is an interface that enables two dissimilar networks to communicate.
   f. "Internet" is a contraction of two words: "internal" and "network."
   g. Modem software refers to such products as America Online and Earthlink.
   h. Coaxial cable consists of a center wire inside a conductive, fiber-optic shield.
   i. Microwaves are radio signals.
   j. Peer-to-peer LANs are often smaller networks than client-server LANs.

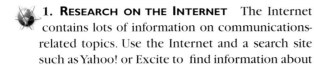

PROJECTS

1. RESEARCH ON THE INTERNET The Internet contains lots of information on communications-related topics. Use the Internet and a search site such as Yahoo! or Excite to find information about any three of the following topics.
Cable modems
Ethernet
Fiber-optic cable
Client-server LANs
Cellular phones
The World Wide Web
Teledesic

Report to the class about the sites you visited and the information that you found at each one.

2. DIGITAL SATELLITES Some exciting new digital satellite services are being pioneered by technologies such as DirecTV (18-inch rooftop dishes that can accept a few hundred television channels with sharp resolution) and DirecPC (digital information downloads from satellite to your PC). What potential do you foresee for these relatively new telecommunications technologies, as television and computing technologies merge together? Can you buy one system that will cater to both TV and PC needs?

3. WIRELESS LANs LANs often use cellular and other types of wireless technologies to link stations. Name three types of applications that work best through wireless LANs, and identify in each case the benefits that result.

4. BECOMING A HIGH ROLLER ONLINE A rapidly growing application on the Internet is personal investing. Users can look up stock prices by computer, maintain lists of their favorite stocks or mutual funds for automatic price quotes, buy and sell stocks and mutual funds online, communicate with other investors about specific companies, access research reports and filings at the Securities and Exchange Commission (SEC), and so on. For this exercise:
   a. Write a paper (three to five pages) about resources available on the Web that cater to ordinary people who want to invest money. Some of the sites listed in the accompanying figure will help get you started.
   b. What, in your opinion, are the three biggest advantages of the Internet for the small investor?

5. LANs Evaluate a client-server LAN on your campus or at a local business, and answer the following questions.
   a. Does the LAN use Ethernet, token ring, or some other LAN architecture?
   b. How many workstations are connected to the LAN?
   c. Identify the servers on the network, and tell what each one does.
   d. How fast can data travel through the LAN?

6. RESEARCH REVISITED A textbook of this sort cannot possibly cover every emerging communications technology. The following list identifies several technologies that have received a lot of attention in the computer press in recent years. For any three of these, explain what the technologies do and their significance.

a. PCS (personal communciations services)
b. GPS (global positioning system)
c. ARCnet
d. Thin clients
e. Baud rate
f. Http (hypertext transfer protocol)

 7. **ISDN** Many telecommunications-industry experts think that ISDN is the next step for residential customers who need more speed than a conventional modem can give them. All of the Baby Bells offer ISDN service, and so do many commercial online services and Internet service providers. Contact your local phone company, and find out the price to install an ISDN line in your home. Be sure to check the following items:

a. Installation charge for 128 kbps service
b. Monthly flat rate to maintain the line
c. Per-minute or per-call charges

Also figure in the cost of an ISDN adapter. Do the installation and monthly maintenance charges cover this cost? Can you buy and install your own to save money?

8. **EXTRANETS** Find an example of an extranet reported in a magazine or newspaper, and report to the class about it. Be sure to cover such details as the name of the company that runs the extranet, the types of users and applications involved, and the method by which unauthorized users are blocked out.

9. **BYTES AND PARITY** Answer the following questions about byte representations of data.

a. Given the following ASCII character representations and the specified parity settings, indicate whether a 0 or 1 should be added to the end of the character:

BYTE REPRESENTATION	PARITY	0 OR 1?
00110101	even	_____
01011010	odd	_____
01001001	odd	_____
00110000	odd	_____
01000001	even	_____

b. What five characters do the bytes in the table represent?
c. You receive the following stream of bits in ASCII. Is odd or even parity in use? What does the message say?

0101011101001111010101111

10. **GLOBAL POSITIONING SYSTEMS** Global positioning systems (GPSs) involve the use of small computing devices combined with special satellites—24 of them that orbit the earth at a height of 10,900 miles. With such a device tucked into a backpack, hikers can retrieve satellite data that tell them their position on Earth within a few feet. GPS devices can also be used in conjunction with maps, by drivers of rental cars, to tell them exactly where they are at any given moment. Using the Internet or other research tools, determine as many uses as you can for GPSs.

INTERACTIVE EXERCISE

CONNECTING YOUR PC TO A NETWORK

Your work PC is to be connected to the company network. Go to the Interactive Exercise at www.harcourtcollege.com/infosys/pcc2e/student/exercise/ to complete this exercise.

ONLINE REVIEW

Go to the Online Review at www.harcourtcollege.com/infosys/pcc2e/student/ to test your understanding of this chapter's concepts.

OUTLINE

Overview
Evolution of the Internet
    From the ARPANET to the World Wide Web
    The Internet Community Today
    Myths about the Internet
What Does the Internet Have to Offer?
    E-Mail
    Information Retrieval and the World Wide Web
    Mailing Lists
    Newsgroups
    Chat
    Online Shopping
Internet Addresses
Desktop Tools for Accessing the Internet
    Browsers and Plug-In Packages
    Search Engines
    Hardware Considerations
Connecting to the Internet
    About Service Providers
    Selecting a Provider
    Setting Up Your System
PC Miniguide: Online Research

INTRODUCTION TO THE INTERNET AND WORLD WIDE WEB

LEARNING OBJECTIVES

After completing this chapter, you will be able to:

1. Discuss how the Internet has evolved to become what it is today.

2. Identify the resources available on the Internet and explain the particular prominence of the World Wide Web.

3. Explain how the Internet benefits individuals and businesses.

4. Name a variety of tools available for working on the Internet.

5. List and evaluate the available options for connecting to the Internet.

OVERVIEW

It's hard to believe that, before 1990, few people outside of the computer industry and academia had ever heard of the Internet. It's a small wonder, though. Hardware, software, and communications tools were not available back then to unleash the power of this tool, to make it the compelling resource it is today.

What a difference a few years make. Today, *Internet* is a household word, and, in many ways, it has redefined how people think about computers and communications. Not since the early 1980s, when **PCs** first swept into homes and businesses, has the general public been so excited about a new technology.

Despite the popularity of the Internet, however, many users cannot answer basic questions about it. What makes up the Internet? Is it the same thing as the World Wide Web? How did the Internet begin, and where is it heading? What types of tools are available to help people make optimum use of the Internet? This chapter addresses such questions.

Chapter 5 begins with a discussion of the evolution of the Internet, from the late 1960s up to the present time. Then it looks into the many resources that the Internet offers—such as e-mail and the World Wide Web—and how individuals and businesses are using the Internet in their work and leisure time. Next, so that you can appreciate how the Internet's content arrives at your desktop, the chapter covers how Internet addresses work. Then, it's on to the software and hardware resources required for access. The final section of the chapter covers connecting to the Internet. Here you will learn about types of organizations that provide Internet links and how to select among them. The **PC Miniguide** foldout within the chapter addresses doing research over the Internet.

EVOLUTION OF THE INTERNET

The **Internet** is a worldwide collection of networks that supports personal and commercial communications and information exchange. It consists of thousands of separate networks that are interconnected and accessed daily by millions of people. Just as the shipping industry has simplified transportation by providing standard containers for carrying all sorts of merchandise via air, rail, highway, and sea, the Internet furnishes a standard way of sending messages across many types of computer platforms and transmission media. While *Internet* has become a household word during the last few years, it has actually operated in one form or another for decades.

For a tutorial on what the Internet and World Wide Web are, go to www. harcourtcollege.com/infosys/ pcc2e/student/tutor/ and click on Chapter 5.

FROM THE ARPANET TO THE WORLD WIDE WEB

The Internet began in 1969 as an experimental project. The U.S. Department of Defense (DOD) wanted to develop a network that could withstand outages, such as those caused by nuclear attack. A principal goal was creating a system that could send messages along alternate paths if a part of the network was disabled. With this purpose in mind, the DOD enlisted researchers in colleges and universities to assist with the development of protocols and message-packeting systems to standardize routing information.

ARPANET   At its start and throughout the first 20 years of its history, the Internet was called **ARPANET** (pronounced *ar-pan-ette*). ARPANET was named for the group that sponsored its development, the Advanced Research Projects Agency (ARPA) of the DOD. During its first few years, ARPANET enabled researchers at a few dozen academic institutions to communicate with one another and with government agencies on topics of mutual interest.

However, the DOD got much more than it bargained for. With the highly controversial Vietnam War in full swing, ARPANET's e-mail facility began to handle not only legitimate research discussions but also heated debates about U.S. involvement in Southeast Asia. As students began to access ARPANET, computer games such as Space War gradually found their way into the roster of applications along with online messaging methods to share game strategies. Such unintended uses led to the development of bulletin boards and discussion groups devoted to other special interests.

As the experiment grew during the next decade, hundreds of colleges and universities tapped into ARPANET. By the 1980s, advances in communications technology enabled many of these institutions to develop their own local networks, as well. These local networks collectively served a mixture of DOS- and Windows-based computers, Apple Macintoshes, UNIX-speaking workstations, and so on. Over the years, ARPANET became a connecting thread of protocols that tied together such disparate networks. Throw in government and private business networks also under development during that time—and add to that the decision to let friendly foreign countries participate—and you can see how ARPANET turned into a massive network of networks.

■ **Internet.** A global network linking thousands of networks and millions of individual users, businesses, schools, and government agencies. ■ **ARPANET.** The forerunner to the Internet, named after the Advanced Research Projects Agency (ARPA), which sponsored its development.

INTERNET RELAY CHAT *Internet relay chat (IRC)* allows people to type messages to others and to get back typed responses in real time (see Figure 5-9). Thus, IRC works like a regular phone call, except that you're typing instead of talking. Two people or several can participate in IRC. Multiperson chats are usually organized around specific topics, and participants often adopt nicknames to maintain anonymity. To participate in IRC, you need a client program that enables you to connect to an IRC server.

IRC takes place in an electronic area called a *chat room.* Chat rooms can be private—that is, reserved only for users who know the proper password to get in—or open to all. A chat room may be run by a service provider like America Online, by a search-engine service such as Yahoo! or Excite, by a community of users with a shared interest, or by virtually anyone else with software and an Internet connection capable of hosting online meetings. While most chat rooms are free, some—such as those where you get to mingle with high-priced business consultants—cost money.

OTHER TYPES OF CHAT Various other, more sophisticated types of chat exist. Several of these are discussed below.

3-D VIRTUAL CHAT This type of chat is a graphical extension of IRC. It enables you to take on the persona of a 3-D character who appears on the screen. In the chat, you mingle with other people having their own onscreen personae. The personae of the chat participants can be seen on the display moving about and interacting in a virtual chat room. To use this feature, you need special 3-D chat software, a speedy computer, and a fast Internet connection.

INSTANT MESSAGING Instant messaging is a cross between the IRC chat room and e-mail. It began around 1996, when America Online popularized buddy lists. A *buddy list* contains the names of your friends and associates; a small window pops up on your screen from your ISP telling you when they're online. At that time, you can invoke *instant messaging* by sending any of them a message that immediately appears on their screen. The receiver can respond in kind, sending an instant message back to you. All of the back and forth communications appear in an onscreen window; thus, the feature works like a two-person chat room. Instant messaging is faster than e-mail because the latter is stored on a server that may not make messages immediately available to recipients.

INTERNET TELEPHONY Sometimes called *voice chat,* this form of chat lets two or more people speak to each other as they would on the phone. The call is routed over the Internet, however, instead of through the regular phone system. There are many varieties of voice chat. At the low end are systems that use half-duplex cards and programs that enable only one person to speak at a time; participants use headsets attached to their computers. At the high end are sophisticated commercial services with fiber-optic lines that enable peo-

---

IRC Chat

<Knuckles> Do you think that the Cubs will ever win a World Series in our lifetimes?

<Rug Rat> Depends on how many decades you plan to live.

<K-Man> Hey, watch what you say about my team. I'm from Chicago.

<Rosie> At least you got your thrill with the Bulls. It'll be a long time before we have a championship pro team here in Phoenix.

<Rug Rat> I'll take the weather you have in the Southwest over a championship, any day.

<Knuckles> So would I. It's only September 3rd and it's freezing here in my part of the world.

<K-Man> Where are you from, Knuckles?

FIGURE 5-9

Internet relay chat (IRC). IRC is like a regular phone call, except that you type instead of talk.

ple to converse over their regular phones. Many industry experts believe that, in the future, all phone calls will be routed like Internet messages.

Like other Internet services, virtually all forms of chat—the exception being high-end Internet telephony—do not involve incurring separate long-distance phone charges. Research has shown that people spend more time at Web sites when they have a chat feature and are more likely to visit again in the future.

ONLINE SHOPPING

In a growing use of the Internet, people have begun to shop online. You can buy products directly from large companies—like Lands' End, L. L. Bean, Dell Computer, Wal-Mart, and Microsoft—at their Web sites, or you can shop at the Web sites of electronic malls (called *e-malls*), where thousands of smaller companies collectively display their wares.

Electronic catalogs on the Web show you color graphics of products. Search tools may help you to locate the product you desire without excessive browsing. If you want to buy a computer, you may be able to configure your system online so that it precisely meets your needs. If you want software, there's a good chance that you'll be able to download a copy of it.

While many businesses have engaged in electronic commerce for years, online shopping by consumers is a relatively new phenomenon. It's also beginning to take off in a big way. Online shopping benefits both businesses and consumers, because businesses don't need salespeople to sell online, and some of the savings in labor costs can be passed on to consumers. Today, the most popular online-shopping categories are PC hardware, travel, entertainment products such as books and music, and flowers and gifts. While most online shopping takes place the same way that shopping does in the physical world, the Internet has made possible an exciting new twist to buying— the cyberauction. *Cyberauctions* enable people to electronically place bids on goods and services from their home PCs, in the hope of snaring a bargain (see Figure 5-10).

One of the major obstacles to electronic commerce so far is consumer concern for *security.* Many customers feel uncomfortable paying by credit card over the Internet, where cyberthieves lurk. To counter this, many commercial

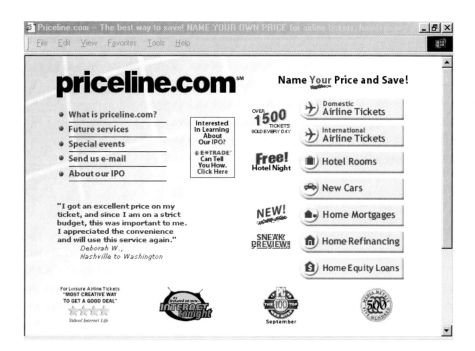

FIGURE 5-10

Electronic commerce. At Web sites like Priceline.com, electronic shoppers can place bids on such items as plane tickets, hotel rooms, rental cars, and mortgage rates.

Web sites also contain toll-free phone numbers that shoppers can use to place orders. Another concern is *privacy*—consumers would rather browse the Web without letting merchants know who they are, but merchants feel that they could do a much better and more pleasant job of selling if they knew the identities and tastes of their customers.

INTERNET ADDRESSES

An **Internet address** performs the same function as a residential or business address in everyday life. It tells where to locate something on the Internet— a particular person, Web site or Web page. Addresses on the Internet are unique; each one is assigned to one and only one person or resource.

MAILBOX ADDRESSES People are most often located on the Internet through their e-mail addresses. An individual's e-mail address usually consists of a user- name (a set of characters, unique to accounts on that person's mail server, assigned to the individual's mailbox) followed by the @ symbol, followed by the mail server's **domain name.** For instance,

mjordan@harcourt.com

tarzan@harcourt.com

are the e-mail addresses of two hypothetical mailboxes at Harcourt College Publishers, the publisher of this textbook, respectively assigned to mjordan and tarzan. The characters "harcourt.com" state the name of Harcourt's server computer. People with e-mail addresses can be reached via private networks or over the Internet.

Note that domain names—and the server computers they represent—func- tion like apartment buildings in everyday life. Each apartment building's address is unique to the mail system, but several individuals may have mail- boxes at the building address.

The set of three letters that generally appears as the rightmost part of a domain name is called the *root domain.* Root domains—such as *com* (for *commercial*), *edu* (for *education*), *gov* (for *government*), and *mil* (for *mili- tary*)—indicate the type of of organization that the domain name represents. Two symbols occasionally follow or replace the root domain to indicate the country of origin. For instance, the domain name:

www.fs.fed.us

suggests a government computer in the United States—the one at the USDA Forest Service.

For a tutorial about access- ing Web pages using Internet addresses, and hyperlinks, go to www.harcourtcollege.com/ infosys/pcc2e/student/tutor/ and click on Chapter 5.

ADDRESSES FOR WORLD WIDE WEB PAGES Web pages and links to infor- mation at Gopher, FTP, and other sites are most commonly located on the Inter- net through **uniform resource locators,** or **URLs** (see Figure 5-11). Every Web page has its own unique URL (sometimes pronounced "earl"). If you know a page's URL, type it in the specified area of your Web browser's screen, and the page will be displayed.

Web-site URLs often contain the three letters *www* preceded by the *pro- tocol identifier* http:// (for *hypertext transfer protocol*). For instance, the Web

---

■ **Internet address.** A unique identifier assigned to a specific location on the Internet, such as a host computer, Web site, or user mailbox. ■ **Domain name.** An ordered group of symbols, separated by periods, that identifies an Internet server. ■ **Uniform resource locator (URL).** A unique identifier representing the location of a specific Web page on the Internet.

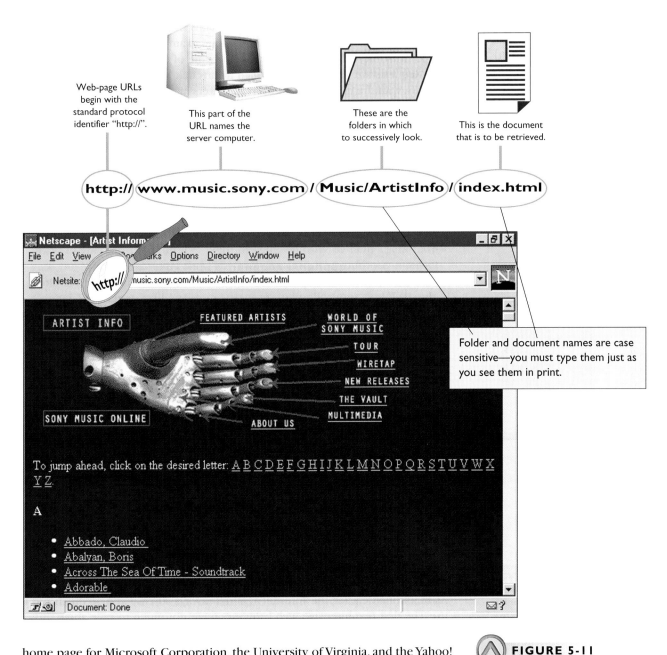

Web-page URLs begin with the standard protocol identifier "http://".

This part of the URL names the server computer.

These are the folders in which to successively look.

This is the document that is to be retrieved.

http:// www.music.sony.com / Music/ArtistInfo / index.html

Folder and document names are case sensitive—you must type them just as you see them in print.

FIGURE 5-11
How URLs work.

home page for Microsoft Corporation, the University of Virginia, and the Yahoo! search site, respectively, have the following URLs:

```
http://www.microsoft.com
http://www.virginia.edu
http://www.yahoo.com
```

The set of symbols after the double slashes—for instance, "www.microsoft.com"—identifies a server by its computer name and domain name.

Often, URLs contain more specific types of information. For instance, the URL

```
http://www.music.sony.com/Music/ArtistInfo/index.html
```

identifies the music section of Sony Corporation's Web site. To the right of the computer and domain name (www.music.sony.com), the URL identifies a sequence of two *folders* (Music and ArtistInfo) that you must open in order to find the specific *document* (index.html). In many contexts, folders are referred to as *directories,* a set of folders is referred to as a *directory path,* and documents are referred to as *files.*

FIGURE 5-20

Adobe Acrobat. Acrobat enables your browser to display a document in a format very similar to the way it appears in print.

If history is a good indicator of the future, expect the next generation of browsers to incorporate many of the best features from the current crop of plug-in and helper programs. What's more, operating systems and software suites are rapidly gaining browser features themselves. The latter trend has led many people to predict that browsers as we know them today may become extinct in a few years, their functions absorbed into other software packages.

SEARCH ENGINES

For a tutorial on searching the Web, go to www. harcourtcollege.com/infosys/ pcc2e/student/tutor/ and click on Chapter 5.

While casual surfing is a popular Web pastime, people often turn to the Internet to find specific types of information as well. When you know generally what you want but don't know at which URL to find it, one of your best options is a search engine. A **search engine** is a software facility that often resembles both a table of contents and an index, with the full power of a computer behind them to electronically locate Web pages on specific topics and make it easy for you to retrieve them.

USING A WEB-RESIDENT ENGINE   You can use many of the best search engines—such as **Yahoo!,** Excite, Lycos, and Alta Vista—free of charge by accessing their Web sites. Once you locate and enter a site (see the PC Mini-guide foldout within the chapter for several addresses), you can perform two types of search operations: (1) selecting successive hyperlinks from categories displayed on the screen or (2) typing in a search string that represents a relevant keyword before you begin selecting hyperlinks (see Figure 5-22).

In the first type of search operation—doing a category search—you will first be presented with several categories on the screen. Then, after you select a hyperlink, you will next see a screen showing a finer breakdown of choices. Eventually, after making choice after choice on a sequence of such screens, you should arrive at an appropriate Web page.

■ **Search engine.** A software tool used to look for specific information over the Internet. ■ **Yahoo!** A widely used search engine.

Package	Vendor	Description
Acrobat	Adobe Systems	Displays documents similar to the way they appear in print
Broadway	Data Translation	Lets you view MPEG videos from your browser
Carbon Copy	Software Publishing	Lets you direct Internet outputs to a computer other than your own
Flash	Macromedia	Used by Web-page authors to create navigational interfaces, animations, and illustrations
Live3D	Netscape	Lets you enjoy virtual-reality worlds
NetMeeting	Microsoft	Adds Internet/intranet telephony, a whiteboard and shared clipboard, a chat area, and the ability to share Microsoft Office applications in a conference
NetShow	Microsoft	Lets you add audio- and video-streaming capabilities to your browser
Pronto96	CommTouch Software	Lets you handle voice messages as e-mail attachments
Quicktime	Apple	Lets you view Quicktime videos from your browser
RealAudio	RealNetworks	Provides realtime audio and FM-quality sound to your browser
RealPlayer	RealNetworks	Lets you add audio- and video-streaming capabilities to your browser
Shockwave	Macromedia	Lets you receive multimedia Web pages
Sizzler	Totally Hip	Enhances your browsing experience with animation
VR Scout	Chaco Communications	Lets you enjoy virtual-reality worlds

FIGURE 5-21

Browser plug-ins.

To understand the second type of search—inputting a search string—let's say you need to find the text of one of the articles of the U.S. Constitution, and you do not see an associated link on the list of categories. You would type *Constitution* into the area of the screen that's specifically provided to enter search strings. Clicking the Search button will retrieve a list of Web pages concerning the Constitution; it may also display some matching categories. By clicking on Web page or category links, you will eventually wind up with a page containing the text of the Constitution.

Specifying strings enables you to do *boolean searches*—that is, searching on multiple keywords using the conditional operators AND, OR, and NOT. For instance, if you wanted a search engine to find all documents that covered *both* the Intel and AMD microprocessor manufacturers, you might specify your request to an engine supporting boolean searches as *Intel AND AMD*. If, instead, you wanted documents that discussed *either* (or both) of these companies, the request *Intel OR AMD* would be your entry. On the other hand, if you wanted documents about microprocessors that are cataloged with no mention of Intel, *microprocessors NOT Intel* is what you would type in the search text box. Every search engine has its own way of letting you do a boolean search, so you should check out the preferred style before conducting one. The chapter foldout looks further at boolean searching as well as other power-searching techniques.

SEARCH DATABASES   At the core of a search engine is a database that resembles a huge index. Typically, the database contains millions of pieces of information about Internet sites throughout the world. When you select a hyperlink or type in a search string, the search engine consults its index to find all URLs that match up to that word. It then provides results of the search within seconds.

Search engines differ in their comprehensiveness. Some, such as Alta Vista, search deeper than others and will produce matches even to obscure references.

DOING A CATEGORY SEARCH

As each menu comes up, you make a selection from it. As you do this, the search progressively narrows until, eventually, you access a specific Web site.

FIGURE 5-22

Using a search engine. Most search engines—such as Yahoo! and Excite—enable you to search either by selecting from menus of categories (left) or by typing search strings (right).

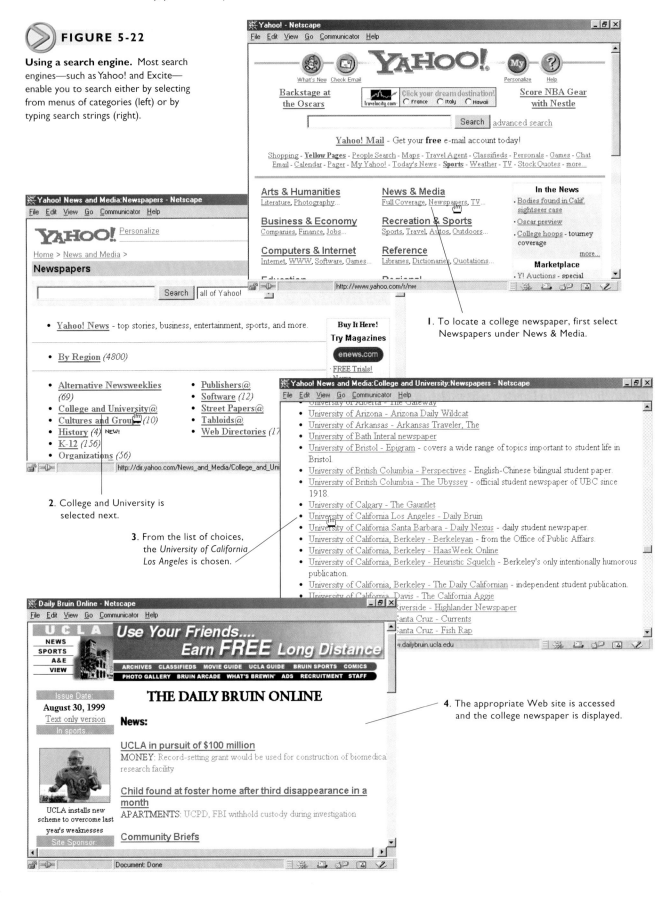

Blockbuster Web Sites for Online Research

IPL Reading Room Newspapers - Netscape
File Edit View Go Communicator Help

the Internet Public Library

Online Newspapers

Africa
Egypt | Ethiopia | Kenya | Madagascar | Mauritius | Morocco | Namibia | Rep
Island | South Africa | Swaziland | Tanzania | Uganda | Zambia | Zimbabwe |

Asia
Bangladesh | Bhutan | China | India | Indonesia | Japan | Laos | Macau | Mala
Korea | Pakistan | Philippines | Singapore | South Korea | Sri Lanka | Taiwan

Caribbean
Aruba | Bahamas | Barbados | Bermuda | Dominican Republic | Grenada | Hai
Antilles | Puerto Rico | Trinidad and Tobago | Virgin Islands |

Central America
Belize | Costa Rica | El Salvador | Guatemala | Honduras | Nicaragua | Panam

Europe
Austria | Belarus | Belgium | Bosnia | Bulgaria | Croatia | Czech Republic | De

Document: Done

COMPUTER JOURNALS

These sites can help keep you up to date on computer technology. Many of the sites allow you to search back issues for articles, and most are free of charge. To locate more journals, or updated addresses if these sites have moved, type "computer magazines" or "computer journals" in a search site or search for a particular magazine, such as "PC World".

SITE	WEB ADDRESS
Byte Online	www.byte.com
Computerworld	www.computerworld.com
Corel Magazine	www.corelmag.com
Family PC	www.familypc.zdnet.com
HotWired	www.hotwired.com
InterActivity Magazine	www.eyemedia.com
InternetWeek	www.internetwk.com
MacWEEK.com	macweek.zdnet.com
Macworld Online	macworld.zdnet.com
PC Computing Online	www.zdnet.com/pccomp
PC Magazine Online	www.zdnet.com/pcmag
PC Week Online	www.zdnet.com/pcweek
PC World Online	www.pcworld.com
Presentations.com	www.presentations.com
TechShopper	www.techweb.com/shopper
Windows Magazine	www.winmag.com
Yahoo! Internet Life	www.zdnet.com/yil
ZDNet	www.zdnet.com

NEWS SITES

These sites contain up-to-date news about c business news, and/or national news.

SITE	WEB AD
ABC News.com	www.abc.
Business Wire	www.busi
CBS.com	www.cbs.
CMPnet	www.cmp
CNet	home.cne
CNN.com	www.cnn.
Forbes.com	www.forb
Information Week	www.info
The Los Angeles Times	www.latir
MSNBC	www.msr
The New York Times	www.nyti
USA Today	www.usat
The Washington Post	www.was

✔ **TRY THIS**
Go to an electronic library site—such as www.ipl.org—
news directory site—such as www.newsdirectory.com—
links to scores of electronic magazines and newspapers.

OTHER RESEARCH-ORIENTED WEB SITES

BIOGRAPHIES

Biography.com	www.biography.com

BOOKSTORES

Amazon.com	www.amazon.com
Borders.com	www.borders.com
Barnes & Noble.com	www.barnesandnoble.com
Fatbrain.com	fatbrain.com

OPEN

Sites of hardware manufacturers, software publishers, and resellers can provide information about computer products. The hardware manufacturer and software publisher sites are useful for obtaining product specifications, as well as to buy products online. The reseller sites can be used to compare prices and buy products online.

SITE	COMPANY DESCRIPTION	WEB ADDRESS
Adobe Systems	Software publisher	www.adobe.com
Apple Computer	Diversified manufacturer	www.apple.com
Beyond.com	Software reseller	www.beyond.com
Buycomp.com	Hardware reseller	www.buy.com/comp
Buysoft.com	Software reseller	www.buy.com/soft
Canon	Diversified manufacturer	www.canon.com
Compaq	Computer manufacturer	www.compaq.com
Computer Discount Warehouse	Reseller	www.cdw.com
Corel	Software publisher	www.corel.com
Dell Computer	Computer manufacturer	www.dell.com
Egghead.com	Reseller	www.egghead.com
Gateway	Computer manufacturer	www.gw2k.com
Hewlett-Packard	Diversified manufacturer	www.hp.com
IBM	Diversified manufacturer	www.ibm.com
Insight	Reseller	www.insight.com
Intel	Computer chip manufacturer	www.intel.com
Iomega	Storage products manufacturer	www.iomega.com
Lotus	Software publisher	www.lotus.com
Microsoft	Software publisher	www.microsoft.com
Oracle	Software publisher	www.oracle.com
Outpost.com	Reseller	www.outpost.com
Seagate	Storage products manufacturer	www.seagate.com
SGI	High-end workstations manufacturer	www.sgi.com
Sony	Diversified manufacturer	www.sony.com

DICTIONARIES, THESAURUSES, ETC.

Bartlett's Familiar Quotations	www.bartleby.com/99
Net Dictionary	www.netdictionary.com
NetLingo	www.netlingo.com
Onelook Dictionaries	www.onelook.com
Thesaurus.com	www.thesaurus.com
WWWebster Dictionary	www.m-w.com/netdict.htm

JOB HUNTING

CareerBuilder	www.careerbuilder.com
CareerMosaic	www.careermosaic.com
CareerPath.com	new.careerpath.com
JobOptions	www.joboptions.com
Jobtrak.com	www.jobtrak.com
Monster.com	www.monster.com
Overseas Jobs Express	www.overseasjobs.co.uk

NEWSGROUPS

Delphi Forums	www.delphi.com
Liszt's Usenet Newsgroups Directory	www.liszt.com/news

PEOPLE AND BUSINESS SEARCHES
(e-mail addresses, phone numbers, etc.)

AnyWho's Directories	www.tollfree.att.net/index.html
BigBook	www.bigbook.com
Bigfoot	www.bigfoot.com
BigYellow	www.bigyellow.com
InfoSpace.com	www.infospace.com
Internet Address Finder	www.iaf.net
Switchboard	www.switchboard.com
Yahoo! People Search	people.yahoo.com

Most people hunting for an ISP have two choices, going with a large, national provider or with a small, local outfit. Some prominent examples of large providers are America Online (AOL), the Microsoft Network (MSN), CompuServe, Prodigy, and EarthLink. An example of a small provider is the Route 66 service out of Albuquerque, New Mexico, whose users are mostly local residents. Typically, rates are comparable between large and small ISPs—between $15 and $25 per month. Often other considerations play heavily in the ISP selection decision. In the next section, we will cover many of these.

Internet access is also being increasingly provided by many deregulated companies in the telephone and television industries. Telephone companies like AT&T (via WorldNet) and television-service providers like DirecTV (via DirecPC) are current players in the ISP arena. Based on the growing success of AT&T's WorldNet, many industry observers are predicting that large national firms like AOL, Earthlink, and other companies will come to dominate the ISP business within the next few years.

Besides the sources already named, you can connect to the Internet in several other ways. For instance, many colleges and universities—and also thousands of companies—are plugged in. Consequently, if you are a student or an employee affiliated with one of these organizations, you may be able to access the Internet through that connection for free. Many libraries also offer their members free access to the Internet. An additional option is a visit to a cyber-café, a coffeehouse with computers for patrons to surf the Internet, or a copy store or other business that offers computer access charged by the minute or hour.

Two popular ways of connecting with an ISP are with SLIP and PPP accounts. A **SLIP** connection (for *serial line Internet protocol)* is the oldest and least expensive method. However, SLIP does not check to see that information arrives to you error free. **PPP** service (for *point-to-point protocol)* checks for errors and also provides better security. Both SLIP and PPP are versions of the **TCP/IP** protocol, a collection of communications protocols that allow PCs accessing the Internet to understand each other and exchange data.

SELECTING A PROVIDER

Many people evaluate service providers with respect to a number of criteria—including those listed here—before making their selections.

OFFERINGS One of the most important steps in choosing an ISP is figuring out what you're getting. ISPs typically differ with respect to access, services, and software.

For instance, not all ISPs will give you full view to all parts of the Internet. On the Web, some ISPs may block access to certain Web sites. Also, not all providers will let you upload files to FTP sites. Consequently, it's important to be prepared ahead of time with a lot of specific questions that help you determine how restricted your Internet usage may be. The smaller providers generally will be able to better customize your access to the Internet.

Subscriber services can also vary dramatically among ISPs. For example, not all ISPs support instant messaging, buddy lists, and e-mail filtering. What's more, many of the large ISPs offer proprietary information and host special events to draw subscribers. You may be offered, say, a free subscription to the *New York Times* Web site, which nonsubscribers have to pay to see. You may also get a chance to engage in online chats with celebrities from time to time.

■ **SLIP.** A version of TCP/IP that enables individuals and organizations to connect to the Internet over ordinary phone lines. ■ **PPP.** A protocol that resembles SLIP but allows more reliable and secure communications. ■ **TCP/IP.** A collection of communications protocols through which PCs accessing the Internet can understand each other and exchange data.

Some ISPs also provide booklets and regular newsletters to their subscribers, thus keeping them educated and informed about useful and new features.

Finally, you will need to check on the software being offered by a prospective ISP. Is free software part of the deal? And if so, are certain brands of software mandated for e-mail, newsreading, FTP uploads and downloads, and Web authoring? Not all software is equal. For instance, the e-mail package you are being given may not support attachments. What's more, this e-mail program may not even be widely used and, consequently, may require extra effort on your part if you have questions on its operation. Also be sure to check the size of your mailbox. Will it be large enough to support the types of data you will be receiving?

ACCESS SPEEDS   An important consideration centers on how fast the service works. While the speed of your Internet application depends in part on the speed of your modem, it also depends on how fast the provider's line moves data to you. A provider offering 56 kbps lines speeds data along to you twice as quickly as a provider offering only 28.8 kbps lines. If you are connecting from a large town or from a business site, you may be able to take advantage of an ISDN or a high-speed T1 line.

SERVICE AND SUPPORT   One of the most important service-related issues is reaching help when you need it. Try calling at 7 P.M. on a Saturday or at 11 P.M. on a weekday. Does anyone answer? Some understaffed providers have earned unsavory reputations for letting users linger on the line half an hour or more and for not returning phone calls or e-mails promptly. The quality of support help is important, too. You want to talk to people who can solve your problems.

Establishing a connection through your provider can also be troublesome at times. Before signing up, ask the provider about the average number of people it has assigned to each modem or line. If that ratio exceeds 15:1, you may wind up too often getting a busy signal when you're trying to connect. A ratio of 10:1 is far more satisfactory. On a related note, look into how often and for how long the provider has had to cut users off from its system due to technical difficulties.

Many people connecting to the Internet as users will eventually want to develop Web pages of their own. If you think that you may become a Web author some day, ask providers what types of support they offer in this area and the cost of such support. Many providers will furnish Web-authoring tools and advice. They will also host a home page for you—and possibly several other pages up to a certain total file size—for free or for a nominal cost.

EASE OF USE   At the least, the service you select should be easy enough to use so that you aren't spending too much time seeking technical assistance. The browser and other packages the service provides should have friendly interfaces and possess features that make sense for your needs.

For links to further information about Internet service providers, go to www.harcourtcollege.com/infosys/pcc2e/student/explore/ and click Chapter 5.

COST   For most people, the bottom line in choosing a provider is what they have to shell out to get on board. Today, most people are on flat-rate plans where they get unlimited hours of **connect time.** Connect time is the amount of time their computer has online Internet access through the provider. Most ISPs charge between $15 and $25 per month. In some cases—and this mostly applies to small, local ISPs—you will also be charged a one-time fee to set up your account, say, $25. Many of the large, national providers offer a free month or a set number of free hours of access to get people to sign on with them.

Some ISPs may also offer variable-rate plans, targeted to subscribers whose Internet usage is relatively modest. For example, $10 per month may entitle you to 15 hours of connect time. If you exceed this usage, you may be billed a $1- to $3-per-hour surcharge for every hour above the basic amount.

You must also consider in your cost evaluation the price of calling up an ISP on a regular basis, to get connected to the Internet. Virtually all providers

■ **Connect time.** The amount of time you spend online with a service provider's computers.

have local phone number that subscribers can dial into so that they won't be billed for long-distance calls. However, not every provider has every geographical area covered with a local phone number. What's more, even though an ISP has a local access number, it might not be equipped with a particularly fast line. So, for instance, that $14.95 monthly rate you're being offered by an ISP might not look so great if you're regularly calling from Santa Fe, New Mexico, with a 56 kpsp modem and the nearest access point is a 28.8 kbps line operated out of Colorado Springs, Colorado.

SETTING UP YOUR SYSTEM

The specific steps that you must follow to connect to the Internet depend on the service provider you choose. Many will supply you with a *startup kit* with installation software stored on a CD-ROM or diskette. All you generally have to do is follow the directions on the disk to begin running the startup program. After the program takes over, it will supply screens that tell you at each step of the way what to do next. In some cases, you won't have to ask for a startup disk at all. Your operating system's opening screens may already display a *setup icon* for your provider. If this is the case, select the icon, and follow the instructions on the screen. Smaller, local providers may just require a Web browser and phone dialing software, and will supply you with instructions on how to set them up properly.

Figure 5-23 shows how getting set up with a service provider is done, by illustrating some of the steps you would actually take to connect to America

FIGURE 5-23

Getting set up with America Online. You can get set up with many national ISPs in a few minutes by supplying information on a series of simple screens.

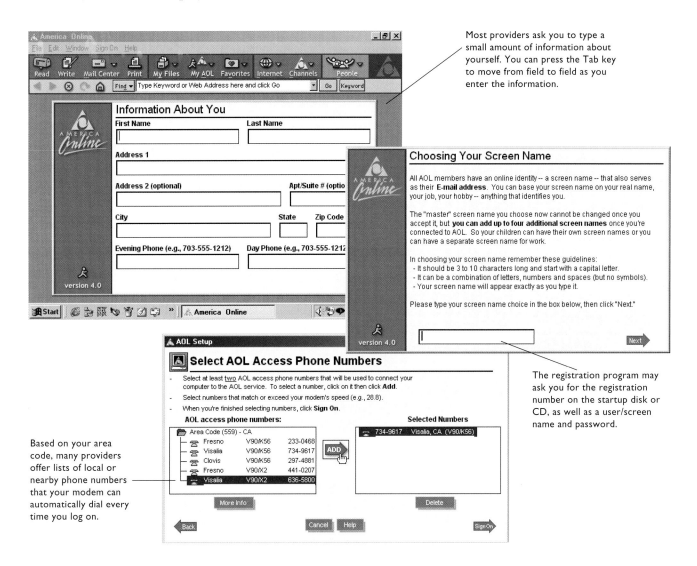

Online (AOL). You would follow very similar setup procedures for other providers. For any of them, you would need to supply identifying information about yourself, select a plan, choose a method of payment, and provide such connect data as your modem speed and home phone number if your computer system can't automatically figure out such information. Connecting to a small, local ISP may involve more steps and complexity, requiring you to select specific protocols and server settings.

After you set up your connection to the provider, you are ready to go. During the setup process, an *access icon* will usually be placed on one of your operating system's opening screens. Every time you turn on your computer system, you can connect to the provider simply by selecting the access icon and logging on. Then, it's just a matter of following directions on the screen to reach the Internet (see Figure 5-24).

FIGURE 5-24

Accessing the Web with America Online (AOL).

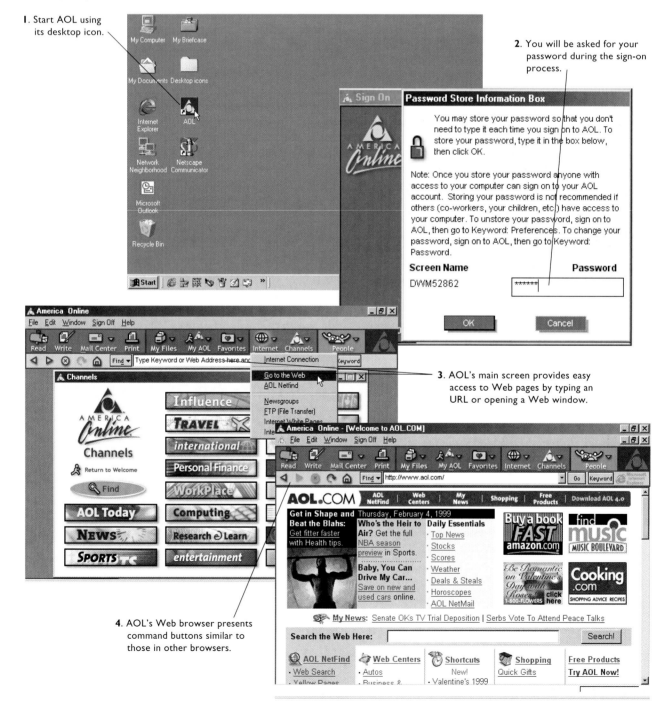

1. Start AOL using its desktop icon.

2. You will be asked for your password during the sign-on process.

3. AOL's main screen provides easy access to Web pages by typing an URL or opening a Web window.

4. AOL's Web browser presents command buttons similar to those in other browsers.

SUMMARY AND KEY TERMS

Go to the Online Glossary at www.harcourtcollege.com/infosys/pcc2e/student/ to review key terms.

Internet has become a household word. In many ways, the Internet has redefined how people think about PCs and communications.

EVOLUTION OF THE INTERNET The **Internet**—a worldwide phenomenon that consists of thousands of linked networks that are accessed by millions of people daily—dates back to the late 1960s. At its start and throughout the first 20 years of its history, the Internet was called the **ARPANET.** It was not until the development of graphical user interfaces and the World Wide Web that public interest in the Internet began to soar.

The Internet community is made up of individuals, companies such as **Internet service providers (ISPs)** and **Internet content providers,** and many other types of organizations. Virtually anyone with a computer that can communicate can be part of the Internet, either as a user or supplier of information or services.

Because the Internet is so unique in the history of the world—and it remains a relatively new phenomenon—several widespread myths about it have surfaced. Three such myths are that the Internet is free, that it is controlled by some central force, and that it is equivalent to the World Wide Web.

WHAT DOES THE INTERNET HAVE TO OFFER? The Internet is home to many features.

Electronic mail, or **e-mail,** was one of the first applications to appear on the Internet, and it is still the most widely used feature.

The **World Wide Web (WWW),** or *Web,* is the feature most people talk about; it is used for *information retrieval.* Information is organized into chunks called *Web pages,* which are connected by **hyperlinks**—indicated onscreen by boldfaced and underlined text or by selectable icons or other images. When a content provider creates one or more Web pages that relate to a specific topic or business, the result is called a **Web site.** A Web site contains anywhere from one to hundreds or thousands of pages, with the starting page of the site called a **home page.** Web sites are hosted at computers called **Web servers.**

The Web is one of many information-retrieval tools on the Internet. **Gopher** is another; it generates hierarchical, text-intensive menus that allow users to access resources by making successive selections with an onscreen pointer. **FTP** sites are good places to visit to get free copies of programs and files. FTP stands for **file transfer protocol,** the procedure that facilitates transfers of files between an FTP server and users' computers. **Telnet** is a protocol that lets a desktop workstation behave like a dumb terminal to a remote server.

A **mailing list** is a discussion group that uses e-mail to communicate. Hundreds of mailing lists on the Internet cover a variety of subjects.

Members of **newsgroups** also share e-mail messages, but with a format somewhat like an electronic newspaper. **UseNet** is the protocol that describes how newsgroup messages are handled between computers. A special etiquette—referred to as **netiquette**—has evolved on the Internet for those who communicate via newsgroups and other forms of electronic mail. Newcomers to newsgroups should read through those groups' **FAQs,** or lists of **frequently asked questions.**

Chat refers to a facility that enables people to engage in interactive conversations over the Internet. The most common type of chat is Internet relay chat.

In a growing use of the Internet, many people now shop online.

INTERNET ADDRESSES An **Internet address** indicates where something on the Internet can be located. Internet addresses are unique; each one is assigned to one and only one resource or person.

People are most commonly reached on the Internet through their *e-mail addresses.* The part of the address before the @ symbol is the person's username; the part following that symbol is the mail server's **domain name.** Web pages and links to information at Gopher, FTP, and other sites are accessed through **uniform resource locators,** or **URLs.**

DESKTOP TOOLS FOR ACCESSING THE INTERNET A **browser,** or *Web browser,* is a software package that enables you to navigate the World Wide Web as well as other parts of the Internet. The first successful browser was and still is called **Mosaic.** Among a variety of browsers on the market today, the most popular commercial products are **Netscape Navigator** and **Microsoft Internet Explorer.**

Browser software is constantly evolving. Some properties that you may want to consider in a browser include functionality, navigational tools, speed, customizability (including the ability to change your **portal** and to control **cookie** files), framing capabilities, a workgroup-computing facility, support for multimedia and virtual-reality applications, Java and ActiveX support, publishing capabilities, and security. A large market has developed for *plug-in packages* and *helper packages,* both of which enable you to add features and functions to your current browsing environment.

When you know generally what you want, but you don't know at which URL to find it, one of your best options is a **search engine.** One of the most popular search engines is Yahoo!, which can be found on the Web and used for free. You can also purchase auxiliary search software to meet additional searching needs.

A more powerful computer system will more likely give you access to the advanced features of the Internet.

CONNECTING TO THE INTERNET Internet service providers (ISPs) furnish Internet connections. Most people hunting for an ISP have two basic choices, going with a large, national provider or with a small, local outfit. Often, you will connect to an ISP through a **SLIP** or **PPP** account, both of which are variations of the **TCP/IP** protocol.

People often select service providers by considering several criteria. Among their priorities are the information a service provides and other features including price, speed, service and support, and ease of use. Fees usually include set monthly amounts and possibly extra charges for **connect time** in excess of the standard amount.

How you connect to the Internet depends on the provider you have chosen, but it usually involves installing a program and choosing the appropriate options or settings.

EXERCISES

1. Define the following terms.
   a. Home page
   b. The Internet
   c. Domain name
   d. Content provider

2. Describe the purposes of the following Internet services.
   a. World Wide Web
   b. Chat
   c. Newsgroups
   d. FTP
   e. E-mail
   f. Telnet

3. Match each term with the description that fits best.
   a. History-list feature
   b. Streaming capability
   c. Framing capability
   d. Webcasting capability
   e. Web-publishing capability
   f. Cookie feature

   _____ Designed to push information to the user while he or she passively sits by and watches

   _____ Enables sound or video images to begin outputting on a client computer before the associated files are fully downloaded

   _____ Permits a user to customize content on Web pages

   _____ Lets you know what sites you've visited on the Web

   _____ Enables users to see two or more pages on the screen at the same time, each page with its own scroll bars

   _____ Lets users create their own Web pages

4. Determine whether the following statements are true or false.
   a. When the Internet was first developed back in 1969, it was called ORACLE.
   b. One of the most prominent browsers available for the Internet is named Yahoo!
   c. On the Internet, an *access provider* and a *content provider* are essentially the same thing.
   d. FAQ files are designed to inform new users about appropriate netiquette.
   e. If the string "mjordan@chicagobulls.com" exists on the Internet, it is most likely the address of a Web page.
   f. The most widely used feature on the Internet is e-mail.

   g. Gopher was originally developed at Microsoft Corporation.
   h. Requests that are part of a URL are context sensitive.
   i. Many browsing environments support multimedia and virtual reality.
   j. Connect time refers to the amount of time your computer is turned on.

5. Fill in the blanks.
   a. Small programs called Java _____ can provide animation to a Web page.
   b. A(n) _____ feature lets you see a low-resolution image on your Web browser before the computer downloads all of the data needed to display the image at full resolution.
   c. _____ is the name of Microsoft's principal browser, whereas _____ is the name of Netscape's principal browser.
   d. The first page you typically encounter at a visit to a Web site is called the site's _____ page.
   e. Newsgroup submissions are called _____, and replies tacked onto the submissions are known as _____.

6. What terms do the following acronyms represent?
   a. IRC
   b. FTP
   c. WWW
   d. FAQ
   e. URL
   f. HTML
   g. ISP
   h. PPP
   i. AOL
   j. VRML

7. Newsgroups are organized by topic, as indicated by their names; for instance, *rec* stands for *recreation* and *sci* for *science*. Name as many other newsgroup classifications as you can as well as their associated three- or four-letter abbreviations.

8. Participants in such Internet services as newsgroups and mailing lists should follow proper netiquette. Identify at least five rules of netiquette.

9. For each of the situations on the following page, name the Internet service you would probably be using. Choose from e-mail, newsgroups, mailing lists, the World Wide Web, Gopher, FTP, Telnet, and chat.

a. You need to find information on virtual reality, in the easiest way possible, for a term paper.

b. You want to send a letter to a friend at Northern Arizona University.

c. You would like to visit the Internet Underground Music Archive at www.iuma.com

d. You want to initiate with other people a series of articles and threads on flying saucers and other extraterrestrial objects.

e. You want to communicate interactively with a friend in real time, with each of you in turn typing something into your computer.

f. You want to download free software.

g. You are communicating with a computer in a foreign country, and it treats your fancy new PC like a dumb terminal.

h. You want to search through government computers to find the locations of downloadable files on Watergate.

10. You are talking with a friend who has some definite misconceptions about the Internet. What can you tell your friend to set him or her straight on the following misconceptions?

a. The Internet is free.

b. The Internet is controlled by the FBI.

c. The World Wide Web is really the same thing as the Internet; purists just like to say they're different.

11. Describe in your own words the difference between the following terms: *Web client, Web site,* and *Web server.* Into which of those three categories—if any of them—would you place the following?

a. A computer that stores thousands of Web pages

b. The home page for television's Discovery Channel

c. The area on a mainframe computer that stores e-mail going to students

d. The browser on your PC

12. A large selection of plug-in programs can enhance browsing environments such as those provided with Internet Explorer and Netscape Navigator. Supply at least five examples of such packages, and describe what each one does.

13. Name at least three Web-resident search engines. What uses do such search engines have?

14. Identify several criteria by which people often choose among service providers.

PROJECTS

 1. INTERNET SERVICE PROVIDERS Find two local or national ISPs that service your area, and compare them with respect to the following criteria:

a. Monthly cost: Assume for sake of comparison that you will need 25 hours of connect time per week.

b. Setup costs, if any.

c. Included software: What software products are the providers offering as part of their servicing package?

d. Local lines: Do you have to dial long distance, or are local lines available? How fast are the lines?

e. Browsers available: What browsers are available, and how do they stack up in comparison?

f. Ease of connecting to the Internet: Compare the procedures involved with both providers.

g. Your "window" to the Internet: To what parts of the Internet do any of the providers deny access?

h. Technical support available: Must you pay any charges for answers to phoned-in questions? During what hours and what days of the week is support available?

2. E-MAIL As mentioned in the chapter text, the most widely used feature of the Internet is electronic mail, or e-mail. For this project, research a stand-alone e-mail package of your own choice, and report to the class about it. Two popular Internet e-mail programs that run on both the Windows and Macintosh platforms are Qualcomm's

Eudora Pro and Pegasus Mail. Windows-only software includes Microsoft Outlook and Outlook Express. Be sure you answer the following questions in your report:

a. What is the name of the chosen program? Who is the program's publisher? How much does the program cost?

b. What are the program's main features?

3. **ONLINE CATALOGS** Online catalogs have become increasingly popular features of the Web and corporate intranets. Many people have speculated that this trend may bring the end of the printed catalog. Answer the following questions, limiting your comments to two pages or less:

a. What compelling advantages do online catalogs have over their printed counterparts?

b. Do you see any advantages of printed catalogs over their online counterparts? If so, name them.

c. How do you feel about the predicted demise of the printed catalog?

4. **NAVIGATING THE WEB** Browsers vary in the way that their *history-list* and *bookmark* features are implemented. For the browser you are using, answer the following questions:

a. How would you return most quickly to the Web page that was on your screen immediately before the one that is there now?

b. How does the history-list feature work?

c. How do you add a bookmark?

d. How do you access a bookmarked page?

e. How can you remove bookmarks when you don't need them anymore?

5. **WEB BROWSER FEATURES** Web browsers come with many exotic features in addition to the standard ones. For the browser you are using in your lab—or, if your lab is not Internet ready, for any browser of your choice (that you can research in a computer journal)—answer the following questions:

a. Is a framing capability available?

b. Are there any webcasting capabilities?

c. Does the browser provide built-in Java support?

d. Can you create your own Web pages with the browser, or do you need some type of plug-in or helper program to do this?

e. What types of security features does the browser provide?

6. **SEARCH ENGINES** You can access several free search engines on the Web, including Yahoo!, Excite, Lycos, and Alta Vista. The URLs of these and other engines can be found in the chapter PC Miniguide foldout.

For this project, choose any two search engines and compare them with respect to the following items:

a. Quantity of information: Observe the number of links each one provides when you search on specific topics. (Do this by selecting some search topics that interest you. Choose some one-word topics like "motorcycles" as well as some multiword, and therefore more complex, ones like "Arizona wildflowers.")

b. Quality of information: Observe how useful the links are. (Use the same single-word and multi-word topics as in part *a* for your searches. Does each search engine locate good links and make them easy for you to access?)

c. Other: Many search sites have added features that go well beyond searching, including e-mail, chat, stock information, and so forth. How do the sites you've chosen compare with respect to such features?

7. **GET A JOB** In recent years, the Internet has become a great place to look for jobs. As your project, find at least one source that posts job announcements in your career area. Describe the source, telling approximately how many jobs are listed and what types of online tools are available to help with job searches. For instance, some sites offer search tools to help you find particular jobs, information about job and salary trends, and calculators that show how much you will need to make in particular geographic areas to maintain a particular standard of living. Note that the Internet hosts both national and regional job-search sites.

To help you to get started, feel free to check out any of the sites in the accompanying table. Also think about using search engines—click on the "Business and the Economy" category—to find more. You may additionally want to look at the "Computer Careers" section that appears in every weekly issue of *Computerworld;* this publication often lists Web sites useful for computer professionals who are hunting for jobs.

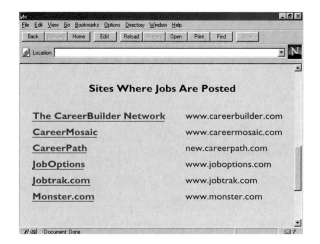

Sites Where Jobs Are Posted

The CareerBuilder Network	www.careerbuilder.com
CareerMosaic	www.careermosaic.com
CareerPath	new.careerpath.com
JobOptions	www.joboptions.com
Jobtrak.com	www.jobtrak.com
Monster.com	www.monster.com

8. CYBERCAFÉS Locate a cybercafé reasonably near your home or school, and pay a visit. Then, answer the following questions:

a. What is the name of the cybercafé? What is its postal address? Its Web and/or e-mail address?

b. What types of hardware does the cybercafé use—fully equipped PCs with diskette drives or dumb terminals that work through a larger computer?

c. What types of browsers are available? What plug-ins or other helper software is available to enhance your Internet experience?

d. How much do you have to pay per hour to use the computers?

e. Does the cybercafé offer classes or individual instruction? If so, what's the cost?

9. PAYING FOR THE INTERNET The chapter mentions the expectation of some industry analysts that pay-per-use Internet access is rapidly approaching. Some have suggested that users should pay charges for the Internet just as they would if they used a toll road—say, paying fees that are proportional to the load they create for Internet resources. Others feel that charges for the Internet by usage are both unnecessary and likely to discourage people from learning to use a critical educational resource. They propose that the Internet's cost could be subsidized by advertisers or by a method similar to the way that many states offer residents free roads—by increasing general taxes slightly or by adding taxes to hardware and/or software purchases.

How do you think the Internet should be supported?

10. THE WEB AS A TRAVEL AGENT I People often use the Internet to shop around for places to go on vacation. The Web is populated with thousands of travel-related sites, blanketing the entire world, and covers airlines, hotels, car-rental agencies, cruise companies, travel agencies, and tourist offices. You can even download travel films that

feature specific vacation destinations, schmooze with travelers who've been there, and reserve airline seats and tourist packages.

Write a paper (three to five pages) about resources available on the Web that cater to people who like to travel. Some of the sites listed in the accompanying table will help get you started.

11. THE WEB AS A TRAVEL AGENT II Want to pick up a $1200 air ticket for less than $200? Try buying it online and at the last minute. In recent years, the Internet has established itself as the place to go for bargain airline tickets.

Unfortunately, you may not have too much advance notice to book a flight and too much flexibility with departure and arrival times. The airline companies try to get full price for tickets, but as departure dates get closer and there are still empty seats, they start cutting prices. For a weekend flight, you may be constrained to leave on Saturday and return on Monday or Tuesday. Still, a rock-bottom price can make the flight a deal.

Visit a site that sells discount airline tickets, and report on what you found in the way of bargains. Some of the sites listed in the accompanying table will help get you started. Do any of the sites you visited also provide bargains on hotel rooms or rental cars?

12. SET UP YOUR OWN CHAT ROOM It's getting easier than ever for computer users to set up their own, private chat rooms, free of charge. An easy way this can be done is through a Web-based search service like Yahoo! or Excite. For this project, set up a private chat room, and conduct a chat between three or more people. Report to the class the means by which you accomplished this, and answer the following questions.

a. How many people participated in the chat room?

b. How did participants gain entry?

c. What types of chat tools were available?

INTERACTIVE EXERCISES

CONNECTING TO AND USING THE INTERNET

 It's time to go online and explore the World Wide Web! Go to the Interactive Exercise at www.harcourtcollege.com/infosys/pcc2e/student/exercise/ to complete this exercise.

DESIGNING, CREATING, AND PUBLISHING A WEB SITE

 You've decided to design and create a Web site. Go to the Interactive Exercise at www.harcourtcollege.com/infosys/pcc2e/student/exercise/ to complete this exercise.

ONLINE REVIEW

 Go to the Online Review at www.harcourtcollege.com/infosys/pcc2e/student/ to test your understanding of this chapter's concepts.

OUTLINE

Overview
The PC Marketplace
    PC Products
    Sales and Distribution
Selecting a PC
    Analyzing Needs
    Listing Alternatives
    Evaluating Alternatives
    Choosing a System
Hardware and Software Installation
Operating a PC
    Backup Procedures
    Equipment Maintenance
    Security
    Troubleshooting and Technical Assistance
Upgrading
    Upgrading Hardware
    Upgrading Software
    Functional versus Technological Obsolescence
Learning More about PCs
PC Miniguide: PC Shopping Checklist

DEVELOPING YOUR OWN PC

LEARNING OBJECTIVES

After completing this chapter, you will be able to:

1. Identify some of the leading companies in critical market segments of the PC industry, as well as the key sales and distribution alternatives for PC products.

2. Explain how to select and install a PC for home or office use.

3. Name some practices designed to protect PC software, hardware, and data resources from damage.

4. List some important guidelines for troubleshooting problems and seeking assistance.

5. Describe some of the ways to upgrade a PC and explain the conditions that justify an upgrade.

6. Name several sources for learning more about PCs.

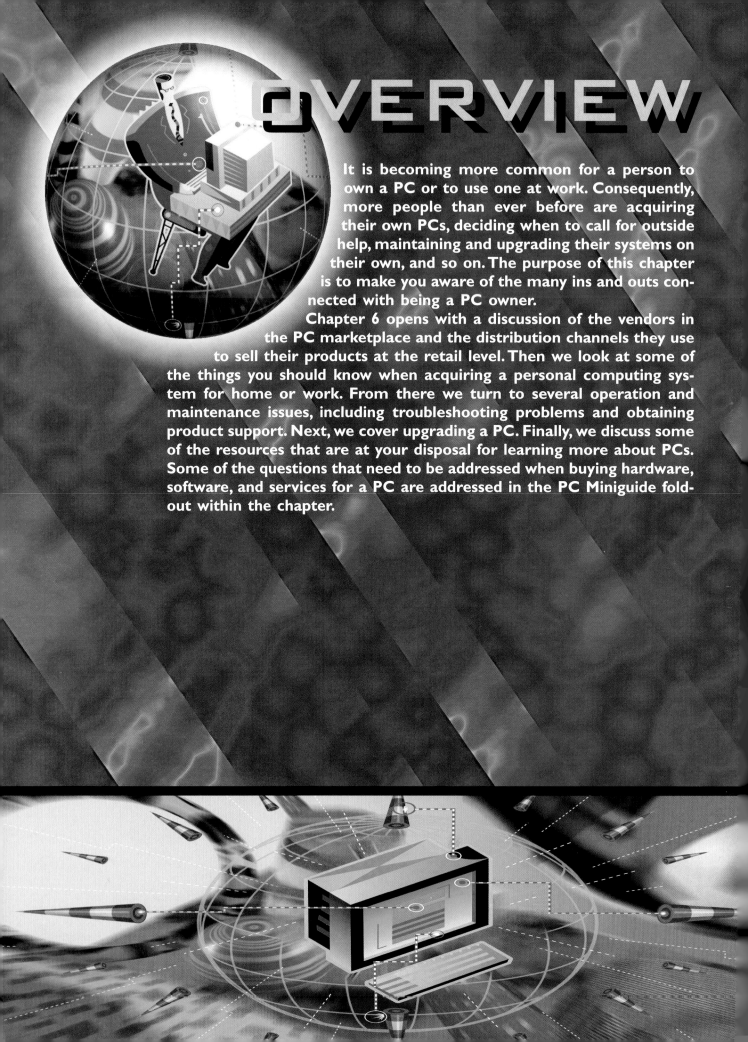

OVERVIEW

It is becoming more common for a person to own a **PC** or to use one at work. Consequently, more people than ever before are acquiring their own **PCs**, deciding when to call for outside help, maintaining and upgrading their systems on their own, and so on. The purpose of this chapter is to make you aware of the many ins and outs connected with being a **PC** owner.

Chapter 6 opens with a discussion of the vendors in the **PC** marketplace and the distribution channels they use to sell their products at the retail level. Then we look at some of the things you should know when acquiring a personal computing system for home or work. From there we turn to several operation and maintenance issues, including troubleshooting problems and obtaining product support. Next, we cover upgrading a **PC**. Finally, we discuss some of the resources that are at your disposal for learning more about **PCs**. Some of the questions that need to be addressed when buying hardware, software, and services for a **PC** are addressed in the **PC** Miniguide foldout within the chapter.

THE PC MARKETPLACE

The PC marketplace comprises a wide variety of firms that make hardware and software products and that sell services. Several other companies are in business solely for product support and distribution purposes.

PC PRODUCTS

A quarter of a century or so ago, many of the companies that make today's most familiar PC products didn't even exist. Today, many of them earn more than $1 billion a year in revenues. Almost overnight, the PC industry has become both the largest and the fastest-growing segment of the computer industry. The following paragraphs mention some of the big names in each major market segment within the PC industry.

SYSTEM UNITS Compaq, IBM, Dell, Hewlett-Packard, Gateway, NEC/Packard Bell, and Apple are among the big names in the PC marketplace. All these companies except Apple have become highly successful largely by producing PC-compatible computers. PC-compatible computers account for more than 90 percent of the systems sold; the remainder are Macintosh systems. Most of the system units sold are of the desktop type, but laptops are gaining fast, and some analysts predict that they may eventually overtake desktop systems for business use.

Vendors of system units are often ranked in *tiers*. The top-tier vendors include longstanding industry firms like Compaq and IBM, whose equipment commands premium prices. Top-tier companies often are involved in extensive research and development efforts, and their equipment is usually top-quality and an all-around safe purchasing bet. Second-tier vendors are less well known and often sell at prices of about 10 to 20 percent less than their top-tier counterparts. Second-tier companies often do little research and development, use less-expensive component parts, and farm out service and support to third-party firms. Nonetheless, the equipment coming out of second-tier companies is usually high quality, service and support are very good, and one's purchase risk is very low.

You might save yet another 10 percent on the purchase price of hardware by going to a third-tier vendor. These companies usually have no name recognition, and many have been in business only a very short period of time. In going with a third-tier company, you have to decide whether saving a couple of hundred dollars or so on a purchase is worth the increased risk. Many large corporations have policies forbidding them to do business with any computer company below what they consider the second tier.

SOFTWARE Among the largest PC software producers (and their leading products) are Microsoft Corporation (Windows and the Office suite of applications), IBM (OS/2, Lotus Notes, and Lotus SmartSuite), and Corel Corporation (the WordPerfect Office suite and Corel DRAW!). Not many years ago, many software companies concentrated on single products. Today, the leaders in this segment have aggressively diversified, internally developing new products and acquiring and partnering with other companies in such diverse fields as communications and entertainment. Many applications programs today are sold as part of *software suites,* which bundle together several full-featured software packages for sale at lower prices than the separate programs would collectively command.

MONITORS AND PRINTERS With the exception of a few U.S. companies such as IBM and Hewlett-Packard, these two segments are dominated by Japanese producers. Major players include Epson, Toshiba, Seiko, Brother, Fujitsu, Canon, NEC, and Okidata.

MICROPROCESSOR CHIPS The microprocessor chip market is ruled largely by Intel and Motorola. Intel makes CPU chips for most of the leading PC-compatible system units, whereas Motorola makes chips for Macintoshes. Also, a number of manufacturers, such as Cyrix and Advanced Micro Devices (AMD), produce Intel-compatible chips. Cyrix and AMD chips are widely used in lower-cost PCs; however, AMD's recent CPU chips—such as the Athlon—are making breakthroughs in the high-end chip area.

DISK SYSTEMS Some familiar firms in the marketplace for diskette drives and hard-disk drives are IBM, Seagate, and Tandon. In the optical-drive marketplace, Canon and Philips are big names. Such companies as Iomega and Imation have done well with superfloppy drives—that is, disk cartridge devices.

A roster of some of the most familiar companies in the PC marketplace appears in Figure 6-1, along with descriptions of the major product offerings that have made these companies famous.

SALES AND DISTRIBUTION

Most users buy PC hardware and software products through computer stores, discount and department stores, the Internet, mail-order houses, manufacturers, and value-added resellers (see Figure 6-2).

COMPUTER STORES When buyers need strong local support in selecting and using PC products, they often turn to *computer stores* such as Computer City and CompUSA (see Figure 6-3). Generally, the salespeople at such places are relatively knowledgeable about computers, and many help buyers try out products before making a commitment. Besides hardware, software, and general advice on purchasing a new system, computer stores also often offer consulting, repair, and other support services to users.

FIGURE 6-1

Who's who in the PC marketplace.
This list shows the products and product lines for which several leading companies are most famous.

Company	Principal Product(s)
America Online	Internet access and content
Adobe	Assorted desktop publishing software products
Apple	Microcomputer systems
Autodesk	AutoCAD design software
Canon	Printers and related products
Compaq	Microcomputer systems
Computer Associates	A wide variety of software products
Corel	A wide variety of software products
Dell	Microcomputer systems
Gateway	Microcomputer systems
Hewlett-Packard	A wide variety of hardware products
IBM	A wide variety of computing products
Intel	Chips for PC-compatible computers
Intuit	Personal finance software
Lotus Development	A wide variety of software products
Macromedia	Multimedia authoring products
Microsoft	A wide variety of software products
Motorola	Chips for Macintosh-compatible computers; wireless products
NEC/Packard Bell	A wide variety of hardware products
Netscape	Internet-related products
Novell	NetWare operating system
Seagate	Storage products
Symantec	A wide variety of utility-software products
Toshiba	A wide variety of hardware products
Yahoo!	Web-based searching and Internet products

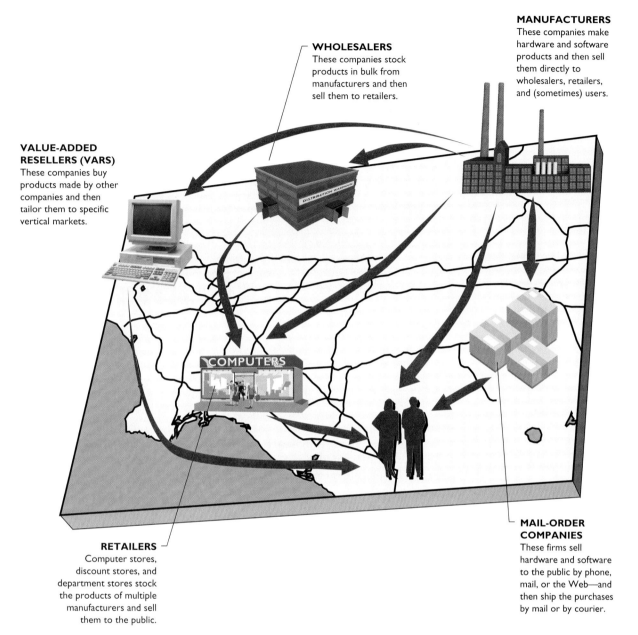

MANUFACTURERS
These companies make hardware and software products and then sell them directly to wholesalers, retailers, and (sometimes) users.

WHOLESALERS
These companies stock products in bulk from manufacturers and then sell them to retailers.

VALUE-ADDED RESELLERS (VARS)
These companies buy products made by other companies and then tailor them to specific vertical markets.

RETAILERS
Computer stores, discount stores, and department stores stock the products of multiple manufacturers and sell them to the public.

MAIL-ORDER COMPANIES
These firms sell hardware and software to the public by phone, mail, or the Web—and then ship the purchases by mail or by courier.

FIGURE 6-2

Distribution channels for computer products.

Computer stores come in many varieties. Most are national or multistate chain stores, but some outfits serve only regional areas such as a single town or a state. Large chains, because they can buy in volume, are likely to have better prices. Many regional stores try to compete by providing superior support. Virtually all computer stores are *resellers*—that is, they sell the hardware and software products made by another company.

While many computer stores are as large as the average mall store, massive *computer superstores* have also become popular. The superstores are probably the best places to browse when you aren't quite sure what you want. Some so-called computer stores such as Radio Shack and Circuit City really amount to *electronics stores,* selling such products as televisions, phones, and electrical supplies in addition to computer hardware and software.

OTHER STORES During the past several years, PC hardware and software products have become so popular that many other types of retail stores have added such items on their showroom floors. Today, you can buy hardware and software at discount stores (such as Wal-Mart), warehouse clubs

 **FIGURE 6-3**

Computer stores. Computer stores are a common sight along highways and in shopping malls. Computer stores are one of the best alternatives for buyers who need strong local support.

(such as Price Club and Costco), department stores (such as Sears), office supply stores (such as Office Depot), and bookstores (such as Walden-books).

As a general rule, the discount stores and warehouse clubs have the best prices, but there is sometimes less of a selection available, and many offer little or no technical support. The smaller selection is often due to deals the store gets on volume purchases and on inventory closeouts—for instance, stock of a printer model the equipment manufacturer wants to get rid of because a replacement model has just come out.

THE INTERNET In a growing trend, many companies sell PC hardware and software over the Internet. To buy a product, you need only go to the seller's Web site and select an item. For software, you can often try out a copy before buying, downloading the program of your choice over the phone lines. If you decide to buy, either the packaged version of the product will be shipped to you immediately, providing you with disks and possibly a user's manual, or you will be given a serial or key number that unlocks the program, converting your trial version to a full version of the program. For hardware, you can often make selections to configure the system of your choice online (see Figure 6-4), receiving it by mail, UPS, or Federal Express a few days or weeks later.

Web sites are not only useful for selling products, but they also can economically disseminate to consumers a lot of valuable marketing and support information that is difficult to organize and distribute by any other means. Companies doing business on the Web may or may not make the products they sell; also, many Web sites distribute freeware and shareware. Additionally, the Web provides an ideal place to hold equipment auctions—called *cyber-auctions*—where buyers submit online bids to a seller to acquire computers or peripherals.

Many computer-industry analysts feel that most people will be meeting their hardware and software needs over the Internet in the near future, which is why sellers are flocking there. One of the most compelling reasons for shopping over the Internet can be price—because customers are placing their own orders and finding answers to their own questions online, orders and information requests cost less for a seller to process than by conventional means. On the downside, many customers do not like to reveal their credit-card numbers over the Internet, and still others prefer shopping in stores.

FIGURE 6-4

Buying on the Web. The Internet's World Wide Web is a good place to shop for PCs. At many Web sites today, you can select how much memory you would like your computer system to have, the size of the hard disk, the size of the monitor, and so on, and immediately see the price of your PC as currently configured.

FIGURE 6-5

Mail-order firms. Several mail-order houses regularly print catalogs that showcase products for PC-compatible or Macintosh computers.

MAIL-ORDER FIRMS Another common source of PC products is mail-order firms. These companies, which are usually resellers, handle products from scores of hardware or software manufacturers and primarily ship goods to a customer after receiving an order by phone or mail or over the Internet (see Figure 6-5). These companies usually have access to an enormous selection of goods and can get almost any item to customers quickly via UPS or Federal Express. Mail-order firms regularly publish price lists in PC journals, in their own product catalogs, or on their Web sites.

Because mail-order companies don't have to pay for a showroom and a staff of knowledgeable salespeople, their prices are usually much lower than those of computer stores and are competitive with discount stores and Internet sellers. A disadvantage of mail-order shopping is that buyers need to know exactly what they want, because most mail-order firms don't maintain showrooms or a large technical staff.

SOFTWARE AND HARDWARE MAKERS Yet another alternative for buying hardware and software is going straight to the product maker.

Hardware companies such as IBM and Compaq manufacture many of the components going into their PCs, whereas companies such as Dell and Gateway merely assemble components made by others into finished PCs. Most PC companies today sell directly to the public, either through advertisements in PC journals or through their Web sites. These companies often do not maintain finished

For links to further information about PC manufacturers and PC buying sites, go to www.harcourtcollege.com/infosys/pcc2e/student/explore/ and click on Chapter 6.

inventories of computers; they build each system to suit a buyer's tastes as they receive each order. Consumers enjoy the advantage of ordering exactly the computer systems they want from a single source—including "free" support and service for a limited period of time. Whether or not they make their own component parts, companies that put their own brand names on hardware devices such as computer systems and peripheral devices and sell the hardware directly to the public are often called **direct manufacturers.**

Many software makers—or **software publishers**—also sell directly to the public. Buyers generally reach publishers through Web sites and through the publishers' toll-free numbers that appear in journal advertisements. Many software publishers will also let you download copies of their products over the Internet for trial purposes.

Buying directly from direct manufacturers and software publishers is not always possible. Many have exclusive selling arrangements with certain wholesalers and with buying consortiums such as schools and large computer clubs. Also, when some companies do sell directly to the general public, they sell only in large quantities—perhaps only *very* large quantities—to chain stores, mail-order firms, value-added resellers, and the like.

VALUE-ADDED RESELLERS (VARs) Value-added resellers (VARs) are companies that buy computer hardware and software from others and make their own specialized systems out of them. For instance, many of the PCs used in the videotape-rental-store business, in medical and dental offices, and in certain other types of *vertical markets* come from VARs. The VAR essentially packages together all of the custom hardware and software needed to run operations in the vertical-market area in which it specializes and often provides full service and support as well. Although going through a VAR is usually more costly than configuring a system on one's own, it is definitely a compelling choice for a small business owner who is not computer savvy or who is too busy with other matters.

USED EQUIPMENT When shopping for a PC, don't overlook used equipment. Ads for used equipment usually appear in the classified sections of local newspapers. If you take this route, ask to try out the equipment before you buy it. If the equipment functions properly during the trial period, it will probably work fine.

When looking at used equipment, be wary of any computer system originally purchased more than 2 or 3 years ago. Technology changes so quickly that a computer built this long ago may have problems running current software today. Also be careful to check how the monitor works over a period of a couple of hours of continuous use, and evaluate the output quality of the printer as well. You should pay considerably less for a used system than you would for a new one.

SELECTING A PC

Chances are good that at some point in your life, you will need to select a PC to better perform your job. Selecting a system for home or for business use must begin with the all-important question: "What do I want the system to do?" Once you've determined the purposes to which the system will be put,

---

■ **Direct manufacturer.** A hardware maker that sells directly to the public. ■ **Software publisher.** A company that creates software. ■ **Value-added reseller (VAR).** A company that buys hardware and software from others and makes computer systems out of them that are targeted to particular vertical markets.

you must choose among the software, hardware, and support alternatives available. Finally, you need a method to evaluate the alternatives and to select a system.

ANALYZING NEEDS

With regard to a computer system, a *need* refers to a functional requirement that the computer system must be capable of meeting. For instance, at a videotape rental store, a computer system must be able to enter bar codes automatically from tapes being checked in and out, identify customers with overdue tapes, manage tape inventories, and do routine accounting operations. All four of these uses are needs. Requiring portability—a computer that you can take with you "on the road"—is another example of a need.

A person owning a PC may find dozens of ways to use it, but he or she may often justify its acquisition on the basis of only one or two needs. For example, many writers find word processing so indispensable to their livelihoods that it matters little what else the PC can do. Sales personnel working out of the office can often justify a notebook computer simply on the basis of its usefulness as a sale-closing tool during presentations at their clients' offices. Figure 6-6 provides a list of several needs that PCs can meet.

If you're not really sure what you want a PC to do, you should think twice about buying one. Computer systems that are configured to match the requirements of certain applications (say, preparing a novel) often perform poorly at others (such as playing power-hungry multimedia games). You can easily make expensive mistakes if you're uncertain about what you want a system to do.

As part of the needs analysis, you should look closely at budgetary constraints. Every user can easily list many needs, but affordability separates real needs from pipe dreams.

LISTING ALTERNATIVES

After establishing a set of needs, the next step is to list some alternative systems that might satisfy those needs. You should almost always consider applications software first, then look for the hardware and systems-software platform that most effectively satisfies your applications-software requirements.

Applications software is selected first because it most directly satisfies needs. For instance, if you want a PC to do commercial art, it would be wise to first look at the various programs available in this area. It makes no sense to choose hardware first and then discover that it doesn't support the type of art software you prefer. Many artists, for instance, prefer a Macintosh platform, so you might completely miss the boat if you buy a PC-compatible computer and then found out later that the Mac is better suited for the work you wanted to do. Also, if you skimped on the CPU and storage and later found out that the programs you selected required a lot of speed, memory, and disk space, again you'd be out of luck or would have to already think about *upgrading,* a topic discussed later in this chapter.

You can get a list of leading software and hardware products from the many PC journals in print and on the Web. Many of these journals also periodically describe the best and worst features of products, rate and compare products, and have industry analysts address product trends (see Figure 6-7). Such information can be useful as input for evaluating products.

LEASING VERSUS BUYING   When looking for a new computer system, you may want to consider leasing one instead of buying outright. Many direct manufacturers—among them Compaq, Dell, and Gateway—both sell and lease computer systems. Over the long run, leasing is usually more expensive than buying but provides greater flexibility; you can switch out of your

Word Processing Word processing is the most common PC application; many people of all types have a need to create memos, letters, manuscripts, and other text-oriented documents.

 Spreadsheets Business users find PCs handy for preparing budgets and other financial schedules and for analyzing information to improve decision making.

 Communications Many people need a computer system to send and receive electronic mail, to download software or exchange documents, and to access the Internet and its World Wide Web.

 Information Retrieval Users of all types find the PC a handy device for looking up information on CDs and on the Internet.

 Transaction Processing Many online service providers let people use their PCs to shop and bank from the home; businesses use PCs too, to process these and other transactions.

 Preparing Slides and Presentation Materials Electronic slide shows, overhead transparencies, multimedia presentations, and handout materials are frequently produced on a PC.

 Art and Design Artists and designers find the PC indispensable for creating products that would be impossible or too expensive to do manually.

 Desktop Publishing Microcomputer systems are useful for preparing books and articles that look like they were created on a professional printer's press.

 Learning An abundance of PC software is available today to provide instruction on virtually any subject.

 Games and Entertainment Electronic games have always been popular on PCs; today, the World Wide Web and digital television are teaming up with PCs.

 Software Development By using PCs with software development tools, programmers develop software for all sizes of computers.

 Portability People like field engineers and salespeople often use PCs away from the office to record data, to perform routine paperwork, and to help sell ideas to clients.

 FIGURE 6-6

PC needs. Most users buy PCs to meet one or two of the needs listed here.

PRODUCT REVIEWS
You can get a review of any particular product by searching for it in any of several computer journals—either the online or printed form.

PRODUCT COMPARISONS
Side-by-side product comparisons are a common sight in computer journals such as *PC Week*. Four tape drives are evaluated here with respect to several criteria.

TECHNOLOGY OVERVIEWS
Many online and printed computer journals feature columnists who provide knowledgeable perspectives about the field.

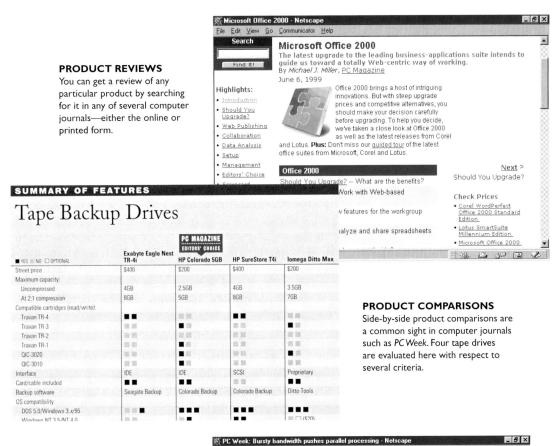
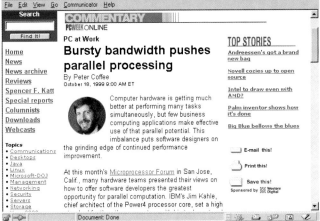

FIGURE 6-7

Product evaluations. You can find out about PC products both in print and on the Web.

current system into a newer model, when necessary, to keep pace with changes in technology. Many leasing plans run for two or three years and provide the lessee the option to buy the system after the lease runs out, at the current market price for used equipment.

EVALUATING ALTERNATIVES

Prospective buyers can evaluate alternative products most effectively by "test driving" them. Keep in mind, however, that you observe the performance of a software package only on a given configuration of hardware. A software package that runs smoothly on a 500 MHz Compaq computer with 128 MB RAM won't necessarily run as well on a Compaq 333 MHz PC with 32 MB RAM, because the varying components used by different manufacturers can affect performance, and because of the difference in CPU chips and the amount of memory in these two systems. Also, the look, feel, and performance of a software package on a computer in the Apple Macintosh line are often noticeably different than they are on a PC-compatible machine. Sometimes it's quite difficult, when selecting a configuration of hardware and software, to see the entire system together, but it's certainly advisable to do this whenever possible.

SELECTION CRITERIA As you evaluate software and hardware products, a number of criteria will help you to make your final selection. The most important selection criterion is *functionality*—the type of work the product does. For many people, ease of learning, ease of use, and the availability of phone support follow closely behind. Also, most people prefer widely used products rather than unknown ones, because the large user base with the more popular products ensures that support will be readily available for a long time. In addition, if you are considering using a PC in an office environment dominated by, say, Apple Macintoshes, choosing that type of computer would probably be more convenient from the standpoint of having local expertise readily available for support. Good written documentation showing how to use the hardware or software is also important. When a helping hand isn't readily available, documentation is often the best alternative for answering a tough question.

Figure 6-8 lists important criteria for selecting a particular PC.

FIGURE 6-8

Important selection criteria. Buyers generally select computer systems on the basis of some combination of criteria.

System Checklist

☑ *Product functionality*
☑ *Ease of learning and use*
☑ *Cost*
☑ *Vendor reputation*
☑ *Support*
☑ *Expandability*
☑ *Meets industry standards*
☑ *Performance*
☑ *Favorable reviews*
☑ *Delivery*
☑ *Documentation*

SHOPPING FOR SOFTWARE AND HARDWARE Before looking over software or hardware products that you might buy, you should make a checklist of features that you want in your eventual system. Also, be sure to watch for these features during the test drive. A rehearsed presentation made by a salesperson is likely to point out only the strengths of a product, not its weaknesses. Also be sure to ask about support. Support has become increasingly important to PC owners in recent years as many of them are realizing it doesn't make sense to save $500 on a system on which they're going to waste $2,000 worth of their time troubleshooting problems on their own. Some of the items that you should watch for, particularly when buying specific types of hardware and software products, are covered in the PC Miniguide foldout within the chapter.

In acquiring hardware, one of the most common mistakes that people make is not thinking enough about the future. You should buy as much processing speed and storage capacity in your initial purchase as you can afford. New software updates—which now come out about every year or two—virtually always require more speed and storage for effective operation. If you buy a bottom-of-the-line system, you might find that the next major upgrade of your favorite software package crawls at a snail's pace. If you buy a system for business use, expect your hardware to last about three years before new software needs force you to buy a new system.

CHOOSING A SYSTEM

After you have considered available alternatives, it's time to choose a system and purchase it. People choose between system alternatives in a number of ways. For instance, some people make a formal list of selection criteria, weigh each criterion with respect to its importance, and quantitatively rate each alternative on each criterion. All other things being equal, they then select the alternative that scores the highest total when the ratings are added.

Others prefer to make their choices less formally. After thinking about their needs and the criteria they apply to evaluate alternatives, they select the first PC they see that "feels right." Although such an acquisition process could be criticized for lack of thoroughness, many people claim that their busy schedules leave no time to spend researching choices with greater care. Of course, rushing to make a selection has a negative side. Just as a car owner can go through years of torture driving around in the wrong type of car, a computer buyer can also wind up with years of headaches resulting from a poor choice.

HARDWARE AND SOFTWARE INSTALLATION

When you buy a computer system, most of the hardware and software you need will probably already be in place. If it isn't, you can usually buy and install it yourself.

INSTALLING HARDWARE Historically, users have not always had an easy time installing new equipment on their PCs. The cover of the system unit had to be carefully taken off and an add-in board inserted correctly. Then, device drivers had to be correctly installed. From start to finish, the process was time consuming and stressful. Something could easily go wrong—an ultrathin circuit could get damaged, or the add-in board might not work with a component on the motherboard. When a problem cropped up, users could waste hours trying to figure out what was causing it.

Fortunately, the scenario just described is rapidly disappearing. To make it easier than ever for PC owners to install hardware on their own, both hardware and software vendors have moved to a *plug-and-play* approach. Consequently, all users of such systems theoretically need to do is plug any new equipment into the system unit—almost as easily as they would plug a lamp into a wall socket—and they're ready to go. When they start their computers after installing the hardware, the operating system "talks to" the new equipment and automatically configures the proper driver for it.

Be aware that not all modern operating systems or equipment support plug and play, and even those that do will often fail to make equipment installation go as smoothly as it could. Hardware and software companies are currently devising a new standard called Simply Interactive PC (SIPC), which they say will someday make PCs as simple to operate as consumer appliances. If computers and the World Wide Web are to reach the mass market as television has, ease of use will be critical.

INSTALLING SOFTWARE Generally, software of any type is relatively easy to install today. When you buy a new program, the package contains one or more *installation disks*. You load the first of the disks into its proper drive, and if instructed to do so on the disk label, enter a command. Then, it's just a matter of following a set of simple instructions on the screen. In most cases, there is very little you have to do beyond entering some identifying information about yourself and deciding what type of installation you would like to do—such as a typical installation, or custom installation (see Figure 6-9).

A *typical install* places most of the files you will need onto your hard disk. A *custom install* enables you to select such options as the location where the program will be installed, whether or not to keep older versions of the program, which optional components to install, whether to run the program or optional components from the CD-ROM, and so forth. Microsoft Office 2000

TYPICAL INSTALLATION
Recommended for most users, it places on your hard disk most of the files you will need, so that they are available for rapid access.

CUSTOM INSTALLATION
Recommended for advanced users, it allows you to change the installation location, keep older versions of the program, and add or delete specific files from the typical-installation option.

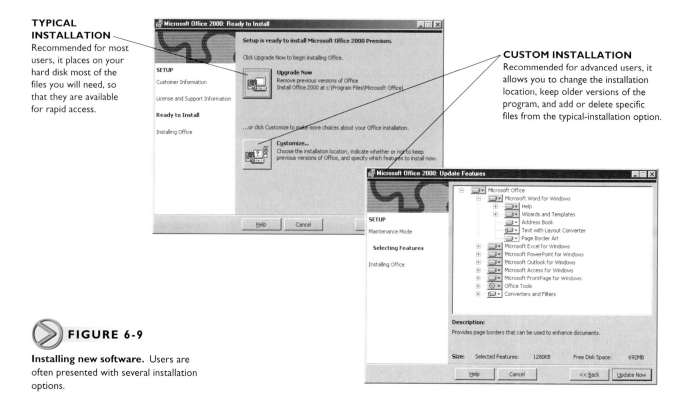

▶ **FIGURE 6-9**

Installing new software. Users are often presented with several installation options.

Premium, for instance, requires about 250 MB of hard-disk space for a typical install, whereas a custom install can require from 100 to over 500 MB, depending on the programs and options installed.

USES FOR YOUR OLD SYSTEM   As you install your new system, consider the risks you take if you prematurely discard your old hardware and software. You may find yourself in a bad situation if you discover problems with your new system after you've given the old system away or sold it. Although new systems are generally extremely reliable, and top- and second-tier vendors will quickly dispatch a new system to you if the one they originally shipped was defective, something else could happen you didn't anticipate. For instance, your new system could get infected by a computer virus during a data download.

Also consider new uses for your old computer system. It could, for instance, serve as a backup device.

OPERATING A PC

Once you acquire a PC, you should develop a set of careful practices to protect your software, hardware, and data from damage and costly mistakes. Four important areas in this regard are backup of programs and data, proper maintenance of hardware and storage media, security, and problem detection and correction.

BACKUP PROCEDURES

Virtually every computer veteran will warn you that, sooner or later, you will lose some critical files. Maybe lightning will strike nearby, zapping your RAM. Perhaps a small brownout will cause the heads on your hard disk to drop out of orbit and crash onto the disk surface, carving a miniature canyon through the electronic version of a 45-page term paper that's due tomorrow. Or maybe you'll accidentally delete or overwrite the file. PC veterans will also tell you that file losses always seem to happen at the worst possible times.

Fortunately, there is a solution to most of these problems—backing up important data and programs. Creating a **backup** means making a duplicate version of any file that you can't afford to lose so that, when the fickle finger of fate causes inadvertent erasure, you're confronted with only a minor irritant rather than an outright catastrophe. Theoretically, you can back up any file on your computer system. The backups you create—through, say, a file-copy, disk-copy, or backup command—can be on diskette, hard disk, tape, or virtually any other type of secondary storage medium.

One common form of backup that everyone should practice is frequently saving to disk a long file that is being developed in RAM. For instance, suppose you are word processing a paper for a class. About every five minutes or so, you should make sure that you save the current version of the file onto disk. That way, if the power goes out on your system, you will have lost only what you typed in since the last Save command. After completing the document, it can then be backed up on another medium, if desired. Many commercial packages provide certain types of automatic backup of files, but unless you know for sure what is being backed up and when, it's safer to do it yourself.

For backup of several files at the same time, many different strategies exist. Some perform **full backups,** storing all files from their hard disks onto tapes or disk cartridges at the end of a day or a week. The advantage to a full backup is that it is relatively straightforward. On the downside, a full backup takes up more storage space and takes longer than a backup in which only selected files are targeted for copying.

An alternative to the full backup is a **partial backup** in which you copy only the files that you have created or altered since the last backup. Users commonly implement two such types of partial backup procedures. A *differential backup* duplicates all files created or changed since the last full backup. In an *incremental backup,* duplicates are made of all files created or changed since the last backup of any type. Both types of partial backup described here enable you, along with the copy of the full backup, to reconstruct the hard disk if it becomes corrupted. Incremental backups are the faster of the two types of partial backup to perform, but result in more work to fully reconstruct the hard disk. Many people who have hard disks will perform a partial backup daily and a full backup weekly. Businesses may perform a full backup every night.

When doing either a full or partial backup, some users back up only document files, since program files are already backed up on the program installation disks.

Whenever you back up files on a disk, make sure to place the backup files on a different disk from the originals. In theory, you shouldn't even keep these copies in the same room or building. That way, if a serious accident such as a fire or flood occurs at one location, the files safely stored at the other location will help you to recover. A variety of accidents that can destroy programs and data—all of them good reasons to back up data stored on disk—are listed in Figure 6-10.

EQUIPMENT MAINTENANCE

PCs consist of sensitive electronic devices that must be treated with care. In this section we discuss protecting your PC with a surge suppressor or UPS

■ **Backup.** A procedure that produces a duplicate version of any file that you can't afford to lose. ■ **Full backup.** A procedure that produces a duplicate copy of all files onto a secondary storage medium. ■ **Partial backup.** A procedure that produces a duplicate copy of selected files onto a secondary storage medium.

Why back up?

- A disk sector goes bad, destroying part of a file.
- A file that you thought you no longer had a need for and erased turns out to be important.
- You modify a file in an undesirable way, and the damage done is irreversible.
- You accidentally reformat a disk.
- The disk suffers a head crash.
- A power brownout or failure at the time of saving a file causes "garbage" to be saved.
- You save a file to the wrong subdirectory, overwriting a different file that has the same name.
- While rushing your work, you make a mistake that causes the wrong files to be erased.
- You unwittingly destroy a file while working on it—say, by deleting parts of it erroneously and then saving the file.
- Malfunctioning hardware or software causes files to be erased.
- A computer virus enters your system and destroys files.
- Your disk is physically destroyed—for instance, a diskette is left in the sun or the hard disk is given a jolt. Alternatively, a fire or flood may destroy the disk.
- Someone steals your diskette or hard disk.

FIGURE 6-10

Reasons for file backup.

FIGURE 6-11

Surge suppressor. The system unit and its support devices feed into the surge suppressor, which is plugged into a standard wall outlet. All of the equipment can be turned on or off by a single switch.

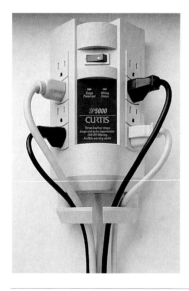

unit; caring for disks; protecting your PC from dust, heat, and static; and protecting monitors.

SURGE SUPPRESSION One of the best devices to have on your PC to minimize the chance of unexpected damage is a surge suppressor. A **surge suppressor,** which is installed between your PC and the electrical outlet providing the power, is a hardware device that prevents random electrical power spikes from impacting your system (see Figure 6-11). Probably the most common problem caused by a spike is loss of data in RAM. Cases have also been reported, however, of loss of data in secondary storage and destruction of equipment.

A surge suppressor cannot guarantee complete electrical protection. If lightning strikes your house, even a top-of-the-line surge suppressor will probably fail to protect your data or equipment. If you are working on your PC when a storm hits, you should save to disk what you've been working on and turn off your system.

Instead of a plain surge suppressor, some people use an **uninterruptible power supply (UPS)** unit (see Figure 6-12). This device is a surge suppressor with a built-in battery, the latter of which keeps power going to the computer when the main power goes off—say, due to a lightning storm, a brownout, or damage to an outside cable. UPSs for PCs often run for a few minutes without outside power before they have to be recharged; UPSs for larger computers may run several hours. In either case, it gives the user a chance to save all open documents, transfer files to a removable storage device, if necessary, and properly shut down the system.

DISK CARE User precautions with diskettes, hard disks, and CDs help to safeguard any data or programs stored on them. Diskettes may look like inert slabs of plastic, but they are actually sensitive storage media that work well only with appropriate care. Never touch the actual diskette surface or bend a diskette. Also, keep diskettes away from magnetic objects, motors, stereo speakers, and extreme temperatures.

■ **Surge suppressor.** A device that protects a computer system from random electrical power spikes. ■ **Uninterruptible power supply (UPS).** A surge suppressor with a built-in battery, the latter of which keeps power going to the computer when the main power goes off.

The most important precaution for a hard disk is placing it in a location where it is not likely to be bumped or subjected to electrical interference. As far as CDs go, make sure that the nonprinted side remains free of dirt, fingerprints, and scratches, which may impair laser reading.

FIGURE 6-12

Uninterruptible power supply (UPS) units.

DUST, HEAT, AND STATIC Each of the tiny processor and memory chips in your hardware units is packed tightly with thousands or millions of circuits. Dust particles circulating in the air can settle on a chip, causing a short circuit. Many people use dust covers that fit snugly over each of their hardware devices when the computer is turned off to prevent foreign particles in the air from causing hardware failure.

Desktop and tower system units also generate lots of heat and require cooling fans. When placing your system unit on a desktop or on the floor, make sure it is in a place where the ventilation is good and the outlet from the fan is not blocked.

Static electricity is especially dangerous because it can damage chips, destroy programs and data in storage, or disable your keyboard. So that the electrical discharges from your fingertips don't wreak havoc, you might consider buying an antistatic mat for under your workstation chair or an antistatic pad to put under your keyboard. Static electricity is more likely in dry areas and in the wintertime, when there's less humidity in the air.

SCREEN SAVERS CRT-type monitors have a phosphorescent inner surface that is lit up by an electronic gun. If you keep your monitor at a high brightness level and abandon it for several hours with an unchanging image on the screen, the phosphorescent surface may get damaged. Ghosty character images can get permanently etched on the screen, making it harder to read. To prevent this from happening, software packages called **screen savers** are available that either dim your monitor or create constantly changing patterns on the screen when the display remains unchanged for a given number of minutes. Today's monitors are better equipped to prevent screen burn than ones made only a few years ago, so sometimes screen savers are useful only for

■ **Screen saver.** A software product designed to protect the phosphor coating on the inside of a display screen from damage when the display is turned on but is not used for an extended period.

their entertainment value or to prevent anyone (by using a screen-saver password) from looking at your computer screen when you are away from your desk.

SECURITY

Security refers to protecting a computer system's hardware, software, and data from unintentional damage, malicious damage, or any type of tampering. There are many ways to secure a PC, including locks on doors and lockplates on equipment, protecting files with passwords that only you know, accessories that block people from seeing what's on your screen or hard disk, encryption algorithms that disguise outgoing messages, and programs that prevent computer viruses from infecting storage devices. The topic of securing computer systems is discussed more thoroughly in Chapter 7.

No matter what type of security strategy you decide to go with, it is important to note that no strategy can give you 100 percent protection. Nonetheless, giving a little thought to some of the things that can go wrong and taking a few simple precautions can save you big headaches later on. Studies made on PC users have shown that they tend not to spend a lot of time thinking about security.

TROUBLESHOOTING AND TECHNICAL ASSISTANCE

If you work with PCs for any length of time, at some point you will probably have an experience when your hardware or software does not work properly. You may turn on your computer system one day and get no response. Perhaps your monitor screen will begin flickering badly every few seconds. Or maybe you will issue a familiar command in a software package that you work with regularly and the keyboard will lock up, the command will remain unexecuted, or the computer will suddenly "crash." When such an event takes place, you will need to troubleshoot to isolate the underlying problem. If the problem is serious enough, technical assistance from an outside source may be necessary.

TROUBLESHOOTING The term *troubleshooting* refers to actions taken to diagnose or solve a problem. Unfortunately, many problems are unique to specific types of hardware and software, so no simple troubleshooting remedy will work all of the time. Nonetheless, the following simple steps and guidelines will help you to identify and correct a number of common problems:

- Try again. A surprising number of procedures work when you try a second or third time. You may have pressed the wrong keys the first time or not pressed the keys hard enough. If the problem persists, attempt to save your work, restart (reboot) your PC, and try again.
- Check to see that all of the equipment is plugged in and turned on and that none of the cables is detached or loose.
- Reboot the system. Many software problems are corrected after the computer is restarted and the program opened again. Some operating systems—such as Windows 98—will also try to reconfigure problem devices when the system is restarted, as well as give you the option of temporarily disabling certain devices if your system crashed, to help you determine the problem device.
- Recall exactly what happened between the time the system was operating properly and the time you began to encounter problems. There might have been an electrical storm outside, and your system was plugged in and damaged by lightning. Or perhaps you installed new systems soft-

---

■ **Security.** A collection of measures for protecting a computer system's hardware, software, and data from damage or tampering.

WHAT SHOULD I LOOK FOR IN
If possible, inspect the output o
before making a purchase to be
read. Most monitors sold today a
are working in an intensely grapl
screen size.

WHAT SHOULD I LOOK FOR IN A KEYBOARD?
If possible, type on the keyboard before buying. Notice, especially before buying a notebook PC, the key spacing and how the keys feel to your touch—some notebook keyboards are cramped and hard to use.

DO I NEED A MOUSE?
A mouse or similar pointing device is a must—you can choose from a mouse, trackball, trackpad, or other pointing device, depending on your preference (try them out first, if possible). Many notebook PCs come today with a built-in pointing stick, trackball, or trackpad in lieu of a mouse, though you can usually add a mouse, if desired.

SOFTWARE

WHAT OPERATING SYSTEM SHOULD I GO WITH?
Most people buying a PC-compatible computer will likely be using Windows, whereas those choosing a Macintosh-compatible platform will be using Mac OS. Make sure the vendor from which you are buying your PC is providing you with the current version of the appropriate operating system—and for that matter, a current version of all other software.

SHOULD I BUY A FULL-FEATURED SOFTWARE SUITE OR AN INTEGRATED SOFTWARE PACKAGE?
While some stand-alone office programs still exist, most people buy office software in the form of suites or integrated software packages. Integrated software packages cost less than suites, yet have most of the features the average user would ever want to utilize. What's more, they require less disk space and memory. Integrated software packages are most suitable for home users. You will probably require a software suite, however, if you work in a business—especially one that uses some of the more sophisticated features of the software and is trying to standardize applications across a broad spectrum of users. The three most popular software suites are Microsoft Office, Corel WordPerfect Office, and Lotus SmartSuite.

WHAT'S THE DIFFERENCE BETWEEN THE PROFESSIONAL AND STANDARD EDITIONS OF A SOFTWARE SUITE?
Most software suites are available in more than one configuration, with the standard editions containing less programs that the professional or premium versions. For example, while all Microsoft Office 2000 editions contain Word, Excel, and a few other core programs, the Professional edition adds Access, a database management system, and the Premium edition adds FrontPage, a Web publishing program.

A DISPLAY SCREEN?
[...] the monitor you are considering [...]ure the display is clear and easy to [...]e of the 17-inch SVGA type. If you [...]cal environment, consider a larger

✔ TRY THIS
When evaluating printers, ask to see sample printouts of text in a variety of sizes and graphical images. Also, check an ink-jet printer's speed for color output—it is usually much slower than for black and white printouts.

WHAT TYPE OF PRINTER IS BEST FOR MY NEEDS?
For most people, the choice will be between an ink-jet and laser printer. Ink-jet printers are especially popular at the low end of the market, and most can produce color output. At the higher end of the market, monochrome laser printers dominate because they are faster and produce better output. When selecting a printer, check the speed (ink-jet printers typically print 3 to 6 pages per minute for black output; laser printers typically print anywhere from 4 to 16 pages per minute), output quality (look for jagged or blurry edges on text or graphics), and the cost of consumable items (paper, color or toner cartridges, etc.) Also consider reading evaluations in PC journals. If you just need color occasionally, you might be better off buying a laser printer and taking your documents on disk to a print shop to print in color, when necessary.

COMMUNICATIONS AND SUPPORT

WHAT DO I NEED TO KNOW ABOUT MODEMS?
Most computers today come with an internal modem. Consider an external modem instead only if you need to use the modem with more than one computer. Also, buy the fastest modem speed available. Most modems sold today come with faxing capabilities.

WHAT SHOULD I LOOK FOR IN SERVICE AND SUPPORT?
Be sure your system comes with at least a one-year warranty and find out if repairs on performed on site, or if you have to deliver a defective system to a local vendor or mail it to the company or manufacturer. Find out if the warranty covers parts and labor or just parts after a period of time. Also check for toll-free technical support—the major PC vendors typically offer several months to several years of toll-free 24 hours a day, seven days a week phone support on both hardware and software.

ware during your last session, and it is affecting the way your current application works.

■ Be observant. If strange noises came out of the disk drives when you unsuccessfully tried to boot up the system, those noises might be important. Even though solving the problem may be beyond your capabilities, you may be able to supply important facts to the people who can assist you in getting your system up and running again. The faster the technicians can diagnose and fix your system, the less money you will spend in help or repair costs, and the sooner you will have your system back.

■ Check the **documentation,** or descriptive instructions, that came with the system. Many products come with a hard-copy manual with a troubleshooting checklist, and many software products have an online help feature that will help you solve many of your own problems.

■ Use diagnostic software. *Diagnostic software* enables you to test your system to see whether parts of it are malfunctioning or are just giving you poor performance. Sometimes, when new equipment is added, compatibility problems arise with existing equipment or software. Also, hard disks can get fragmented with use over time and may need to be sped up with a *defragmentation utility.* A file becomes fragmented when it's too large to be stored in contiguous locations on disk. When this happens, the file is split by your PC and stored in noncontiguous locations. The defragmentation utility will check your hard disk for degree of fragmentation. It can also speed disk access by rearranging files and free space on your disk, so files are stored in contiguous locations, and free space is consolidated into a single block. Figure 6-13 shows how such a utility consolidates fragmented files. Many operating systems have their own defragmentation utilities.

■ Use your system's boot disk. Many computer systems come with—or allow you to create—a special boot disk that can be used to start the computer when it will no longer boot from the hard drive. After booting the computer, diagnostic software or other procedures can be used to try to identify and correct the problem.

FIGURE 6-13

Diagnostic software. Many operating systems include a defragmentation utility program that can, if necessary, rearrange files on a hard disk for faster access.

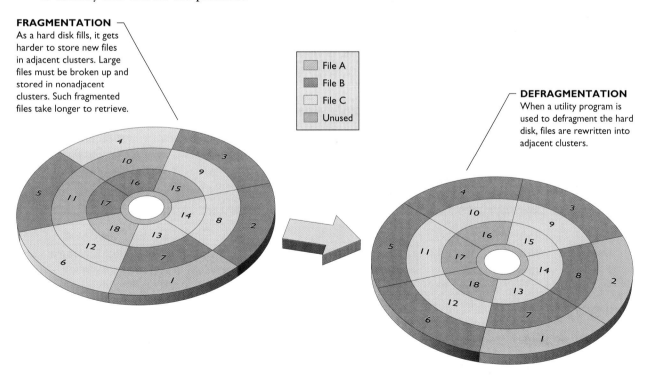

FRAGMENTATION
As a hard disk fills, it gets harder to store new files in adjacent clusters. Large files must be broken up and stored in nonadjacent clusters. Such fragmented files take longer to retrieve.

File A
File B
File C
Unused

DEFRAGMENTATION
When a utility program is used to defragment the hard disk, files are rewritten into adjacent clusters.

■ **Documentation.** A detailed written description of how a program, procedure, or system works.

You should weigh the time that it takes to solve a problem yourself against the cost of outside help. It's not a disgrace to give up if the problem is more than you can handle. It is simply an admission that your time is valuable and that you are wise enough to know when to call in a professional for assistance.

TECHNICAL ASSISTANCE WITH HARDWARE AND SOFTWARE One of the most important items in working with hardware or software products is getting technical assistance when you need it. Three such sources of assistance are discussed below.

THE MANUFACTURER One of the best prospects for support is turning to the company that made the hardware or software with which you are working. Probably nobody knows more about correcting problems than the people who may have created them in the first place. It's that very thought that leads personal computer owners to contact the hardware manufacturer or software publisher first whenever something bad happens.

Many manufacturers provide toll-free phone numbers, fax numbers, e-mail addresses, and Web or newsgroup sites for users to contact to get help with technical problems. To reach others, you will have to make a toll call or, worse yet, dial a 900-area-code number where you get charged by the minute. Some vendors are notorious for keeping users on hold and may keep users waiting a half-hour or more. Check to see whether some type of premium service is available where you can get a faster and perhaps higher level of response. Also check if phone support is still covered under your warranty.

With the cost of support escalating, hardware and software makers are increasingly devising more ways to provide assistance over the Web (see Figure 6-14). IBM, for instance, has placed on the Web a vast storehouse of technical-support knowledge, one that used to be available only to its own

FIGURE 6-14

Web-based technical support.
Gateway's Web site provides buyers with information on products as well as customer support.

support staff. One of its features is a software agent that travels over the phone lines to repair remote computer systems. Intel has a combination Web- and human-based system called AnswerExpress. The Web part of the system does an online inventory of your computer system's vitals and relays it to a live support technician, who will call you back within minutes.

THIRD-PARTY SUPPORT Products are often supported through *third-party firms* that specialize in giving assistance. You can contact one of these firms yourself, or you may be put in touch with them by a hardware or software maker. Many of the latter, incidentally, do not have their own in-house technical support groups but instead farm out customer support to third-party firms.

Third-party firms often have toll-free or 900-area-code phone numbers that you call to get help. In the case of the 900 area codes, many firms will cap charges at a limit—say, $25 or $50—so that your bill doesn't become outrageous. When dealing with anyone who charges for support, check to see whether any follow-up calls you make once a problem is theoretically corrected will incur an additional charge.

USER SUPPORT If you don't know anyone personally who can give you help, take solace in the fact that many users post problems on the Internet or on public bulletin boards. The message you post might be read by literally hundreds of other users, and there's a good possibility that someone out there has encountered and solved the problem you are now wrestling with. While you may get the answer you are seeking without paying a dime, however, don't be surprised if you have to wait a week or more to have your plea for help read by the right person.

With the more widely used products, you will also find formal user groups. *User groups* enable you to meet other users in person and to talk about common problems and creative ways to use hardware and software.

EQUIPMENT REPAIRS In some cases, a problem is simple enough that no equipment repair is necessary. However, when a repair is required and is beyond the scope of your capabilities, you will need to seek professional help. Likely sources of such help are the party that sold you the problematic hardware, computer stores in your area, and computer repair technicians listed in the *Yellow Pages* of your local phone book.

Keep the following questions in mind when asking someone else to diagnose or repair your system:

- Is it better to repair old equipment or to buy new equipment? For instance, if the PC to be repaired is worth less than $500, it may be cheaper to buy a completely new computer system.
- Will the repair work be done under **warranty?** Most new equipment is sold with a warranty stating that the manufacturer will pay for certain repairs if the equipment fails within a given number of days or months after purchase. If the warranty hasn't expired, the repair may cost you nothing. Be aware that many manufacturers state in their warranty that the warranty becomes void if you attempt to repair the equipment yourself or if a repair is attempted by an unauthorized person or shop. Most hardware manufacturers publish a list of authorized repair shops.
- Can you get an estimate before proceeding with the work? In many cases, repair technicians can provide a free estimate of what the repair will cost. If they can't, you might want them to diagnose the problem first and to

For links to further information about technical support sites, go to www.harcourtcollege.com/infosys/pcc2e/student/explore/ and click on Chapter 6.

■ **Warranty.** A conditional pledge made by a manufacturer to protect consumers from losses due to defective products.

FIGURE 6-15

Contracts. A good warranty or maintenance contract should cover the clauses listed here.

Warranty and Maintenance
Coverage The contract should state clearly if both parts and labor are covered.
Contract Period Many contracts cover a period of one to three years. Some vendors provide a "lifetime" guarantee on certain types of parts or services.
Repair Procedure A procedure should spell out clearly what steps will be taken when a problem occurs. Often, the vendor will first try to diagnose the problem over the phone. If this fails, either you will have to bring or send the unit to an authorized repair center or a technician will be dispatched to your home or office within a certain number of hours or days. If you can't afford to be without your computer system for an appreciable period, this part of the contract may be the most critical. Some contracts will provide you with a "loaner" system while yours is being repaired.
Support Hotline Many companies provide a hotline for you to call when you have a question or a problem. Sometimes you can call toll free, and sometimes you won't be billed for the vendor's time. It's a good idea to check out how easy it is to reach the hotline; some of them are so understaffed it takes days for a call to be returned.
Other Clauses Most contracts will be void if you attempt to repair the equipment yourself or let someone who's not an authorized repairperson do it.

call you when they are able to provide an estimate. You never, ever want to put yourself in a situation in which you are presented with an unexpected, outrageously expensive repair bill.

■ Is priority service available? People who use PCs as part of their jobs often need repairs immediately. Many repair shops realize this and will provide same-day or next-day turnaround for an extra fee. Some will even lend you equipment while repairs are being made.

When you buy a PC, you can often choose to buy an extended maintenance contract to cover certain types of repairs beyond those stated in the warranty. Figure 6-15 lists a number of the points covered by both warranties and maintenance contracts.

UPGRADING

Hardware and software generally need to be upgraded over time. **Upgrading** a PC means buying new hardware or software components that will extend the life of your current system. The question you must ask when considering an expensive upgrade is the same one that you would ask when considering costly repairs to a car: Should I spend this money on my current system or start fresh and buy a completely new system?

When you acquire a new PC, it is extremely important to formulate an upgrade strategy. Ideally, you should buy a PC that adheres to a well-supported standard. This and other considerations will give you flexibility to upgrade it to meet reasonable future needs over the course of its lifetime.

■ **Upgrading.** The process of buying new hardware or software in order to add capabilities and extend the life of a computer system.

Of course, you cannot anticipate all of your future needs, but you invite unnecessary and expensive upgrades later on by spending no time thinking about system growth.

UPGRADING HARDWARE

Some common types of hardware upgrades include adding more RAM or a second hard disk to a system, installing a faster modem, adding boards that provide new types of functionality, and adding new peripheral equipment, such as an image scanner or a DVD drive. Unless your system is powerful enough to handle growth, many upgrades will not be possible. For instance, if you have an Intel 80486-based processor and you want to do a serious upgrade, you should probably just purchase a new PC. You cannot bring a 486 computer up to the level of today's mainstream desktop computers without replacing the motherboard and virtually every other item inside the system unit. With some new PCs selling for $500 or less, it would cost less to buy an entirely new machine.

Today, some PCs sold in the marketplace are touted as *upgradable PCs*. These devices are designed with modest and predefined types of replacement in mind, making it possible to swap out components like the CPU chip or the internal hard disk as more powerful ones become available. For instance, many PCs come with special sockets in the system board that make it possible to plug in an Intel *overdrive chip* that takes over the duties of the resident CPU chip.

UPGRADING SOFTWARE

Many PC software vendors enhance their products in some major way every year or two, prompting users to upgrade. Each of these upgrades—which are called **versions**—is assigned a number, such as 1.0, 2.0, 3.0, and so on. The higher the number, the more recent and more powerful the software. Minor upgrades, called **releases,** typically increase their numbers in increments of 0.1—say, 1.1, 1.2, and 1.3—or .01, such as release 3.11 following release 3.1. Releases are usually issued in response to bugs or shortcomings in the version. Recently, the versions and releases of many software products began being assigned numbers that correspond exactly or approximately to the year of issue—such as Office 97 (for the 1997 version of Microsoft Office) and Office 2000 (for the 2000 version, which actually came out in 1999).

With computer networks now reaching into many homes and offices, many companies are making upgrades available to users with increasing frequency. Thus, between official versions and releases of a product, you may be able to take advantage of free enhancements for only the effort it takes to download them. Often, the cost of enhancements is built into the price that you originally pay when you buy or license the software. Companies also may make such enhancements available for nonnetworked users through the mail, for a nominal fee that covers the cost of a disk, handling, and mailing.

Each version of a software product is virtually guaranteed to be more sophisticated and complex and to require more RAM than its predecessors. For example, it's not unusual for a product that only a decade ago fit on one or two diskettes and worked with 256 KB of RAM to now require a CD and 16 or more megabytes of RAM. The technical documentation accompanying the software is much more extensive than it was a few years ago, too, and

■ **Version.** A major upgrade of a software product. ■ **Release.** A minor upgrade of a software program.

generally more sophisticated. Fortunately, however, both the quality of software and user training has increased dramatically.

Virtually all software products tend to be *upward compatible.* This means that applications developed on earlier versions of the software will also work on later versions. *Downward compatibility* is also commonplace. For example, WordPerfect 9 enables users to save files, say, in either WordPerfect 9 or any of several earlier WordPerfect formats. So, if you are using WordPerfect 9 on your desktop computer but the magazine you are sending an article to requires it in WordPerfect 6.1, there is no problem.

Cross compatibility is also widely found today. This feature enables you to, say, turn a WordPerfect 9 document into a Microsoft Word 2000 document. When translating documents from one vendor's software package into another, you must be aware that certain details can get lost in the translation. For instance, sometimes boldfacing and italicizing may not be picked up.

Generally, new software will be offered to current users at a reduced price to make an upgrade more attractive. The potential user has to weigh the benefits of using the new package against its costs. The costs include the sticker price of the software, additional training, setting up new standards for use, and, possibly, equipment upgrades due to the increased sophistication of the software. As a result of these practical considerations, organizations often take a longer time to upgrade than many people expect.

FUNCTIONAL VERSUS TECHNOLOGICAL OBSOLESCENCE

As suggested in earlier paragraphs, PC products can serve user needs for several years before they must be replaced. A product becomes **functionally obsolete** when it no longer meets the needs of an individual or business. Improvements to hardware and software products are continuous, however, and often a product is replaced in stores with a newer version or release well before it is functionally obsolete. A product in this latter class is said to be **technologically obsolete.**

In upgrading, a common problem is that users believe the product they are using is functionally obsolete when it is merely technologically obsolete. Because of the rapid pace of technology, virtually anyone buying a PC today will have at least one technologically obsolete component within a matter of months. What's more, it's often smart not to jump into a new version of a product immediately but instead to wait for the initial bugs in it to be fixed. A user may switch from a technologically obsolete product to a newer version for any of several valid reasons, some of which are listed below:

- The older product is also functionally obsolete.
- The older product results in much higher operating costs than the newer one.
- The newer product has an attractive feature that makes conversion worthwhile.
- Support is no longer available for the older product.

The term **legacy system** is often used for technologically obsolete products. Most companies have a variety of legacy systems on their hands today, and many of these systems will be capable of years of further use before they have to be replaced.

For links to further information about upgrading a PC, go to www.harcourtcollege.com/infosys/pcc2e/student/explore/ and click on Chapter 6.

■ **Functionally obsolete.** A term that refers to a product that no longer meets the needs of an individual or business.
■ **Technologically obsolete.** A term that refers to a product that still meets the needs of an individual or business, although a newer version or release has superseded it in the marketplace. Also called a **legacy system.**

LEARNING MORE ABOUT PCS

A wide range of resources fulfills the needs of those who want to learn more about PCs and their uses. Classes, computer clubs, computer shows, magazines, newspapers, newsletters, books, and electronic media—such as the World Wide Web—are all sources of information.

CLASSES A good way to learn any subject is to take an appropriate class. Many four-year colleges and universities and community colleges offer PC-oriented courses for undergraduate, graduate, and continuing-education students. Probably the fastest way to find out about such courses is to phone a local college and speak to the registrar or to someone in a computer-related academic department. Your local computer stores and Internet-enabled coffeehouses (cybercafés) may also organize classes. Some stores provide classroom support as part of system purchases.

CLUBS Computer clubs are another effective way to get an informal education in PCs. They are also a good place to get a relatively unbiased and knowledgeable viewpoint about a particular product or vendor. Generally clubs are organized by region, product line, or common interests. For instance, Apple computer enthusiasts join clubs such as Apple-Holics (Alaska), Apple Pie (Illinois), or Apple Core (California). Many clubs also function as buying groups, obtaining software or hardware for members at reduced rates. Computer clubs range in size from two or three members to several thousand.

SHOWS A computer show gives you a firsthand look at leading-edge hardware and software products. Such shows typically feature numerous vendor exhibits as well as seminars on various aspects of computing. Every November, Las Vegas hosts one of the largest trade fairs in the world, the Computer Dealer Expo (COMDEX) show (see Figure 6-16). This weeklong event commonly attracts hundreds of vendors and around 200,000 visitors, many of them from foreign countries. COMDEX is a spectacular event and undoubtedly will remain popular for several years. However, today's trend favors smaller, more specialized exhibitions.

 FIGURE 6-16

Computer shows. The weeklong Computer Dealer Expo (COMDEX) attracts hundreds of thousands of enthusiasts to Las Vegas from around the world.

PERIODICALS Periodicals are another good source of information about PCs. Scores of them fill newsstands, collectively catering to virtually every conceivable interest area. Computer magazines and newspapers can vary tremendously in reading level. You can generally browse through a variety of computer-related publications at your local bookstore or computer store; evaluate them carefully to determine their appropriateness to your needs. Many PC periodicals also maintain online versions on the World Wide Web. Online periodicals enable users to electronically search for information on specified topics and often give access to back issues.

For links to further information about **PC magazines** and other sites for **PC information**, go to www.harcourtcollege.com/infosys/pcc2e/student/explore/ and click on Chapter 6.

BOOKS One of the best ways to learn about any aspect of personal computing is to read a book on the subject. A host of softcover and hardcover books is available, covering topics ranging from the simple to the highly sophisticated. Included are how-to books on subjects such as using the more widely known productivity software packages, programming in PC-based languages, and the technical fundamentals of PCs. You can find such books in your local library, computer stores, and bookstores. Many books are also published on the World Wide Web. Always check the copyright date of a book before you use it; computer technology moves along rapidly, and books in the field can go out of date just as fast.

ELECTRONIC MEDIA One easy way to learn a subject in our electronic age is to pick up a training disk or view a videotape or television show devoted to the subject. Today many PC-oriented software packages are sold with CDs that provide screen-oriented tutorials, showing you how to use the program. Other types of professionally prepared *courseware* from a third-party vendor may also be available. Videotapes are plentiful for standard videocassette players, so you can see how something works simply by watching your television. In addition, many television shows—especially on cable and satellite—are oriented toward computer education and knowledge. As if all of these sources weren't enough, the World Wide Web is a veritable treasure trove for all sorts of free information about computers (see Figure 6-17).

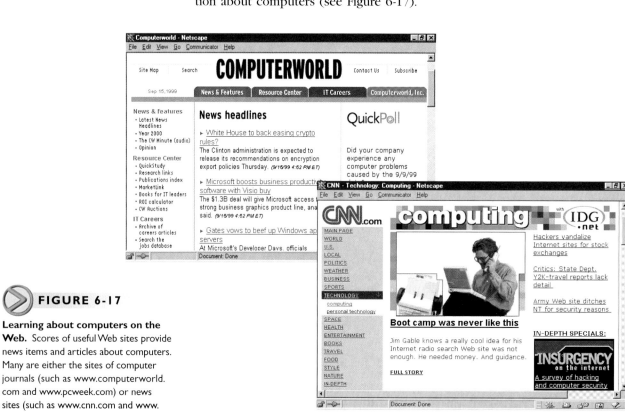

FIGURE 6-17

Learning about computers on the Web. Scores of useful Web sites provide news items and articles about computers. Many are either the sites of computer journals (such as www.computerworld.com and www.pcweek.com) or news sites (such as www.cnn.com and www.msnbc.com).

SUMMARY AND KEY TERMS

 Go to the Online Glossary at www.harcourtcollege.com/infosys/pcc2e/student/ to review key terms.

Chapter 6 covers such related activities as users acquiring their own PC resources, taking care of their own systems, upgrading systems on their own, and educating themselves about PCs.

THE PC MARKETPLACE The PC marketplace is composed of a wide variety of firms that make hardware and software products. One important market segment, the manufacturing of PC system units, is dominated primarily by Compaq, IBM, and a handful of other companies that make PC-compatible computers. System-unit makers are commonly divided into top-tier, second-tier, and third-tier firms.

Most users get their PC hardware and software from retail stores of various sorts, the Internet, mail-order houses, **direct manufacturers** and **software publishers,** and **value-added resellers (VARs).**

SELECTING A PC Steps for selecting a PC include analyzing needs, listing system alternatives, evaluating alternatives, and choosing a system. Although applications software is normally selected before a computer-system platform, software and hardware choices for PCs are often interrelated so that you must consider them jointly. Also, for many PC owners, service is becoming an increasingly important selection criterion.

HARDWARE AND SOFTWARE INSTALLATION When you buy a PC today, most of the hardware and software you need will probably already be in place. To make it easier than ever for PC owners to install any new hardware on their own, both hardware and software vendors have moved to a *plug-and-play* approach.

OPERATING A PC **Backup** refers to procedures for making duplicate copies of valuable files. Two types of backup methods are **full backup** and **partial backup.**

PCs are sensitive electronic devices, so they need careful treatment and protection from damage. A **surge suppressor** will prevent most random electrical spikes from entering your PC and causing damage. An **uninterruptible power supply (UPS)** unit is a surge suppressor with built-in reserve power to let you operate your PC when the main power to your home or office fails. Precautions taken with diskettes and hard disks help to safeguard any data stored on them. Other practices can protect your PC from dust, heat, and static. Software called **screen savers** can protect your monitor.

Security measures protect a PC's hardware, software, and data from unintentional and malicious damage and tampering. No matter what type of security strategy you choose, it is important to note that no strategy can give you full protection.

Although no two problems with a computer system are ever totally alike, some useful guidelines can be followed when troubleshooting problems or when seeking outside technical assistance. For instance, just trying a procedure out a second time or checking the **documentation** that comes with a product often solves the problem. Three sources of software assistance are support from the software publisher, third-party support, and user support. When considering an equipment repair, you should check first to see what protection the manufacturer offers under **warranty.**

UPGRADING You can **upgrade** your PC by buying new hardware or software components that add capabilities and extend its useful life. When considering a hardware upgrade, you must consider such things as your current system's storage capacity, the number of expansion slots, and the power of the system unit. Software upgrades are often accomplished by acquiring a new **release** or **version** of the program that you are currently using. You need to ask yourself whether upgrading is better than starting fresh and buying a new PC. You also must consider whether you are planning to replace a product that's only **technologically obsolete** instead of **functionally obsolete.** Technologically obsolete systems are sometimes called **legacy systems.**

LEARNING MORE ABOUT PCs   A wealth of resources is available to those who want to learn more about PCs and their uses. Classes, computer clubs, computer shows, magazines, newspapers, newsletters, books, and electronic media are all sources of information about PCs.

EXERCISES

1. Fill in the blanks.
   a. A(n) _____ is a program designed to protect your monitor against damaging the phosphorescent coating on its screen.
   b. _____ refers to making, for security purposes, a duplicate copy of a file.
   c. A(n) _____ is a hardware device designed to stop power spikes from damaging a PC.
   d. A(n) _____ usually states that a product manufacturer will correct defects in software or hardware for a given period of time under certain conditions.
   e. A product that no longer meets the needs of a user is said to be _____ obsolete.

2. Match each company name with the description that fits best.
   a. Compaq
   b. Corel
   c. Intel
   d. Microsoft
   e. Iomega
   f. Motorola
   g. Seagate
   h. Apple
   _____ Makes CPU chips for the Apple Macintosh line of computers
   _____ A large, U.S.-based maker of PC-compatible computers
   _____ A producer primarily of hard-disk drives
   _____ The maker of Windows as well as a wide variety of other software products
   _____ The maker of most CPU chips for PC-compatible computers
   _____ The company that publishes WordPerfect
   _____ A producer of superfloppy drives
   _____ The biggest producer of PCs that are not PC-compatible

3. Name as many types of sources as you can for buying PC hardware and software. Which of these sources would you consult in the following situations?
   a. You want to look over a lot of products but don't have time to spend browsing around a store.
   b. You just opened a taco restaurant and need a PC that specializes in keeping track of fast-food operations.
   c. You want a new PC but don't want to spend the premium prices the more famous companies charge.
   d. You're nervous about buying a PC and need a seller that will hold your hand to help you through any problems.
   e. You want to get a brand-name printer at a low price, and you must have it today. You're willing to accept equipment that just became technologically obsolete when a new model came out last month.
   f. You need a printer and want to see as many printer specifications as you can within the next few hours.
   g. All you need is a 166 MHz Pentium computer that will help you write your novel, and you'll be darned if you'll pay for anything more.
   h. You need a software product immediately, and your local computer store does not stock the product.

4. Define each of the following terms:
   a. Legacy system
   b. UPS
   c. Software publisher
   d. Value-added reseller
   e. Third-tier manufacturer
   f. Incremental backup
   g. Partial backup

5. Name several selection criteria that are important to consider when evaluating alternative PC purchases.

6. Provide at least eight reasons that illustrate the importance of backing up files.

7. What is the difference between technological obsolescence and functional obsolescence?

8. Name at least five sources from which users can learn more about PCs. Also, identify the types of learning resources that are available over the Internet.

9. Each of the following definitions is not strictly true in some regard. In each case, identify how the definition is false. Then correct the error by defining the term in the right way.

a. Software publisher: A company that sells the software that other companies create

b. Legacy system: Technologically obsolescent hardware or software that has been around for a while in a company, even though it continues to be updated regularly by its maker

c. Release: A particular version of a software package

d. Value-added reseller: A company that sells computer systems made by others

e. Surge suppressor: A device that keeps a computer system running in the event of a power shortage

10. Why is it sometimes better to lease a PC than to buy it outright?

PROJECTS

1. **BUYING A DESKTOP PC**   The figure below shows an ad for a desktop PC. To demonstrate your knowledge of computing terms in the figure, most of which have been covered in various chapters of this textbook, respond to the questions below and on the following page.

a. What types of storage devices come with the computer system? What is the capacity of each type of storage device?

b. What type of CPU chip comes with the system? How fast is the CPU chip?

c. Is the system PC-compatible?

d. Is the system a "multimedia" computer system?

e. What type of local bus unit does the system contain?

f. Can the monitor display photographic-quality images? What do *noninterlaced* and *.26 dp* mean?

g. What software comes with this system?

h. Does a word-processing program come with this system? If it does, what's its name?

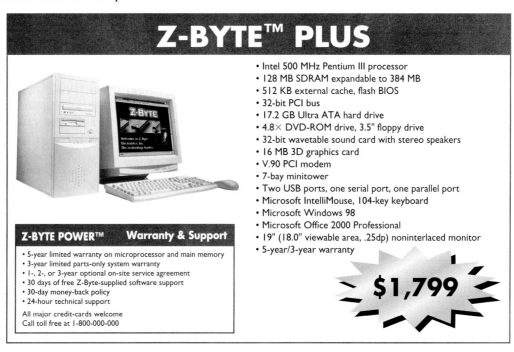

i. Does a printer come with this system? If it does, who is its manufacturer?

j. What options do you have available if the hard disk fails after one year of use?

k. What options do you have available if the operating system isn't responding properly after six weeks of use?

2. **BUYING A NOTEBOOK COMPUTER** The figure at the top of this page shows an ad for a notebook PC. To demonstrate your knowledge of computing terms, most of which have been covered in various chapters of this textbook, respond to the following questions.

a. What types of storage devices come with the computer? What is the capacity of each type of storage device?

b. Do each of the storage devices offer more or less capacity than the corresponding ones in the computer system detailed in Project 1?

c. Why isn't the system offered with a mouse?

d. Is the system a "multimedia" computer system?

e. What does the ad mean by a *Type II PCMCIA slot?*

f. What is the purpose of the infrared port?

g. Would you recommend buying this computer system to gain access to the Internet? Why or why not?

h. What software comes with this system?

i. What's the significance of this computer's lithium ion battery feature? How does this technology compare with other types of batteries?

j. Can you hook up a printer directly to this computer system? Explain why or why not.

k. What options do you have available if the hard disk fails after one year of use?

l. Can you run Windows on this computer? Why or why not?

3. **BUYING A PRINTER** You need a printer for your PC and want to spend no more than $600.

a. Find an ink-jet printer and a laser printer that you can buy for this price. In what important ways do these printers differ?

b. Cut out or copy an ad for a printer from a PC magazine. What does the ad tell you about the features of the printer? Where can you go to get additional information?

c. A call to a local computer store reveals that you can get a product demonstration. What sorts of questions should this demonstration answer?

 4. **BUYING PC HARDWARE OVER THE INTERNET** Many companies that sell PC hardware maintain sites on the World Wide Web. Such sites often showcase product offerings, offer users the chance to configure hardware and buy it, provide technical support, and so on. Visit two such Web sites—one representing a computer maker and the other an equipment reseller—and report to the class about them, making sure that you cover the following points:

a. What are the names of the companies you visited?

b. What types of hardware do they sell?

c. What objectives are served by each of the Web sites—for instance, providing product information, enabling people to buy equipment, offering technical support, and so on?

d. Do the sites offer any types of search or query tools to help you shop online—tools that might lead to better purchase decisions than those you might make after looking at hard-copy advertisements?

e. Do the sites include any "fun" features that might attract shoppers to make return visits?

f. How do people place orders and pay for the equipment?

Some of the Web sites in the accompanying figure may interest you.

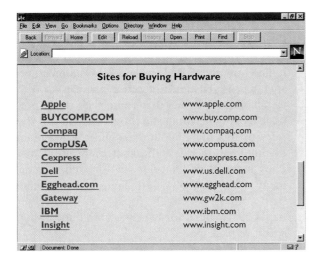

While the sites of computer makers like IBM and Compaq feature their own equipment, sites of resellers like BUYCOMP.COM enable you to select from a large variety of products and scores of manufacturers.

5. BUYING PC SOFTWARE OVER THE INTERNET Many companies that sell PC software maintain sites on the World Wide Web. Such sites often showcase product offerings, offer users the chance to try out or buy software, provide technical support, and so on. Visit two such Web sites—one representing a software publisher and the other a software reseller—and report to the class about them, making sure that you cover the following points:

a. What are the names of the companies you visited?

b. What types of software are sold at the sites?

c. What objectives are served by each of the Web sites—for instance, providing information about software products, enabling users to buy software, letting users download software on a trial basis, offering technical support, and so on?

d. Do the sites offer any types of search or query tools to help you shop online—tools that might lead to better purchase decisions than those you might make after looking at hard-copy advertisements?

e. How do people place orders and pay for the software?

Some of the Web sites in the accompanying figure may interest you.

While the sites of software publishers like Microsoft and Corel feature their own programs, sites of resellers like Egghead.com enable you to select from a large variety of products and scores of publishers.

6. ONLINE PC MAGAZINES You can subscribe to or read for free online versions of many popular PC magazines. For this project, research at least two PC magazines published in Web versions, and answer the following questions:

a. How much does an online subscription cost, relative to a hard-copy subscription of the same magazine?

b. What types of features do the online versions of these magazines have that you can't get in the hard-copy versions?

c. What types of features do the hard-copy versions of these magazines have that you can't find in the online versions?

7. TECHNOLOGY NEWS ON THE INTERNET Several Web sites report on news events regarding technology. Three such sources are MSNBC at www.msnbc.com, CNET News.com at news.cnet. com, and the technology news section of CNN at www.cnn.com. Visit any two of these Web sites and report to your class about what you find. What future prospects do you anticipate for interactive news received on your PC, as opposed to getting news through television or print outlets like newspapers and magazines?

8. **BOOK REPORT** Microsoft Corporation has been one of the most written-about technology companies of the past decade. For this project, write a report, not to exceed 15 pages, discussing some aspect of the company that has made it famous. A variety of books are available to help you gain information for your report, including those below:

   ■ *The Microsoft File: The Secret Case Against Bill Gates,* by Wendy Goldman Rohm. Times Books, 1998.

   ■ *Barbarians Led by Bill Gates: Microsoft from the Inside,* by Jennifer Edstrom and Martin Eller. Henry Holt and Company, 1998.

   ■ *Overdrive: Bill Gates and the Race to Control Cyberspace,* by James Wallace. Wiley, 1997.

   ■ *The Microsoft Way: The Real Story of How the Company Outsmarts Its Competition,* by Randall E. Stross. Addison-Wesley, 1996.

   ■ *Microsoft Secrets: How the World's Most Powerful Software Company Creates Technology, Shapes Markets, and Manages People,* by Richard W. Selby. Free Press, 1995.

Also consider PC newspaper and journal articles to help you in your research as well as information gathered over the Internet.

 9. **PC HISTORY** Many important people have shaped the history of PCs. Several of them are listed below. For this project, choose any three and, for each one, write a sentence or two about his contribution to the history of PCs.
   a. Bill Gates
   b. Steve Jobs
   c. Scott McNealy
   d. Marc Andreesen
   e. Gary Kildall
   f. Phillipe Kahn
   g. Dan Bricklin.
   h. Brian Bastian
   i. Ted Hoff
   j. Tim Berners-Lee

10. **HARD-DISK REQUIREMENTS** Select a software suite, minisuite, or integrated software package, and report to the class the recommended number of bytes required to do a typical installation, a run installation, and a custom installation. Note that the names of these installation options may vary from product to product. Also answer the following questions.
   a. Are any other installation options available?
   b. In addition to the amount of storage needed, what other types of hardware or software requirements are stated by the software publisher for the package you have chosen?

11. **ONLINE DOCUMENTATION** Increasingly, software publishers are putting the documentation telling how their products work—documentation such as tutorials and reference manuals—on the installation CD-ROMs that come with those products. When you install the programs, you can then refer to this documentation online. While online documentation saves the cost of printing hard-copy manuals and supports automated searches, many users have objected. Some feel that online help cannot effectively replace a well-written, hard-copy manual for learning about and using a software package.

   For this project, list the advantages and disadvantages of online documentation relative to hard-copy documentation, from your own perspective as a user. What kind of documentation would provide the most help for you to learn or use a software package?

 12. **SURGE SUPPRESSORS AND UPSS** Affordable surge suppressors and UPSs are widely available to PC users. For this project, find both an inexpensive surge suppressor and an inexpensive UPS that are currently on the market, and report to the class about them. In your presentation, be sure to cover the following:
   a. The name and model number of each item
   b. The price of each item
   c. The characteristics of each item. For instance, how much of a shield does the surge suppressor provide? How many outlets does it have in which to plug in devices? How long will the UPS operate after the main power to the computer is lost?
   d. Which of the two products you have chosen appears to be the better buy? Why?

ONLINE REVIEW

 Go to the Online Review at www.harcourtcollege.com/infosys/pcc2e/student/ to test your understanding of this chapter's concepts.

OUTLINE

Overview
Computers, Work, and Our Well-Being
    Stress-Related Concerns
    Ergonomics-Related Concerns
    Environment-Related Concerns
Computer Crime
    Types of Computer Crime
    Minimizing Computer Crime
    Crime Legislation
Computers and Privacy
    Privacy and Electronic Mail
    Privacy and Marketing Databases
    Privacy and the Internet
    Caller Identification
    Privacy Legislation
Ethical Issues Regarding Computers
    Some Examples
    Why Study Ethics?

SOCIAL ISSUES INVOLVING COMPUTERS

LEARNING OBJECTIVES

After completing this chapter, you will be able to:

1. Describe several work-related and well-being-related concerns that people have regarding computers.

2. Explain what computer crime is, give several examples of it, and describe how computer crime can be prevented.

3. Appreciate how computer technology can encroach on people's privacy and describe some of the legislation enacted to prevent such abuses.

4. Explain what is meant by ethics and provide several examples of ethical misbehavior in computer-related matters.

OVERVIEW

Since the era of commercial computing began about 50 years ago, computers of all sizes and types have rapidly woven their way into the fabric of modern society. In the process, they've created both opportunities and problems. Consequently, they've been both cursed and applauded —and for good reason.

So far in this text, we've focused on the opportunities more than the problems. Although the computer revolution has brought undeniable benefits to society, it has also produced some troubling side effects. Like any fast-paced revolution, it has been disruptive in many ways. Some jobs have been created, others lost, and still others threatened. In addition, an increasing variety of health-related concerns have surfaced that affect people who work with computers and related technologies. Computers have also immensely increased access to sensitive information, creating new possibilities for crime and threatening personal privacy. Clearly, some controls to limit the dangers that these awesome devices pose will always be needed.

In this chapter, we highlight four important problem areas: computers and our well-being in the workplace, computer crime, computers and privacy, and ethical uses of technology. PCs have been around only since the 1970s, so many of the problems covered in this chapter have been inherited rather than initiated by their use. However, PCs have added an important dimension to the social concerns posed by technology. Because so many of them are in use and they are so easy to operate, PCs have made many problems far more pervasive and dangerous.

COMPUTERS, WORK, AND OUR WELL-BEING

Computers have been said to pose a threat to our mental and physical well-being. Although the body of scientific evidence supporting this claim is far from conclusive and is likely to be that way for many more years, we should all be aware of the major concerns raised about the possible effects of computers on our health.

STRESS-RELATED CONCERNS

Emotional problems such as financial worries, feelings of incompetence, and disorientation often produce emotional *stress*. This stress, in turn, may have been triggered by a computer-related event.

LAYOFF OR REASSIGNMENT One of the first criticisms leveled at computers upon their entry into the workplace was that their very presence resulted in job-related stress. When computers were introduced, many people were no longer needed and subsequently were laid off and forced to find new jobs. Workers at the lowest rungs worried most about job security. Many feared the full potential of computers in the office or on the factory floor and spent much of their time never knowing whether machines might replace them. Such fears are still widespread today.

Even people who were not laid off found that their jobs had changed significantly and that they had no choice but to retrain. Airline agents, for example, had to learn how to manipulate a database-retrieval language. Secretaries were pressured into learning word processing and other office-related software to keep in step. Even the pace of work has become faster and far less personal than it was earlier. Many workers never made the transition successfully.

A growing fact of life is that, because of computers, fewer people are needed to do many types of work today. Computers also change the way work is done, often in ways that seem impersonal and that are difficult to predict. For instance, modern computer networks are posing a new threat to workers in that companies no longer have to staff as many physical locations as in the past. Networks also mean that work can be transferred to foreign countries more easily. Also, the Web is threatening to put many small travel agencies, realtors, and booksellers out of business.

FEAR OF FALLING BEHIND The PC boom that has taken place since the early 1980s has put computing power of awesome dimensions at almost everyone's fingertips. Many researchers perceive a widespread fear that failure to learn how to use PCs will make one fall behind. One example is the numerous non-computer-oriented executives, managers, and educators who see themselves being upstaged by their PC-knowledgeable colleagues. There are so many big advances occurring on so many new technology fronts these days that the pace of change is fast enough to make even computer experts—especially those working on mainframe computers—feel they are falling behind.

BURNOUT Burnout is caused not by fear of computers *(cyberphobia)* but by overuse of them *(cyberphelia)*. The infusion of such technologies as PCs, video CDs, e-mail, pagers and wireless phones, and the Web into home and office has raised new concerns about emotional health. What will happen to children who withdraw into their computer systems, to computer-bound managers who are being inadvertently swept into the tide of the computer revolution and its relentless pace, or to families whose intimacy is threatened by overuse of computers in their homes?

To date, little research has been done on computer burnout. What makes this area so controversial is the compelling flip-side argument that most victims of computer burnout would burn out on something else if computers didn't exist.

ERGONOMICS-RELATED CONCERNS

Ergonomics is the field that addresses making products and work areas comfortable and safe to use. With respect to technology, ergonomics covers the effects on workers of things such as display devices, keyboards, and workspaces.

DANGERS POSED BY DISPLAY DEVICES For more than a decade, large numbers of data-entry operators have reported a variety of physical and mental problems stemming from their interaction with display devices. The complaints have centered on visual, muscular, and emotional disorders resulting from long hours of continuous display device use. These disorders include blurred eyesight, eyestrain, acute fatigue, headaches, and backaches. In response to these problems, several states and cities have passed laws that curb display device abuse. Also, hardware vendors have redesigned their products with features such as screens that tilt and swivel to make them more comfortable to use.

Keep in mind that it is not displays alone that cause physical problems. Humans are often part of the equation, too. Operator-induced factors that play a large part include poor posture, not taking frequent breaks, poor exercise habits, bad placement of the display on the desktop, and the like.

DANGERS POSED BY KEYBOARDS Years ago, computer keyboards frequently were built into display units, making it difficult for operators to move them about as freely as they could if the keyboards had been detached. Most claims that a computer keyboard could result in injury seemed to be put to rest after keyboard manufacturers started making detachable keyboards—that is, until the last few years or so.

Today, some people are experiencing a condition known as *carpal tunnel syndrome,* a painful and crippling complex of symptoms affecting the hand and wrist that has been traced to the repetitive finger movements routinely made when using a keyboard. Carpal tunnel syndrome is an example of a *repetitive stress injury,* in which hand, wrist, shoulder, and neck pains can result from performing the same types of physical movements over and over again. Physicians recommend that to minimize the chance of such injuries you should take breaks every hour or so and relax or stretch your body. Recently, a number of innovatively designed keyboards have come to the fore that claim to reduce stress in the hands and wrists (see Figure 7-1).

FIGURE 7-1

Stress-reducing keyboards.

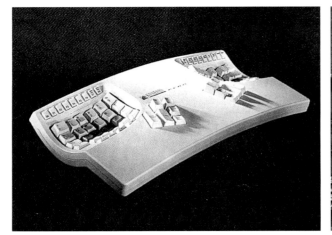

■ **Ergonomics.** The field that studies the effects of things such as computer hardware, software, and workspaces on peoples' comfort and health.

WORKSPACE DESIGN Display devices and keyboards are not the only things that can torture people at workstations. The furniture may be nonadjustable, forcing the user into awkward postures that are guaranteed to produce body kinks. Or the lighting may be so bright that it causes a headache-producing glare on the display screen. Even disconcerting noise levels, present due to poorly designed office equipment or acoustics, may be the culprits. Ergonomics researchers are constantly studying such problems, and the results of their efforts are becoming apparent in the consumer products now being offered to the ergonomics-conscious buyer. Figure 7-2 illustrates some principles of good workspace design.

ENVIRONMENT-RELATED CONCERNS

The surge in PC use during the past several years has caused a variety of environmental concerns.

Take power use. The U.S. Environmental Protection Agency (EPA) estimates that home and office PCs now annually consume billions of dollars worth of electricity. This indirectly has resulted in the discharge of tons of pollutants into the atmosphere. The PC industry responded by adding a variety of energy-saving devices into computer hardware. Among these devices are power-management software that puts the CPU, hard-disk drive, display, and printer into a sleep mode when they are not being used; low-power-consumptive chips and boards; and flat-panel displays.

The environmental threat goes much deeper than just the higher electrical use. For instance, the so-called paperless office that many visionaries predicted for the computer age has become largely a myth. Because computer output is so easy to produce, more paper than ever is now consumed. It is estimated that U.S. businesses generate close to a trillion pages a year—an amount that would stack more than 50,000 miles high!

FIGURE 7-2

Workplace design. Features such as detachable keyboards, tilt capabilities on both keyboards and display devices, and adjustable furniture have contributed to added comfort for display device users.

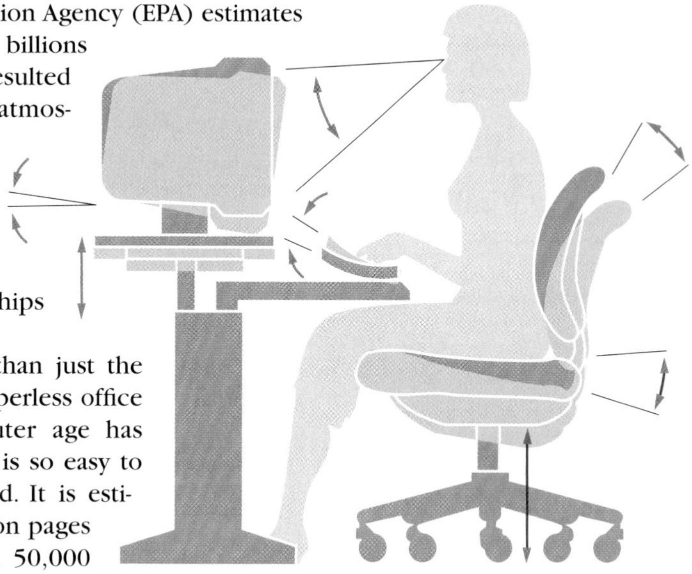

COMPUTER CRIME

Computer crime is defined as the use of computers to commit criminal acts. The law is spotty on computer crime. The U.S. government has made it a felony to access in a prohibited way confidential programs or data in federal-level computers. Most states also have laws that address some aspects of computer crime. But such laws notwithstanding, computer crime is hard to pin down.

One reason is that it is often difficult to decide when a troubling act is really a crime. No one doubts that a bank employee who uses a computer system to embezzle funds from customers' accounts is committing a crime. But what about an employee who steals time on a company PC to balance a personal checkbook for a home or business? Or someone who repeatedly uses a company PC to play games or e-mail jokes to friends? Aren't those acts also "cheating" the company? Where does one draw the line?

Another problem in pinning down computer crime is that judges and juries—not to mention law-enforcement personnel—are often bewildered by

For a tutorial on computer crime, go to www.harcourt college.com/infosys/pcc2e/ student/tutor/ and click on Chapter 7.

■ **Computer crime.** The use of computers to commit criminal acts.

the technical issues involved in such cases. Thus, many companies lack confidence that computer crimes will be investigated and prosecuted successfully, and they don't report them. Also, companies that discover computer criminals among their employees frequently are reluctant to press charges because they fear even more adverse publicity. Why get clients worried?

TYPES OF COMPUTER CRIME

Computer crime has many forms. Some cases involve the use of a computer for theft of financial assets, such as money or equipment. Others concern the copying of information-processing resources, such as programs or data, to the owner's detriment. Still other cases involve manipulation of data such as grades for personal advantage. By far, the majority of computer crimes are committed by insiders.

The cost of computer crime to individuals and organizations is estimated at billions of dollars annually. No one knows for sure what the exact figure is because so many incidents are either undetected or unreported. As in many fields, a specialized jargon has evolved in the area of computer-related crime.

DATA DIDDLING *Data diddling* is one of the most common ways to perform a computer crime. It involves altering key operations data on a computer system in some unsanctioned way. Data diddlers often are found changing grades in university files, falsifying input records on bank transactions, and the like.

THE TROJAN HORSE A **Trojan horse** is a procedure for adding concealed instructions to a computer program so that it will still work, but will also perform prohibited duties. For example, a bank worker can subtly alter a program that contains thousands of lines of code by adding a small patch that instructs the program not to withdraw money from his or her account.

Trojan horses are frequently found today on the Internet to host *computer viruses,* which we'll talk about shortly. They are also being increasingly used for spoofing. A *spoof* is a program buried in a legitimate application that tricks an unsuspecting user into revealing confidential information, such as an access code or credit-card number.

SALAMI SHAVING *Salami shaving* involves manipulating programs or data so that many small dollar amounts—say, a few cents' worth of interest payments in a bank account—are shaved from a large number of transactions or accounts and accumulated elsewhere. The victims of a salami-shaving scheme generally are unaware that their funds have been tapped, because the amount taken from each individual is trivial. The recipient of the salami shaving, however, benefits from the aggregation of these small amounts, often substantially. Supermarkets have been occasionally accused of salami shaving at the checkout counter by not conscientiously updating computer-stored prices to reflect lower shelf prices.

TRAPDOORS *Trapdoors* are diagnostic tools used in the development of programs that enable programmers to gain access to various parts of a computer system. Before the programs are marketed, these tools are supposed to be removed. Occasionally, however, some blocks of diagnostic code are overlooked—perhaps even intentionally. Thus, a person using the associated program may be provided unauthorized views of other parts of a computer system. Recently, a trapdoor was discovered in a well-known browser that enabled snoopers to remotely view the hard-disk contents of any browser users. In 1998, several trapdoors traced to foreign countries were discovered in computer systems in U.S. Air Force and Navy bases, legitimizing the fear

---

■ **Trojan horse.** Adding concealed instructions to a computer program so that it will still work but will also perform prohibited duties.

that computer-system break-ins may become a new battlefield between nations in the 21st century.

LOGIC AND TIME BOMBS *Logic bombs* are programs or short code segments designed to commit a malicious act as soon as the unsuspecting program user performs some specific type of operation. In one documented case, a programmer inserted into a system a logic bomb that would destroy the company's entire personnel file if his name was removed from it. A *time bomb* works just like a logic bomb, except that a date or time triggers the criminal activity.

COMPUTER VIRUSES A **computer virus** is a small block of code—often transmitted to a computer system from a diskette or from data or a program downloaded off a network—that is designed to cause malicious damage to the system or to pull a harmless prank. Malicious damage includes destroying programs and data or gumming up your PC so that it's difficult or impossible to continue working. Pranks include flashing messages on your display screen and beeping your audio unit from time to time to let you know that your PC has been invaded by someone who delights in this sort of sad joke.

Computer viruses often work by copying their harmful code into memory or onto disks, spreading infection like a human virus to any other computer those disks are inserted into. Some computer viruses also contain a mechanism that at a specific time or moment destroys data. Unfortunately, with so many people today downloading programs and data from the Internet, the computer virus problem has gotten much worse.

Thousands of computer viruses of one sort or another are now in existence. All computer viruses are also technically Trojan horses; after all, who would load a virus onto their computer system unless they thought they were dealing with a legitimate application? Figure 7-3 illustrates some additional facts about the behavior of computer viruses. An upcoming section within the chapter addresses protecting a computer system from virus attacks.

For links to further information about computer crime, go to www.harcourtcollege. com/infosys/pcc2e/student/ explore/ and click on Chapter 7.

EAVESDROPPING Examples abound involving the use of technology to *eavesdrop* on information intended for others. One of the earliest types of eavesdropping, and still one of the most common, was wiretapping. Modern computer systems have made it possible to eavesdrop in new ways—for instance, by simply having access to an identification number, an unauthorized user can peek into files and even steal from them. Tools such as *sniffer programs* enable criminals to intercept data and access codes on a network, without anyone being any the wiser that they have been intruding. Two other examples of eavesdropping are using descrambling systems to intercept satellite transmissions and using scanners to overhear calls made over wireless phones.

CELLULAR PHONE FRAUD The goal of *cellular phone fraud,* which takes eavesdropping a step further, is to make calls without paying for them—sticking either the cellular-phone owner or the phone company for the charges. The scam works as follows: Each cellular phone uses a unique internal electronic serial number for verification and billing purposes. This number is broadcast when the phone is in use or even just turned on. Criminals using scanners stake out spots along highway overpasses or in airport parking lots, pluck numbers out of the air, and then use black-market software to program other cellular phones with the stolen numbers (see Figure 7-4).

Cellular phone fraud collectively costs the public hundreds of millions of dollars a year. In New York, some bandits have been reported to make as much as $1,000 a day by allowing others to make illegitimate calls—many of them

---

■ **Computer virus.** A small block of unauthorized code, concealed and transmitted from computer to computer, that performs destructive acts when executed.

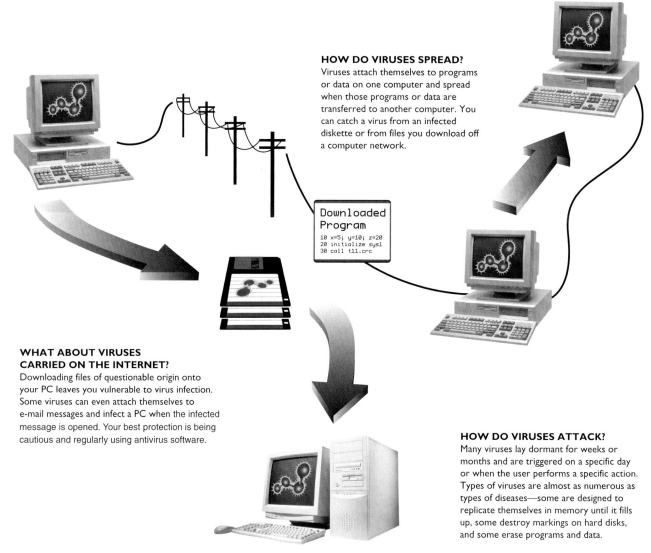

HOW DO VIRUSES SPREAD?
Viruses attach themselves to programs or data on one computer and spread when those programs or data are transferred to another computer. You can catch a virus from an infected diskette or from files you download off a computer network.

Downloaded
Program

```
10 x=5; y=10; z=20
20 initialize sys1
30 call t11.crc
```

**WHAT ABOUT VIRUSES
CARRIED ON THE INTERNET?**
Downloading files of questionable origin onto your PC leaves you vulnerable to virus infection. Some viruses can even attach themselves to e-mail messages and infect a PC when the infected message is opened. Your best protection is being cautious and regularly using antivirus software.

HOW DO VIRUSES ATTACK?
Many viruses lay dormant for weeks or months and are triggered on a specific day or when the user performs a specific action. Types of viruses are almost as numerous as types of diseases—some are designed to replicate themselves in memory until it fills up, some destroy markings on hard disks, and some erase programs and data.

 **FIGURE 7-3**

Computer viruses. A computer virus is harmful computer code that can alter programs or destroy data. Viruses can copy themselves onto legitimate programs and data, thereby spreading damage.

to foreign countries. Cellular-phone owners can request their carriers to block foreign or long-distance calls if they aren't planning on making any.

SOFTWARE PIRACY **Software piracy,** the unauthorized copying or use of a computer program, is often a crime. It is definitely a crime to copy a program and then attempt to sell it for profit. If an individual just uses an illegitimate copy that was made by someone else, such usage is a crime as well, although many types of infractions are rarely discovered or prosecuted. Anyone knowingly involved with unauthorized copies of a program can be found guilty of breaking copyright laws. A number of companies have been successfully prosecuted for buying one or a few copies of a software package and distributing many more copies to employees.

■ **Software piracy.** The unauthorized copying or use of computer programs.

HACKING **Hacking** is a computer term referring to the activities of people who get their kicks out of using computers or terminals to crack the security of remote computer systems. It's a serious problem. For instance, U.S. Department of Defense computers are attacked by hackers hundreds of thousands of times a year, with probably many more times that number of attacks going undetected. Some people engage in hacking purely for the challenge of cracking codes. Others do it to steal computer time, to peek at confidential information, or to cause damage. Intentions aside, hacking often is considered by the courts to be a breaking-and-entering crime similar to forced entry into someone's car or home.

In the early days of PCs, the typical profile of a hacker was a propellerheaded teenager who was in it purely for the excitement that came from snooping and bragging about it. Today's hacker is just as likely to be a well-trained professional who aims to steal or destroy computer resources. Favorite targets these days are credit-card numbers and other sensitive financial information that travel over the Internet.

Cellular phone fraud. Criminals often use stolen serial numbers to make long-distance calls. Using special equipment, they can pluck these numbers right out of the air if they are near legitimate callers who are using their cellular phones.

COUNTERFEITING Desktop publishing and color-printing technology are so sophisticated today that they have opened the door to a relatively new type of computer crime—*counterfeiting*. Take desktop publishing. By using a scanner to read in a corporate logo and then a standard desktop publishing program, producing checks that look genuine is something even a novice can do. As far as color technology goes, the total number of phony U.S. bills being produced on color copiers and printers—now estimated in the billions of dollars—rose eightfold in just the first three years of the 1990s.

Would-be counterfeiters, beware. Financial instruments are being redesigned with watermarks, special inks, and reflective elements that cannot be copied. Also, many color copiers now print invisible codes on outputs, making counterfeit money easier to identify and trace.

COVERUPS In recent years, technology has been deployed to cover up criminal activity—which itself is a crime. For instance, many criminals now booby-trap PCs containing potential evidence so that data are destroyed if the computer is commandeered by the authorities. For instance, the clicking of a mouse could send a command to erase hard disk data at a rate of 50 megabytes per second. Another trick is rigging the door frame in a computer room with magnetic strips, so that a computer's disk storage is demagnetized (and the disk contents destroyed) as soon as someone tries to cart the computer outside.

INTERNET-RELATED CRIMES The rise of the Internet has contributed to new varieties of criminal activity that most people scarcely could have imagined only a few years ago. For instance, several individuals have been arrested in recent years for systematically *stalking* children through computer newsgroups. Web sites and e-mail have made possible *cyberporn,* the distribution of pornographic material over computer networks. In another type of case, a university student was indicted for running an Internet bulletin board over which copyrighted software was allegedly distributed for free.

Today, with so much talk about building even more electronic links to connect users everywhere, new fears have arisen about the potential for computer crime. Especially worrisome to many individuals are the risks involved to both their finances and their privacy when using the Internet to engage in electronic commerce.

■ **Hacking.** Using a PC or computer terminal to penetrate the security of a remote computer system.

MINIMIZING COMPUTER CRIME

It's impossible to achieve 100-percent protection from criminal activities; consequently, the emphasis is on minimizing losses. To achieve this end, organizations can combat computer crime in many ways.

ASSESS RISKS The most important way an organization can minimize crime is by having a good plan for security. The centerpiece of any such plan is an assessment of which operations are most vulnerable to attack. Employers should make a list of disaster-level events that can occur to their operations and make sure that key areas are protected from the most costly and likely types of mishaps.

HAVE A RECOVERY PLAN Because no security plan can guarantee 100-percent safety, one should assume that the worst can, in fact, happen. Thus, organizations should specifically take steps to have backups ready if or when disruptive events such as thefts, fires, floods, or computer outages occur. Backup provisions should include having copies of all important programs and data stored at another site as well as making arrangements for resuming normal, day-to-day operations at a backup site. A plan that spells out what an organization will do to recover from highly disruptive events is called a **disaster-recovery plan.**

HIRE TRUSTWORTHY PEOPLE Employers should carefully investigate the background of anyone being considered for sensitive computer work. Some people falsify résumés to get jobs. Others may have criminal records. Despite the publicity given to groups such as hackers, studies have consistently shown that most computer crimes are committed by insiders.

BEWARE OF MALCONTENTS The type of employee who is most likely to commit a computer crime is one who has recently been terminated or passed over for a promotion or who has some other reason to get even with the organization. In cases in which an employee has been terminated and potential for computer crime exists, the former employer should update its records immediately to show that the person involved is no longer employed and to terminate that employee's company computer access.

SEPARATE EMPLOYEE FUNCTIONS An employee with many related responsibilities can commit a crime more easily than one with a single responsibility. For example, the person who authorizes adding new vendors to a file should not be the same one who authorizes payments to those vendors.

RESTRICT SYSTEM USE People who use a computer system should have access only to the things they need in order to do their jobs. A computer operator, for example, should be told only how to execute a program and not what the program does. Also, users who need only to retrieve information should not also be given updating privileges. High-risk situations such as using software and diskettes of questionable origin should be avoided to prevent the spread of computer viruses.

PASSWORD PROTECT PROGRAMS AND DATA On many systems, users can restrict access to programs and data with **passwords**. For example, a user might specify that anyone wanting access to file AR-148 must first enter the password é5775jummm. To modify the file, a second password may be required. Users are recommended to choose passwords carefully, to change passwords frequently, and to protect particularly sensitive files with several passwords (see Figure 7-5).

■ **Disaster-recovery plan.** A plan that maps out what an organization or individual does to prepare for and react to disruptive events. ■ **Password.** A word or number used to permit selected individuals access to a system.

Many organizations use measures such as access cards and biometric security devices in place of or in combination with passwords. **Access cards**, such as those used in automatic teller machines at banks, activate a transaction when they are used with a password or number. **Biometric security devices** provide access by recognizing some unique physiological characteristic of a person—such as a fingerprint or handprint—or some unique learned characteristic—such as a voice or signature (see Figure 7-6). Because of its reliability and the amount of business beginning to be conducted over the Internet, biometric security is predicated to be a very high-growth area in the near future. According to Iris-Scan, a firm that uses the human eye's iris to verify people's identity, the chance of two different people's irises matching using their scanner is one in 1078, which makes it more effective than DNA testing.

Passwords, access cards, and biometric security devices are all examples of authentication systems. *Authentication* refers to the process a computer system uses to determine whether someone is actually the person he or she claims to be. Biometric devices have been gaining in favor because, while passwords and access cards may be intercepted or stolen, it is exceedingly more difficult for a criminal to replicate a unique personal characteristic.

BUILD FIREWALLS To ward off the threat of hackers, more and more organizations are creating firewalls. A **firewall** is a collection of hardware or software intended to protect computer networks from attack. Historically, network attacks originated outside the organization, from hackers. As intranet creation has intensified, however, security experts are advising organizations to build internal firewalls, too, to keep nosy employees from browsing through data that they don't need in order to perform their jobs.

SECURE TRANSMISSIONS WITH ENCRYPTION Some users and vendors encrypt data and programs to protect them, especially if those resources are going to be traveling over a public network like the Internet. **Encryption**—or *cryptography*—involves scrambling data and program contents through some type of coding method (see Figure 7-7). The encrypting procedure provides *keys,* or passwords, for both coding and decoding. One key locks the message at the sending end of the transmission to make it unintelligible to a snoop, and only a person who is authorized to see the message can decrypt it with a key at the receiving end. The sender and receiver keys do not have to necessarily be the same. Many software packages today have built-in encryption routines.

Several forms of encryption exist. One of the most common is *public-key encryption,* used to send secure data over such unsecured networks as the Internet. Let's see how this works in electronic banking: Two types of keys are used, one public and one private. *Public keys* are kept in the bank's directory, and certain employees will have access to them

RULES FOR PASSWORDS

■ Make the password as long as you possibly can. A four- or five-character password can be cracked by computer program in less than a minute. A ten-character password, in contrast, has about 3,700 trillion possible character permutations and could take a computer decades to crack.

■ Choose an unusual sequence of characters for the password—for instance, mix in numbers and special characters with words from other languages or unusual names. The password should be one that you can remember yet one that doesn't conform to a pattern a computer can readily figure out.

■ Keep a written copy of the password in a place where no one but yourself can find it. Many people place passwords on post-it notes that are affixed to their monitors or taped to their desks—a practice that's almost as bad as having no password at all.

■ Change the password as frequently as you can. Sniffer programs that criminals frequently use can read passwords being entered into unsecured systems.

FIGURE 7-5

Passwords.

FIGURE 7-6

Biometric security. Biometric security devices enable transactions by recognizing some unique physiological characteristic of a person—such as a fingerprint or handprint—or some unique learned characteristic, such as a voice or signature.

■ **Access card.** A plastic card that, when inserted into a machine and combined with a password, permits access to a system. ■ **Biometric security device.** A device that, upon recognition of some physiological or learned characteristic that is unique to a person, allows that person to have access to a system. ■ **Firewall.** A collection of hardware or software intended to protect a company's internal computer networks from outside attack. ■ **Encryption.** A method of protecting data or programs so that they are unrecognizable to unauthorized users.

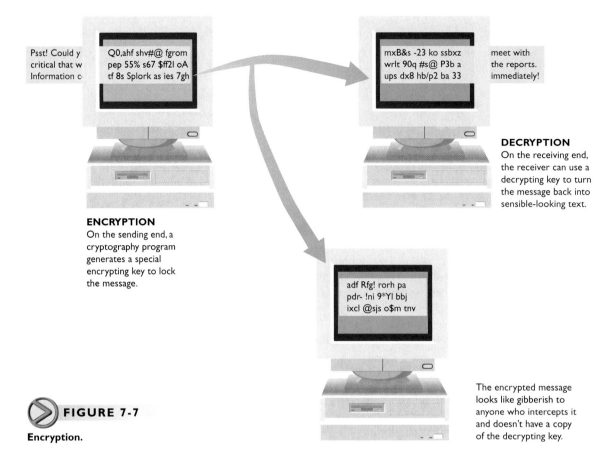

Psst! Could y
critical that w
Information c

Q0,ahf shv#@ fgrom
pep 55% s67 $ff2l oA
tf 8s Splork as ies 7gh

mxB&s -23 ko ssbxz
wrlt 90q #s@ P3b a
ups dx8 hb/p2 ba 33

meet with
the reports.
immediately!

DECRYPTION
On the receiving end,
the receiver can use a
decrypting key to turn
the message back into
sensible-looking text.

ENCRYPTION
On the sending end, a
cryptography program
generates a special
encrypting key to lock
the message.

adf Rfg! rorh pa
pdr- !ni 9*Yl bbj
ixcl @sjs o$m tnv

FIGURE 7-7

Encryption.

The encrypted message
looks like gibberish to
anyone who intercepts it
and doesn't have a copy
of the decrypting key.

FIGURE 7-8

Browser security warnings. In some
secure environments, your browser will
send you a message box such as the one
shown here before it downloads an
uncertified Java applet or ActiveX
control, or transmits data to an
unsecured site.

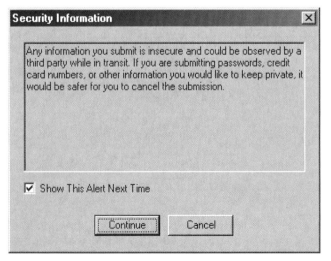

when an encrypted message needs to be sent to a customer. Each customer has access to a *private key,* known only to him or her, which is used to decrypt the message coming from his or her public key. When a customer sends a message back to the bank, the bank uses its own private key to decrypt the message.

Another popular form of encryption uses *digital certificates* that authenticate a sender as a preapproved or legitimate source. If your browser sends you a warning that the sender has not signed a digital certificate, it should immediately put you on notice that you could be communicating with a thief, a hacker, or a person trying to implant a virus on your system.

For sensitive Internet transactions involving credit card information, banking or other financial information, and the like, Web pages that use encryption or some other approved security method should be used. Most browsers indicate on the toolbar or status bar when a secure Web page is being viewed and often the URL will begin with *https* instead of *http.* When performing a sensitive transaction, if you notice that the page is not secured, think very carefully before continuing—virtually all companies doing business on a regular basis over the Internet will use secure Web pages. Many browsers will display a warning when you are about to send data to an unsecured site (see Figure 7-8).

USE CRIME-PREVENTION SOFTWARE A variety of software products are available to help in the fight against computer crime. For instance, **antivirus software** is available to help detect and eliminate the

■ **Antivirus software.** Software used to detect and eliminate computer viruses.

Most antivirus programs will provide you with a list of known viruses.

By clicking on a virus in the list, you can learn about its characteristics.

Antivirus programs will scan memory and any disk drives that you specify. At the end of the scan, they will report their findings.

Antivirus programs should be updated regularly. Every year, hundreds of new viruses are introduced, many of which older programs are not equipped to handle.

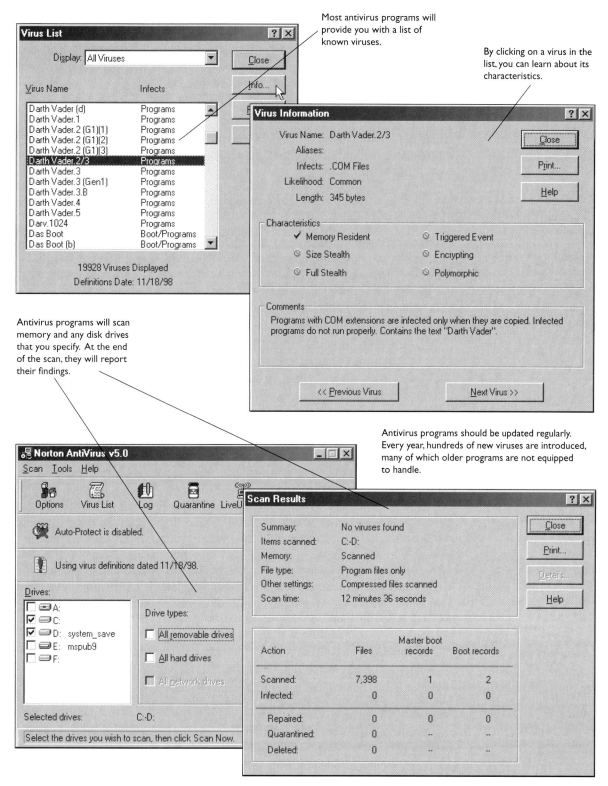

presence of computer viruses (see Figure 7-9). Also, because computers are often used to file false claims, computer programs using artificial-intelligence techniques have been deployed by businesses and government agencies to analyze claims for suspicious patterns. Some of these programs use an artificial-intelligence technique called *neural-net computing,* which enables a computer system to imitate the pattern-recognition process of the human brain.

FIGURE 7-9

Antivirus software. The Norton AntiVirus program illustrated here has almost 20,000 viruses cataloged for which varying degrees of protection are provided.

DEVISE STAFF CONTROLS Overtime work should be carefully scrutinized, because computer crimes often occur at times when the criminal thinks he or she is unlikely to be interrupted. Sensitive documents that are no longer needed should be shredded. Access to computer facilities or the program/data library should be strictly limited to authorized personnel. **Callback devices**, which hang up on and call back people phoning in from remote locations, should be used in communications systems to deter hacking and virus implantation.

MONITOR IMPORTANT SYSTEM TRANSACTIONS The systems software in use should include a program for maintaining a log of every person gaining or attempting to gain access to a system. The log should contain information on the workstation used, the data files and programs used, and the time at which the work began and ended. Such a log allows management to isolate unauthorized system use.

CONDUCT REGULAR AUDITS Unfortunately, many crimes are discovered by accident. Key elements of a system should be subjected to regular **audits**—inspections that certify that the system is working as expected—to ensure that there is no foul play. Auditing often involves two key components, looking for security loopholes and inspecting system-activity logs to ascertain nothing unusual is taking place.

EDUCATE EMPLOYEES One of the best ways to prevent computer crime is to educate employees about security matters. People should be told about various types of computer crime and the conditions that foster them, informed of the seriousness and consequences of computer crime, and instructed on what to do when they suspect a computer crime is taking place or is about to occur.

CRIME LEGISLATION

Federal law has also sought to deter computer crime, with mixed results. The main piece of legislation regarding using computers in criminal ways—the *Computer Fraud and Abuse Act*—has been regularly amended to broaden its scope and to clarify its intent. The law currently outlaws unauthorized access to data stored in computers of the federal government and federally regulated financial institutions. It also outlaws the deliberate implantation of computer viruses in those computers. Actions taken with intent to harm are classified as felonies, while actions performed merely with reckless disregard are considered misdemeanors. Critics say the law doesn't go far enough in that a hacker who is merely curious may not be guilty of a crime at all.

The rapid growth of the Internet has recently pushed the issue of network legislation into the forefront. There have long been laws addressing such offenses as sending indecent material through the mail, libel, harassment, inciting hatred, and the like, but how should those laws apply to computer networks?

One problem is jurisdictional. Because networks can be global, it can be hard to determine where a crime is legally being committed and whose laws apply. A second problem is that many existing laws do not transfer well to networks. Should, say, inflammatory comments over a network be treated like casual chat in a telephone conversation or like carefully crafted words sent through the mail? A third problem deals with responsibility and enforcement issues. Whose job should it be to monitor the massive number of messages

---

■ **Callback device.** A device on the receiving end of a communications network that verifies the authenticity of the sender by calling the sender back. ■ **Audit.** An inspection used to determine whether a system or procedure is working as it should or whether claimed amounts are correct.

sent over computer networks daily? Will the right to personal privacy be compromised? Will the public be willing to pay for the potentially exorbitant cost of having networks policed? Some of these issues are addressed in the next section of this chapter.

COMPUTERS AND PRIVACY

Almost all of us have some aspects of our lives that we prefer to keep private. These may include a sorry incident from the past, sensitive medical or financial facts, or certain tastes or opinions. Yet we can appreciate that sometimes selected people or organizations have a legitimate need for some of this information. A doctor needs accurate medical histories of patients. Financial information must be disclosed to credit card companies and college scholarship committees. The government may need to probe into the lives of people applying for unusually sensitive jobs.

No matter how legitimate the need, however, there is always the danger that information will be misused. Stored facts may be wrong. Facts may get to the wrong people. Facts may be taken out of context and used to draw distorted conclusions. Facts may be collected and disseminated without one's knowledge or consent. Victims can be denied access to incorrect or inappropriate data. As it applies to information processing, **privacy** refers to how information about individuals is used and by whom.

The problem of how to protect privacy and ensure that personal information is not misused was with us long before electronic computers existed. But modern computer systems, with their ability to store and manipulate unprecedented quantities of data and to make those data available at many locations, have added several new wrinkles to the privacy issue. The trend for a long time has been for more and more sensitive data to be put online and for such data to be packaged and sold to others. Thus, it is not unusual that more public concern than ever exists regarding privacy rights.

For a tutorial on privacy issues, go to www. harcourtcollege.com/infosys/ pcc2e/student/tutor/ and click on **Chapter 7.**

PRIVACY AND ELECTRONIC MAIL

Two issues currently dominate the area that covers privacy and electronic mail, the use of electronic mail within companies and Internet spamming.

COMPANY ELECTRONIC MAIL Many people believe that the objective of e-mail within companies is to promote a free-flowing dialogue between workers—that is, to increase the effectiveness of communication. They claim that e-mail should be viewed as the modern-day version of informal chatting around the water cooler, and that e-mail messages should not in any way be confused with official company records. Others claim that any business document created on the premises of an organization is not the property of the individual but of the organization. The issue has largely been resolved in favor of the latter viewpoint; what you say in your e-mail can be legally seized by others and used against you. What's more, you can be prosecuted for destroying e-mail evidence if you deliberately do it to avoid retribution, and your company can get into legal trouble for not taking the proper precautions with employee e-mail (see Figure 7-10).

The issue of employees creating potentially damaging e-mail messages has reached crisis proportions in many companies. In the United States alone, close

---

■ **Privacy.** In a computer processing context, refers to how information about individuals is used and by whom.

FIGURE 7-10

E-mail and the courts. It is against the law to knowingly destroy e-mail messages to avoid punishment for a criminal act.

to 100 million people use e-mail, and the average worker/user sends or receives several electronic messages a day. The growing use of e-mail has made it easier for anyone—clients, employees, disgruntled people, and regulators—to file a lawsuit against a company. Charges already filed have ranged from sexual and racial discrimination to stolen secrets and uncompetitive practices. The latter charge, incidentally, has been one route the Justice Department has chosen to try to nail Microsoft on antitrust charges. The Feds have sorted through years and years of the company's e-mail messages, hoping to find the "smoking gun" that could prove its allegations against Microsoft.

To protect themselves, companies often rely on a formal e-mail policy and software to help enforce it. For instance, at Amazon.com, the online bookseller, a recent policy is that all nonessential documents "should be destroyed when they are no longer current or useful." To help companies carry out or enforce policies, the software industry has responded with various types of products. *E-shredders,* for instance, are programs that claim to completely obliterate e-mail messages. *Snooping software* monitors what users are doing at their PCs. *Nanny programs* alert workers with flashing onscreen warnings when the contents of incoming or outgoing e-mail may be in violation of a company's e-mail policy.

Precautions notwithstanding, a large part of the problem is that companies aren't sure what's expected of them. What type of e-mail is appropriate and what's not? What constitutes being prudent and careful in the eyes of the law? How long must e-mail legally be kept?

The matter of whether or not companies should be allowed to eavesdrop on their employees' e-mail messages is a matter of very heated debate. Companies are quick to point out that they have to protect themselves from unauthorized use of their e-mail systems. After all, a careless comment in a memo could make the company liable. Privacy-rights advocates often counter that companies don't casually rifle through people's desks or file cabinets, so why should they peek at their computer files? Also, the advocates point out, e-mail monitoring can be used for political purposes. Currently, eavesdropping by companies on their e-mail systems is totally legal, and the law doesn't even require that employees be informed that their messages could be monitored. Nonetheless, it makes good business sense to have a computer-resource-usage policy in effect and to have it read by all employees.

SPAMMING   **Spam** refers to unsolicited bulk electronic mail sent over the Internet. The electronic equivalent of junk mail, spam most often originates from commercial sources. At best, it is an annoyance to recipients and can clog a mail network so as to slow down the delivery of important messages. At worst, it can disable a mail network completely.

Internet service providers such as America Online often have millions of pieces of spam clogging their networks each day, and the problem is growing worse. Many people use *e-mail-filtering programs* that automatically discard incoming messages if they appear to contain spam. Currently, legislation is being drafted at both federal and state levels to curb spam abuse.

One of the principal dangers of spam is that the spammer need not worry about carefully targeting a specific audience, because there is virtually no cost difference between sending 500 e-mails versus 500,000. Every time you register your e-mail address at a Web site, you open yourself up to spam.

■ **Spam.** Unsolicited, bulk electronic mail sent over the Internet.

HOW MARKETING DATABASES WORK

When you make an electronic transaction, information about who you are and what you buy is recorded.

The identities of people and what they buy are sold to a micromarketer.

The micromarketer uses its computers to reorganize the data in a way that might be valuable to others.

Companies buy the reorganized data and use it for their own purposes.

PRIVACY AND MARKETING DATABASES

Marketing databases are repositories that contain information about the consuming public. They record where people live, what they are inclined to do, and what they buy. Using such facts, companies attempt to determine the best way to promote specific products to specific types of people. Virtually any time you leave traceable information about yourself anywhere, there's a good chance that it will eventually find its way into somebody's marketing database and on to a company that wants to sell to you (see Figure 7-11).

When you buy a house, for example, your name, address, and the sales price are recorded in a county courthouse. These records are available to the public, including micromarketers. *Micromarketers* are companies that specialize in creating marketing databases and passing on the information to companies that sell products or services. The micromarketer typically breaks down the neighborhoods in a region into several dozen categories. Consumers are placed into one of these categories according to their address. For instance, a "Blueblood Estates" category might be a neighborhood in which the very wealthy live. A "Shotguns and Pickups" category, by contrast, might refer to a rural area where trailers are the likely abode. There are also categories for urban professionals, the elderly, and so on.

Each category is correlated in the micromarketer's computer system with certain buying preferences, a profiling technique known as *geodemographics.* "Blueblood Estates" types are likely to buy expensive cars and take trips to places such as Aspen and St. Thomas. Those of the "Shotguns and Pickups" sort are more likely to be into country music, chainsaws, and Elvis collectibles. This information helps companies customize a direct-mail campaign to consumers' specific tastes. Consumers, of course, often look at unsolicited direct mail as junk mail and resent it as an intrusion on privacy.

In addition to geodemographic data, micromarketers also collect data showing consumers' past purchasing behavior. Every time you make a computerized purchase, valuable data can be gathered about your purchasing tastes and entered into a computer system. Records kept by stores, credit-card companies, banks, the companies whose magazines you subscribe to, and other organizations are sold to the micromarketer. Even the government sells information.

PRIVACY AND THE INTERNET

The First Amendment to the U.S. Constitution guarantees a citizen's right to free speech. This protection allows people to say or show things to others

FIGURE 7-11

Marketing databases.

■ **Marketing database.** An electronic repository containing information useful for niche-marketing products to consumers.

without fear of arrest. People must observe some limits to free speech, of course, such as prohibitions of obscenity over the public airwaves and dealing in child pornography.

But how should the law react to alleged patently offensive or indecent materials on the Internet, where they can be observed by surfing children and by adults who see this as an "in-your-face" invasion to their privacy? The courts recently struck down the Communications Decency Act, which proposed making such actions illegal. The courts have so far had difficulty defining just what is "patently offensive" and "indecent." What's more, they have concluded that numerous self-policing mechanisms now available at the PC-workstation level reduce the need for new laws that restrict Internet content. For instance, a large selection of **blocking software** on the market allows users to block from their own view materials on the Internet that are objectionable to them or to family members.

Blocking software packages work in a variety of ways. The software may provide a list of subjects or keywords that will automatically trigger a system for preventing access to a site; typically, a user can trim or add to this list. For instance, parents could block their home PCs from displaying information on sex, drugs, bomb making, or hate literature if any of those topics were not already censored by their access provider. Many of the latest browsers also allow users to restrict access (see Figure 7-12).

Despite the failure so far of the Communications Decency Act, the censorship battle surrounding the Internet continues to rage. Arguments against censorship point out that policing the Internet effectively would require a prohibitively expensive and difficult effort. Arguments for censorship claim that blocking software assumes computer-literate parents, and many do not and never will meet this standard. In all likelihood, say many industry experts, the Internet will eventually police itself, as the movie industry does with its rating system, at least in the short run.

Momentum has been building within the Internet community to create a universal rating system for Web sites. For instance, a site might voluntarily rate its content on a scale of 0 to 4 on each of several dimensions—such as language, nudity, sex, and violence. (Users could automatically assign noncomplying sites a 4 rating on all dimensions.) Enabled desktop software, such as a browser, would let users establish the maximum number on each dimension that they would tolerate, placing these controls in password-protected files, out of the reach of children. When anyone navigated the Internet from the user's account, the software would read a site's ratings and block access if any single rating exceeded its allowable value.

Another Internet-related and potentially far more serious privacy concern is that people make themselves vulnerable to being spied upon any time they log on to the Internet. This concern is more than justified; as mentioned earlier, a trapdoor was recently found in a well-known browser that enabled remote snoopers to peer at the contents of a Web user's hard disk as the user downloaded Web pages. Conceivably, a snooper could read your electronic mail and peek at any electronic financial records on your PC. The trapdoor has since been closed, but fears linger.

For links to further information about privacy, go to www. harcourtcollege. com/infosys/pcc2e/student/ explore/ and click on Chapter 7.

CALLER IDENTIFICATION

Caller identification, or *caller ID,* refers to a technology in which a telephone device contains a tiny display that will output the phone number and

---

■ **Blocking software.** A program that blocks access to certain parts of the Internet deemed objectionable, based on predetermined criteria. ■ **Caller identification.** Refers to the use of a telephone or answering device that displays the origin of incoming calls.

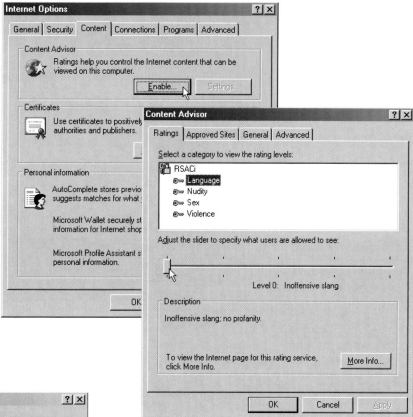

INTERNET OPTIONS
Internet Explorer's censoring options are accessed through the Internet Options dialog box.

CONTENT ADVISOR
When the Content Advisor is enabled, you can specify the maximum allowable level of language, nudity, sex, and violence for rated sites.

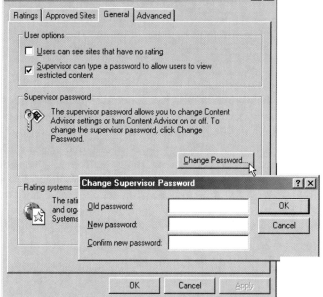

PASSWORD PROTECTION
A supervisor password will prevent the Content Advisor from being changed or disabled by anyone else.

name (or organization) of an incoming caller (see Figure 7-13). Thus, the party receiving the call can identify the person at the other end of the line before picking up the phone, regardless of whether the caller is aware of this. Callers can, however, block caller ID by entering a special code number before dialing a phone number.

Many people have praised caller identification systems as a good way of screening or cutting down on unwanted calls. Also, businesses such as takeout restaurants are guaranteed a measure of protection against callers who order food and then don't show up. Some people, however, have been less enthusiastic, seeing these systems as a potential invasion of privacy. For

FIGURE 7-12

Using a browser to censor content on the Internet.

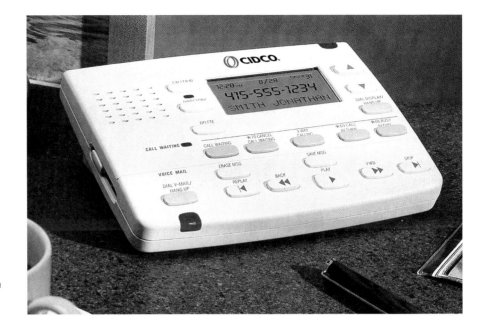

FIGURE 7-13

Caller ID. With a caller ID display, you can tell who's at the other end of the line before answering.

instance, a person living in an apartment in a dangerous neighborhood might be afraid to report a crime taking place outside, fearing that his or her identity could be leaked and cause the criminal to take revenge at some point in the future. Not everyone, of course, is aware that caller ID can be blocked.

Caller identification is not available everywhere. While most states permit its use, some do not.

PRIVACY LEGISLATION

Since the early 1970s, the federal government has sought to protect citizens' rights by passing legislation to curb privacy abuses. Some important laws enacted for this purpose are described in Figure 7-14.

Many people inside and outside the computer industry feel that privacy legislation is woefully out of date and due for an overhaul. Many major privacy laws were enacted more than two decades ago and largely apply to the conduct of the federal government and the organizations to which it supplies aid. A lot has changed since then. Twenty-five years ago, most information was centralized on mainframes and available only in hard-copy form, whereas today it is much more common for data to travel over networks and never make it into print.

ETHICAL ISSUES REGARDING COMPUTERS

The term **ethics** refers to standards of moral conduct. For example, telling the truth is a matter of ethics. An unethical act isn't always illegal, but sometimes it is. For example, purposely lying to a friend is unethical but nor-

■ **Ethics.** A term that refers to standards of moral conduct.

Date	Law and Description
1970	**Freedom of Information Act** Gives individuals the right to inspect data concerning them that are stored by the federal government
1970	**Fair Credit Reporting Act** Prevents private organizations from unfairly denying credit to individuals and provides individuals the right to inspect their credit records for truthfulness
1974	**Education Privacy Act** Stipulates that, in both public and private schools that receive any federal funding, individuals have the right to keep the schools from releasing such information as grades and evaluations of behavior
1974	**Privacy Act** Stipulates that the collection of data by federal agencies must have a legitimate purpose
1978	**Right to Financial Privacy Act** Provides guidelines that federal agencies must follow when inspecting an individual's bank records
1984	**Computer Fraud and Abuse Act of 1984** Makes it a crime to break into computers owned by the federal government
1984	**Cable Communications Policy Act** Limits disclosure of customer records by cable TV companies
1986	**Electronic Communications Privacy Act** Extends traditional privacy protections to include e-mail, cellular phones, and voice mail
1986	**Computer Fraud and Abuse Act of 1986** Amends the 1984 law to include federally regulated financial institutions
1988	**Video Privacy Protection Act** Limits disclosure of customer information by video-rental companies
1988	**Computer Matching and Privacy Act** Limits the use of government data in determining federal-benefit recipients
1991	**Telephone Consumer Protection Act** Requires telemarketing companies to respect the rights of people who do not want to be called and significantly restricts the use of recorded messages
1992	**Cable Act** Extends the Cable Communications Policy Act to include companies that sell wireless services
1994	**Computer Abuse Amendments Act** Extends the Computer Fraud and Abuse Act to include computer viruses
1996	**National Information Infrastructure Protection Act** Punishes information theft crossing state lines and cracks down on network trespassing
1997	**No Electronic Theft (NET) Act** Expands computer piracy laws to include distribution of copyrighted materials over the Internet
1998	**Telephone Anti-Spamming Amendments Act** Applies restrictions to unsolicited, bulk commercial e-mail

FIGURE 7-14

U.S. laws relating to privacy.

mally is lawful, but perjuring oneself as a courtroom witness is a crime. Whether or not criminal behavior is involved, ethics plays an important role in shaping the law and in determining how well we get along with other people.

For a tutorial on ethical issues, go to www. harcourtcollege.com/infosys/ pcc2e/student/tutor/ and click on Chapter 7.

SOME EXAMPLES

Today, computers present a number of ethical concerns. Several examples of these are listed below:

■ A small business owner regularly uses for personal purposes a software package that she isn't licensed to use, claiming she is doing so just to get the feel of it. Although most vendors encourage limited experimentation with their products, they frown on someone who hasn't bought the software using it regularly, and such use is, at a minimum, ethically questionable.

■ On a university PC network, a student casually eavesdrops on data not intended for his use. Snooping may entail neither a prosecutable crime nor a major security threat, but that makes the act no less ethically reprehensible.

■ A computer professional working for one software company leaves to take a job for a competing company. Almost immediately, the professional divulges secrets that were entrusted in confidence by the former employer, giving the new employer an unfair competitive advantage.

■ A medical programmer is assigned to code a software routine that is to be part of a system that monitors the heart rate of hospital patients. Before the program can be fully tested, the programmer is ordered to hand it over so that the system can meet its promised deadline. The programmer tells the project supervisor that the code may contain serious bugs. The supervisor responds, "It's not our fault if the program fails because the deadline is too tight."

■ A large software company, hearing that a small competitor is coming out with a new product, spreads a rumor that it is working on a similar product. Although the large company never provides a formal release date for its **vaporware**—software that's announced long before it's ready for market—it unfairly leaves potential users with the mistaken impression that they will be taking a major risk by purchasing the small competitor's product.

WHY STUDY ETHICS?

Why has ethics become such a hot topic? Undoubtedly, ethics has taken on more significance in recent years because the workplace has become increasingly multicultural and diverse. Different cultures have different values, and what might seem ethically problematic to a person in the United States might be a normal way of doing business in other countries, or vice versa. Take bribes, for instance. In the United States, both bribing and taking bribes are generally considered morally off base. Bribes are also illegal. In some other countries, bribing is not only culturally tolerated, but the salaries of workers are adjusted downward to reflect that bribes are an understood part of the compensation package. Such phenomena as increasing divorce rates and changing family structures have also tended to broaden ethical norms within cultures over time.

Many scholars think that educating people about ethical matters is being pushed aside today in the rush to achieve measurable results. A movement is afoot to change this, however. In recent years, professional computer organizations and some 90 percent of the largest U.S. corporations have established *codes of conduct* covering unauthorized uses of software, hardware, and communications networks (see Figure 7-15). Also, ethics is frequently a topic in computer journals and at professional conferences today.

Whose job is it to teach ethics? The consensus seems to be that primary responsibility lies with parents. With regard to schools, many people feel that

---

■ **Vaporware.** Software that is announced long before it is ready for market.

CODE OF CONDUCT

1. Employees should not copy or use software that belongs to someone else.

2. Employees should not deploy their computers to browse, use, read from, or write to programs of files that are not meant for them.

3. Employees should use computers only to perform job-related tasks.

4. Employees should not use the computers of others, unless authorized or specifically given permission.

5. Employees must not engage in inappropriate electronic communications and are required to read the company's formal e-mail policy.

6. Employees should take reasonable precautions in protecting their computer resources.

7. Employees suspecting inappropriate computer activity within the company should report it immediately to their superiors.

8. Employees must not do anything on their computers that would interfere with larger goals or programs within the company.

9. Employees should not use their computers to engage in activities considered either criminal or in any way harmful to others.

10. Employees must ultimately bear legal and moral responsibility for their actions on the computer.

ethics should be part of the curriculum, but a debate rages over where it should be taught. Should special classes be devoted to ethical behavior, or should an ethics component be a part of each course?

 FIGURE 7-15

Codes of conduct. Illustrated here is a list of computer-usage guidelines that an employer may distribute to employees.

SUMMARY AND KEY TERMS

Go to the Online Glossary at www.harcourtcollege.com/infosys/pcc2e/student/ to review key terms.

Since the early 1950s, when the era of commercial computing began, computers have rapidly woven their way into the fabric of modern society. In the process, they have created both opportunities and problems.

COMPUTERS, WORK, AND OUR WELL-BEING One of the first criticisms leveled at the entry of computers into the workplace was that their presence resulted in stress. Stress-related concerns include fear of layoff or reassignment, fear of falling behind, and job burnout. In addition to these problems, other concerns related to **ergonomics** issues, such as display-device usage and workspace design, have surfaced. Many people also worry about environment-related issues, such as energy usage and the paperwork glut, as well as computer programs going haywire in the year 2000.

COMPUTER CRIME **Computer crime** is defined as the use of computers to commit criminal acts. In practice, even though there are laws that deal with computer crime, it is hard to pin down. It is sometimes difficult to decide when a troubling act is really a crime, people are bewildered by the technical issues involved, and companies frequently are reluctant to press charges.

Computer crime may take many forms. Types of computer crime include data diddling, the **Trojan horse** technique, salami-shaving methods, unauthorized use of trapdoor programs, logic bombs and time bombs, **computer viruses,** eavesdropping, cellular-phone fraud, **software piracy, hacking,** counterfeiting, coverups, and Internet-related crimes.

Organizations can minimize computer crimes in many ways: assessing risks; having a **disaster-recovery plan;** hiring trustworthy people; taking precautions with malcontents; separating employee functions; restricting system use; limiting access to programs and data with **passwords, access cards, biometric security devices,** and **firewalls;** devising staff controls; concealing the contents of particularly sensitive programs and data through **encryption;** using **callback devices;** monitoring important system transactions; conducting regular **audits;** educating employees; and using **antivirus software** and similar programs.

COMPUTERS AND PRIVACY Most people want some control over the kinds of facts that are collected about them, how those facts are collected, their accuracy, who uses them, and how they are used. Modern computer systems, with their ability to store and manipulate unprecedented quantities of data and make those data available to many locations, have added a new dimension to the personal **privacy** issue. Recently, several new concerns about privacy have been voiced with respect to electronic mail (including intracompany mail and **spam**), **marketing databases,** Internet **blocking software,** and **caller identification** phone systems.

ETHICAL ISSUES REGARDING COMPUTERS The term **ethics** refers to standards of moral conduct. Today one of the most important ethical concerns regarding computers is using someone else's property in an improper way. Another is leading people to believe something that's more fiction than fact when it works to one's advantage—such as the case with **vaporware.**

EXERCISES

1. Fill in the blanks.
   a. Fear of computers is known as _____.
   b. _____ is the field that covers the effects of factors such as equipment and computer workspaces on the productivity and health of people in the workplace.
   c. _____ refers to a phone-system feature that can display the phone number and name of a caller.
   d. _____ is a crime that involves manipulating programs or data so that many small dollar amounts are trimmed from a large number of transactions or accounts and accumulated elsewhere.
   e. _____ are companies that specialize in creating marketing databases and passing the information contained in them to companies that sell directly to people.

2. Match each term with the description that fits best.
   a. Computer virus   d. Hacking
   b. Data diddling   e. Trapdoor
   c. Spoof   f. Sniffing
   _____ An example of a Trojan horse
   _____ Refers to software that can glean passwords and other data from a computer system
   _____ Is transmitted through a copy operation
   _____ A diagnostic tool that allows the viewing of computer storage
   _____ The altering of an organization's operations data

   _____ Using a computer terminal or PC to illegally break into a remote computer system

3. Describe some ways in which computers may adversely affect our health or well-being.

4. Define the following terms.
   a. Vaporware
   b. Firewall
   c. Authentication
   d. Biometric security device
   e. Geodemographics
   f. Encrypting key

5. Answer the following questions about computer viruses.
   a. What is a computer virus?
   b. Describe as many ways as you can that your computer can become infected by a virus.
   c. How do you prevent catching a computer virus?
   d. How do you get rid of a computer virus?

6. Computer crime can exist in many forms. In each case below and on the following page, describe the type of computer crime taking place.
   a. A person working for the Motor Vehicle Division deletes a friend's speeding ticket from a database.
   b. A brokerage business overcharges by one fiftieth of one percent on all commissions made on the buying and selling of stocks.

c. A group of people make copies of U.S. software whose rights are owned by others and sell the software overseas for a profit.

d. A disgruntled employee places a program on the company mainframe that instructs key data to be erased on March 15.

e. A person uses a desktop publishing system to create phony checks.

f. A systems programmer implants code into a program that would cause all phone numbers in the company to become inoperative if the company vetos a pay raise.

g. A repairperson implants a device on a company network that enables him to pick up from a remote phone all transmitted account numbers and passwords.

7. What fundamental rights of the individual have computer privacy laws tried to protect?

8. Below are described several situations regarding the use of computers. In the check boxes provided, mark whether each act is *unethical, criminal,* or *neither* of these. The "neither" category can include both ethical acts or acts that, while not morally wrong, are not commendable either.

UNETHICAL CRIMINAL NEITHER

a. A company spokesperson tells employees that the company doesn't monitor e-mail messages, knowing full well it does. ❏ ❏ ❏

b. A programmer rigs his company's network so that on April 19 everyone gets a message when they log on telling them that the government was wrong to use force with the Branch Davidians at Waco. ❏ ❏ ❏

c. The executive of a company with no policy as regards e-mail confidentiality randomly snoops messages to make sure that employees are not goofing off. ❏ ❏ ❏

d. A brokerage house sells a list of clients to a micromarketer, not really caring who the micromarketer deals with. Later, the micromarketer sells the list to a telemarketing company it suspects is involved in shady investing practices.
   Brokerage house: ❏ ❏ ❏
   Micromarketer: ❏ ❏ ❏

e. A worker is given the job of building a system that will deliver a new computer service to consumers, signing a legally binding agreement not to disclose facts about it to outsiders. She is so fascinated by the service that she immediately quits her job and interests a competitor to hire her on at twice her former salary, in order to develop a competitive service. ❏ ❏ ❏

UNETHICAL CRIMINAL NEITHER

f. A software developer creates an antivirus program. To finance the advertising campaign for this product, the developer calls several computer executives at large firms and gets them to put up $10,000 each. This, the developer believes, will produce the funds needed and make the executives more likely to buy the product.
   Developer: ❏ ❏ ❏
   Computer executives: ❏ ❏ ❏

g. A fund raiser for a hospital has access to a continually updated database that reveals the recent deaths of people who were able to afford expensive medical care. The fund raiser frequently uses the database to target bereaved families for contributions. ❏ ❏ ❏

h. A teenager gets a demon dialer—a program that rapidly generates passwords and tries them out—and uses it to break into the computer of a local business. Once inside the system, the teenager looks around for a few minutes and then leaves, disturbing nothing. When his friends ask him about the incident the next day, he confides, "It was no big deal. I just wanted to see for myself if the demon dialer did what everyone said it could do." ❏ ❏ ❏

9. Determine the differences between the following terms.
   a. Caller identification and a callback device
   b. A computer crime and an ethical impropriety regarding computers
   c. Encrypting data and password-protecting data
   d. Software piracy and hacking
   e. A time bomb and a logic bomb

10. Determine whether the following statements are true or false.
   a. Carpal tunnel syndrome is a disability that evolves from poor use of display technology.
   b. Cellular phone fraud is a prime example of software piracy.
   c. A disaster-recovery plan maps out what an organization does to prepare for and react to disruptive events.
   d. Access cards are typically used in combination with passwords.
   e. The Computer Fraud and Abuse Act is the main piece of legislation governing an individual's right to privacy as regards computer databases.

PROJECTS

1. OFF TO THE RACES A clerk in a steel company uses a company-owned, networked PC—on company time—to handicap horses for a local racetrack.
   a. Is a crime being committed?
   b. Where do you draw the line between a criminal and noncriminal act?
   c. From a privacy standpoint, how do you feel about the steel company randomly checking the contents of files on its network, from time to time, to ensure that employees are using its computers for work-related tasks?

2. COMPUTER CRIMES Computer crimes are regularly reported in the press. For this project, find an example of a computer crime covered in a newspaper or magazine, and report to the class about it. Be sure to cover such details as the nature of the crime, the dollar amount of loss resulting from the crime, how the criminal act was discovered, and the like.

3. ACCEPTABLE USE POLICIES Many schools have a code of conduct governing acceptable uses of their computers. The policies often address such issues as what types of information can and cannot be stored on the computers and what types of uses are considered objectionable. For this project, create what you feel is an ideal acceptable-use policy for your campus. Make sure the policy addresses the following issues:
   a. Who the policy covers—students, faculty, administrators, alumni, anyone else?
   b. What types of uses are forbidden. Make sure you are specific; vague usage of words creates loopholes and will effectively leave you with no policy at all.
   c. Any penalties that are to be levied for first infractions and repeat infractions.

If your school already has an acceptable-use policy, compare yours with theirs, and comment on the differences.

4. ANTIVIRUS PROGRAMS Many antivirus programs currently exist on the market. For this project, choose such a program, answering the following questions in the process.
   a. What is the name of the product? Who makes it?
   b. How much does the product cost?
   c. How many types of viruses can the program detect?

   d. How are updates received on the product? How much do such updates cost?
   e. How should the product be used—at the beginning of a work session, continuously throughout a work session, or what? _____

Three Web sites that you might want to visit for product information are listed below.

COMPANY	WEB ADDRESS
Dr. Solomon's	www.drsolomon.com
MacAfee	www.mcafee.com
Symantec	www.symantec.com

5. ERGONOMICS One of the problems with diseases like carpal tunnel syndrome and other types of repetitive stress injuries is that their causes are not fully understood by the medical profession. Thus, the vendors of many ergonomic products have no scientific evidence at all to any claim that the products lead to any sort of cure or alleviation of pain. (When a product makes no claims that it can cure illnesses, incidentally, it does not need approval from the Food and Drug Administration.) For this project, find an ad for a product that claims to be ergonomic.
   a. What is the product, and who makes it?
   b. In what way is the product claiming to be ergonomic?
   c. Is any sort of research evidence being cited as to the ergonomic effectiveness of the product?

6. STEP UP TO THE BEEF BOX This chapter and others have touched upon a lot of controversial social issues regarding computers. Here's your chance to sound off with your own ideas on one of them. A recent statement made by the American Association of University Professors (AAUP) said of colleges forbidding certain uses of the Internet,

> ...On a campus that is free and open, no idea can be banned or forbidden ....No viewpoint or message may be deemed so hateful or disturbing that it cannot be expressed.

Respond to this with your own opinions on the matter. Do you think colleges are crossing any sort of a line when they try to prohibit certain types of speech on their Internet sites or try to block sites accessed through their computers?

7. **"DUMPING" PRODUCTS** Over the past several years a number of large computer companies have been accused by others of *dumping* their products—that is, putting them in the hands of consumers for below actual cost—to achieve competitive advantage over smaller rivals. For example, a multibillion dollar company, facing a threat from a small upstart company with far fewer resources, may decide to distribute a product for free for a certain period. This action would force the rival to take a similar action and possibly drive it out of business or in a new direction. Once the smaller rival is out of the way, the larger company can then gradually raise prices and achieve normal profit margins.

   a. Is dumping, as described here, an ethical problem, a crime, or merely a smart, aggressive business practice?

   b. In what ways do consumers benefit or lose when dumping takes place?

   c. Is "dumping" just an ugly word for "price war"? Tell why or why not.

   d. What's the difference between a computer company selling a product for below cost, in an effort to draw users, and a supermarket giving away free turkeys before Thanksgiving to any shopper making a $25 purchase?

   e. Extra credit: Locate an article in the computer press that describes an alleged dumping incident and report to the class about it.

8. **SOFTWARE PIRACY** In a recent editorial in *Computerworld*, a software consultant touched off a flood of fiery protest by remarking that software piracy is overblown as an issue. He argued that:

   a. Most people who pirate software wouldn't have bought the software in the first place, so the aggregate value of pirated software doesn't necessarily represent lost revenue.

   b. Pirates who like a product often legitimately buy future releases of it to access new features, so pirating often has a positive effect on future sales.

   c. The value of stolen software—which is estimated to be in the billions of dollars annually—overstates the real drain on profits because it multiplies the number of illegal copies times sales price.

Respond to these comments.

9. **MARKETING DATABASES AND YOU** The chapter hints that there is considerable fear that marketing databases can be used to invade a person's privacy.

   a. What important issue areas do you feel should be addressed by the government to ensure that the privacy of individuals isn't invaded by micromarketers? For instance, one critical issue area concerns *access;* that is, who will have access to the marketing data, and under what circumstances will access be granted?

   b. If you were able to write laws that governed the creation and use of marketing databases, what would they allow or prohibit?

10. **Privacy** Privacy issues regarding computers are regularly reported in the press. For this project, find an example of a privacy issue covered in a journal or newspaper, and report to the class about it. Be sure to cover such details as the alleged privacy violation and whose privacy is being compromised.

11. **Disaster Recovery** Many organizations have disaster-recovery plans that are used to get them back on track if a traumatic event strikes. Each plan begins with an evaluation of risks that organization faces and a list of precautions it should be taking immediately to minimize losses in the event of a disaster. For this project, let's assume that your school asks you to set up a disaster-recovery plan for its campus computer operations. What types of disaster situations are possible? What sorts of precautions would you recommend for minimizing the effects of such disasters? Write a paper (five to eight pages) outlining your plan and defending it. Feel free to use computer journals, books, or information from the Internet to do your background research.

12. **THE ELECTRONIC FRONTIER FOUNDATION** The Electronic Frontier Foundation, or EFF, is a nonprofit organization devoted to the protection

of privacy, free expression, and access to public resources and information online—as well as to the promotion of social responsibility in computer-related matters. Visit the EFF's Web site at www.eff.org, and write a summary (one to three pages) describing how the site is organized and the types of information you found there.

13. **BLOCKING SOFTWARE** As mentioned in the chapter text, blocking software can prevent access to objectionable materials. For this project, find a software product that blocks Internet content, and write a paper (three to five pages) about it. Your paper should cover the following issues:
    a. The name of the product and the company that makes it
    b. The cost of the product
    c. How the product works with other computer-system resources; in other words, is it a browser plug-in, a stand-alone product that works independently of a browser, or something else?
    d. The method by which the product blocks parts of the Internet that the user deems objectionable

14. **SOFTWARE ERRORS** An underlying fear that many people have about computer systems is that they sometimes make mistakes that a human of reasonable intelligence would never make. Software errors are, in fact, frequently covered by the press. As this book was being written, for instance, an interesting error had just been reported as having been made by a midwestern bank. Into each of 826 depositor checking accounts, a program had erroneously deposited $924.8 million dollars—collectively, several times the bank's total assets. Just a couple of years before that, incidentally, an eastern bank made a similar error, erasing half of the balances in thousands of checking accounts. A culprit often cited for such errors is the multitude of systems that banks use to process deposits and withdrawals—human tellers, ATM machines, wire transfers, PC-based systems, and so on—all of which have to be coordinated.

For this project, find an example of a software error covered in a newspaper or magazine, and report to the class about it. Be sure to cover the nature of the error, the consequences or dollar amount resulting from the error, and the likely cause of the problem.

15. **INVOKE YOUR PRIVACY RIGHTS** Tired of junk mail, marketing databases, and—perhaps most of all— telemarketers who call you in the middle of your supper? The U.S. Federal Trade Commission (FTC) has a Web site (www.ftc.gov/privacy) to inform people how to put a stop to the marketing of their personal information. Other advice on privacy matters can be found at the nonprofit Privacy Rights Clearinghouse Web site at www.privacy rights.org. For this project, visit one of these sites, and report its contents to your classmates.

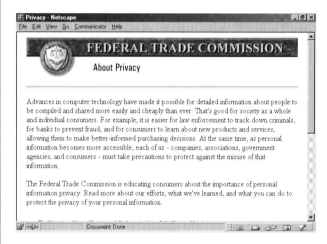

16. **ONLINE PRESCRIPTIONS** The explosion of commerce on the Internet has led to some businesses few people could have imagined only a decade ago. One of these is a new method of health-care delivery: online medical prescriptions. In this high-tech form of health care, doctors with Web sites who have never seen their patients can make prescription drugs available to them through an online questionnaire. For instance, a patient requesting the drug Viagra fills out a form on his home PC and e-mails it back, with a consultation fee, to the doctor. If the request is approved, an electronic prescription can be sent to an online pharmacy, and the drugs can often cost the patient far less than had the prescription been filled at a conventional, local pharmacy.
    a. The American Medical Association has officially frowned on such online prescriptions, whereas others see it as the wave of the future. What do you think?
    b. Do you see any legal or ethical issues involved in such online health care? Be specific.

INTERACTIVE EXERCISE

SAFEGUARDING YOUR COMPUTER

You'd like to practice some basic security methods, such as checking for viruses and backing up files. Go to the Interactive Exercise at www. harcourtcollege.com/infosys/pcc2e/student/exercise/ to complete this exercise.

ONLINE REVIEW

Go to the Online Review at www.harcourtcollege.com/infosys/pcc2e/student/ to test your understanding of this chapter's concepts.

GLOSSARY

The terms shown in boldface are presented in the text as key terms. Numbers in parentheses after the definitions of terms indicate pages on which the terms are boldfaced in the text. The terms shown in boldfaced italic are other commonly used and important words often encountered in computing environments. Numbers in parentheses after the definitions of bold-faced italic terms indicate the pages on which the terms are mentioned.

A

Access card.
A plastic card that, when inserted into a machine and combined with a password, permits access to a system. (247)

Accounting package.
A software package that processes an organization's business transactions, such as those coming from payroll, order entry, accounts receivable and payable, and so forth. (110)

Active-matrix.
Refers to a flat-panel display technology that provides very sharp screen images. Contrasts with passive-matrix. (59)

ActiveX.
A set of controls that enables programs or content of virtually any type to be embedded within a Web page. (184)

Add-in board.
A circuit board that may be inserted into a slot within a desktop computer's system unit to add one or more functions. (45)

Address.
An identifiable location in storage where data are kept. Both memory and disk are addressable. (49)

AI.
See Artificial intelligence. (36)

Analog.
Transmission of data as continuous-wave patterns. Contrasts with digital. (135)

Antivirus software.
Software used to detect and eliminate computer viruses. (248)

Applet.
A small program that provides a dynamic or interactive quality to a Web page. (182)

Applications.
See Applications software. (10)

Applications software.
Programs that help with the type of work that people buy computer systems to do. Contrasts with systems software. (10, 100)

ARPANET.
The forerunner to the Internet, named after the Advanced Research Projects Agency (ARPA), which sponsored its development. (161)

Artificial intelligence (AI).
The ability of a machine to perform actions that are characteristic of human intelligence, such as reasoning and learning. (36, 112)

ASCII.
A fixed-length, binary coding system widely used to represent data for computer processing and communications. (36)

Asynchronous transmission.
The transmission of data over a line one character at a time, with variable time intervals between characters. Contrasts with synchronous transmission. (148)

Audit.
An inspection used to determine whether a system or procedure is working as it should or whether claimed amounts are correct. (250)

Authentication.
The process of determining that a person is who he or she claims to be. (247)

B

Backbone.
The part of a network that carries the most traffic. (139)

Backup.
A procedure that produces a duplicate version of any file that you can't afford to lose. (219)

Bandwidth.
The difference between the highest and lowest frequencies that a transmission medium can accommodate. (135)

BBS.
See Bulletin board system. (124)

Binary.
The numbering system with two possible states. (34)

Biometric security device.
A device that, upon recognition of some physiological or learned characteristic that is unique to a person, allows that person to have access to a system. (247)

Bit.
A binary digit, such as 0 or 1. (34)

Bits per second (bps).
A measure of a transmission medium's speed. (135)

Blocking software.
A program that blocks access to certain parts of the Internet deemed objectionable, based on predetermined criteria. (254)

Bookmark.
A place in a program or application that you can immediately go to after selecting an associated menu choice. (179)

Boolean search.
Retrieval of data by using keywords such as AND, OR, and NOT when specifying filtering conditions. (189)

Boot.
The process of loading the operating system into the computer system's RAM. (20)

Bps.
See Bits per second. (136)

Bridge.
An interface that enables two similar networks to communicate. Contrasts with gateway. (146)

Browser.
A program that makes it easy for users to find and display Web pages. (109, 178)

Bulletin board system (BBS).
A computer file shared by several people that enables them to post or broadcast messages. (124)

Bus.
Any electronic path within a computer system along which bits are transmitted. (46)

Bus network.
A telecommunications network consisting of a transmission line with lines dropped off for several devices. (140)

Byte.
A configuration of 8 bits that represents a single character of data. (36)

C

Cache memory.
A storage area, faster than RAM, where the computer stores data it has most recently accessed. (42)

CAD software.
See Computer-aided design software. (111)

Callback device.
A device on the receiving end of a communications network that verifies the authenticity of the sender by calling the sender back. (250)

Caller identification.
Refers to the use of a telephone or answering device that displays the origin of incoming calls. (254)

Cartridge tape.
Magnetic tape in which the supply and take-up reels are contained in a small plastic case. (56)

Cascading.
The overlapping of windows on a display. Contrasts with tiling. (86)

Cathode-ray tube (CRT).
A display device that projects images on a long-necked display tube similar to that in a television set. (59)

CD-ROM.
A low-end optical disk that can be read but not written to. (55)

Cellular phone.
A mobile phone that transmits calls through special ground stations that cover areas called *cells* to communicate with the regular phone system. (133)

Central processing unit (CPU).
The piece of equipment, also known as the computer, that interprets and executes program instructions and communicates with support devices. (5)

Chat.
An Internet feature that supports interactive discussion groups on selected topics. (173)

Check box.
A screen choice that requires the user to toggle an accompanying check mark on or off, respectively indicating whether the choice is selected or not. (90)

Client.
A device designed to receive service in a client-server network. Contrasts with server. (142)

Client-server LAN.
A LAN composed of *client* devices, which receive network services, and server devices, which provide the services. Contrasts with peer-to-peer LAN. (142)

Cluster.
An area formed where a fixed number of contiguous sectors intersect a track. (51)

Coaxial cable.
A transmission medium, consisting of a center wire inside a grounded, cylindrical shield, capable of sending data at high speeds. (131)

Communications medium.
The intervening link, such as a telephone wire or cable, that connects two physically distant hardware devices. (129)

Communications satellite.
An earth-orbiting device that relays communications signals over long distances. (132)

Compiler.
A language translator that converts an entire program into machine language before executing it. Contrasts with interpreter. (99)

Computer.
The piece of equipment, also known as the *central processing unit (CPU),* that interprets and executes program instructions and communicates with peripheral devices. (5)

Computer-aided design (CAD) software.
A general term applied to the use of computer technology to automate design functions. (111)

Computer crime.
The use of computers to commit criminal acts. (241)

Computer system.
A collection of elements that includes the computer and components that contribute to making it a useful tool. (5)

Computer virus.
A small block of unauthorized code, concealed and transmitted from computer to computer, that performs destructive acts when executed. (243)

Concentrator.
A communications device that combines control and multiplexing functions. (146)

Connect time.
The amount of time you spend online with a service provider's computers. (194)

Context sensitive.
A characteristic of a user interface that adjusts program actions to accommo-

date the type of operation the user is currently trying to perform. (87)

Cookies.
Small files stored on your hard drive by your browser at the request of the Web servers you visit. (182)

Coprocessor.
A dedicated processor chip that is summoned by the CPU to perform specialized types of processing. (42)

CPU.
See Central processing unit. (5)

Cross compatibility.
The ability of a software or hardware product to work with products from other vendors. (228)

Crosshair cursor.
An input device that you move over hard-copy images of maps and drawings to enter them into computer storage. (33)

CRT.
See Cathode-ray tube. (59)

Cryptography.
The field that deals with the art and science of encryption. (247)

Cyberphobia.
The fear of computers. (239)

D

Data.
A collection of raw, unorganized facts. (6)

Database.
A collection of related files. (14)

Database management system (DBMS).
A software product designed to integrate data and provide easy access to them. (106)

Data bus.
The path that links the CPU to RAM. (46)

DBMS.
See Database management system. (106)

Default.
The assumption that a computer system makes when the user indicates no specific choice. (80)

Defragmentation.
The process of rewriting a program that is stored in noncontiguous clusters into contiguous clusters. (223)

Desktop computer.
A computer system that is designed to reside on an ordinary desktop. Contrasts with portable computer. (15)

Desktop publishing.
A PC-based publishing system that can fit on a desktop. (109)

Dialog box.
A box that requires the user to supply information to the computer system about the task being performed. (90)

Digital.
Transmission of data as 0 and 1-bits. Contrasts with analog. (135)

Direct access.
Reading or writing data in storage so that the access time involved is independent of the physical location of the data. Also known as *random access.* Contrasts with sequential access. (49)

Direct manufacturer.
A hardware maker that sells directly to the public. (212)

Directory.
A collection of files that is grouped under a name of its own. Also commonly called a *folder* in a graphical user interface. (93)

Disaster recovery plan.
A plan that maps out what an organization or individual does to prepare for and react to disruptive events. (246)

Disk drive.
A direct-access secondary storage device that uses a magnetic or optical disk as the principal medium. (51)

Diskette.
A low-capacity, removable disk made of a tough, flexible plastic and coated with a magnetizable substance. Also called a *floppy disk.* (49)

Display device.
An output device that contains a viewing screen. Also called a *monitor.* (57)

Display terminal.
A piece of hardware that consists of a display (for output) and a keyboard (for input). (136)

Document.
Any single piece of work created with software and then given a name by which it may be accessed. (12)

Documentation.
A detailed written description of how a program, procedure, or system works. (223)

Domain name.
An ordered group of symbols, separated by periods, that identifies an Internet server. (176)

Dot-matrix character.
A character composed from a rectangular matrix of dots. (60)

Dot pitch.
The distance between display-screen pixels, in millimeters. (58)

Downloading.
The process of transferring a file from a remote computer to a requesting computer over a network. Contrasts with uploading. (145)

Downward compatibility.
The ability of a software product to save files in a form that is acceptable to an earlier version or release of the product. Contrasts with upward compatible. (228)

Dragging and dropping.
The process of moving an item from one part of the screen to another with a mouse. (32)

Drop-down menu.
See Pull-down menu. (80)

Dumb terminal.
A workstation, consisting of a display and keyboard, that can do little more than send and receive data. (140)

DVD.
An optical-disk standard that enables very high capacities. (55)

E
EDI.
See Electronic data interchange. (129)

Electronic data interchange (EDI).
A computer procedure that enables firms to electronically exchange standard business documents—such as purchase orders and invoices. (129)

Electronic mail.
The computer-to-computer counterpart for interoffice mail or the post office. Also called e-mail. (109, 123, 166)

Electronic mailbox.
A storage area on a hard disk that holds messages, memos, and other documents for the receiver. (123)

E-mail.
See Electronic mail. (109, 123, 166)

Encryption.
A method of protecting data or programs so that they are unrecognizable to unauthorized users. (247)

Ergonomics.
The field that studies the effects of things such as computer hardware, software, and workspaces on people's comfort and health. (240)

Ethernet.
A collection of protocols that specify a standard way of setting up a bus-based LAN. (149)

Ethics.
A term that refers to standards of moral conduct. (256)

Expansion bus.
The path that extends the data bus so that it links with peripheral devices. (46)

Expansion slot.
A socket inside the system unit into which an add-in board is plugged. (45)

Expert system.
A program or computer system that provides the type of advice that would be expected of a human expert. (112)

Extranet.
An extension of an organizational intranet onto the Internet itself. (144)

F
Facsimile.
A method for transmitting text documents, pictures, maps, diagrams, and the like over the phone lines. Abbreviated as fax. (124)

FAQs.
See Frequently asked questions. (173)

Fax.
See Facsimile. (124)

Fiber-optic cable.
A transmission medium composed of hundreds of hair-thin, transparent fibers along which lasers carry data as light waves. (131)

Field.
A collection of related characters. (14)

File.
A collection of related records. (14)

File directory.
A listing on a storage medium that provides such data as name, length, and starting address for each stored file. (51)

File transfer protocol (FTP).
A communications protocol that facilitates the transfer of files between a host computer and a user's computer. (170)

Firewall.
A collection of hardware or software intended to protect a company's internal computer networks from outside attack. (247)

Flat-panel display.
A slim-profile display device. (59)

Floppy disk.
See Diskette. (49)

Folder.
A container for documents. (13)

Formatting.
The process of organizing a disk so that it is usable in a particular operating environment. (51)

Freeware.
Software offered for use without charge. (76)

Frequently asked questions (FAQs).
Typical questions asked by newcomers to Internet newsgroups, mailing lists, and chat rooms, accompanied by the answers to those questions. (173)

FTP.
See File transfer protocol. (170)

Full backup.
A procedure that produces a duplicate copy of all files onto a secondary storage medium. Contrasts with partial backup. (219)

Full-duplex transmission.
A type of transmission in which messages may travel in two directions simultaneously along a communications path. (147)

Functionally obsolete.
A term that refers to a product that no longer meets the needs of an individual or business. (228)

Function key.
A special keyboard key that executes a preprogrammed routine when pressed. (31)

G

Gateway.
An interface that enables two dissimilar networks to communicate. Contrasts with bridge. (146)

GB.
See Gigabyte. (37)

Ghosted.
Refers to a menu choice that has a faded appearance, indicating that the choice is unavailable in the current context. (81)

Gigabyte (GB).
Approximately one billion bytes. (37)

Gopher.
An information-retrieval tool for the Internet that generates hierarchical, text-intensive menus; successive topic choices narrow a search to a particular resource. (170)

Graphical user interface (GUI).
A term that refers to the graphical screens that make it easier for users to interact with software. (78)

Graphics tablet.
An input device that consists of a flat board and a pointing mechanism that traces over it, storing the traced pattern in computer memory. (33)

Groupware.
Software that enables several people to collaborate in their work. (126)

GUI.
See Graphical user interface. (78)

H

Hacking.
Using a PC or computer terminal to penetrate the security of a remote computer system. (245)

Half-duplex transmission.
Any type of transmission in which messages may move in two directions—but only one way at a time—along a communications path. (147)

Hard copy.
A permanent form of computer system output—for example, information printed onto paper or film. Contrasts with soft copy. (57)

Hard disk.
A system consisting of one or more rigid platters and an access mechanism. (52)

Hardware.
Physical equipment in a computing environment, such as the computer and its peripheral devices. Contrasts with software. (9)

Helper package.
A program designed to work alongside another program. (187)

Hierarchical local network.
A local network in which a relatively powerful host CPU at the top of the hierarchy interacts with workstations at the bottom. (144)

History list.
A browser feature that stores descriptions and addresses of the last several Web sites you visited. (179)

Home page.
The starting page for a Web site. (169)

Host computer.
The main computer in a network. (140)

Hot swappable.
Refers to a hardware device that can be brought online or offline without power to the main computer system shut off. (47)

HTML.
See Hypertext markup language. (186)

HTML converter.
A program designed to produce Web pages from documents already existing in other formats. (186)

HTML Wizard.
A program that automatically generates Web pages from screen selections made by the user. (186)

Hyperlink.
An icon, image, or specially marked text that represents a link to a new document, application, or Web page. Also called *hypermedia* (84, 168)

Hypermedia.
See Hyperlink. (84)

Hypertext markup language (HTML).
The most widely used language for developing Web pages. (186)

I

Icon.
A graphical image on a display screen that invokes some action when selected. (82)

Imagemap.
A screen image with embedded hyperlinks. (83)

Image scanner.
A device that can read into computer memory a hard-copy image such as a text page, photograph, map, or drawing. (33)

Impact printing.
A technology that forms characters by striking a pin or hammer against an inked ribbon, which presses the desired shape onto paper. Contrasts with nonimpact printing. (60)

Information.
Data that have been processed into a meaningful form. (7)

Infrared technology.
A communications medium in which data are sent as infrared light rays. (134)

Ink-jet printer.
A printer that forms images by spraying small droplets of charged ink onto a page. (61)

Input.
What is supplied to a computer process. Contrasts with output. (3)

Input device.
Equipment that supplies materials to the computer. Contrasts with output device. (4)

Insertion point.
A cursor character that shows where the next key pressed will appear on-screen. (57)

Instruction set.
The set of machine-level instructions available to a computer. (40)

Integrated software program.
A collection of abbreviated software products bundled together into a single package and sold at a price that is less than the sum of the prices of the individual components. (100)

Internet.
A global network linking thousands of networks and millions of individual users, businesses, schools, and government agencies. (123, 161)

Internet address.
A unique identifier assigned to a specific location on the Internet, such as a host computer, Web site, or user mailbox. (176)

Internet content provider.
An organization or individual providing information for distribution over the Internet. (164)

Internet relay chat (IRC).
A feature that allows people to type messages to others and to get responses in real time. (174)

Internet service provider (ISP).
An organization that sells basic online access to the Internet. (164)

Interpreter.
A language translator that converts program statements line by line into machine language, immediately executing each one. Contrasts with compiler. (100)

Intranet.
A private network—often one set up by a company for employees—that implements the infrastructure and standards of the Internet and World Wide Web. (143)

IRC.
See Internet relay chat. (174)

ISA.
A popular PC bus standard; stands for Industry Standard Architecture. (46)

ISDN.
A digital phone service that offers high-speed transmissions over ordinary phone lines. Stands for *integrated services digital network.* (139)

ISP.
See Internet service provider. (164)

J

Java.
A programming language, created at Sun Microsystems, that is used to add interactive or dynamic features to Web pages. (182)

Joystick.
An input device that resembles a car's gear shift. (32)

K

KB.
See Kilobyte. (37)

Keyboard.
An input device composed of numerous keys, arranged in a configuration similar to that of a typewriter, that generate letters, numbers, and other symbols when pressed. (31)

Kilobyte (KB).
Approximately 1,000 bytes (1,024 to be exact). (37)

L

LAN.
See Local area network. (142)

Language translator.
Systems software that converts applications programs into machine language. (99)

Laptop computer.
A portable personal computer weighing about 8 to 15 pounds. (16)

Laser printer.
A printer that works on a principle similar to that of a photocopier. (60)

Legacy system.
See Technologically obsolete. (228)

Light pen.
An electrical device, resembling an ordinary pen, used to enter computer input. (32)

List box.
A screen-window panel that requires the user to select an item from a predetermined list. (90)

Local bus.
A path that connects the CPU directly to peripheral devices that require the most speed. (47)

Local network.
A privately run communications network of several machines located within a few miles or so of one another. Contrasts with wide-area network. (140)

Local area network (LAN).
A local network without a host computer, usually composed of PC workstations and shared peripherals. (142)

M

Machine language.
A binary-based programming language that the computer can execute directly. (40)

Machine-readable form.
Any form that represents data so that computer equipment can read them. (5)

Mac OS.
The operating system for Apple's Macintosh line of computer systems. (97)

Mailing lists.
A service through which discussion groups communicate via shared e-mail messages. (171)

Mainframe.
A large computer that performs business transaction processing chores. (18)

Marketing database.
An electronic repository containing information useful for niche-marketing products to consumers. (253)

Maximize.
Enlarging a window so that it fills the entire screen. Contrasts with minimize. (87)

MB.
See Megabyte. (37)

Megabyte (MB).
Approximately 1 million bytes. (37)

Memory.
Also known as *random access memory (RAM)*, the section of the computer system that temporarily holds data and program instructions awaiting processing, intermediate results, and processed output. (8)

Menu.
A set of options from which the user chooses to take a desired action. (80)

Menu bar.
A horizontal list of choices that appears on a highlighted line, usually below the window title. Often called the *main menu.* (80)

Message box.
A dialog box that pops up on the screen to warn the user or to provide status information. (91)

Microcomputer system.
A computer system driven by a microprocessor. (5)

Microprocessor.
A CPU on a silicon chip. (3, 5)

Microsoft Internet Explorer.
A widely used Web browser. (179)

Microwave.
An electromagnetic wave in the high-frequency range. (132)

Midrange computer.
An intermediate-sized and medium-priced computer. (18)

Minimize.
Reducing a window to an icon on the taskbar. Contrasts with maximize. (87)

Modem.
A communications device that enables digital computers and their support devices to communicate over analog media. (137)

Monitor.
A display device without a keyboard. (57)

Monochrome.
A term used to refer to a device that produces outputs in a single foreground color. (38)

Mosaic.
A freeware tool that was the first GUI Web browser to gain wide acceptance; most commercial browsers today are enhanced forms of Mosaic. (178)

Motherboard.
See System board. (41)

Mouse.
A common pointing device that you slide along a flat surface to move a pointer around a display screen and make selections. (31)

Mouse pointer.
An onscreen, context-sensitive symbol that corresponds to movements made by a mouse. (31, 81)

MS-DOS.
An operating system widely used on early PC-compatible computers. (94)

Multimedia.
A term that refers to computer systems and applications that involve a combination of text, graphics, audio, and video data. (185)

Multiplexer.
A communications device that interleaves the messages of several low-speed devices and sends them along a single high-speed path. (146)

Multitasking.
A capability of a single-user operating system to execute two or more programs or program tasks concurrently. (94)

N

Netiquette.
Proper etiquette for exchanges on the Internet. (173)

Netscape Navigator.
A widely used Web browser. (178)

NetWare.
The most widely used operating system on local area networks (LANs). (98)

Network.
A system of machines that communicate with one another. (17)

Network computer.
A stripped-down desktop PC that is optimized for the Internet and intracompany communications. (16)

Network interface card (NIC).
An add-in board though which a workstation connects to a local network. (137)

Network operating system (NOS).
An operating system that enables the network administrator in an organization to control network tasks. (94)

Neural-net computing.
An expert-system technology in which the human brain's pattern-recognition process is emulated by a computer system. (249)

Newsgroup.
A service that works like an electronic newspaper, carrying *articles* posted by subscribers and responses to them (together called *threads*). (172)

NIC.
See Network interface card. (137)

Nonimpact printing.
A technology that forms characters and other images on a surface by means of heat, lasers, photography, or ink jets. Contrasts with impact printing. (60)

Noninterlaced.
Refers to a monitor that draws every screen line of pixels on each screen refresh; contrasts with interlaced monitors, which draw in every other line. (58)

Nonvolatile storage.
Storage that retains its contents when power is shut off. Contrasts with volatile storage. (42)

NOS.
See Network operating system. (94)

Notebook computer.
A portable computer system that is roughly the size of a 1- or 2-inch-thick notebook. (16)

O

Object module.
A program that is compiled. Contrasts with source module. (99)

OCR.
See Optical character recognition. (33)

Offline.
A state that *does not* allow a device to send data to or receive data from other devices. Contrasts with online. (18)

Online.
A state that allows a device to send data to or receive data from other devices. Contrasts with offline. (18)

Operating environment.
A term that refers to a user interface or operating system—for instance, DOS, DOS-with-Windows, Windows 95, and Windows 98. (94)

Operating system.
The main collection of systems software that enables the computer system to manage the resources under its control. (92)

Optical character recognition (OCR).
The use of reflected light to input marks, characters, or codes. (33)

Optical disk.
A disk read by reflecting pulses of laser beams. (54)

Output.
The results of a computer process. Contrasts with input. (3)

Output device.
Equipment that accepts materials from the computer. Contrasts with input device. (4)

P

Packet switching.
A transmission technique that breaks messages into smaller units that travel to a destination along possibly different paths. (152)

Palette.
A menu that enables users to choose such attributes as color and texture. (85)

Palmtop computer.
A portable personal computer that you can hold in your hand. (16)

Parallel transmission.
Data transmission in which each bit in a byte follows its own path simultaneously with all other bits. Contrasts with serial transmission. (135)

Parity bit.
An extra bit added to the byte representation of a character to ensure that either an odd or an even number of 1-bits transmitted with every character. (149)

Partial backup.
A procedure that produces a duplicate copy of selected files onto a secondary storage medium. Contrasts with full backup. (219)

Passive-matrix.
Refers to a flat-panel display technology that provides adequate but not outstandingly sharp screen images. Contrasts with active-matrix. (59)

Password.
A word or number used to permit selected individuals access to a system. (246)

Path.
An ordered list of directories that lead to a particular file or directory. (93)

PC.
See Personal computer. (5)

PC card.
A small card that fits into a slot on the exterior of a portable computer to provide new functions. Also called a *PCMCIA card*. (45)

PC compatible.
A personal computer based on Intel microprocessors or compatible chips. Contrasts with Macintosh compatible. (16)

PC-DOS.
The operating system designed for and widely used on early IBM microcomputers. (94)

PCI.
A widely adopted local-bus standard; stands for Peripheral Component Interconnect. (47)

PCMCIA.
An acronym for *Personal Computer Memory Card International Association.* See PC card. (45)

PDA.
An acronym for personal digital assistant. See Palmtop computer. (16)

Peer-to-peer LAN.
A LAN in which all of the user workstations and shared peripheral devices operate on the same level. Contrasts with client-server LAN. (143)

Peripheral equipment.
The devices that work with a computer. (4)

Personal computer (PC).
A microcomputer system designed to be used by one person at a time. (5)

Personal computer system.
See Personal computer. (5)

Pixel.
A single dot on a display screen. (38)

Platform.
A foundation technology by which a computer system operates. (16)

Plotter.
An output device that prints such output as posters, graphs, and diagrams. (64)

Plug-and-play.
The ability of a computer to detect and to help configure new hardware components. (45)

Plug-in package.
A program that updates another program with features the latter doesn't have. (186)

Pointing device.
A piece of input hardware that moves an onscreen pointer such as an arrow, cursor, or insertion point. (31)

Pointing stick.
A trackball-like device placed between the keys of a portable computer. (33)

Port.
A socket on the exterior of a computer's system unit into which a peripheral device can be plugged. (44)

Portable computer.
A PC that is compact and light enough to be carried about easily, for use at different locations. Contrasts with desktop computer. (16)

Portal.
The page your browser first displays when you turn it on. (182)

PPP.
A protocol that resembles SLIP but allows more reliable and secure communications. (193)

Presentation graphics software.
A program used to prepare bar charts, pie charts, and other information-intensive images and to present them to an audience. (108)

Primary storage.
See Memory. Contrasts with secondary storage. (8)

Printer.
A device that records computer output on paper. (59)

Privacy.
In a computer processing context, refers to how information about individuals is used and by whom. (251)

Processing.
The conversion of input to output. (3)

Productivity software.
Computer programs, such as word processors and spreadsheets, designed to help make workers more productive in their jobs. (11, 100)

Program.
A set of instructions that causes the computer system to perform specific actions. (7)

Programming language.
A set of rules used to write computer programs. (7)

Prompt.
Displayed text or symbols indicating the computer system's readiness to receive user input. (78)

Proprietary software.
A software product to which someone owns the rights. (75)

Protocol.
A set of conventions by which machines establish communication with one another in a telecommunications environment. (147)

Pull-down menu.
A menu of subcommands that drops down vertically from a horizontal menu bar or appears alongside another pull-down menu. Also called a *drop-down menu.* (80)

R
Radio button.
A panel of alternative choices—preceded by round, graphical screen elements—in which one and only one choice can be selected by the user. (90)

RAM.
See Random access memory. (8, 42)

Random access.
See Direct access. (49)

Random access memory (RAM).
The computer system's main memory. (8, 42)

Read-only memory (ROM).
A software-in-hardware module from which the computer can read data but to which it cannot write data. (42)

Read/write head.
The component of a disk access mechanism or tape drive that inscribes or retrieves data. (48)

Realtime processing.
Processing that takes place quickly enough so that results can guide current and future actions. (185)

Record.
A collection of related fields. (14)

Release.
A minor upgrade of a software program. (227)

Repeater.
A device that amplifies signals over a network. (145)

Rewritable CD.
An optical disk that allows users to repeatedly write to and read from its surface. (55)

Ring network.
A telecommunications network that connects machines serially in a closed loop. (140)

ROM.
See Read-only memory. (42)

Root directory.
The topmost directory in a directory structure. (93)

Router.
A device used on WANs to decide the paths along which to send messages. (145)

S
Scalable.
Refers to hardware components whose speed or storage capacity can be increased incrementally. (144)

Screen saver.
A software product designed to protect the phosphor coating on the inside of a

display screen from damage when the display is turned on but is not used for an extended period. (221)

Scroll bar.
A horizontal or vertical bar along an edge of a window that allows the user to view information that does not currently fit within the window. (87)

Search engine.
A software tool used to look for specific information over the Internet. (188)

Secondary storage.
Storage on media such as disk and tape that supplements memory. Contrasts with primary storage. (8)

Sector.
A pie-shaped area on a disk surface. (51)

Security.
A collection of measures for protecting a computer system's hardware, software, and data from damage or tampering. (222)

Sequential access.
Fetching stored records in the same order in which they are physically arranged on a storage medium. Contrasts with direct access. (49)

Serial transmission.
Data transmission in which every bit in a byte must travel down the same path in succession. Contrasts with parallel transmission. (135)

Server.
A computer that manages shared devices, such as laser printers or high-capacity hard disks, in a client-server network. Contrasts with client. (142)

Shareware.
Software that people can copy and use in exchange for a nominal fee. (76)

Shortcut keystrokes.
Keystrokes that make it possible for commands to be entered with minimal keystroking. (78)

SIMM.
An acronym for single in-line memory module, a SIMM is a board upon which RAM chips are mounted. (42)

Simplex transmission.
Any type of transmission in which a message can move along a path in only a single, prespecified direction. (147)

SLIP.
A version of TCP/IP that enables individuals and organizations to connect to the Internet over ordinary phone lines. (193)

Soft copy.
A nonpermanent form of computer system output—for example, information

sent to a display. Contrasts with hard copy. (57)

Software.
Computer programs. Contrasts with hardware. (9)

Software license.
An agreement that enables someone to use a proprietary software product. (75)

Software piracy.
The unauthorized copying or use of computer programs. (244)

Software publisher.
A company that creates software. (212)

Software suite.
A collection of software products bundled together into a single package and sold at a price that is less than the sum of the prices of the individual components. (100)

Source module.
A program before it is compiled. Contrasts with object module. (99)

Spam.
Unsolicited, bulk electronic mail sent over the Internet. (252)

Speaker.
An output device that produces sound. (62)

Spreadsheet.
A productivity-software product that supports quick creation and manipulation of tables and financial schedules. (101)

Star network.
A telecommunications network consisting of a host device connected directly to several other devices. (140)

Storage.
An area that holds materials going to or coming from the computer. (3)

Storage media.
Objects that store computer-processed materials. (5)

Streaming.
A term often used to describe audio or video transmissions that can begin to be played at a client workstation before their associated files have been fully downloaded. (185)

Subdirectory.
Any directory below the root directory. (93)

Subnotebook computer.
A portable personal computer weighing about 2 to 6 pounds. (16)

Supercomputer.
The fastest and most expensive type of computer. (18)

Surge suppressor.
A device that protects a computer system from random electrical power spikes. (220)

SVGA.
A display-device standard widely used on Pentium-class computers. (59)

Synchronous transmission.
The timed transmission of data over a line one block of characters at a time. Contrasts with asynchronous transmission. (148)

Syntax.
The grammatical rules that govern a language. (78)

System board.
The main circuit board of the computer to which all computer-system components connect. Also called a *motherboard*. (41)

System unit.
The hardware unit that houses the CPU and its memory as well as a number of other devices. (33)

Systems software.
Background programs that enable applications programs to work with a given set of hardware. Contrasts with applications software. (11, 92)

T

Tape drive.
A secondary storage device that reads from and writes to mounted magnetic tapes. (56)

Taskbar.
In Windows 95 and 98, a bottom-of-screen area that enables you to launch applications and observe system status information. (79)

TB.
See Terabyte. (37)

TCP/IP.
A collection of communications protocols through which PCs accessing the Internet can understand each other and exchange data. (193)

Technologically obsolete.
A term that refers to a product that still meets the needs of an individual or business, although a newer version or release has superseded it in the marketplace. Also called a legacy system. (228)

Telecommunications.
Transmission of data over a distance. (123)

Telecommuting.
Working through one's home and being connected by means of electronic devices to coworkers in remote locations. (127)

Teleconferencing.
Using computer and communications technology to carry out a meeting between people in different locations. (127)

Telnet.
A communications protocol that lets workstations serve as terminals to a remote server computer. (170)

Terabyte (TB).
Approximately 1 trillion bytes. (37)

Terrestrial microwave station.
A ground station that receives microwave signals, amplifies them, and passes them on to another station. (132)

Text box.
A space in a dialog box in which the user is expected to type information. (90)

Tiling.
Arranging screen windows so that they appear side by side. Contrasts with cascading. (86)

Token ring.
A ring-based LAN that uses token passing to control transmission of messages. (149)

Toolbar.
An icon menu comprised of small graphics called buttons that stretches either horizontally or vertically across the screen. (83)

Track.
A path on a storage medium where data are recorded. (50)

Trackball.
An input device that exposes the top of a sphere, which the user moves to control an onscreen pointer. (33)

Trojan horse.
Adding concealed instructions to a computer program so that it will still work but will also perform prohibited duties. (242)

Twisted-pair wire.
A communications medium consisting of wire strands twisted in sets of two and bound into a cable. (129)

U

Uniform resource locator (URL).
A unique identifier representing the location of a specific Web page on the Internet. (176)

Uninterruptible power supply (UPS).
A surge suppressor with a built-in battery, the latter of which keeps power going to the computer when the main power goes off. (220)

Universal serial bus (USB).
A relatively new bus standard that allows enabled devices to hook up to a single, hot-swappable port. (47)

Unix.
A long-standing operating system most commonly used on midrange computers, PC networks, graphics workstations, and the Internet. (97)

Upgrading.
The process of buying new hardware or software in order to add capabilities and extend the life of a computer system. (226)

Uploading.
The process of transferring a file from a local computer to a remote computer over a network. Contrasts with downloading. (145)

Upward compatible.
Refers to the ability of an application to work in a later version or release of the software than the version in which it was created. Contrasts with downward compatibility. (228)

UPS.
See Uninterruptible power supply. (220)

URL.
See Uniform resource locator. (176)

UseNet.
A protocol that defines how newsgroups are handled by server computers. (173)

User.
A person who needs the results that a computer produces. (164)

User interface.
The manner in which a computer product makes its resources available to users. (77)

Utility program.
A general-purpose program that performs some frequently encountered operation in a computer system. (98)

V

Value-added reseller (VAR).
A company that buys hardware and software from others and makes computer systems out of them that are targeted to particular vertical markets. (212)

Vaporware.
Software that is announced long before it is ready for market. (258)

VAR.
See Value-added reseller. (212)

Version.
A major upgrade of a software product. (227)

Vertical-market software.
Productivity software products designed to meet the needs of niche markets, such as medical and dental offices and videotape-rental stores. (111)

VGA.
The display device standard most widely used on 386 and 486 computers. (59)

Virtual reality.
A hardware-and-software technology that allows computer systems to create illusions of real-life experiences. (186)

Voice chat.
A feature that enables you to speak to others over the Internet. (174)

Voice mail.
An electronic mail system that digitally records spoken phone messages and stores them in an electronic mailbox. (123)

Volatile storage.
Storage that loses its contents when power is shut off. Contrasts with nonvolatile storage. (42)

W

WAN.
See Wide area network. (145)

Warranty.
A conditional pledge made by a manufacturer to protect consumers from losses due to defective products. (225)

Web server.
A computer that stores and distributes Web pages upon request. (169)

Web site.
A collection of related Web pages belonging to an individual or organization. (168)

Wide area network (WAN).
A network that spans a large geographic area. Contrasts with local network. (145)

Window.
A box of related information that appears overlaid on a display screen. (86)

Windows NT.
An operating system designed by Microsoft Corporation for both workstation and network applications within organizations. Beginning in 1999, Microsoft started naming this operating system Windows 2000. (96)

Windows 3.x.
A graphical operating environment created by Microsoft Corporation to run in conjunction with DOS. Two widely used versions are Windows 3.1 and Windows 3.11. (94)

Windows 9x.
The operating system that succeeded the combination of DOS with Windows. Two versions are Windows 95 and Windows 98. (95)

Windows 95.
The operating system that succeeded the combination of DOS with Windows 3.x. (95)

Windows 98.
The upgrade to Windows 95. (95)

Windows 2000.
Microsoft's high-end operating system, formerly known as Windows NT. (96)

Word processing.
The use of computer technology to create, manipulate, and print text materials such as letters, legal contracts, and manuscripts. (101)

Workgroup computing.
Several people using desktop workstations to collaborate in their job tasks. (126)

World Wide Web (WWW).
A network within the Internet consisting of data organized as pages with hyperlinks to other data. (168)

WORM.
An optical disk that allows the user's drive to write data only once and then read it an unlimited number of times. (55)

WWW.
See World Wide Web. (168)

WYSIWYG.
An acronym for the phrase what you see is what you get, indicating a display screen image identical or very close to the look of the eventual printed output. (79)

Y
Yahoo!
A widely used search engine. (188)

Z
Zip disk.
A removable disk capable of storing 100 or more megabytes of information. (52)

INDEX

Access cards, 247
Access icon, 196
Access keys, 80, 81
Access provider, 18, 125
Access speeds, 194
Accounting software, 110–111
Active and default choices, 80–81
Active command, 80, 81
Active-matrix color display, 59
ActiveX, 182, 184–185
Add-in boards, 41, 45
Addressable memory, 49
Addresses, Internet, 176–178
Analog signals, 135
Antivirus software, 248–249
Applets, 182
Applications software, 10–11, 21–22, 82, 100–108, 123–129
ARPANET, 161–163
Arrows, 81, 82
Articles, 172
Artificial intelligence (AI), 112
ASCII, 35
Asynchronous transfer mode (ATM), 139
Asynchronous transmission, 148
Audio data, 6, 40
Audits, 250
Authentication, 247

Backbones, 139, 140
Backup, 48, 218–219
Bandwidth, 135
Bays, 42
Beta test, 76
Biometric security devices, 247
Bitmap, 38
Bits (binary digits), 34–35
Bits per second (bps), 135
Blocking software, 254
Bookmark, 179
Books, PC, 230
Boolean searches, 189
Booting, 20
Bridge, 146
Browser; *See* Web browsers
Buddy list, 174
Buffer, 148
Bulletin board systems (BBS), 124
Burnout, 239–240
Bus, 46–47
Bus networks, 140
Bytes, 34–35

Callback devices, 250
Caller identification, 254–256

Carpal tunnel syndrome, 240
Cartridge tapes, 56–57
Cascaded windows, 86
Case sensitive, 178
CD-ROM, 55
Cellular phones, 133–134
    fraud and, 243–244
Central processing unit (CPU), 5
Channels, 185
Chat, Internet, 173–175
Chat room, 174
Check boxes, 90, 91
Checkmarks, 81, 82
Classes, PC, 229
Client, 142
Client-server LANs, 142–143
Clone chips, 42
Clubs, PC, 229
Cluster, 51
Coaxial cable, 130, 131
Codes of conduct, 258
Collaborative computing, 126–128
Color coding, 39
Color display, 58
Color fiber-optics, 132
Color graphics, 39
Command buttons, 83
Command separators, 81, 82
Command syntax, 77–78, 79
Communications media, 129
Communications protocols, 146–152
Communications satellites, 132–133
Communications software, 109
Compiler, 99
Computer-aided design (CAD), 111
Computer crime, 241–251
    cellular phone fraud, 243–244
    computer viruses, 242, 243
    counterfeiting, 245
    coverups, 245
    data diddling, 242
    eavesdropping, 243
    hacking, 245
    Internet-related, 245
    legislation, 250–251
    logic bombs, 243
    minimizing, 246–250
    salami shaving, 242
    software piracy, 244
    time bombs, 243
    trapdoors, 242–243
    Trojan horse, 242
    types of, 242–246
Computer(s), 5
    animation, 6
    networks, 17–18

and privacy; *See* Privacy
    stores, 208–210
    superstores, 209
    systems, 5
    telecommunications, 134–139
    viruses, 242, 243
    work, and our well-being, 239–241
Concentrator, 146
Conferencing software, 127
Connect time, 194
Content providers, Internet, 164
Context sensitive, 87
Continuous waves, 135
Conversion, 37
Cookies, 182
Cost, ISPs, 194–195
Counterfeiting, 245
Coverups, 245
CPU chip, 41
Crawlers, 192
Crime-prevention software, 248–250
Cross compatibility, 228
Crosshair cursor, 33
CRT (cathode-ray tube), 58–59
Cryptography, 247
CSMA/CD, 149
Customizability, 182
Cyberauctions, 175
Cyberphelia, 239
Cyberphobia, 239–240
Cyberporn, 245

Daisy chains, 140
Data, 6–7, 12–15, 135–136
Database management, 11
Database management systems (DBMs), 21, 106–108
Databases, 13, 14
Database searches, 189–192
Data bus, 46
Data diddling, 242
Dedicated lines, 136
Default command, 81
Defragmentation, 223
Demodulation, 137
Desktop computers, 15–16
Desktop publishing, 109
Desktop tools, Internet, 178–192
    browsers, 178–188
    plug-in packages, 186–188
    search engines, 188–192
Diagnostic software, 223
Dialog boxes, 86, 90–91
Dial-up lines, 136–137
Differential backup, 219
Digital certificates, 248

Digital signals, 135
Digital signature, 186
DirecPC, 139
Direct access, 49
Direct manufacturers, 212
Directories, 93, 177
Directory path, 177
Disaster recovery plan, 246
Discrete states, 135
Discussion groups, 124
Disk care, 220–221
Disk drive, 19, 51, 208
Diskettes, 49–52
Display terminals, 19, 57, 136, 240
Documentation, 223
Documents, 12–13, 93
Domain name, 176
DOS, 94
Dot-matrix printers, 60
Dot pitch, 58
Double-density diskettes, 50
Downloading, 145
Downward compatibility, 228
Dragging and dropping, 32
Drop-down list boxes, 91
Drop-down menu, 80
Drum plotters, 64
Drum scanner, 36
DSP chips, 43
Dumb terminals, 140
Dust, 221
DVD, 55–56
DVD-ROM, 19, 55

Eavesdropping, 243
E-faxing, 125
Electronic data interchange (EDI),
    129
Electronic mail (e-mail), 11, 109, 123,
    166
    filtering programs, 252
    mailboxes, 123
    privacy and, 251–253
Electronic media, 230
Electronics stores, 209
Electrostatic plotter, 64
Ellipses, 81, 82
E-malls, 175
Encryption, 247
Equipment repairs, 225–226
Ergonomics, 240–241
E-shredders, 252
Ethernet, 149
Ethics, 256–259
Expansion bus, 46
Expansion slots, 41
Expert systems, 112
External cache, 43
External devices, 48
External hard disk, 52
External modems, 138
Extranets, 144

Facsimile (fax), 45, 124–125, 142
Falling behind, fears of, 239
Fast Ethernet, 149
Favorites (bookmarks), 179
Fax modems, 45, 125
Fax servers, 142
Fax software, 125
FDDI, 151
Fiber-optic backbone, 140
Fiber-optic cable, 131–132
Fields, 13, 14
File(s), 13, 14, 21, 177
    directory, 51
File server, 142–143
File transfer protocol (FTP), 170
Filtering programs, 252
Firewalls, 247
Fixed-media secondary storage, 48
Flatbed plotters, 64
Flatbed scanner, 36
Flat-panel display devices, 59
Floppy disks, 49–52, 208, 220–221
Folders, 13, 93, 177
Formatting, 51
Frame-relay service, 139
Framing, 182
Freeware, 76–77
Frequently asked questions (FAQs), 173
Full backup, 219
Full-duplex transmission, 147
Full-motion video, 6
Functionality, 216
Functionally obsolete, 228
Function keys, 31, 32

Gateway, 146
Geodemographics, 253
Geosynchronous orbits, 133
Ghosted commands, 81–82
Gigabit Ethernet, 149
Gigabyte (GB), 36
Gopher, 170
Graphical user interface (GUI), 78–91
Graphics, 6
Graphics accelerator chips, 43
Graphics board, 45
Graphics data, 38–39
Graphics standards, 59
Graphics tablet, 33, 35
Graphics workstations, 17
Grayscale images, 38
Groupware, 126

Hacking, 245
Half-duplex transmission, 147
Hand-held computers, 16
Handheld scanner, 36
Handshaking, 147
Hard copy, 57
Hard-disk drive, 41
Hard disks, 19, 41, 52–53
Hardware, 9, 19, 29–71, 192, 216

cartridge tapes, 56–57
companies, Internet, 164
diskettes, 49–52
hard disks, 52–53
image scanners, 33
input, 31
installation, 217
monitors, 57–59
optical disks, 54–56
output, 57–64
plotters, 64
pointing devices, 31–33, 35
printers, 59–61
processing, 33–47
producers, 211–212
secondary storage, 48–57
speakers, 62
system unit, 42–47
technical assistance with, 224–225
upgrading, 227
Heat, 221
Helper packages, 187
Hierarchical local networks, 144–145
High-density diskettes, 50
History list, 179
Home page, 21, 169
Host computer, 140
Hot swappable, 47
HTML (hypertext markup language),
    186
HTML converters, 186
HTML wizard, 186
Hubs, 140, 146
Hyperlinks, 84, 168
Hypermedia, 84, 168
Hypertext menus, 84

Icons, 18, 32, 82–84
Imagemaps, 83
Image scanners, 33
Impact printing, 60
Incremental backup, 219
Information retrieval, 125–126,
    168–171
Infrared technology, 134
Infrastructure companies, Internet, 164
Ink-jet plotter, 64
Ink-jet printers, 61
Input, 3
I/O devices, 4, 6, 31–33
Insertion point, 57
Installations, 217–218
Instant messaging, 174
Instruction set, 40
Integrated software program, 100–101
Intelligent agent, 21
Interlaced monitor, 58, 59
Internal bus, 46
Internal cache, 43
Internal devices, 48
Internal hard disk, 52
Internal modems, 137–138

Internet, 11, 18, 84, 125; See also World Wide Web (WWW)
  addresses, 176–178
  chat, 173–175
  computer crime and, 245
  connecting to, 192–196
  content providers, 164
  desktop tools; See Desktop tools, Internet
  e-mail; See Electronic mail (e-mail)
  evolution of, 161–166
  information retrieval and, 168–171
  infrastructure companies, 164
  mailing lists, 171
  myths about, 165–166
  newsgroups, 172–173
  online shopping, 175–176
  PC sales via, 210–211
  service providers, 18, 125, 164, 192–195
  setting up systems, 195–196
  software and hardware companies, 164
  users, 164
Internet relay chat (IRC), 174
Internet Society, 165
Internet telephony, 174–175
Interorganizational systems (IOSs), 129
Interpreters, 100
Intranet, 143–144
IRIDIUM project, 133
ISDN, 139

Java, 182
Joystick, 32, 35

Keyboards, 19, 31, 32, 240
Kilobyte (KB), 36

Language translators, 40, 99–100
Laptop computers, 16
Laser printers, 60–61
Layoffs, 239
Leasing vs. buying, 213–215
Legacy system, 228
Legislation
  computer crime, 250–251
  privacy, 256
Light pen, 32
Linux, 97–98
Liquid crystal display (LCD), 59
List boxes, 90–91
Local area networks (LANs), 142–145, 149–151
Local bus, 47
Local networks, 137, 140–145, 149–151
Logic bombs, 243
Log on, 18
Low-density diskettes, 50
Low-Earth orbit satellites, 133

Machine language, 40
Machine-readable form, 5

Macintosh compatible, 16
Mac OS, 97
Mailbox addresses, 176
Mailing lists, 171
Mail-order firms, 211
Mail servers, 142
Mainframes, 18
Main menu, 80
Maintenance, of PCs, 219–222
Manufacturers, 224–225
Marketing databases, privacy and, 253
Marketplace, PCs, 207–212
Maximizing windows, 87
Megabyte (MB), 36
Megahertz, 43
Memory, 6, 8
Memory (RAM), 41
Menu bar, 80, 81
Menus, 80–86
Message boxes, 91
Messaging, 123
Metaengines, 192
Microcomputer system, 5
Micromarketers, 253
Microprocessor chips, 42, 208
Microsoft Internet Explorer, 179
Microwave technology, 132–133
Midrange computers, 18
Minimizing windows, 87
Minisuites, 100
Modems, 18, 21, 135, 137–139
Modulation, 137
Monitors, 19, 57–59, 136, 140, 208
Monochrome, 38
Mosaic, 178
Motherboard, 42
Mouse, 31–32, 34, 81
Mouse pad, 34
Mouse pointer, 31–32, 34, 81
MS-DOS, 94
Multimedia computing, 7, 185
Multiplexer, 146
Multitasking, 94

Nanny programs, 252
Natural languages, 34
Navigation bars, 83–84
Needs analysis, PCs, 213
Netiquette, 173
Netscape Navigator, 178
NetWare, 98
Network architecture, 149
Network computers (NCs), 16
Network interface cards (NIC), 136–137
Network operating systems (NOS), 94
Network topologies, 140
Neural-net computing, 249
Newsgroups, 124, 172–173
Newsreader, 173
Nonimpact printing, 60
Noninterlaced monitor, 58, 59
Nonremovable media storage, 48

Nontext data, 38–39
Nonvolatile memory, 43
Notebook computers, 16
Numeric (math) coprocessor chips, 43

Object module, 99
Offline, 18
Online, 18
Online help, 91
Online shopping, 175–176
Operating environment, 94
Operating systems, 11–12, 92–98
Optical character recognition (OCR), 33
Optical disks, 54–56
Option buttons, 90
Output, 3–4
Output devices, 4, 57–64

Packet switching, 152
Paging, 125
Palettes, 85
Palmtop computers, 16
Parallel ports, 44–45
Parallel transmission, 135–136
Parity bit, 148–149
Partial backup, 219
Passive-matrix color display, 59
Passwords, 246
Path, 93
PC cards, 45
PC compatible, 16
PC-DOS, 94
PCMCIA card, 45
Peer-to-peer LANs, 143–144
Periodicals, PC, 230
Peripherals, 4, 48
Personal computers (PCs), 3–6, 15–17, 207–236
  backup procedures, 218–219
  functional vs. technological obsolescence, 228
  maintenance of, 219–222
  marketplace, 207–212
  operating, 218–226
  products, 207–208
  sales and distribution, 208–212
  security, 222
  selecting, 212–217
  technical assistance with, 224–226
  trouble shooting, 222–224
  upgrading, 213, 226–228
Personal digital assistants (PDAs), 16
Pixels, 38
Platforms, 16
Plotters, 64
Plug-and-play, 45, 217
Plug-in packages, 186–188
Pointing devices, 31–33, 35
Portable computers, 16
Portal, 182
Ports, 44–45
Power supply, 41

PPP (point-to-point protocol), 193
Presentation graphics, 10, 108–109
Primary storage, 8
Printers, 59–61, 208
Print servers, 142
Privacy, 176, 251–256
    caller identification, 254–256
    e-mail and, 251–253
    the Internet and, 253–254
    legislation, 256
    marketing databases and, 253
Private key, 248
Processing, 3
Processing hardware, 33–47
Productivity software, 10, 11, 100
Products, PC, 207–208
Programming language, 7
Programs, 6, 7, 40, 82; See also
        Applications software; software
Progressive graphics capability, 179
Prompt, 78
Proprietary software, 75–76
Protocol, 140, 147, 176
Protocol identifier, 176
Public-domain software, 76
Public-key encryption, 247–248
Pull-down menu, 80–82

Radio boxes, 91
Radio buttons, 90
RAM (random access memory), 8, 43
Random access, 49
Read/write head, 48
Realtime processing, 185
Reassignment, 239
Receiver, 129
Records, 13, 14, 21
Red-green-blue (RGB) monitors, 57
Refreshed, 58
Relational databases, 107
Release, 12, 227
Removable media secondary storage, 48
Repeaters, 145
Repetitive stress injury, 240
Request, 178
Resellers, 209
Resolution, 36, 58
Rewritable CDs, 55
Ring networks, 140
Robots, 192
ROM (read-only memory), 43–44
Root directory, 93
Root domain, 176
Routers, 145–146

Salami shaving, 242
Sales and distribution, PCs, 208–212
Samples, 40
Scalable superserver computers, 144
Scanners, 36
Screen savers, 221–222
Scroll, 32

Scroll arrow, 89
Scroll bar, 87–90
Search engines, 188–192
Secondary storage, 8, 48–57
Sector, 51
Security, 48, 175, 186, 222
Sender, 129
Sequential access, 49
Serial ports, 44
Serial transmission, 135–136
Servers, 18, 142
Service providers, 18, 125, 164, 192–195
Set up, Internet systems, 195–196
Setup icon, 195
Shareware, 76
Shortcut keystrokes, 78, 79, 81, 82
Shows, PC, 229
SIMMs, 43
Simple list boxes, 90–91
Simplex transmission, 147
Site license, 76
Sizing handle, 86
Slider, 91
SLIP, 193
Sniffer programs, 243
Snooping software, 252
Social issues, 237–265
    computer crime; See Computer crime
    computers, work, and our well-being,
        239–241
    environment-related concerns, 241
    ergonomics-related concerns,
        240–241
    stress-related concerns, 239–240
Soft copy, 57
Software, 9–12, 73–119, 216
    accounting, 110–111
    antivirus, 248–249
    applications, 10–11, 100–108
    communications, 109
    computer-aided design (CAD), 111
    crime-prevention, 248–250
    database management, 11, 106–108
    desktop publishing, 109
    e-mail, 11
    freeware, 76–77
    installation, 217–218
    language translators, 99–100
    modem, 139
    operating systems, 11–12, 92–98
    packages, 12
    PC, 207–208
    presentation graphics, 10, 108–109
    producers, 211–212
    productivity, 10, 11
    proprietary, 75–76
    shareware, 76
    software suites, 100–101, 207–208
    spreadsheets, 10, 101
    systems, 11–12, 92–100
    technical assistance with, 224–225
    upgrading, 227–228

user interface; See User interface
    utility programs, 98–99
    vertical-market, 111–112
    Web browsers, 11
    word processing, 10, 101
Software companies, Internet, 164
Software license, 75
Software piracy, 244
Software publisher, 212
Software suites, 100–101, 207–208
Sound board, 45
Source module, 99
Spam, 252
Speakers, 62
Speed, of browsers, 179
Speed, of data transmission, 135
Spiders, 192
Spin boxes, 91
Spoof, 242
Spreadsheets, 10, 21, 101
Stalking, 245
Star networks, 140
Startup kit, 195
Static, 221
Storage, 3
Storage bays, 41
Storage devices, 6
Storage media, 5, 48
Streaming, 185
Stress-related concerns, 239–240
Subdirectories, 93
Subfolders, 13, 93
Subnotebook computers, 16
Supercomputers, 18
Superdiskettes, 51–52
Surge suppression, 220
Synchronous transmission, 148
Syntax, 78
System board, 41, 42
System expansion, 45–46
Systems, PC, 207
Systems Network Architecture, 151
Systems software, 11–12, 92–100
System unit, 33, 42–47

Tab menus, 85
Tape drive, 56
Taskbar, 79
TCP/IP, 151, 193
T1 dedicated line, 139
Technical assistance, 224–226
Technologically obsolete, 228
Telecommunications
    applications, 123–129
    media, 129–139
Telecommuting, 127
Teleconferencing, 127
Teledesic, 133
Telnet, 170
Terabyte (TB), 36
Terrestrial microwave stations, 132
Text, 6

Text boxes, 90, 91
Text data, 35–37
T3 fiber-optic dedicated lines, 139
Third-party firms, 225
Threads, 173
3-D virtual chat, 174
Tiled windows, 86
Time bombs, 243
Title bar, 86
Token ring, 149–151
Toolbars, 79, 83, 179
Track, 50, 51
Trackball, 33, 35
Transaction processing, 110, 128–129
Transportability, 48
Trapdoors, 242–243
Trojan horse, 242
Trouble shooting, 222–224
Twisted-pair wires, 129–130

Uniform resource locator (URL),
    176–177
Uninterruptable power supply (UPS),
    220
Universal serial bus (USB), 47
Unix, 97–98
Unlimited storage capacity, 48
Upgrading, 213, 226–228
Uploading, 145
Upward compatibility, 228

UseNet, 173
User groups, 225
User interface, 77–91; See also
    Graphical user interface (GUI)
Users, Internet, 164
User workstations, 18
Utility programs, 98–99

Value-added reseller (VAR), 212
Vaporware, 258
Versions, 12, 227
Vertical markets, 111–112, 212
Video-adapter boards, 45
Videoconferencing, 127
Video data, 6, 40
Virtual reality, 186
Voice chat, 174–175
Voice mail, 123–124
Volatile memory, 43

Warranty, 225
Waveform audio, 40
Wavelength division multiplexing
    (WDM), 131–132
Web browsers, 11, 109, 162, 169,
    178–188
Webcasting, 185
Web clients, 169
Web-page organization, 14
Web-publishing capabilities, 186

Web servers, 163, 169
Web site, 21, 168
Web surfing, 169
Wide area networks (WANs), 137,
    145–146, 151–152
Windows, 86–90
Windows 2000, 96
Windows CE, 95–96
Windows NT, 96
Windows 3.x, 94
Windows 9X, 95
Wireless media, 132–134
Wire media, 129–130
Word processing, 10, 21, 101
Words, 38
Workgroup computing, 126–127, 185
Workspace design, 241
World Wide Web (WWW), 11, 14, 84,
    161–163, 165–166; See also
    Internet
    addresses for web pages, 176–178
    information retrieval and, 125–126,
        168–171
WORM, 55
Write-protect square, 50
WYSIWYG, 79

Yahoo!, 188

CREDITS

Chapter 1

Figure 1-1 (top right) Photo provided courtesy of Proxima Corporation

Figure 1-1 (top left) Photo courtesy of Hewlett-Packard Company

Figure 1-1 (bottom right) Photo courtesy of Hewlett-Packard Company

Figure 1-1 (bottom left) Advertisement for Oldsmobile Aurora, "Caught Their Eye," Director Bob Giraldi, Giraldi Suarez for the Leo Burnett Agency USA. Visual Effects by R/Greenberg Associates, used by permission.

Figure 1-2 ©L.L.Bean, Inc. www.llbean.com

Figure 1-3 Photo courtesy of Hewlett-Packard Company

Figure 1-5 (top) Word 2000 screen shot reprinted by permission from Microsoft Corporation

Figure 1-5 (middle) Excel 2000 screen shot reprinted by permission from Microsoft Corporation

Figure 1-5 (bottom) PowerPoint 2000 screen shot reprinted by permission of Microsoft Corporation

Figure 1-5 (top) p.11 Access 2000 screen shot reprinted by permission of Microsoft Corporation.

Figure 1-5 (middle) p.11 Pegasus Mail System, Copyright ©1990–1999, David Harris

Figure 1-5 (bottom) p.11 ©Disney Enterprises, Inc.

Figure 1-8 (all) Courtesy of International Business Machines Corporation. Unauthorized use not permitted.

Figure 1-10 Word 2000 screen shots reprinted by permission from Microsoft Corporation

p.26 (top) ©Amazon.com, Inc.

p.26 (bottom) ©L.L.Bean, Inc. www.llbean.com

Chapter 2

Figure 2-3 (top left) Courtesy of Intermec Technologies Corporation

Figure 2-3 (top right & Bottom left) ©Logitech. All rights reserved. Used with permission from Logitech.

Figure 2-3 (bottom right) Wacom Technology

Figure 2-4 Photo courtesy of Hewlett-Packard Company

Figure 2-10 Courtesy of Xircom

Figure 2-16 (top left) Courtesy of Iomega Corporation

Figure 2-16 (top right) Courtesy of Imation Corporation. Used with permission

Figure 2-17 Courtesy of International Business Machines. Unauthorized use not permitted.

Figure 2-18 Courtesy of Iomega Corporation

Figure 2-19 (bottom left) Courtesy of Imation Corporation. Used with permission.

Figure 2-19 (bottom right) Courtesy Maxell Corporation

Figure 2-20 Courtesy of Imation Corporation. Used with permission.

Figure 2-21 (all) Courtesy of International Business Machines Corporation. Unauthorized use not permitted.

Figure 2-25 Photo courtesy of Panasonic Communications & Systems Co.

Figure 2-26 Photo courtesy of Hewlett-Packard Company

Figure 2-27 Photo courtesy of Hewlett-Packard Company

Figure 2-28 ©CalComp Corporation

p.68 (left) ©Intel Corporation

p.68 (right) ©Apple Computer, Inc.

p.70 (top) Courtesy Epson America, Inc.

p.70 (bottom) Photo courtesy of Hewlett-Packard Company

Chapter 3

Figure 3-1 User License reprinted by permission from Microsoft Corporation

Figure 3-4 Excel 2000 screen shot used by permission from Microsoft Corporation.

Figure 3-11 ©Lotus SmartSuite

Figure 3-10 Microsoft ®Paint Windows 98 Screen shot reprinted with permission of Microsoft Corporation

Figure 3-13, 3-14, 3-21 Windows screens reprinted with permission of Microsoft Corporation

Figure 3-25 Word 2000 screen shots reprinted by permission from Microsoft Corporation

Figure 3-26 Excel screen shots reprinted by permission from Microsoft Corporation

Figure 3-27 Access screen shots reprinted with permission of Microsoft Corporation

Figure 3-29 PowerPoint 2000 screen shots reprinted by permission from Microsoft Corporation

Figure 3-30 Publisher 2000 screen shot reprinted by permission from Microsoft Corporation.

Figure 3-31 Peachtree Software, Inc.

Figure 3-32 (top left) Image courtesy of Intergraph Corporation

Figure 3-32 (top right) ©Lightscape/Autodesk

Figure 3-32 (bottom left & right) Engineering Animation, Inc.

p.118 Excel 2000 screen shots used by permission from Microsoft Corporation

Miniguide1 3-1, 3-11, 3-12, 3-20 Word 2000 screen shot used by permission from Microsoft Corporation.

Chapter 4

Figure 4-3 Photo courtesy of Motorola

Figure 4-6 (top & middle) Photo courtesy of Hewlett-Packard Company

Figure 4-6 (bottom) Courtesy of International Business Machines Corporation. Unauthorized use not permitted.

Figure 4-21 Hewlett-Packard Company

p.157 ©MiniStor Peripherals

Chapter 5

Figure 5-5 *www.discovery.com*. Used by permission of Discovery Communications, Inc. Discovery Channel Online updates website design and content regularly. Screen captures shown are for the purpose of example only and may not reflect what is currently appearing online.

Figure 5-11 ©SONY Electronics, Inc.

Figure 5-12 (bottom) Microsoft ®Internet Explorer. ©1999 Microsoft Corporation. All rights reserved.

Figure 5-19 (top) From RealPlayer Plus. Used with permission from RealNetworks, ©1999. www.real.com

Figure 5-23 Used courtesy of Yahoo! Inc. www.yahoo.com

Figure 5-24 America OnLine. www.aol.com

Figure 5-25 America OnLine. www.aol.com

Miniguide3 6-2 Courtesy of International Business Machines Corporation. Unauthorized use not permitted.

Chapter 6

Figure 6-3 Courtesy of CompUSA Inc.

Figure 6-4 (top) ©Dell Computer Corporation. Prices and lease quotes may vary with date of sale and models and options available.

Figure 6-5 (bottom left) ©PC Mall. www.pcmall.com

Figure 6-5 (bottom right) ©MacZone. Courtesy of www.zones.com

Figure 6-7 (middle) From "First Looks: Summary of Features, Tapes Backup Drives," PC Magazine, January 6, 1998, p. 48. Used by permission from PC Magazine, ©1998 Ziff-Davis

Figure 6-7 (bottom) ©PC Magazine/ZD Net. www.zdnet.com/pcmag

Figure 6-9 Office 2000 screen shots reprinted by permission from Microsoft Corporation.

Figure 6-10 (top underlay) Courtesy of International Business Machines Corporation. Unauthorized use not permitted.

Figure 6-11 Courtesy of Curtis Manufacturing Company, Inc.

Figure 6-12 Courtesy of American Power Conversion

Figure 6-16 ©ZD Events Comdex/Fall '98, Las Vegas, Nevada

p.233,234 ©Z-Byte™ Prices may vary with date of purchase and model and options available.

Miniguide3 6-1 Courtesy of International Business Machines Corporation. Unauthorized use not permitted.

Miniguide3 6-3 Courtesy Maxell Corporation

Miniguide3 6-3 Courtesy of Imation Corporation. Used with permission

Miniguide3 6-5 Courtesy of International Business Machines Corporation. Unauthorized use not permitted.

Miniguide3 6-7 Photo courtesy of Hewlett-Packard Company

Miniguide3 6-8 Courtesy of International Business Machines Corporation. Unauthorized use not permitted.

Miniguide3 6-9 Used by permission from Microsoft Corporation

Miniguide3 6-10 Photo courtesy of Hewlett-Packard Company

Chapter 7

Figure 7-1 (left) Glide Point Wave by Cirque Corporation. http://www.glidepoint.com

Figure 7-1 (right) Kinesis Keyboard by Kinesis Corporation. http://www.kinesis-ergo.com

Figure 7-6 Recognition Systems, Inc. Used with permission.

Figure 7-13 Used with permission from CIDCO® – www.cidco.com